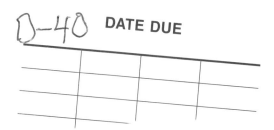

DATE DUE

D1563509

Prairie Birds

Prairie

*Fragile Splendor in
the Great Plains*

University Press of Kansas

Paul A. Johnsgard

Birds

Published by the University Press of Kansas (Lawrence, Kansas 66049), which was
organized by the Kansas Board of Regents and is operated and funded by Emporia
State University, Fort Hays State University, Kansas State University, Pittsburg State
University, the University of Kansas, and Wichita State University

Library of Congress Cataloging-in-Publication Data

Johnsgard, Paul A.
    Prairie birds : fragile splendor in the Great Plains / Paul A. Johnsgard.
        p.   cm.
    Includes bibliographical references and index. (p. 329).
    ISBN 0-7006-1067-7 (cloth : alk. paper)
    1. Birds—Great Plains.   2. Prairie animals—Great Plains.   I. Title.

QL683.G68 J633 2001
598′.0978—dc21   00-043754

British Library Cataloguing in Publication Data is available.

Printed in the United States of America

10 9 8 7 6 5 4 3 2 1

The paper used in this publication meets the minimum requirements of the
American National Standard for Permanence of Paper for Printed Library Materials
Z39.48-1984.

To the memory of Aldo Leopold,
who transformed a decaying woodlot
into a conservation theology,
and to Annie Dillard,
who made sitting beside an obscure creek
a religious experience

Contents

Figures, Tables, and Charts

Tables

Charts

Preface and
Acknowledgments

Each spring, the sun swings slowly northward until it reaches the vernal equinox in late March. Then for a singular day it rises above the horizon at exactly due East and also sets precisely twelve hours later at due West. At such times I am reminded of Eos, Greek goddess of the dawn, her presunrise presence projected above the eastern horizon as pinkish fingers of radiant light. We have a collective cultural memory of her to thank for the Old English word East, meaning the direction of sunrise, as well as for the original pagan springtime celebration of Easter. It is an auspicious time to be alive—a time above all to watch birds—the word auspicious is similarly of pre-Christian origin (from the Latin in this case), meaning to divine the future by watching the movements of birds.

And so I turn my eyes toward the east and west each spring, making sure that I am witness to at least one sunrise and sunset in the company of grassland birds. At times it is a shared sunrise with greater prairie-chickens on a rounded hilltop crowned by bluestem prairies. Often it is shared with sandhill cranes gathering in Nebraska's Platte Valley, and occasionally with migrating wildfowl, who also are stirred to move northward, following the annual northward sweep of the sun. In some special places, and at such precious times, it is easy to imagine that one is a part of a different world, where warfare and famine are far removed and the combined noises of wind, uncounted wings, and a chorus of skyward voices are little if at all different from the sounds that were present an ice age or two ago. I suspect that the migrating cranes of a pre–ice-age period some 10 million years ago would fully understand every nuance of the crane conversation going on today along the Platte. Cranes have scarcely changed in these millions of years although the world around them now would be scarcely recognizable to birds of that era.

As spring has moved forward in eastern Nebraska, with the first crab apple and redbud blossoms breaking optimistically into bloom, I knew I must return to the Platte one last time to look for the first returning prairie migrants. Easter weekend seemed a perfect choice; a strong, persistent south wind the previous week was blowing the snow geese northward toward the edges of their own known world, and I also knew that the sandhill cranes wouldn't be able to resist much longer the urge to leave the Platte Valley. The moon was ripening to its monthly fullness, and owls were starting to appear at twilight, hunting for mice to feed their growing broods of young. A few nights previously I had watched entranced, as male woodcocks did their graceful sky dances by moonlight while small and nearly invisible flocks of ducks sliced noisily through a star-struck sky.

Driving from Lincoln to the Platte Valley is like driving backward in time. One begins by passing over rolling hills of glacial till, sprinkled with rounded and ice-scarred boulders that were dropped randomly across the landscape as the last glacier retreated about 11,000 years ago. Within fifty miles the land is flatter, and the wind-carried loess soil underneath the grassy mantle dates back at least a half-million years. Great flocks of blackbirds move like dust clouds though the sky, sometimes briefly stopping to decorate a leaf-bare tree, then moving on like some restless spirit searching endlessly for a suitable final resting place.

The first meadowlarks are starting to break into song from fenceposts along low meadows, and northern harriers sweep low over these same meadows. The meadowlarks singing here are westerns, the easterns being seemingly unable or unwilling to leave their familiar patches of remnant tall-grass prairie to the east. Horned larks scatter like wind-blown leaves from the edges of dusty roads, and a vesper sparrow peers warily from the shelter of a wild plum in the ditch. Migrating Swainson's hawks soar lazily above, their wingtips delicately seeking out the faint updrafts coming from the sun-warmed earth, their circling paths reminding one that all of life consists of repeated circles and that the earth's orbit has gone full circle one more time since their return the previous spring.

I drive down country roads far more familiar to me than are most back streets of Lincoln, noting new houses rather magically appearing around sandpit lakes that only a few years before supported least terns and piping plovers, and the remains of old, abandoned farmsteads that similarly have nearly disappeared since the previous spring. Century-old cottonwoods lie sprawled and broken in gigantic, chaotic heaps, where either old age or the need to clear more land for center-pivot irrigation has dictated their removal. At last I reach my destination: a stretch of privately owned meadows and river shoreline miles from the nearest public access. Grabbing my binoculars and camera, I head out to locate the tallest grasses I can find near the river. Lying down, I am surrounded by last year's growth of Indian grass and big bluestem, the Indian grass now rich golden copper and the bluestem with a reddish tinge that has always seemed to me to be the very hallmark of native prairie. It is now nearly sundown. Song sparrows are singing occasionally from a willow thicket near the river, and newly arrived red-winged blackbirds sit rather aimlessly and silently about, perhaps wondering where the females are, while keeping a wary eye out for great horned owls in the deepening afternoon light. The cranes are now returning to the river, with great and endless waves of birds passing overhead, their jubilant calls carrying with them the authority of almost 60 million years of history, plus the excitement of the moment.

As I lie there, drinking in the sights, sounds, odors, and touch of prairie, I wonder how many others have known the magic of spending a spring evening alone with birds, beside a prairie river, and if they have also had the urge to try to burn it into memory, to be recalled at times and places far removed. And so, even while sitting in a small, windowless university office, I feel compelled to begin writing this book, to try to share the wonder of the Great Plains prairies and their life, especially the lives of the birds that evolved in company with the prairie grasslands over eons of time.

In the late 1970s, when I wrote a book on the breeding birds of the Great Plains, the literature on the ecology and behavior of most nongame birds was abysmally limited. Thus, in choosing suggested readings with regard to the thirty-three grassland-adapted species emphasized in this book, I was forced to include the old, although classic, life histories written by A. C. Bent as primary or secondary reading choices for no fewer than twelve of these species. With the proliferation of nongame divisions or natural heritage programs of state and provincial conservation agencies, the amount of recent research on these nonhunted species has exploded. No fewer than eight distributional surveys or breeding bird atlases for individual states and provinces (Alberta, Saskatchewan, Ontario, South Dakota, Wyoming, Iowa, Missouri, and Colorado) within the Great Plains region have been produced since my regional book was published in 1979. Additionally, breeding bird atlases for several peripheral states (Michigan, Kentucky, and Tennessee) in the adjoining central lowlands region have appeared, and a Nebraska breeding birds atlas is finally in press. Furthermore, individual accounts for more than two-thirds of the grassland endemics discussed in detail in this book have now been published in the *Birds of North America* series of single-species monographs sponsored by the American Ornithologists' Union (Poole and Gill 1990 et seq.). This recognition of the importance of nonhunted species in understanding natural ecosystems is of course a situation only to be celebrated, and one can further hope such studies will continue.

There is also a slight downside to this proliferation of new information. If anything, there is now far too much data to try to assimilate and summarize in a few pages for most of the grassland species, and I have necessarily been highly selective in what I have decided to include. Habitat modeling and effects of management on grassland birds are topics that now are being intensively addressed by many federal, state, and provincial conservation agencies; the resulting literature fairly overflows my vertical files. Rather than attempting, as I originally had planned, to write a somewhat technical if highly abbreviated summary of all that is known of each of the grassland species' habitat needs and population studies, I have elected to undertake a more readable if less comprehensive approach. In keeping with this less formal approach, I have given ecological and geographical measurements using the English system rather than the less familiar metric system. Using metrics for such subjective data as estimated territory sizes and population densities seems to me to convey a sense of accuracy that is usually unjustified, and even NASA has a recent history of being badly confused by them.

I have therefore concentrated in this book on producing readable, and even occasionally first-person chapters primarily describing each grassland species' breeding-season ecology and behavior, with a corresponding reduction in discussions of such relatively specialized topics as taxonomy, physiology, nonbreeding biology, and theoretical niche modeling. Although I have avoided using in-text references for purely literary reasons, I have provided lists of references to the relevant literature at the end of each chapter and assembled a rather extensive bibliographic section of more than 600 references, including many theses and dissertations. These also include a substantial number of literature reviews, especially the species accounts for grassland birds published in the *Birds of North America* series and the similar Department of Interior series on the effects of habitat management on grassland birds (Dechant et al. 1998 et seq.). Where factual statements are made in the text that are not readily attributable as to their origin, the basis for such statements can usually be found in one or the other of these two sources or in Bent's older life histories accounts. I have also tried to include five to ten primary and relatively recent literature references for each of the typical grassland species, with an emphasis on their reproductive biology and behavioral ecology.

Among the people I must personally thank for their help on this project are Barbara Voeltz of the Nebraska Game and Parks Commission Library, for her undaunted and heroic efforts in performing internet literature searches; the staff of the University of Nebraska libraries; and many other librarians. There are likewise too many biologists who advised or helped me to acknowledge each of them individually, but I must mention S. K. Davis, Cheri Gratto-Trevor, Joe Hartman, Scott Johnsgard, Douglas Johnson, David Rintoul, Mary Romanjal, Janet Ruth, John Sullivan, Daniel Svingen, and Maiken Winter. The manuscript was critically read in part or in total by Linda Brown, John Zimmerman, and another anonymous reviewer, but I take responsibility for any and all weaknesses. Fred Woodward of the University Press of Kansas took an immediate interest in the book when I first mentioned that I might write it and persisted in his optimism throughout. To all these people and institutions I offer my sincere thanks.

part one

The
Land:
Its
History
and Biota

An Ancient Sea of Grass

The Beginnings

All stories need beginnings, but unless one happens to believe the biblical Creation tale, it is difficult to know where to start a narrative history of the grasslands and their vertebrate fauna. As good a time as any is about 75 million years ago, near the end of the Mesozoic era, the last act in the long Age of Dinosaurs. At that time most of the interior of what is now North America was still submerged under a great inland sea, the Western Interior Seaway (Fig. 1). This sea extended from what is now the Gulf of Mexico to what would eventually become the Arctic Ocean. But there was nothing arctic about this or any other ocean at that time. And although the birds present in the earlier Mesozoic era such as *Archaeopteryx,* as long ago as nearly 150 million years, would have been much more appealing to a herpetologist than to any ornithologist, those birds present near the end of the Mesozoic would seem only slightly out of place in a modern field guide.

Most of what is now eastern North America consisted of lowlands that were covered by vast tropical or subtropical forest consisting of hardwoods such as ancestral oaks and magnolias, but there were

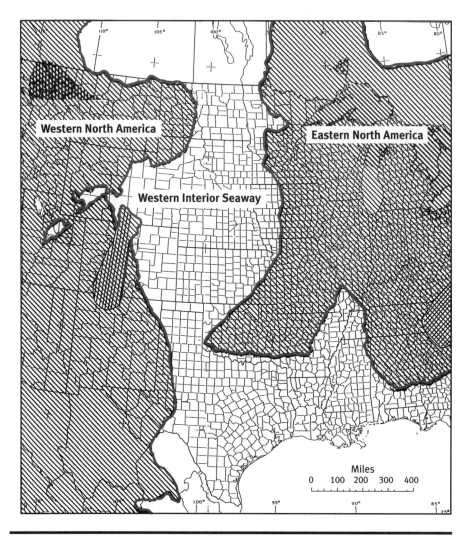

1. Presumptive geography of North America during the late Mesozoic era (ca. 74 million years ago). Cross-hatched areas indicate mountain ranges. Adapted from a map ("North America in the Age of Dinosaurs") published by the National Geographic Society, January 1993.

also conifers and primitive fernlike but seed-bearing cycads present. The Appalachian Mountains, which had begun to rise in much earlier Precambrian times, were already ancient. To the west and northwest of these oldest ranges were newer elements, dating from Paleozoic times. In the western component, which extended north to connect with the eastern areas of what is now Asia, there were more elevated areas. The Rocky Mountains were already starting to rise, as well as the Sierra Nevadas and the coastal ranges of the Pacific Northwest. The last half of the Mesozoic era marked the start of massive mountain-building in the Central Rockies, in a process called the Larimide Orogeny. From regions west and southwest of the Rockies, in locations as far away as what is now Nevada, uplifts of the earth's mantle began to buckle its crust, producing waves of new mountain ranges rising progressively to the east. These wrinkles in the earth's crust extended from what is now Alaska to northern Mexico, in a discontinuous pattern. Volcanic action was also under way, but most of the Rocky Mountains' rise can be attributed to folding and faulting effects rather than to the primary result of volcanic activity.

This period was the last heyday of the dinosaurs, which had dominated the earth for 100 million years. These included enormous, plant-eating sauropods and terrible carnivores such as the famous *Tyrannosaurus rex*. There were also semiaquatic duckbills with high-placed nostrils that may have allowed them to wade in shallows, and bone-headed dinosaurs with hollow head chambers that probably served to resonate their calls. Along the edges of the Western Interior Seaway were giant marine lizards called mosasaurs and long-necked plesiosaurs, which consumed both fish and squids.

Fish of all sizes were abundant, and along the coastlines of what is now western Kansas and Montana were several loonlike but flightless species of *Hesperornis*. Like those of loons, their feet were placed far to the rear for maximum diving and underwater swimming efficiency. This leg position allowed their webbed feet to be oriented sideways, in an oar-like manner, and provided for rapid propulsion and quick turns. Nearly 100 teeth were present, ensuring a good grip on slippery fish. These birds were about five feet in length and must have been able to capture rather large fish. Above the waves, and foraging in a ternlike manner, were several species of the much smaller *Ichthyornis*. Most of these birds were about as large as a modern-day pigeon, but, even as compared with modern pigeons, the brains of *Ichthyornis* species were quite small and reptilian.

At this time there were a few small, often shrewlike mammals lurking about in the shadows of these huge reptiles. They probably survived by a combination of their wits; their agility, a result of their longer legs and a more efficient upright stance that was associated with an improved hip and shoulder structure; and their diversified teeth and jaws, which allowed for a similarly diversified diet. Certainly insects were a part of their diet, and perhaps small reptiles or their eggs may also have been eaten. Still, their day had not yet arrived, for their hairy coats were not of any special value as insulating devices, since the climate was still essentially tropical. Probably their development of excellent olfaction, as well as refined hearing abilities associated with large external ears and a much more complex inner-ear structure, gradually adapted the early mammals to a more nocturnal lifestyle. This would have helped take them well out of harm's way from the slower and more diurnal predatory reptiles. The development of large eyes with efficient light-reflecting retinas for nighttime vision and special sensory hairs, or vibrissae, around their muzzles perhaps also facilitated efficient nocturnal survival mechanisms.

The uplifting of the Rocky Mountains, as well as that of the mountain ranges farther to the west, had major geological and climatic effects on the regions to their east. As soon as these mountains began to rise they also began to erode away; their river-carried residues gradually began filling in the lowlands to the east and eventually also even filled in the shallow interior seas. Moisture-laden winds coming from the warm Pacific Ocean were increasingly intercepted by these rising mountains, causing the air currents to rise and cool, thus discharging much of their moisture on the leeward western slopes. Thus the winds, after cresting the peaks, were relatively moisture deficient, and as they warmed up on their return to lower altitudes they were even more unlikely to discharge any additional moisture. These two interacting phenomena, the increased or "orographic" precipitation on the windward sides of the mountains, and the "rain-shadow effect" on their leeward sides, were to have a major molding effect on the climate of the developing Great Plains.

The Cenozoic Era

The end of the Mesozoic era came not with a whimper, but with a bang. About 65 million years ago an event occurred that was simply world-shattering in its effects. At that time an enormous asteroid, perhaps ten miles in diameter, evidently struck the planet in a region roughly coinciding with the Yucatan Peninsula of Mexico. Its initial impact must have been lethal to everything for hundreds of miles around, but its major effect was much more long-lasting and universal. A great cloud of iridium-rich asteroid dust arose, spreading out and drifting about in the earth's atmosphere for decades if not centuries. This cloud effectively blocked the sun's rays, probably killing or at least influencing the growth of much of the light-dependent vegetation and thus reducing food supplies for the largest of the plant-eating reptiles. Carnivorous reptiles dependent on the plant-eaters soon lost their food base, too. The dust itself may also have directly influenced the animals' respiratory efficiencies, hastening their deaths. Whatever were the direct causes, the age of reptiles was rather quickly brought to an ignominious end, and the great majority of reptilian families that had dominated the earth's Mesozoic history simply disappeared, both on land and sea.

By the early parts of the Cenozoic era, roughly 60 to 65 million years ago, the climate of the world was already significantly changing, becoming both drier and cooler. Most of eastern North America was covered by a temperate forest (the Arcto-Tertiary Geoflora), which was rich in such familiar trees as oaks, maples, willows, and sycamores. It was much like the hardwood forests of the southern Appalachians of today, but conifers such as pines were also present. Much of the western and southwestern regions of North America consisted of a more tropical forest (the Neotropical-Tertiary Geoflora), whose typical trees such as laurels are still well represented in Mexico and farther south. Relatively less moisture evaporated from the cooler oceans, bringing less water to their adjoining land masses, and the rising mountains to the west increasingly caused regional variations in rainfall patterns across interior and eastern North America. By then the interior lowlands had filled in, in part probably facilitated by some buckling or deformations of the floor of the ancient inland sea. In any case, the beginning of drainage patterns that would eventually give rise to the Mississippi and Missouri Rivers had probably begun.

The long mountain ranges of the western American coast extended south into what is now Mexico and finally terminated in a low peninsula representing what would eventually become Honduras and Nicaragua. To the east of these mountains, the Sierra Madre Occidental, in what are now the uplands of Mexico, a more xeric and warm climate developed. Within this region a group of relatively drought-tolerant plants gradually evolved, probably in the rain shadow of these mountains as well as being in a latitudinal region that is still characterized by having a permanent high-pressure zone, with its attendant almost cloudless skies and persistently dry climate. This ancestral plant community, the Madro-Tertiary Geoflora, was to become the evolutionary center of the desert-adapted North American flora and the associated fauna of southwestern North America. Probably it consisted initially of various relatively drought-tolerant trees, shrubs, and perhaps also some grasses, although the grass component has left almost no fossil record. The earliest known North American grass fossils date back to 58 million years ago, but grass fossils from the Great Plains first appear in the late Oligocene epoch, about 24 to 30 million years ago.

Birth of the Great Plains Grasslands

As regions to the north and northeast of Mexico became progressively drier, the Madro-Tertiary Geoflora extended northward into the areas immediately to the east of the Sierra Nevada Range, eventually producing the arid Great Basin flora. More important from the standpoint of our story, it also moved northeastwardly into the expanding plains and lowlands lying in the rain shadow of the still-expanding Rocky Mountains. This northern migration and establishment of a definably distinct grasslands ecosystem perhaps underwent its major northward movement during the Miocene and especially the later Pliocene epochs, i.e., during the past 5 to 20 million years or so, as the Northern Hemisphere continued its drying and cooling trend. The arid oak and juniper woodlands and associated chaparral communities of southwestern America thus differentiated, as did true scrub desert and sage-dominated semidesert, and perhaps finally the somewhat less arid but more widespread interior high plains grasslands lying in the Rocky Mountains' rain shadow. Although this arid-adapted flora was probably the source of the steppelike components of the Great Plains flora of today, the more mesic tall-grass prairies may have formed independently, perhaps as savannalike offshoots of the temperate hardwood forests far to the east, in areas too dry to support closed forests.

This expansion of the plains grasslands did not go unnoticed by the mammals, which by now had diversified into essentially all the major family types with which we are familiar, even though the actual species were variably different. The abundant and nutritious grass cover provided the basis for an explosion of large herbivorous and highly mobile mammals on the open grasslands, ranging in the American plains from early horses and camels to elephants and rhinos. There were also cranes, similar in appearance to the modern crowned cranes of the African savannas, as well as some somewhat related but more carnivorous birds that stalked the plains in search of small reptilian or mammalian prey. By 25 million years ago there were clawed horses (chalcotheres) running about on the plains of what is now Nebraska; 16 million years ago barrel-bodied rhinos were present; and by 14 million years ago mastodons and four-tusker elephants had also appeared. By 10 million years ago the camels were disappearing from the plains, but single-hoofed horses were abundant, as were prong-horned antelopes and four-tusked elephants.

Just about 10 million years ago, volcanic action from somewhere in the western mountains, perhaps in what is now Wyoming, brought with it a massive cloud of volcanic dust that settled on some areas of northern Nebraska. The choking clouds evidently did not cause immediate death to the unlucky herds of rhinos, camels, horses, and other large mammals that were exposed to it. Yet certainly within a few weeks they had all died, the mother rhinos often with babies curled up next to them. The fine, glasslike particles of volcanic dust, while proving deadly to lungs, provided a basis for perfect fossilization, to the point that not only small bones but also fragile body parts, such as the windpipes of the fossilized cranes, can be easily seen.

Although humankind may trace it earliest roots to the tropical African forests at least 6 million years ago, it was the grasslands of that continent that made us human. Moving from the forests into the expanding grassy savannas during the Pliocene epoch about 5 million years ago forced us to stand upright to see above the grasses around us and to run erect, with our arms and hands freed for wielding tools or weapons. And it was the discovery that grasses could be counted upon to provide crops of small but nutritious seeds within a few months after planting that gave humans the economic basis for attaining a stable, sedentary existence. Rather than relying on harvesting the irregular and usually nonstorable forest fruits and berries, or risking life and limb in stalking large animals, we were eventually transformed by the existence of grasses from enduring chance survival as mobile, risk-taking hunters (and sometimes also becoming the hunted) into becoming simple but more secure and productive farmers. It is probably not by chance that three great centers of historic civilizations, in the Orient, in northern Europe, and in the New World, came about in association with the developing cultivation of the world's three greatest cereal crops: rice, wheat, and maize.

The Pleistocene

Life changed for everybody with the advent of the Pleistocene epoch, almost 2 million years ago. The cooling trend that had characterized virtually the entire Cenozoic era on earth reached its ultimate endpoint. Ice masses at the northern and southern poles increased in size and thickness, not only cooling the world's climates but also capturing some of the ocean water, converting it to ice. This caused a gradual lowering of ocean levels worldwide, eventually lowering shorelines by as much as several hundred feet. In this process many shallow seas became dry land, and some long-standing ocean barriers to migration by terrestrial animals and plants disappeared. Thus the waters of the Bering Strait that had long separated Asia from North America became a lowland corridor for migration that was used both by humans and other animals.

Warm-blooded birds and mammals responded to these cold temperatures by becoming larger in mass—large, bulky animals lose temperature more slowly than do smaller and more lanky ones having more exposed surface area relative to their body mass. Longer hair produced luxuriant pelages that were better at trapping body heat, as did layers of body fat and, in the case of birds, thicker, longer, and down-supplemented plumages. White hair or feathers serve to retain heat much better than do brown- or black-colored ones and also provide better visual protection against a snowy backdrop. Seasonal movements, either up and down mountain slopes, or longer ones crossing zones of latitude, became increasingly common mammalian and avian adaptations for dealing with seasonal temperature extremes and food-availability variations.

The Pleistocene epoch of the last 1.77 million years is commonly referred to as the Ice Age. Yet in both North America and in Europe there were at least four major periods of continental glaciations, each of which was followed by a much milder and about an equally long interglacial interval lasting for as much as several hundred thousand years.

The first of the major continental glaciations in North America is known as the Nebraskan. It began less than 2 million years ago and lasted nearly 300,000 years. It was named for the fact that at its maximum southern limits it reached what would become northeastern Nebraska. This period was followed by a similarly long interglacial interval (the Aftonian). About 1.4 million years ago, the Kansan glacial period began and lasted for nearly .5 million years. At its maximum its southernmost lobe reached what is now eastern Kansas, depositing rich glacial till this far south as it slowly melted. A second interglacial interval (the Yarmouth) followed, lasting about 300,000 years. Then came the Illinoian glacial, again named for the glacier's southern limits, and lasting about 200,000 years. The following interglacial interval (the Sangamon) lasted longer than the glacier that preceded it, bringing us up to about 150,000 years ago.

Finally came the Wisconsinian glaciation, the best-studied because its numerous tracks may still quite literally be seen all around the northern half of North America. By the time of its maximum extent, some 18,000 years ago, ice had helped scour out the present-day Great Lakes and covered virtually all of Canada as well as most of the northern United States north of the Missouri, Mississippi, and Ohio Rivers (Fig. 2). Indeed, these great river valleys formed the drainages for the vast amounts of ice and snowmelt produced when the glacier began to retreat about 15,000 years ago. Meltwaters also temporarily formed many enormous impounded lakes such as glacial Lake Agassiz, which covered much of easternmost North Dakota and adjacent Minnesota, in the present-day Red River Valley, and Lake Bonneville, in the vicinity of the present-day Great Salt Lake.

The vegetation of that era is considerably more conjectural than are the landforms, since its direct evidence is mostly preserved in fossil pollen profiles and similar inconspicuous records. Nevertheless, a fairly likely vegetational map can be drawn (Fig. 3) for the period approximating the time of the maximum Wisconsinian glaciation. Although not shown on the map, it is very likely that a narrow zone of tundralike conditions existed along the boundary of the ice sheet, with mammoths, musk oxen, caribou, woolly rhinos, and similar Arctic-adapted mammals moving about along these snowy edges. Arctic breeding birds, such as various sea ducks, geese, and sandhill cranes probably also bred in and around the abundant meltwaters at the glacier's edges. Other than in such areas, grasslandlike conditions were probably relatively confined to the Great Basin, the southern Great Plains, and perhaps a few other local areas, such as the Nebraska Sandhills. Coniferous parklands, consisting of pine forests with scattered open areas of grasses, may also have

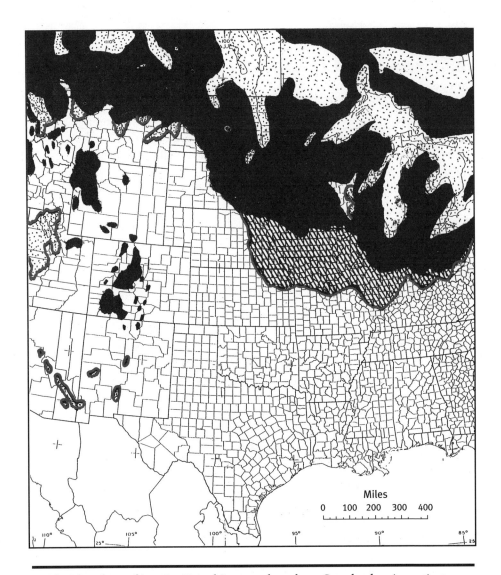

2. Glacial geology of interior United States and southern Canada, showing extinct
glacial lakes (*stippled*), southern limits of earlier (Nebraskan, Kansan, and Illinoian)
glaciations (*hatched*), and maximum extent of last (Wisconsinian) glaciation (*solid black*).
Adapted from a map in the *National Atlas of the United States of America* (U.S. Geological
Survey, 1970).

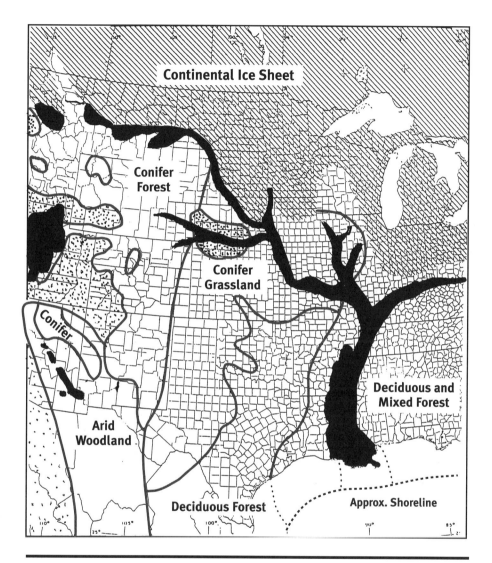

3. Conjectural vegetation of the Great Plains region during the late Wisconsinian glaciation (ca. 18,000 years ago). Black areas show lakes and rivers, stippling indicates grasslands (lighter stippling shows arid grasslands and semideserts), and clear areas indicate montane regions. Mainly after Kendeigh (1974).

been widespread. Coniferous forests covered much of the western half of the country as well as the Appalachian Mountains region and the lower but cooler ice-free lands to the north. Deciduous forests occupied most of the midwestern and southeastern regions, with a broad zone of mixed coniferous and deciduous forests filling the areas of the Great Plains between the purer stands of coniferous and deciduous forests.

This period, near glacial maximum, was presumably an important time for the bird fauna evolving in conjunction with the interior grasslands. Professor Robert Mengel has noted that the typical grassland birds that are the central focus of this book number less than three dozen species, a rather surprisingly low number considering the vast area that is now occupied by the interior grasslands. This paucity of species diversity might reflect the rather late geographic differentiation of the grassland ecosystem, which has mostly occurred during the past 10 million years. This comparatively short timespan has left relatively little time for species proliferation, at least as compared with the much older scrub, woodland, and forest communities, which average about 3.0 species per genus, rather than the grassland's average of 1.1 species per genus. In Mengel's view, the grasslands of the central plains, rather than being a major center for internal speciation, have served more significantly as a geographic isolating agent, allowing speciation to occur in forests and woodlands lying both to the east and west of the grasslands.

As an example of the grassland's isolating effects, we can see many closely related forest- or edge-dwelling east-west species pairs that are to varying degrees now isolated by the plains grasslands. These pairs include the Baltimore and Bullock's orioles, indigo and lazuli buntings, rose-breasted and black-headed grosbeaks, eastern and western woodpewees, and also some well-marked subspecies (the yellow-shafted and red-shafted races of the northern flicker). Among the grassland endemics there is only a single comparable east-west species pair, the eastern and western meadowlarks. Most of the geographic separations of these avian taxonomic pairs, some of which have barely attained species-level differences, must have occurred during the late Pleistocene, or even in post-Pleistocene times in the case of the most closely related forms such as the flickers.

Until about 18,000 years ago, there were still spruces growing in what is now northeastern Kansas. As recently as 11,000 years ago spruces also still dominated the uplands of western Iowa and occurred widely in the Dakotas and the northern Sandhills of Nebraska. By 15,000 years ago the glacier covering what is now the interior of southern Canada was starting to melt, producing vast meltwater lakes along its southern margins (Lake Regina in what is now Saskatchewan, Lake Souris along the Manitoba–North Dakota border, and Lake Agassiz, extending at maximum from southern Manitoba south to northeastern South Dakota). At that time grasses, sedges, and other herbaceous plants probably slowly began to replace the coniferous spruce forests of the northern plains. Some species remained and survived as isolated relict pockets, such as groves of aspens in the cool, shaded slopes of the Niobrara River Valley of northern Nebraska, along with some accompanying forest-adapted birds, such as American redstarts and black-and-white warblers in the same area.

Glacial melting proceeded quite rapidly, and the woolly mammoths that had been roaming about the tundralike fringes of Lake Agassiz began to retreat northward. By slightly more than 10,000 years ago the spruce forests of what would become eastern North Dakota were being replaced by prairie grasslands and deciduous forests of elms and oaks. This parkland community of deciduous forests and savannas may have persisted for a few thousand years in the northern plains, but slowly the climate began to become much drier, and the pendulum swung inexorably in favor of the more drought-tolerant grasses, thereby converting large areas of the northern and central plains from deciduous parkland and savanna to open prairie. Fossil floras from the Great Plains suggest that its annual precipitation may have dropped from about forty inches per year around 17 million years ago to only half as much annually some 5 million years ago, and deciduous forests correspondingly became increasingly restricted to gallery forests along streamsides. To the east of the Rockies, most of this precipitation began to fall as spring and summer rains, brought up from Gulf Coast sources; to the west of the Rockies a summer-dry and winter-wet climate developed, producing a quite different array of grassland types in the separately evolving Palouse prairies of the Pacific Northwest. By the end of this last glaciation, the physiography of interior North America was comparable to that of the present day (Fig. 4).

The climate of the entire northern hemisphere continued to become progressively warmer from about 10,000 years ago onward, producing a long "hypsithermal" period that lasted from about 7,500 B.C. to 1,000 B.C. Ocean levels rose as the continental ice sheets and polar ice caps melted, reestablishing the Bering Sea connection between the Pacific and Arctic Ocean and effectively shutting down easy migration between

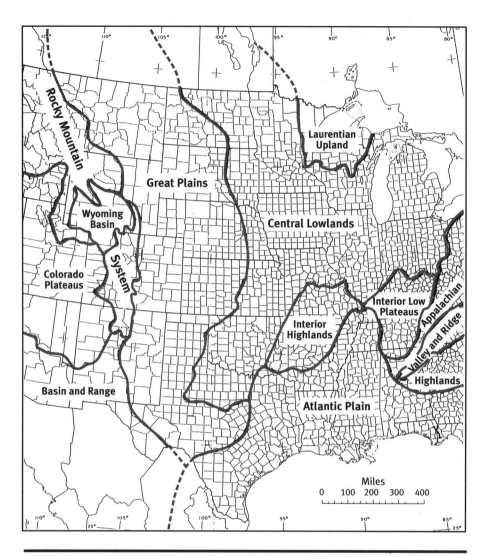

4. Major physiographic regions of the interior United States, after N. Fenneman, in *National Atlas of the United States of America* (U.S. Geological Survey, 1970).

Asia and North America for land-based animals. The climate of North America reached a maximum of warmth and dryness about 3,000 B.C., the so-called xerothermic period.

The vegetation of central North America during the xerothermic period (Fig. 5) was greatly different from that typical of the preceding glacial maximum. By then the deciduous forests had retreated eastwardly, and a "prairie peninsula" gradually penetrated beyond Lake Superior. At least in some areas there were small, forest-bounded islands of grassland as far east as Lake Erie. To the north, deciduous forests blended into coniferous forests in what would become southeastern Ontario, and a broad area of aspen parklands formed along the northern edge of the prairie in what is now Saskatchewan and Manitoba. Still farther west, coniferous forests probably covered much of what is now Alberta and certainly extended south along the Rocky Mountains in much the way they presently do. But the grasslands held sway over virtually the entire Great Plains region, no doubt gradually merging in the southwest with desert grasslands and scrub desert.

No avian or mammalian range maps exist for this long, dry period, but speculations are always possible. This era must have been a wonderful period for the large plains-grazing mammals. A smaller species of bison (*Bison antiquus*) had replaced earlier and larger forms associated with colder times during the Pleistocene. This bison extended its eastern range all the way to the Atlantic coast and even south to Florida. With it such species as the brown-headed cowbird and the eastern meadowlark probably thrived. Eastern outlying populations of basically western bird species probably split off then, such as the heath hen, an isolated (and eventually doomed) Atlantic coastal race of the greater prairie-chicken. The Florida race of the burrowing owl may also have found its way there during these arid times. Probably some of the species that are now limited to the southwestern grasslands, such as Cassin's sparrow, also moved upward into the central or even northern plains. The northern limit of the Cassin's sparrow's breeding range is still inclined to oscillate during periods of wetter and drier years.

Oscillating periods of wet years and droughts have continued on the interior plains since the end of the hypsithermal period. In general, the climate has become somewhat more moist, but droughts have tended to recur with increasing frequency. Part of these fluctuations seems to be related to periodic changes in Pacific Ocean currents, alternately bringing unusually colder or warmer waters northward along the Pacific

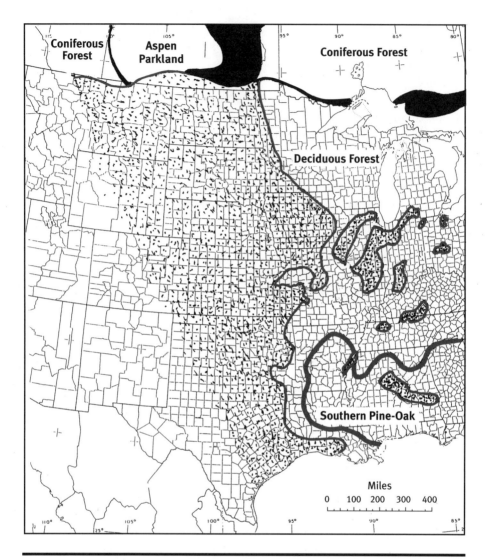

Coniferous Forest

Aspen Parkland

Coniferous Forest

Deciduous Forest

Southern Pine-Oak

Miles

0   100   200   300   400

5. Conjectural vegetation of the Great Plains region during the post-Pleistocene xerothermic period (ca. 5,000 years ago). Stippling indicates grasslands (western limits not defined); solid black areas are forest transition zones. Mainly after Kendeigh (1974).

There are seven or eight categories of phenomena in the world that are worth talking about, and one of them is the weather.

—Annie Dillard,
Pilgrim at Tinker Creek

coast, and with them variations in storms and precipitation patterns. There has also been a trend toward renewed planetary warming during the past century, perhaps at least in part caused by the burning of fossil fuels and by the increased atmospheric heat retention, the so-called "greenhouse effect," resulting from accumulations of carbon dioxide in the upper atmosphere.

Suggested readings

Askins 1999; Axelrod 1985; Graham 1999; Kendeigh 1974; Kurten and Anderson 1983; Leopold and Denton 1987; Mengel 1970; Wells 1970.

2

The Biotic Communities of the Central Plains

For as long as grass has existed, it has been wedded to the wind. Unlike most flowers, it needs neither insects nor other organisms to achieve its pollination. It needs only the wind, of which there is an endless supply on the prairie. Grasses are almost univer- sally wind-pollinated and have many adap- tations related to this feature. They have evolved abundant, light, and easily dissemi- nated pollen. They also have modifications of their flower parts that not only help cap- ture this pollen but that also cause the flo- rets to open whenever the air conditions are favorable for wind dispersal. A few grasses have seeds with woolly tufts at their bases that probably help the seed to be- come attached to mammalian hair and thus to be transported to new sites. Some bristly headed grasses such as needle-and- thread have bent and twisted awns that al- ternately tighten and relax again under varying degrees of moisture, causing the seed to be literally drilled into soft earth, as if each were propelled by its own individ- ual screwdriver.

And grasses have another, almost invis- ible secret that has allowed them to survive and thrive. The secret lies in the fact that grasses have their germinal growing points, called meristems, at the bases of their leaves and of their stems. In broad-leaved plants other than grasses and sedges, such cell-division areas are located toward the tips of their stems, and their terminal growth is effectively stopped by upperpart removal or death. However, fire, freezing, or the devouring of the above-ground parts of grasses does not stop their growth and either kill or significantly retard the plants. Instead, such events simply stimulate new growth from the protected base of the plants, typically located just above ground level. Thus, even as plant-loving mammalian grazers and browsers of the Cenozoic era came to dominate the earth's terrestrial ecosystems, the grasses survived. This unique regenerative ability of grasses may frustrate those modern home owners having large lawns, yet it has produced nothing but success for the grasses. Indeed, they have responded to all the earth's traditional calamities such as fire, flood, glaciers, and drought by simply waiting them out and then resprouting and inheriting much of the wasteland left by the often-defeated forests or other less adaptable vegetation types.

Grasses also know how to deal with summer heat. Some prairie grasses such as western wheatgrass have waxy surfaces that reduce evaporation; additionally, its leaves curl up in hot weather, so that each blade forms a closed tube, through the ends of which gas exchange can continue to occur but which also reduces exposure to needless evaporation.

Another secret of grasses is that, unlike trees, they safely store their annual profit of organic matter mostly underground, so that about two-thirds of the plant's so-called biomass is usually out of sight and unavailable to most large animals. Over long periods of time these soils become increasingly rich in inorganic nutrients and water-holding organic humus, the product of untold generations of storage and gradual breakdown of the grasses' root systems. The grassland soils of the world, which are now the world's breadbaskets for cereal grain cultures, are this way simply because they are the planet's best-preserved biological graveyards.

Unlike grasses, trees and tall shrubs are like ostentatious capitalists, building ever larger structures yearly and storing relatively little of their annual profits in their roots. In tall-grass prairies, from two to four times more biomass may be present underground than in their above-ground parts. When grass burns, its above-ground parts die back from drought or freezing; its ashes or dead leaves remain largely where they were and are rather quickly broken down into nutrients that can rapidly be resorbed back into the living plant. Cutting or burning trees results in a sudden loss of most of their stored-up nutrients, which may be blown away as ash or hauled away as timber. In either case the result is often catastrophic for the trees, which patiently must rise again as seedlings or saplings. Thus fires are typically the greatest enemy of forests and shrub-dominated communities, and even a single burn may transform a forest or shrub-dominated community into a continuous grassland, at least temporarily.

The spreading of grasses across landscapes is aided not only by their abundant seed crops but also especially by the lateral expansion of their coverage by means of horizontal underground roots, called rhizomes, and by similar lateral but above-ground stems, or stolens. Plants that spread out in this manner often take the form of clumped "bunchgrass," in that the separate plants have definite gaps between them. Or a grass species may be of the sod-forming type, in which the roots of separate plants grow together and interconnect to form a continuous above-ground mantle of greenery, with little or no space between for other plants to take root.

Armed with these simple survival strategies, grasses have come to develop a long-term tolerant coexistence with grazing animals. Unlike many low-growing broad-leaved plants such as shrubs and forbs, grasses have never evolved thorns or leaves with noxious chemicals that might prevent or seriously reduce grazing by large mammals, although a few have seeds protected with irritatingly sharp coatings or long and sharp awns. Many grasses also have substantial amounts of silica present in their leaves, probably serving as a leaf-strengthening adaptation, to which the grazing mammals have readily adjusted by developing higher, stronger, and more effectively grinding teeth. The entire local mammal megafauna of horses, rhinos, camels, and other large mammals in the 10-million-year-old volcanic ash strata of Ashfall Geologic Park in north-eastern Nebraska was destroyed in a very short time by that single calamitous event. Not so the grasses, which have long since reclaimed and even today still quietly cover the site. Appropriately, the fossil rhinos found still have fossil grass seeds and grass leaf remnants lodged between their teeth.

Grasses not only now cover this small Nebraska site but indeed originally probably covered more than 90 percent of the entire Great Plains during historic times (Fig. 5). I once estimated that in the Great Plains states between North Dakota and the Texas panhandle, representing an area of about 500,000 square miles, the native vegetation originally con-

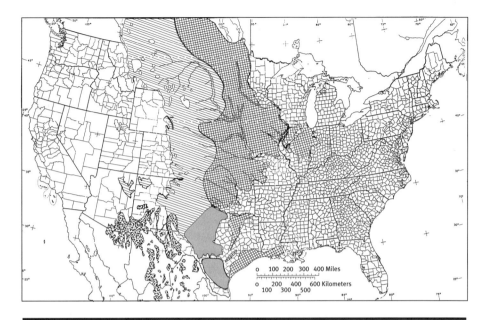

6. Presettlement grassland vegetation of interior North America, after Shantz and Zon (1924). Includes tall-grass prairies (*cross-hatched*), short-grass plains (*hatched*), mesquite and desert grassland savannas (*light shading*), and desert grasslands (*stippled*). Mostly after Shantz and Zon (1924), but Mexican desert grasslands after McClaren and Van Devander (1995).

sisted of about 80 percent grasslands. Most of the rest was either hardwood forest or a forest-grassland mosaic, so that about 400,000 square miles of native grasslands (short grass, mixed grass and tall grass) might have been present within that multistate region, which makes up about one-third of the entire original grassland biome of North America.

Almost everyone who has tried to map the grasslands has provided a somewhat different set of terms and mapped boundaries. Nearly all tend to divide the grasslands into a western, drier, short-grass prairie or steppe component (Fig. 6) and a more easterly and more mesic tall-grass category that, at least as fragmented elements, still extends as far east as Illinois and western Indiana. These are the remnants of the "prairie peninsula" that once (during the postglacial xerothermic period) extended much farther east but that since has been largely replaced by hardwood forest (and more recently, by corn), as a result of improved

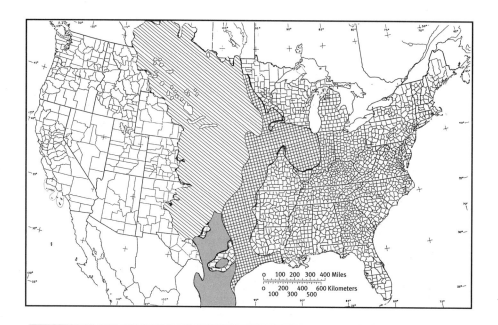

7. Original grasslands (*hatched*) of interior North America, plus eastern oak savanna transition region (*cross-hatched*) and southern mesquite grasslands (*light shading*). The clear areas in Texas are pinyon-juniper woodlands; those in the northwestern plains are coniferous forests. After Aldrich (1966).

moisture conditions and protection from recurrent prairie fires. This entire area, from about Iowa eastward, has at times been classified as "oak savanna" (Fig. 7). Among the native Missouri Valley hardwords, oaks such as bur oaks are the most resistant to periodic droughts and fires, and they, more than any other forest tree, are more likely to extend westward into the treeless prairies as lone outliers, in places where other hardwood species are likely to be confined to stream valley shorelines or other similar wetland situations.

To the northeast and northwest the grasslands meet the transcontinental boreal coniferous forest of Canada, but it is unusual for the grasslands to abut directly against evergreen forests. Instead, aspens typically form a transitional boundary between these two types, either as discontinuous groves or as more continuous parklands, within which the prairies often exist as isolated islands. It is perhaps true that aspens are scarcely more resistant to fires than are the pines, spruces, and firs, but aspens are famous for their ability to regenerate as sapling shoots fol-

lowing death or removal of their upperparts. Indeed, the groves of aspens that are so common in this northern region and similar ones
bounding the front ranges of the Rocky Mountains are probably each
largely clones of a single genetic type, which has gradually spread out
from what may have been a single tree to constitute a sort of spreading
superorganism.

To the west, the arid short-grass plains gradually become transformed into "sageshrub," as various species of sagebrush, especially big
sage and other arid-adapted shrubs begin to share dominance with the
grasses. Under even drier conditions, the shrubs gain ascendancy over
the grasses and make up a shrub semidesert community. Locally drier
conditions also sometimes prevail somewhat farther east, where the soil
substrate is distinctly sandy. Here, sandsage replaces the various sage
species that are more typical of harder soils and together with grasses
form a fairly distinctive "sandsage-steppe" mixed shrub and grassland
community. Even farther west, in the intermontane basins west of the
Rockies, a similar dry desert grassland is present that perhaps is a relict
of the Sierra Madre Geoflora, whereas in the northern prairie states of
the Dakotas, eastern Montana, and eastern Wyoming some boreal plant
and bird elements appear (Fig. 8).

To the south and southwest the short-grass prairies merge gradually with the desert grasslands of New Mexico and Mexico (see Figs. 6
and 7). The desert grassland is a community type that extends well into
the Mexican highlands, the presumed ancestral home of the North
American grassland community. Especially in Texas, the grasslands also
form a distinctive savannalike mixture of desert grass and mesquite, a
thorny, arid-adapted, and leguminous tree somewhat similar in appearance to the thorny acacias of the African savanna. The western edge of
the tall-grass and midgrass prairies roughly corresponds with the
twenty-inch annual precipitation isohyet; west of this, short-grass
species dominate. Similarly, few areas of tall-grass prairie exist in areas
receiving more than forty inches of precipitation; this is the region now
dominated by forests (Figs. 9 and 10). Nearly all the surviving native
grasslands are encompassed by the regions west of the twenty-inch isohyet and east of the Rockies.

Like the spines of these African trees, mesquite thorns help to reduce
browsing by large mammals, and in both cases this adaptation has
evolved in climates where the trees can ill-afford to altruistically donate
any of their valuable photosynthetic parts to mammalian passers-by.

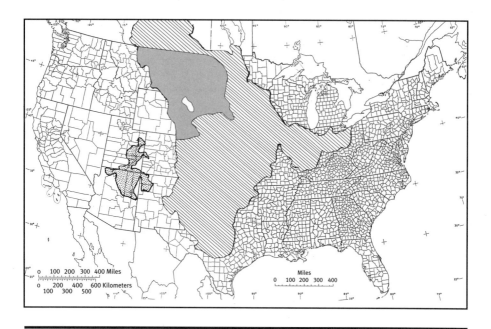

8. Original distribution of Great Plains (*hatched*) and Great Basin (*stippled*) grasslands. After Robbins et al. (1986). The upland northern plains region of the United States, as defined by Kantrud (1982), is shown as shaded overlay.

Succulent water-storing but spiny plants, or those having edible leaves but thorny spines, become more common here too, as do generally non-thorny shrubs having distasteful or even poisonous leaves that are sometimes very high in absorbed soil salts. By having salt concentrations in their cells that are more concentrated than that of the surrounding environment, salt-tolerant plants can absorb water in quite strongly saline soils. The excess salts may be excreted by special glands on their leaves or may remain in the leaves until they drop off at the end of the growing season, thus depositing a salty blanket under the plant canopy that may inhibit other less salt-tolerant plant species from germinating there. This adaptation is not known to occur in grasses, but some drought-tolerant grasses such as certain grama grasses, needle-and-thread, and wheatgrasses have high concentrations of proteins and carbohydrates in their cytoplasm that help to bring in water by osmosis.

If these widely spread grasslands have any single genus of grass that ecologically and sometimes quite literally binds them together, it is perhaps the bluestems, in the genus *Andropogon* (Fig. 11). Big bluestem largely dominates the tall-grass prairies of the eastern plains, and little bluestem is equally important in mixed-grass prairie. Sand bluestem is the dominant type in the Sandhills grasslands of central Nebraska as well as occurring in other localized sandy areas from North Dakota to Texas. At least seven other species of *Andropogon* also occur in the Great Plains region. The stems of bluestem grasses are not so much blue as they are somewhat purplish, at least when the above-ground leaves and stems are dead. This distinctive color provides a somewhat purplish-red sheen to native prairies in fall and winter and blends perfectly with the coppery-red tones of Indian grass, another typical tall-grass species. By this color alone anyone can often recognize bluestem prairie remnants

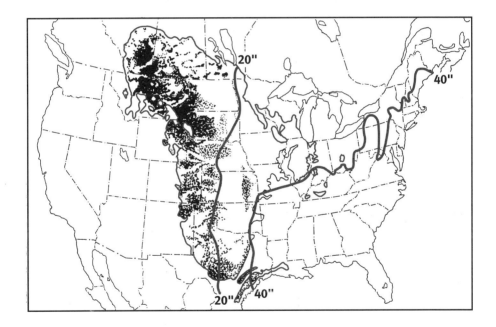

9. Current distribution of remaining grassland remnants in interior North America (*shaded areas*), relative to 20 inches (51 cm.) and 40 inches (102 cm) annual precipitation isohyets (from the *National Atlas*, U.S. Geological Survey, 1970). The approximate original limits of native grasslands in interior North America (mainly after Shantz and Zon 1924 and Küchler 1966) are also shown (*heavy lines*). The Flint Hills region of Kansas is apparent as a vertical band through eastern Kansas, and the Nebraska Sandhills region is also evident.

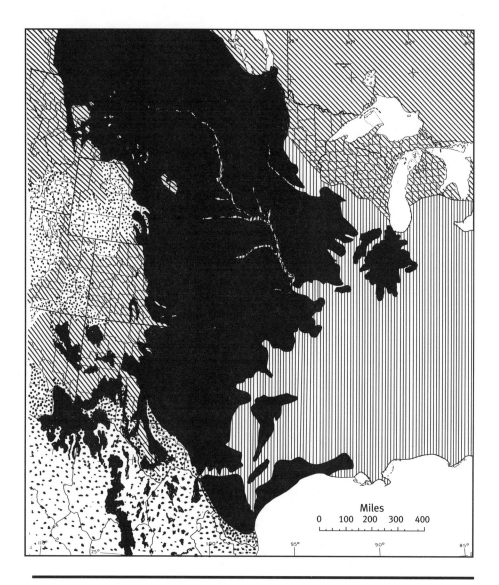

10. Nongrassland vegetation types surrounding interior grasslands (*black*) of North America, including coniferous forest (*diagonal hatching*), deciduous forest (*vertical hatching*), sage-scrub desert (*fine stippling*), and creosote bush or other arid scrub desert types (*heavier stippling*). Mainly after Shantz and Zon (1924); Mexican desert grasslands after McClaren and Van Devender (1995).

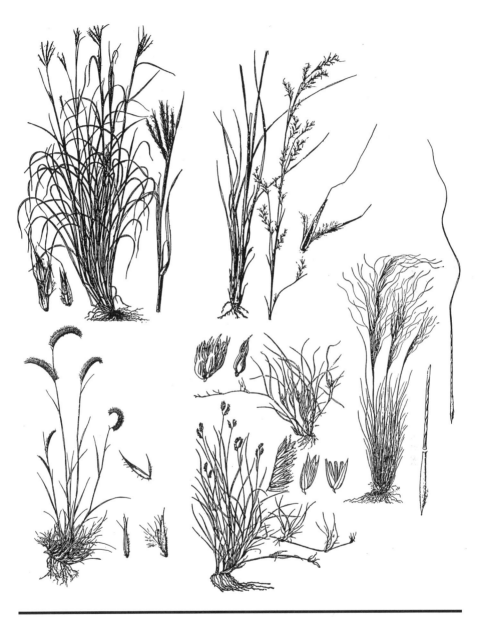

11. Drawings of five prairie grasses, including (A) big bluestem, (B) little bluestem, (C) blue grama, (D) buffalo grass, and (E) needle-and-thread. The enlarged view of the last species shows its twisted and highly elongated awn. From *Grasses, U.S. Yearbook of Agriculture,* 1948.

from nearly a mile away, as it contrasts so strongly with the more buffy-yellow, dead-grass color of annual grasses such as downy brome and other similar nonnative grasses.

Another important soil-binding grass genus, that of grama grass or *Bouteloua,* has a North American range that also rather neatly circumscribes the Great Plains grasslands. Side-oats grama, a beautiful and relatively tall species whose florets hang down from the stem like the feathers on a Sioux warrior's spear, is most common in mixed-grass prairies. Blue grama, hairy grama, and black grama are shorter and progressively more arid-adapted and thus are more western or southwestern in their distributions. A similar-sized grass, appropriately called buffalo grass, is another of the important short-grass species of wide distribution on the high plains. It is likely that bison have relished the taste of buffalo grass, bluestems, and grama grasses for millions of years, just as cattle do now.

Although it is not apparent from such taxonomic groupings, an important difference between the generally mesic-adapted and taller-grass species, and the shorter, more arid-adapted ones, is that two quite different metabolic pathways are present in these two general types. Many green plants, including not only grasses but also forbs (herbaceous plants that are neither grasses nor sedges) and woody plants such as conifers that grow where moisture is not a serious problem synthesize their basic six-carbon carbohydrates such as simple sugars via a pathway involving certain intermediary molecules with three carbon atoms in their photosynthetic process. Such plants are most abundant in cool and moist habitats. These plants are thus called three-carbon or C_3 species and are often simply described as "cool-season" species. Most of their growth occurs early in the growing season, when they often provide important nesting cover for birds and fresh green leaves for grazing animals. The well-named Junegrass of early summer is an example.

In plants adapted to warmer and drier habitats, the first stable molecule in the same photosynthetic process is a four-carbon compound; such plants can use water more efficiently than can species of the other category, and a critical enzyme operates more efficiently at a higher temperature. Additionally, C_4 plants build up carbon dioxide within their cells to much higher levels than do C_3 plants, allowing their leaf pores (stomata) to remain closed longer, thus reducing water loss to the atmosphere. These so-called "warm-season" or C_4 plants include about half the world's roughly 10,000 species of grasses and such prairie grasses as little bluestem, grama grass, and buffalo grass.

Both groups of prairie grasses and forbs tend to have deep root systems, generally extending farther below the soil surface than their above-ground parts attain at maximum height. Most prairie plants thus have root systems that allow them access to moisture far below even when surface soil levels become completely dry (Fig. 12). Some short-grass species such as blue grama grass have rather shallow root systems that seem to be adapted for capturing the moisture from brief summer rains, whereas many of the tall-grass plants have very deep roots that are at least partly nourished by late winter snowmelt or heavy spring rainfall. The Great Plains species of *Andropogon* are warm-season grasses, but in the genus *Panicum*, another major member genus of the Great Plains prairie community comprising more than twenty species, there are variations among species as to their C_3 or C_4 pathways. There are even some species of grasses known that use both pathways. Surprisingly, not only the arid-adapted short-grass prairie grasses are of the C_4 type but many of the tall-grass species are also. Tall grasses such as the bluestems bloom in late summer and thus need to use midsummer moisture for their flowering. In areas where summer rains exceed spring rains, tall grasses using C_4 metabolism are likely to predominate.

There is also a third type of photosynthesis, typical of desert-adapted plants such as some cactuses but apparently not of grasses. These plants, all of which have thick leaves, shut down their leaf pores during the heat of the day so that no water can escape. However, no carbon-dioxide gas can then enter the leaves, so photosynthesis cannot be completed. During the day the plant builds up intermediate acidic three-carbon molecules, which are not converted to six-carbon sugars until nightfall, when their leaf pores open up and allow carbon dioxide to enter and complete the photosynthetic process. These relatively slow-growing plants are called CAM plants because of one of their intermediate acid molecules. The commercially grown pineapple plant has this type of metabolism, and its fruits are harvested during early morning hours rather than midday, to avoid the acid taste that would otherwise be present.

Through these adaptations, the grasses have come to terms with the vicissitudes of the Great Plain's climate, its animals, and its premechanized agricultural history. They have reshaped the soils of the plains to their own ends, thereby enriching it for everyone. However, the metal plow was outside their range of evolutionary experience or their ability to cope. Hundreds of species of grasses then silently began to disappear from the plains.

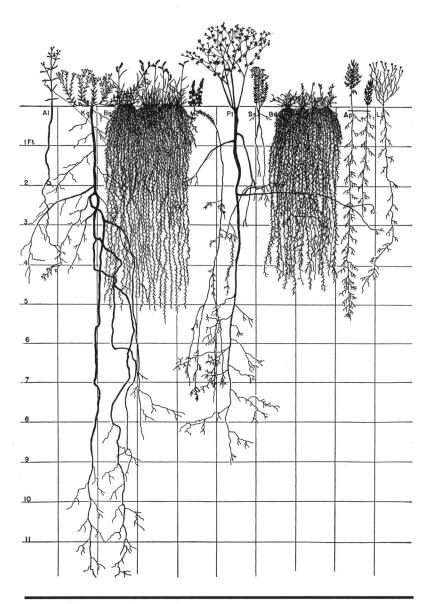

12. Root profiles of various mixed-grass prairie plants, including (*left to right*), narrowleaf four-o'clock, prairie false boneset, blue grama, globemallow, wild alfalfa, cutleaf ironplant, buffalo grass, western ragweed, and skeletonweed. From *Grasses, U.S. Yearbook of Agriculture, 1948.*

Many native forbs also disappeared, including such interesting and conspicuous native perennial forbs as the beautifully yellow-blossomed compass-plant, a plant whose larger leaves consistently orient themselves vertically in a north-south direction, which allows the leaves to perform photosynthesis during hot weather without becoming water-deficient and wilted. This trait was sufficiently precise as to be used by early explorers of the West for helping to judge directions. The compass-plant was also a favorite food of bison and was well known to the Native Americans as well as to early settlers, who regularly used it as a source of medicine (its generic name *Silphium* refers to a traditional Greek medicinal plant). Scarcely one Nebraskan in a thousand would now recognize a compass-plant, and perhaps not a single farmer in the entire state would admit to the possibility that the presence of such a plant might be a welcome discovery on his or her property.

> *What a thousand acres of Silphiums looked like when they tickled the bellies of the buffalo is a question never again to be answered, and perhaps not even asked.*
>
> —Aldo Leopold,
> *Sand County Almanac*

Bird Communities of the Grasslands

Do not venture into the prairie if you are attracted only to colorful and conspicuous forest birds, such as orioles, tanagers, and warblers. And you must not only look down into the grass but also search high above, for the prairie birds are as likely to be singing their fine melodies when nearly out of sight above as from the earth below. But be careful where you step, lest you tread on the hidden nest of a sparrow or crush a fragile prairie violet.

Just as the prairie has its own distinctive array of grasses and forbs, so too it has its characteristic birds and mammals and no doubt also its abundant but less-studied insects and other animal groups. Charles Kendeigh listed twenty-five species of birds (including all of those described in this book) and thirty-one species of mammals that are common and widespread grassland species in North America. Only a few members of each of these two groups are entirely confined (that is, wholly endemic) to grasslands. Instead, they often also occur during early successional stages of adjoining community types such as various

Table One   Grassland Bird Species of the Great Plains

	U.S. Great Plains[a]	North America[b]	Northern Plains[c]	Canadian Plains[d]
Northern harrier	X	Secondary (P)	X	X
Swainson's hawk	X	Secondary		X
Ferruginous hawk (+***)	X	Primary	X	X
Prairie falcon	X	Secondary		X
Greater prairie-chicken	X	Secondary (P)		X
Lesser prairie-chicken	X	Secondary		
Sharp-tailed grouse	X	Secondary	X	X
Mountain plover (−**)	X	Secondary	X	Primary
Long-billed curlew	X	Primary	X	Primary
Upland sandpiper (+***)	X	Secondary (C)	X (I)	X
Marbled godwit	X	Primary		Primary
Wilson's phalarope (−**)	X	Primary		
Franklin's gull	X	Primary		
Burrowing owl	X	Secondary	X	X
Short-eared owl	X	Secondary		X
Horned lark (−***)	X	Secondary (P)	X	Primary
Sprague's pipit (−***)	X	Primary	X (I)	X
Dickcissel (−***)	X	Secondary (C)		X
Cassin's sparrow (−***)	X	Primary		
Clay-colored sparrow(−***)	X	Secondary	X (I)	X
Brewer's sparrow (−***)	X	Secondary	X (I)	X
Vesper sparrow	X	Secondary	X (I)	X
Lark sparrow (−***)	X	Secondary		X

forest communities. They can also opportunistically spread into the grasslands from various more desertlike community types, to which they may be equally or perhaps even better adapted.

In an earlier book on the breeding birds of the Great Plains states, I identified about forty species as typical of the Great Plains grasslands, i.e., those species that are closely associated with grasslands and are not only most common there but also tend to be variably limited to the plains grasslands. Thirty-three of these species are tabulated here (Table 1), excluding six species (Chihuahuan raven, Bachman's sparrow, field sparrow, LeConte's sparrow, Nelson's sharp-tailed sparrow, and Brewer's blackbird) that in retrospect probably are best classified elsewhere and

Table One   (continued)

	U.S. Great Plains[a]	North America[b]	Northern Plains[c]	Canadian Plains[d]
Lark bunting (–***)	X	Primary	X	Primary
Savannah sparrow (–**)	X	Secondary	X(I)	X
Grasshopper sparrow (–***)	X	Primary (C)	X(I)	X
Baird's sparrow	X	Primary	X(I)	Primary
Henslow's sparrow (–***)	X	Secondary (P)		X
McCown's longspur	X	Primary	X(I)	Primary
Chestnut-collared longspur	X	Primary	X(I)	Primary
Bobolink (–***)	X		X(I)	
Eastern meadowlark (–***)	X	Secondary (C)		
Western meadowlark (–***)	X	Secondary	X	X

[a] Includes those species identified by Johnsgard (1979) as grassland species of the Great Plains states, except for six species that were not listed by any of the other authors tabulated here. Asterisks indicate increasingly higher levels of statistical significance (* = $p < 0.10$, ** = $p < 0.05$, *** = $p < 0.01$) as to apparently improving (+) or declining (–) overall populations of each species, based on breeding bird surveys in the United States and Canada done between 1966 and 1996 (see Table 12).

[b] Identified by Mengel (1970) as North American grassland avifauna species, including all "primary" and most "secondary" species. Six secondary (mostly sage-scrub) species not on Johnsgard's list are excluded. Species identified as (C) were classified by Zimmerman (1993) as regularly present "core species" on a remnant prairie (Konza Prairie) in eastern Kansas; those listed as (P) were less frequently present as summer residents.

[c] Identified by Kantrud and Kologiski (1983) as typical Northern Great Plains grassland species. Those marked parenthetically (I) were considered indicator species for various subregions.

[d] Identified by McNicholl (1988) as Canadian endemic grassland ("steppe") species. Secondary steppe species are indicated by X.

that also were not chosen by others who have tried to identify the grassland avifauna. Foremost among these is Robert Mengel, who produced a list (thirty-seven total species, twelve of which he considered as grassland endemics) similar to mine. He also included six peripheral and mostly sage-scrub species (Mississippi kite, sage grouse, common poorwill, sage thrasher, green-tailed towhee, sage sparrow) that were not part of my list. Mengel excluded the bobolink, which I have somewhat reluctantly accepted, but which he believed to have invaded the central plains from more eastern meadow habitats during early historic times. Both of us excluded the brown-headed cowbird; although it historically was strongly associated with the bison, it is now actually rare to absent on completely treeless areas of grassland. From a geographic species-density viewpoint, the region centered in north-central Montana has the highest number of sympatric grassland endemics (ten to twelve), using Mengel's terminology (see Fig. 16, chap. 3). This distributional pattern suggests that the grassland avifauna of the Great Plains had their evolutionary origins in an environment of short- and mixed-grass prairies rather than in an ancestral tall-grass prairie ecosystem.

In his recent survey of grassland species, Fritz Knopf largely adopted Mengel's list of prairie birds but excluded three wetland-associated species (marbled godwit, Wilson's phalarope, and Franklin's gull) as well as four peripheral western forms (sage grouse, green-tailed towhee, Brewer's sparrow, and sage sparrow), only one of which I have retained on my list.

The U.S. Fish and Wildlife Service has additionally classified as grassland species the ring-necked pheasant, barn owl, LeConte's sparrow, and sedge wren when analyzing their breeding bird survey data but excluded the Swainson's hawk, prairie falcon, Wilson's phalarope, Franklin's gull, burrowing owl, clay-colored sparrow, and Brewer's sparrow.

Two other more regional listings of grassland endemic birds are included in Table 1. One list consists of grassland birds typical of the northern plains states (from Montana's and North Dakota's Canadian borders south to northwestern Nebraska), and the other is a list of grassland birds typical of the Canadian high plains and "steppe" grasslands.

Nearly half of the thirty-three grassland species in Table 1 are nonpasserines, consisting of several species each of shorebirds, raptors, and grouse. The passerine birds also include one transhemispheric species (the horned lark), but most of the others have clear affiliations with the interior grasslands of North America. Nineteen of the total appear on all four of the lists summarized in the table and probably thus constitute the truest central plains grassland endemics. The breeding ranges of the thirty-three species are highly variable, and it is clear that not a single one has a breeding range whose limits correspond exactly with that of the historic central plains grasslands. However, massive ecological changes have occurred within these grasslands in historic times, and many corresponding range adjustments by the birds have no doubt occurred as well.

Not only do the ranges of the grasslands birds differ, but their relative abundances also vary greatly (Table 2). It will surprise no one who has been raised on the prairie to learn that its most common breeding birds are the two species of meadowlarks, especially the western meadowlark. Meadowlarks are the largest and most conspicuous of the prairie songbirds. Their flutelike songs also proclaim them as among the prairie's most characteristic birds and the species most strongly identified with grasslands by farmers and ranchers. Meadowlarks, together with the less widely recognized horned lark, are ground-foraging insectivores with fairly long legs, and all three species also exhibit white outer tail feathers that are conspicuous during flight, especially during aerial display. The meadowlarks have the longest, most tapering, and straightest beaks among the prairie songbirds, which are useful probing tools. The horned lark, the much more restricted-range Sprague's pipit, and the bobolink have relatively shorter and more sparrowlike beaks, the bobolink in effect becoming ecologically little more than a large, seed-eating sparrow (Fig. 13).

Although never so abundant as the meadowlarks and horned larks, the grassland sparrows compose the grassland group having the largest species diversity; more than one-third of all the grassland endemic birds are part of the sparrow assemblage. These species differ relatively little in total body mass or beak size, but, as will become apparent in the later species accounts, they effectively manage to subdivide the grasslands both geographically and ecologically. Yet all of them are to varying degrees dependent on the seeds of grasses and other prairie plants, even though they additionally consume and even depend upon insect foods during the summer breeding season. Grasshopper sparrows, vesper sparrows, and Savannah sparrows are among the most abundant and widespread of the grassland sparrows, but dickcissels (in eastern tallgrass prairies) and lark buntings (in western short-grass steppe) are often the most abundant sparrow species within their more limited ranges. All have very similar sparrowlike bills and feet (Fig. 14).

One doesn't normally think of shorebirds as typical grassland birds, but several of the most attractive of the grassland avifaunal species are among this group, including the long-billed curlew, upland sandpiper, marbled godwit, and mountain plover. By stretching the concept of grasslands slightly to include prairie marshes, the Wilson's phalarope and Franklin's gull also need to be included. Three of these, the Franklin's gull, upland sandpiper, and Wilson's phalarope, are true Neotropical migrants, passing to the equator or beyond during their fall migrations. The long-billed curlew and mountain plover are also fairly

Table Two   Breeding Densities and Frequencies of Grassland Endemics

	Great Plains Densities[a]	Northern Plains Frequencies[b]	Overall 1977 Index[c]
Western meadowlark	73.7	77%	18.7
Eastern meadowlark	17.1		16.5
Horned lark	44.2	62%	12.3
Savannah sparrow	5.0	7%	6.0
Dickcissel	18.0		5.3
Lark bunting	25.9	38%	4.3
Grasshopper sparrow	5.7	33%	3.2
Vesper sparrow	8.0	32%	2.9
Lark sparrow	3.9		1.8
Cassin's sparrow	4.2		1.6
Clay-colored sparrow	6.0	9%	1.2
Chestnut-collared longspur	6.4	44%	0.9
Brewer's sparrow	1.8	25%	0.89
Upland sandpiper	2.0	15%	0.68
Franklin's gull	4.9		0.40
Long-billed curlew	0.6	10%	0.18
Northern harrier	0.7	tr.	0.17
Swainson's hawk	0.6		0.17
Wilson's phalarope	0.7		0.14
Burrowing owl	0.4	tr.	0.14
Marbled godwit	0.7		0.12
Baird's sparrow	0.7	15%	0.09
Sharp-tailed grouse	0.2	tr.	0.08
Sprague's pipit	0.2	12%	0.08
McCown's longspur	1.0	15%	0.03
Greater prairie-chicken	0.2		0.03
Henslow's sparrow	tr.		0.03
Bobolink	1.1	4%	0.03
Ferruginous hawk	0.1		0.02
Short-eared owl	0.2		0.02
Prairie falcon	tr.		0.01
Mountain plover	tr.	tr.	0.01
Lesser prairie-chicken	–		0.003

[a] Estimated average number of birds per twenty-five-mile (forty-km) route, for all breeding bird survey routes in seventeen Great Plains states and provinces (see Chart 3). Data derived from Robbins et al. (1986). Values of less than 0.1 are shown as tr.

[b] Incidence of occurrence (as percentage) in 615 study plots (mostly of 65 ha., or 160 acres) throughout the northern Great Plains (Kantrud 1982). Species too rare to be quantified are shown as tr.; other unlisted grassland species were absent or were not included in the survey.

[c] Index represents mean number of birds seen per route on all routes where species was detected × the numerical incidence of its occurrence among the 1,832 breeding bird surveys done during 1977 (Robbins et al. 1986).

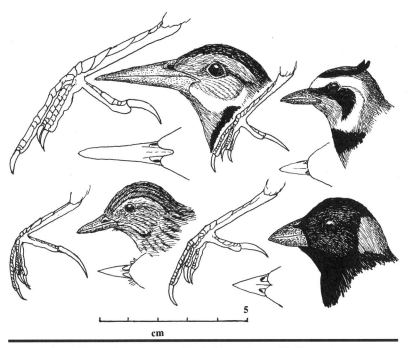

13. Heads and feet of eastern meadowlark (A), horned lark (B), Sprague's pipit (C), and bobolink (D). Drawing by author, in part after Ridgway (1902, 1904, 1907).

strongly migratory but often winter no farther south than northern Mexico.

These species have distinctive bill shapes and varied bill lengths; examining this feature alone provides strong clues as to their food habits. The ploverlike birds, including the upland sandpiper (originally called the upland plover), have short, fairly stout bills and large eyes; they forage for surface foods, typically on dry sand or harder surfaces, and do little probing. The sandpipers, including the curlews and godwits, have bills designed for probing in soft, usually wet, sand. Their eyes are relatively smaller, and their bills are well supplied with tactile receptors for detecting subsurface movements not apparent to their eyes. Watching a long-billed curlew on its nesting grounds trying to capture and pick up insects with the tip of its incredibly long and curved bill is like

14. Heads and feet of lark bunting (A), dickcissel (B), lark sparrow (C), McCown's longspur (D), Baird's sparrow (E), grasshopper sparrow (F), vesper sparrow (G), and Savannah sparrow (H). Drawing by author, in part after Ridgway (1901).

watching someone trying to eat with chopsticks for the first time; it seems there should be a better way. Yet on its coastal wintering grounds, the curlew's long, decurved bill becomes a perfect probing tool in deep sand, and it would seem that in this case, as in the grassland sparrows, evolution has responded more to its wintering habitat needs (where it is in competition with many more shorebird species) than to its possible nesting-ground requirements. The Wilson's phalarope has a long, straight, and delicate bill that is used for plucking small items from the water surface or from just beneath it as the bird runs about at the water's edge or, more often, swims in a tight circle, stirring up small items from the subsurface with its foot actions and using the water's surface tension to sip up particles from its bill-tip into its mouth. The Franklin's gull has an all-purpose bill that is not greatly different in shape or function from that of crows and jays and that similarly is adapted for handling a wide variety of foods.

There are two owls characteristic of the American grasslands, the short-eared owl and the burrowing owl. The short-eared owl also occurs in Eurasia, and the burrowing owl extends south as far as temperate South America. The short-eared owl is a rodent specialist, which usually feeds from late afternoon into the evening hours, when it is replaced by truly nocturnal specialists such as the barn owl. Like those of most owls, its facial feathers are shaped like paired parabolic disks surrounding its large lateral ear openings, and few birds are better adapted at locating the exact source of prey sounds than are these owls. Unlike the short-eared owl, the burrowing owl is largely insectivorous during summer months, and the area around the nesting burrow is often littered with regurgitated pellets containing the exoskeletons of beetles that the birds have consumed. Its facial disks may be poorly developed, but there is nothing wrong with its daytime eyesight. I have watched burrowing owls twist their heads skyward and intently watch hawks that were so high in the air that I could scarcely see them without my binoculars.

Probably no single grassland bird species is as fascinating to observe for hours on end than is the burrowing owl. It is an owl that doesn't seem to accept the fact that owls should sleep during the day and hunt at night. Instead, it sits interminably on fenceposts or large boulders, carefully surveying its daytime surroundings with all the solemnity of a spindly-legged Bible-belt preacher in his pulpit, constantly scanning his flock to make certain they are all paying proper attention. Also like many such self-righteous preachers, it typically produces a large, un-manageable brood of youngsters in progressive stair-step sizes, who seem too prone to leave the confines of their burrow and wander away at the earliest opportunity, thereby often encountering trouble enough on their own.

Six raptors are especially typical of the North American grasslands. Besides the two owls, there are four hawks: the northern harrier, Swainson's hawk, ferruginous hawk, and prairie falcon. All are daytime hunters, primarily using their keen eyesight but also employing their fine hearing. The northern harrier probably has the best hearing of any of this group, and its facial feathering is somewhat owl-like, in that facial disks around the eyes are slightly developed. The Swainson's hawk is the only Neotropical migrant among these raptors. Its wintering grounds are at least 6,000 miles away in the temperate grasslands of southern South America. It is also the most insectivorous of these hawks, especially on its wintering grounds. Although the northern harrier is not strongly migratory, its transatlantic breeding range extends well into Eurasia, where it is part of a rather large group of similar marsh- and grassland-adapted harriers.

The ferruginous hawk's Latin name, *Buteo regalis,* gives some hint as to its imperial nature. The only raptor on the American grasslands that is more majestic than the ferruginous hawk is the golden eagle, and both are closely associated with two other basic grassland mammalian types, the prairie dog and the jackrabbit. The prairie falcon is simply a peregrine cloaked in grassland camouflage. I once sat on the very edge of Scott's Bluff in western Nebraska, looking almost vertically downward 800 feet, searching the rocks and grass with my binoculars for any possible birds. It wasn't until I first located the swiftly moving shadow of a falcon, perfectly projected on the grasslands below, that I was able to locate the low-coursing falcon itself, its brown dorsal colors blending perfectly with the still-dormant short grasses.

Being at the top of the grassland food chain, the raptors are necessarily rare. The average Great Plains collective densities for the six raptors total only 2.0, as compared with well over 200 for all the other avian types (see Table 2). Thus, seeing any raptor on the plains is something not to be expected every day, and to see one as impressive as a ferruginous hawk, as swift as a prairie falcon, or as majestic as a golden eagle is an event to be remembered for a lifetime.

Finally, there are three species of prairie grouse: the greater and lesser prairie-chickens and the sharp-tailed grouse. These wonderful birds capture, in my opinion, the very essence of the prairie. Their plumages are a marvelously intricate but extremely well-camouflaged pattern of pale buff and various tones of earth brown. The males' haunting courtship calls seem to have much the same air of wildness and sense of ancient wisdom as do those of loons and cranes. I can still vividly remember the first prairie-chicken I ever saw, when I was about eight years old. It was among a group of dead ring-necked pheasants that my father had shot on one of his regular hunts during the depression, in eastern North Dakota. He seemed almost embarrassed to have shot the prairie-chicken, since by then they already were becoming rare in North Dakota. However, in those bleak days meat was meat, and prairie-chickens were still legal game. But I looked at it intently, trying to fix its beauty in my memory in case I never saw another. It wasn't until I moved to Nebraska, over twenty years later, that I was able at last to see and hear live prairie-chickens in the wild and began to come under their particular mystical spell.

Almost all of these grassland species have drab or dun-colored plumages that closely correspond in hue to that of dead grass; don't search for birds-of-paradise in the prairie. Yet one should also be alert to the fact that prairie birds may appear more colorful and brilliant to one another than we are inclined to assume. It is now known that many birds, perhaps most, have visual ranges extending into the ultraviolet portion of the spectrum. Therefore, white or even brown feathers may reflect these very short wavelengths in ways humans can't appreciate but that are probably completely visible to birds. It is a revelation to examine the plumages of even some rather common prairie birds with a good source of UV light. The seemingly black plumage of an American crow becomes brilliantly illuminated with shimmering iridescent highlights, and the black dorsal spots and the tiny black teardrops on a mourning dove's cheeks become intensely violet. The male brown-headed cowbird appears almost as colorful as an American crow, but the fe-

You must not be in the prairie, but the prairie must be in you. . . . He who tells the prairie's mysteries must wear the prairie in his heart.

—William Quayle,
The Prairie and the Sea

male remains as drab as ever. Most vegetation absorbs rather than reflects UV light. Thus, birds that may seem virtually invisible to us may reveal or hide parts or all of their plumage in a way so as to make themselves more or less visible to others in a vegetational environment, as the situation may require. Life on the prairie stage is never so dull, and the plot line is never so simple, as it might seem to the casual observer.

Suggested Readings

Barbour and Billings 1988; Bennett and Cuthill 1994; Burkhardt 1989; Gayton 1990; Johnsgard 1979; Kendeigh 1974; Knight 1994; Knopf 1996b; McClaren and Van Devender 1995; Mengel 1970.

3   Lessons in Survival

Every species that now exists on our planet is a testimony to long-term survival; they are the visible evidence of unbroken generational reproduction. The uncounted biological failures that the earth has seen have generally long since disappeared, save perhaps for a few fragmentary fossils that show that failure has been a far more common story than success, and even the most successful of our species have left mostly invisible trails of continuous death extending back before time immemorial. As humans, we are only the most recent blip on that long durational time screen, in which even a century's span is scarcely noticeable. The maximum lifespan of a wild bird does not even register. But we don't yet know how long a single clump of grass might survive. It is very likely to surprise us.

Long-term Survival Lessons: Climate, Fire, and Drought

Weather has existed for long before it ever gave people an opportunity to complain about it; weather is to climate what a small and quickly melting chocolate tidbit is to an all-day sucker. An individual plant or animal may often not be able to adapt to the extremes of daily weather, but the

Forests decay, harvests perish, flowers vanish, but grass is immortal.

—John Ingalls, "Blue Grass"

species must certainly adapt to the average long-term climate if it is to survive. In simplest evolutionary terms, genes mutate; individuals are selected; populations adapt. Whether a given individual is selected for or against, and thus lives or dies, may be no more predictable than the single toss of a coin. Nevertheless, with enough available coin tosses, natural selection makes its choices known.

On the central plains, fire, floods, drought, and blizzards have represented the traditional Four Horsemen of the Apocalypse, perhaps with an occasional tornado thrown in as a Cosmic Trickster, seemingly just to make life more exciting. Grasses have adapted to all of these stresses remarkably well; after all, that is why at least remnants of the North American grasslands still exist. Clearly, they are highly adapted to regular but moderate grazing and for millions of years have thrived under the hooves of bison, horses, antelope, elk, and countless other grazing ungulates. Fire has always been one of their best friends, blizzards occur when their above-ground parts are inactive, and neither periodic floods nor occasional droughts do any permanent damage to them. Grasses truly are, as John Ingalls, pioneer U.S. senator from Kansas once poetically said, immortal.

The long-term consequences of grazing, burning, and other disturbances to the grassland landscape are manifold and include direct effects on the plants themselves as well as indirect effects on the avifauna, mostly as a reflection of these vegetational changes. To a large degree such rather broad-scale vegetational changes are fairly predictable, even though individual species may react somewhat differently (Chart 1). For example, fire suppression invariably favors woody (tree or shrub) species over herbaceous ones, and increased fire rates or intensities similarly tend to eliminate woody plants from an area. However, moderate grazing normally favors grasses and sedges, to the corresponding disadvantage of palatable forbs and shrubs. Grazing may have varied effects on tree survival and reproduction, favoring it in the case of unpalatable seedlings but perhaps having little or no adverse effect on rapidly growing but more palatable types.

These vegetational changes may have both short-term and long-term influences on grassland bird populations (Chart 2) and may be quite complex. John Zimmerman has concluded that in the Flint Hills of

Chart One   Typical Patterns of Plant Succession Associated with Grazing and Burning in Prairies

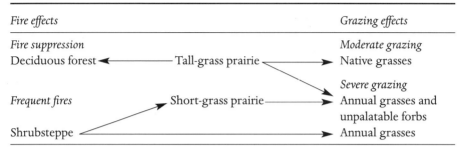

Fire effects	Grazing effects
Fire suppression	Moderate grazing
Deciduous forest ◄——————— Tall-grass prairie ———————►	Native grasses
	Severe grazing
Frequent fires ——————► Short-grass prairie ———————►	Annual grasses and unpalatable forbs
Shrubsteppe ———————————————————►	Annual grasses

Kansas grazing does not lower nesting success in grassland-dependent passerine birds, but grazing plus burning may reduce both nest survival and nestling production. In some cases, such as reduction of tick, mite, or other parasite populations after fires, the effects may well be similar for all the grassland birds. Other changes, including short-term litter and thatch reduction also as a general result of fires, may have quite opposite effects on the breeding of grassland species of conservation concern, such as the litter-dependent Baird's sparrow versus one or both longspurs. On the other hand, long-term ecological changes such as growth stimulation of grasses brought about by burning may result in an increase in litter and thatch two or more years into the future. In such cases a Hobson's choice may arise for land managers, and the degree of local or immediate conservation needs of a single species may provide the best alternative, perhaps at the expense of some other less endangered form or even possible long-term disadvantages.

For a summary of some of the observed positive or negative effects of grazing or burning on specific grassland species, see Table 3 and Chart 3. Clearly, with over thirty grassland bird species of potential concern, the wisdom of Solomon may at times be required to make the best judgments possible in achieving the most desirable techniques for managing bird populations on natural areas.

Short-term Survival Lessons: Corn, Cows, and Cowbirds

Recently I drove through the Pawnee National Grasslands of northeastern Colorado. It was one of those blue-sky October days, with the

Fire

Immediate effects

1. Reduced woody cover may adversely affect tree- or shrub-dependent species (Cassin's sparrow, Brewer's sparrow) but may benefit others by reducing hiding places or arboreal perches for predators.
2. Reduced herbaceous litter may decrease shelter for ground nesters (many sparrows) but may make walking and running easier.
3. Increased bare ground may improve foraging for some ground-foraging species (hawks, lark sparrow, mountain plover) but may also expose active nests to predators. However, reduced cover around burrowing owl nests makes them less vulnerable to sneak attack by predators.
4. An increase in large-seeded herbaceous forbs (such as dock and smartweeds) favors some seed-eaters (several sparrow species, sharp-tailed grouse).
5. Populations of ticks and other parasites may be reduced.

Long-term effects

1. There will be a gradual shift to more grasses, but fewer shrubs and trees will prolong effect no. 1 above, reducing nesting tree sites for species such as Swainson's hawks.
2. New growth is often both succulent and of high nutrient quality, at least for a few months.
3. Increased availability of herbaceous forage will benefit granivorous species.
4. Increased long-term visibility may affect both prey escape routes and hunting techniques of predators.
5. Small mammal populations (rodents) often increase for one to two years after burns, improving food supplies for hawks and owls.

Grazing

Light to moderate grazing

1. A more open canopy is created, affecting microclimate (temperature and humidity), possibly thus influencing nesting success.
2. Herbivores concentrate nutrients in urine and feces, affecting localized insect populations and foraging opportunities for insectivores.
3. Ground-trampling may increase soil-packing and ease of digging or probing for food.
4. Weedy "invader" species (including large-seeded annual forbs) tend to increase while more succulent species tend to decrease.

Intense grazing

1. Reduced biodiversity and plant cover affect nesting success, food availability, and amount of escape cover for prey species.
2. Patchy vegetation and warmer, drier soils favor grasshopper reproduction, thus improving food supplies for insectivores but reducing it for granivores.

Chart Two   (continued)

Cultivation of Grain Crops

1. The overall nesting habitat is reduced.
2. Crowding into field edges and ditches increases.
3. Exposure to pesticides and herbicides increases.
4. Vulnerability to predators using travel lanes increases.
5. Vulnerability to brood parasites increases.
6. Biodiversity of native plant foods and arthropods is reduced.
7. Sheltering cover, perch sites, and nest sites are reduced.
8. Direct mortality by disking, mowing, threshing, and so on increases.
9. Foods for granivorous spp. (grouse, sparrows, and so on) increases.
10. Irrigation may improve local water supplies.

Source: In part after Knight (1994), McClaren and Van Devender (1995), Bock et al. (1993), and Collins and Wallace (1990).

scattered golden cottonwoods looking like a Colorado tourist brochure cover, but the sere grasses had already assumed their khaki-tan winter cloaks. There were perhaps almost as many annual weeds and corn, wheat, or wheatgrass remains evident as there were grama grasses and other prairie forbs, the persistent remnants of failed farming practices. Here and there little groups of rather scrawny cattle dotted the rolling

Table Three   Positive Effects of Grazing and Burning on Some Breeding Birds of Northern Mixed-grass Prairies and Shrubsteppe

No Grazing; Burning ca. Every 5 to 10 Years	Moderate Grazing	Heavy Grazing
Upland sandpiper	Lark sparrow	Mountain plover
Long-billed curlew	Vesper sparrow	Horned lark
Short-eared owl	Chestnut-collared longspur	McCown's longspur
Baird's sparrow		(Brown-headed cowbird)
Lark bunting		
Grasshopper sparrow		
Savannah sparrow		
Brewer's sparrow		
Clay-colored sparrow		
Western meadowlark		

Source: Largely adapted from Dobkin (1994).

Chart Three   Population Responses by Grassland Birds to Grazing

Positive responses in taller and shorter grasslands	
Mountain plover	Lark sparrow
Burrowing owl	McCown's longspur
Horned lark	
Negative responses in taller and shorter grasslands	
Northern harrier	Baird's sparrow
Short-eared owl	Henslow's sparrow
Cassin's sparrow	
Positive responses in tall grasslands, negative in short grasslands	
Sprague's pipit	Chestnut-collared longspur
Dickcissel	Bobolink
Lark bunting	Eastern meadowlark
Grasshopper sparrow	Western meadowlark
Responses mixed, uncertain, or lacking	
Ferruginous hawk	Brewer's sparrow
Long-billed curlew	Vesper sparrow
Clay-colored sparrow	

Source: After Bock et al. 1993.

landscape, and overhead there were occasional flocks of blackbirds and cowbirds heading south toward a land of warmer nights and fewer prairie falcons.

It was a perfect visual combination of all the vicissitudes that have been suffered by the Great Plains grasslands in modern times. But there was also a golden eagle imperiously gazing downward from the struts of an old windmill tower, a prairie falcon that seemingly delighted in proving its prowess in scaring the daylights out of the myriad horned larks that at times almost carpeted the landscape, and a circling ferruginous hawk on the outlook for any rodents foolish enough to be out in the daylight hours. It was a fragmentary scene from an Eden that once was, a once magnificent garden now largely infested by weeds but still haunting, nevertheless. It was a shadowy view of times past, like the full-body castings of people suddenly trapped almost 2,000 years ago in Pompeii when Vesuvius erupted. Fragments of Pompeii itself also re-main, its floor and wall mosaics telling of happier times, just as fragments of the original short-grass prairie grasslands still defiantly persist in the American West, in spite of all that has happened there.

The effects of ungulate grazing on bird populations have already been described, but the differential effects of bison and cattle on the flora, and thus on the avifauna, need to be mentioned, too. Bison typically move gradually through an area, remaining only as long as their preferred plants are abundant, then go on to greener pastures. Domesticated cattle are typically confined and will eat the more desirable species of grasses until they are virtually eliminated before turning to the less palatable plants. Thus, the distasteful, thorny, or even toxic plants tend to increase under the impact of confined grazing while preferred species decline. Furthermore, continuous grazing of the above-ground parts of plants eliminates the annual production of litter, which would normally be recycled back into the soil as organic matter. The annual productivity of the plants is instead converted into beef, which in turn is removed from the land and marketed far away. Eventually the fertility of the soil will be depleted, just as the continuous cutting of trees will destroy the fertility of forest soils. Furthermore, the constant presence of confined cattle will tend to harden and pack the surface soil, reducing water penetration and eventually starving the plants above.

These factors have sometimes predictable effects on the bird life, but none of these effects is as severe as a conversion of native pastures to crops, especially to highly cultivated and rigidly weed-controlled row crops such as wheat or corn.

Some of the deleterious effects of farming on the productivity of Neotropical migrant birds have been summarized by Nicholas Rodenhouse and others. They pointed out that Neotropical migrants make up about 70 percent of the birds using farmlands for breeding and 86 percent of the bird species identified as breeding there. However, compared with the number in uncultivated areas, the number of nesting species is relatively low in farmlands. Both species richness and relative abundance are greatest in uncultivated edge habitats with trees or shrubs, less in uncultivated grassy edges, and least in row crops. Of the five Neotropical migrant species associated with grasslands that were studied by these authors (Table 4), all exhibited low annual productivity. These losses mainly were associated with high predation or direct agricultural influences, but with brood parasitism of seemingly smaller importance. The five grassland species had a lower estimated productivity than the 3.0 fledglings per pair per year judged to be minimal for population maintenance.

Table Four   Productivity of Grassland Birds Nesting in Farmlands

Species	No. of Nests	Nesting Losses (%)			Total	Reference
		Preda-tion	Agri-culture	Para-sitism		
Vesper sparrow	90	41	14	9	64	Three studies cited in Rodenhouse et al. 1993
Grasshopper sparrow	41	80	2	2	84	Basore and Best (in Rodenhouse et al. 1993)
Dickcissel	130	28	27	11	66	Three studies cited in Rodenhouse et al. 1993
Bobolink	33	9	85	0	94	Bollinger et al. 1990
Western meadowlark	24	50	17	0	67	Two studies cited in Rodenhouse et al. 1993
Total	318	38	25	7	70	

Source: Adapted from Rodenhouse et al. (1993). The average nesting losses of twelve species of open-nesting temperate-zone passerines is 44.6%, or a 55.4% success rate (Ricklefs 1969). Estimated fledgings produced per year were 1.4 to 2.9 for vesper sparrow, 0.8 for grasshopper sparrow, 0.2 to 2.2 for dickcissel, 0.3 for bobolink, and 0.1 to 0.7 for western meadowlark. At least 3.0 fledged young annually are needed to balance average annual mortality of adults and fledged young.

Agricultural crop or land-use types with numerous, predominantly positive, significant species-occurrence associations at the county-area level included Conservation Reserve Program (CRP) lands (nineteen positive species associations, two negative associations), followed by winter wheat (twenty positive, five negative), all wheat types (fourteen positive, two negative), and barley (fourteen positive, three negative). Soybeans and sorghum had nearly equal numbers of positive and negative associations. High positive associations between specific crops and the presence of a bird species, however, are not necessarily also correlated with high nesting density or nesting success. In a five-year study involving six midwestern states, Louis Best and others found that CRP fields supported thirty-three species of nesting birds, as compared with ten species in row-crop fields. Furthermore, the number of nests found was more than 143 times greater in CRP fields than in row crops. In another recent analysis, Douglas Johnson and Michael Schwartz studied the summer birds of CRP lands in nine counties in the northern prairies, recording seventy-three species on these lands. Of the twenty most commonly occurring species, only the horned lark had appreciably higher densities on croplands than on CRP lands, and eight grassland species (grasshopper sparrow, western meadowlark, Savannah sparrow, clay-colored sparrow, bobolink, chestnut-collared longspur, dickcissel, and Baird's sparrow) were considerably more common on CRP lands than on croplands.

One indirect effect of farming is the fragmentation of grasslands into areas too small to support viable populations of grassland species. Minimum areas of grassland species are still only imperfectly known, but Peter Vickery and others examined this question for ten grassland and early successional species in Maine and reported that most of them are area-sensitive. They found that upland sandpipers reached a 50 percent incidence of abundance in areas of about 500 acres, grasshopper sparrows at about 250 acres, and vesper sparrows at about 50 acres. Bobolinks and eastern meadowlarks also showed a positive relationship with area, but their populations were too low to measure these effects clearly. Other studies in Illinois by James Herkert have suggested that minimum areas of these two species may range from about 25 to 250 acres. Similarly, Illinois surveys by Jeffery Walk and Richard Warner have suggested that there are minimum area requirements for several grassland species: grasshopper sparrow, 30 acres; northern harrier, 135 acres; greater prairie-chicken and upland sandpiper, 160 acres; and Henslow's and Savannah sparrow, 185 acres. It is likely that minimum areas of at least 250 to 500 acres should be present for maintaining populations of grassland species.

It is difficult if not impossible to separate the influence of farming practices from that of brood parasitism on the productivity of grassland birds. The brown-headed cowbird's overall geographic range and its relative abundance greatly increased during the twentieth century, as forest fragmentation, livestock-raising, and grain-crop production increased during this time. The current breeding distribution of the brown-headed cowbird (Fig. 15) in the Great Plains region shows that even today it has its maximum breeding densities in the region that approximates the one-time limits of the original tall-grass prairie, but it is also a region that currently has been converted to more than 95 percent agricultural land, especially that devoted to corn production for food or silage.

Presumably most of the grassland avifauna (Fig. 16) of interior North America have been exposed to the effects of the brown-headed cowbird for centuries, if not millennia, but few have yet evolved fool-proof

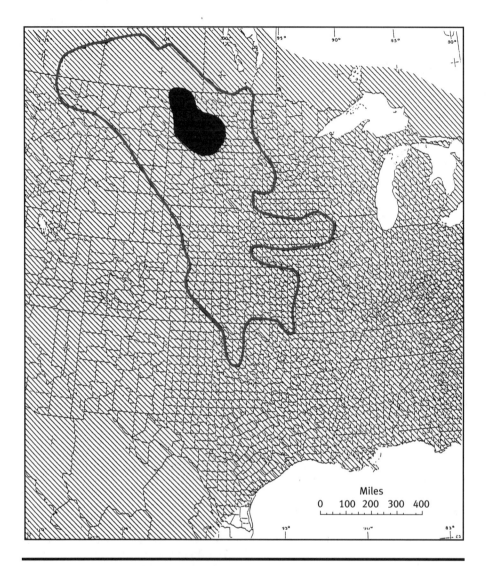

15. Brown-headed cowbird, approximate breeding distribution. The solid black area represents densest breeding areas between 1982 and 1996, the continuous line less dense populations. Mainly after Sauer et al. (1997).

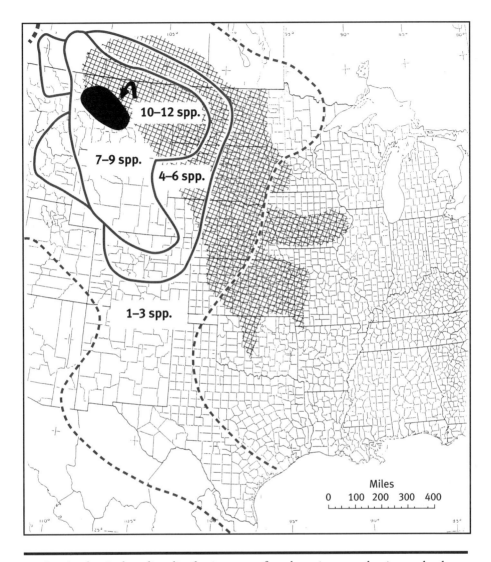

16. Species density breeding distribution map of twelve primary endemic grassland birds (after Mengel 1970). The cross-hatched area shows the densest breeding concentration of the brown-headed cowbird, from 1982 to 1996.

Table Five   Grassland Cowbird Hosts and Extent of Brood Parasitism

Hosts	Parasitism Rate (N)	Location	Source
Dickcissel (300+)	69.4 (620)	Kans.	Lowther 1977
	90.8 (65)	Kans.	Hatch 1983
	31.1 (61)	Okla.	Wiens 1963
	50.0 (28)	Kans.	Hill 1976
Western meadowlark (200+)	18.4 (76)	Minn.	Johnson and Temple 1990
	43.0 (65)	Manit.	Davis and Sealy 2000
Vesper sparrow (70+)	8.0 (112)	Ohio	Hicks 1934
	10.1 (89)	Mich.	Southern and Southern 1980
	2.6 (77)	Wash.	Vander Hagen and Walker 1999
Clay-colored sparrow (50+)	10.8 (204)	Manit.	Hill and Sealy 1994
	36.2 (232)	Manit.	Knapton 1978
	10.4 (135)	Minn.	Johnson and Temple 1990
	32.5 (40)	Minn.	Buech 1982
	39.4 (33)	N. Dak.	Friedmann et al. 1977
	14.9 (174)	?	Lorenzana and Sealy 1999
Eastern meadowlark (30+)	10.1 (69)	Midwest	Lowther 1977
	70.0 (40)	Kans.	Elliott 1978
Grasshopper sparrow (25+)	11.8 (51)	Ont.	Friedmann et al. 1977
	6.5 (46)	Minn.	Johnson and Temple 1990
	50.0 (18)	Kans.	Elliott 1978
	22.2 (18)	Kans.	Hill 1976
Chestnut-collared longspur (20+)	22.6 (62)	N. Dak.	Friedmann and Kiff 1985
	14.2 (56)	Manit.	Lorenzana and Sealy 1999
Horned lark (20+)	45.2 (31)	Kans.	Hill 1976
	18.7 (16)	Midwest	Lowther 1977
Lark bunting (20+)	15.5 (142)	Kans.	Hill 1976
	54.5 (22)	Manit.	Sealy 1999
Baird's sparrow (20+)	36.0 (76)	Manit.	Davis and Sealy 1998
Savannah sparrow (20+)	37.0 (46)	Minn.	Johnson and Temple 1990
	32.0 (31)	Manit.	Davis and Sealy 2000

Apparently rare to infrequent fostering hosts (up to 20 host records)

	Parasitism Rate (N)	Location	Source
Lark sparrow	45.5 (33)	Okla.	Newman 1970
	5.9 (17)	Okla.	Weins 1963
	81.8 (11)	Kans.	Hill 1976

Table Five   (continued)

	Parasitism Rate (N)	Location	Source
Sprague's pipit	18.0 (17)	Manit.	Davis and Sealy 2000
Brewer's sparrow	12.5 (16)	Idaho	Rich and Rothstein 1985
	5.0 (281)	Wash.	Vander Hagen and Walker 1999
Bobolink	34.0 (47)	Minn.	Johnson and Temple 1990
	10.3 (58)	Ont.	Friedmann et al. 1977
Henslow's sparrow	5.3 (59)	Mo.	Winter 1998

Source: Mostly after summaries in Ortega (1998) and Johnsgard (1998); additional small samples for some species can be found in Ortega. Seemingly insignificant or inadequately studied hosts—

Upland sandpiper: an inappropriate host, as the young are not fed by parents.

Wilson's phalarope: an inappropriate host, as the young are not fed by parents.

Sprague's pipit: three of seventeen Manitoba nests parasitized (Davis and Sealy, in press; cited by Lorenzana and Sealy 1999).

Cassin's sparrow: fewer than ten cases known (Friedmann 1963; Friedmann et al. 1977); three of ten nests parasitized (Schnase 1984).

McCown's longspur: very few cases known (Krause 1968).

defenses against it. Most of the grassland passerines have short bills that are too small to pick up and remove the cowbird egg, and none seems to be able to pierce its relatively thick shell with their rather blunt bills even if they should be able to recognize its presence. The brown-spotted eggshell pattern of the cowbird closely approximates those of several sparrow species, especially those of the lark and vesper sparrows. Furthermore, although its somewhat larger size is readily apparent to humans, the cowbird egg may simply be accepted by the birds as within their acceptable innate limits or perhaps may even be favored over their own eggs as a superoptimal visual stimulus.

The apparently relative reproductive impacts of the cowbird on North American grassland bird species have been summarized in Table 5. Extremely high parasitism rates seem to be associated with the dickcissel (whose geographic breeding range is a fairly close counterpart of the denser breeding range of the cowbird) and with the grasshopper, clay-colored, Baird's, and Savannah sparrows. Rather surprisingly, the vesper sparrow is evidently not a highly parasitized species, even though it nests in rather exposed sites and its egg pattern rather closely corre-

Table Six   Breeding Data for Grassland Passerine Birds

Species	Mating System[a]	Total Days Required			Broods/ Fledging	Season
		Nest-Building	Egg-Laying	Incubation[b]		
Horned lark	Monog.	3–6	3–4	11–12 (F)	9–12	2+
Sprague's pipit	Monog.?	?	4–5	? (F?)	10–11+	2?
Dickcissel	M. or P.	4	3–5	12–13 (F)	ave. 9	1 or 2
Cassin's sparrow	Monog.	?	3–5	11–12 (F)	ca. 9	1 or 2
Brewer's sparrow	Monog.	4–5	3–4	11–13 (F)	8–9	1 or 2
Vesper sparrow	Monog.	?	3–4	11–13 (B)	ave. 9	2(1–3)
Lark sparrow	Monog.	3–4	4–5	11–12 (F)	9–10	1
Lark bunting	M. or P.	?	4–5	11–12 (F or B)	9–12	1 or 2
Savannah sparrow	M. or P.	1–3	3–5	12–13 (B)	7–10	2
Grasshopper sparrow	Monog.	2–3	4–5	11–12 (F)	9	2
Baird's sparrow	Monog.[c]	?	4–5	11–12 (F)	8–11	2
Henslow's sparrow	Monog.?	5–6	3–5	11 (F)	9–10	2+
McCown's longspur	Monog.	2–5	3–4	12 (F)	10–12	2
Chestnut-collared longspur	Monog.	4–12	3–5	10–13 (F)	9–14	2
Bobolink	M. or P.	1–2	5–6	10–13 (F)	10–14	1
Eastern meadowlark	M. or P.	6–8	3–5	13–15 (F)	11–12	1 or 2
Western meadowlark	M. or P.	6–8	4–6	13–15 (F)	12	1 or 2

[a] Denotes apparently most typical system; M. or P. indicates monogamous or polygynous. See relevant text for possible exceptions.

[b] F indicates incubation by female; B indicates both female and male evidently participate.

[c] Mate-switching may occur between broods.

sponds to the cowbird's. Parasitism rates in the lark sparrow appear to be quite variable in different regions. Meadowlarks, whose bills are certainly large enough to pick up a cowbird egg and sharp enough to pierce it, perhaps fail to recognize the cowbird's slightly smaller but very similarly patterned egg, and they are sometimes heavily parasitized in spite of their well-concealed nests.

These variably parasitized species have breeding characteristics that make them potential candidates for cowbird parasitism, at least in terms of their incubation and fledging periods (Table 6). The cowbird has an incubation period of eleven to twelve days and a fledging period of ten days. It begins laying in early April at the southern part of its range and in mid-May in northern portions. There is roughly a two-month period of intensive laying, centering in May or June, depending upon latitude. During this fairly long egg-laying period the males continue to court females, forming monogamous pair bonds, polygynous ones, or promiscuously courting all available females. Likewise, females may be monogamous, polyandrous, or promiscuous. Males display to females or toward other males with bowing displays (Fig. 17D–E) and interact agonistically with other males with upward bill-tilting postures (Fig. 17C). The bowing display, accompanied by a rather loud whistled and slurred song, is more strongly performed toward other males than toward females, and sometimes three or more males may perform it almost simultaneously. Both sexes assume a downward-tilted head when soliciting preening from others (Fig. 17A).

Female cowbird behavior is otherwise largely oriented toward successful parasitism. She spends a great deal of time watching the nest-building activities of potential hosts, often from a well-hidden location in a tree or bush. During the host's egg-laying period she is able to visit its nest quickly when the host is absent and deposits an egg in a very short time, almost always in less than a minute (Fig. 18A). She then usually picks up a host egg and flies off with it (Fig. 18B). Eggs are laid in daily sequences of about one to seven eggs, usually around sunrise each day. Females never lay more than one egg in a single nest, but multiple parasitism may result from two or more females exploiting the same nest. Because of the nestling cowbird's strong begging behavior and associated loud calls, it is usually fed more than are host young and often causes the starvation of one or more of the host young (Fig. 18C).

It is a kind providence that has withheld a sense of history from the thousands of species of plants and animals that have exterminated one another to build the present world.

—Aldo Leopold,
Sand County Almanac

Life on the prairie never has been easy, but few humans who were born and raised there would ever trade prairie sunsets for montane alpenglow or the gentle sounds of wind whispering through the grasses for the pounding surf of ocean shorelines. Prairies are thus an acquired taste, but for the grassland birds they are the only game in town, and the birds reliably play the game of survival and reproduction every

17. Brown-headed cowbird displays, including preening-invitation display by
female (A) and male (B), low-level and intense bill-tilting by males (C), and
middle (D) and late (E) stages of song-spread display of male, including
sonogram of vocalization. Drawing by author, adapted from Johnsgard
(1997).

18. Brown-headed cowbird behavior, including female egg-laying in a red-eyed vireo nest (A), removing an egg from host's nest (B), and cowbird (*behind*) and red-winged blackbird nestlings, both ten days old (C). Drawing by author, adapted in part from Johnsgard (1997), and in part from author's photographs.

year in spite of all odds. We can ask no more of them. But we can ask ourselves to try every means possible to prolong their opportunities for doing so.

Suggested Readings

Basore et al. 1968; Best et al. 1997; Bock and Bock 1987, 1992; Bowen and Kruse 1993; Coupland 1958; Dale 1984; Daubenmire 1968; Ensign 1983; George et al. 1992; Gibson and Hulbert 1987; Herkert 1991b, 1994; Kantrud 1981; Kantrud and Kologiski 1982; Kirch et al. 1978; Lowther 1993; Johnson 1996; Ortega 1998; Owens and Myers 1973; Pylypec 1991; Reynolds and Trost 1981; Rohrbaugh et al. 1999; Rodenhouse et al. 1993; Ryder 1980, Smith et al. 2000; Vickery, Hunter, and Scott 1994; Walk and Warner 1999; Zimmerman 1996.

part two

The
Grassland
Avifauna

4

Broad Wings over Short Grass: *Swainson's and Ferruginous Hawks*

One fine mid-September day a few years ago, I drove west out of Corpus Christi, Texas, away from the seemingly endless petroleum refineries and confusing limited-access highways into the low hills bordering the south shoreline of the Nueces River. I was looking for Hazel Bazemore Park, a relatively obscure county park and site of one of the most famous hawk-watching locations in America. After I finally found the entrance and drove in, it didn't look especially promising. There were no steep cliffs to provide uplift for migrating birds, and the lazy, seemingly second-rate river itself didn't offer any obvious north-south orientational benefits or provide any other especially distinctive landmarks. Yet many other binocular-bearing and serious-looking people were already there, standing, sitting, or even lying about on the ground, their eyes turned skyward. It took only a few moments to see what was happening. Someone would suddenly shout out, "Hawk at ten o'-clock," and the binoculars would quickly jump to attention. Soon dark specks would appear in the north, often initially fairly low in the sky but gaining altitude after they crossed the river and, ascending on outstretched wings and catching topography-based or thermal updrafts, they passed by overhead. They were a mixture of migrating Swainson's hawks, Mississippi kites, and broad-winged hawks, plus a smattering of turkey vultures, accipiters, and other raptors. They were either traveling as single individuals or were aggregated in loose, often slowly rotating "kettles." The locals were far more competent than I in identifying each of the species at what seemed impossibly far distances; I simply kept my mouth shut and absorbed the show. As many as 10,000 broad-winged hawks might pass overhead during a single day in late September, the birds often grouped in great swirling masses riding invisible thermals, although on most days a few hundred birds might be a more typical tally.

Swainson's Hawk

William Swainson (1789–1855) was a British naturalist and lithographer, who illustrated and wrote the series, *Zoological Illustrations* (1820–1833). He later (1832) also coauthored and illustrated the bird volume component of the multivolume *Fauna Boreali-Americana* with Sir John Richardson, who had served as a naturalist on Sir John Franklin's 1818 Arctic expedition (see Franklin's gull account, chapter 8). This monograph included several newly described species from northern North America. Swainson later emigrated to New Zealand, where he had a series of misfortunes and eventually died in relative obscurity.

The Swainson's hawk was first collected by John Richardson in 1827 at Fort Carlton, in western Canada. It was illustrated by William Swainson but was initially identified and described under the same Latin name as the one then in use for the European common buzzard, a species very similar to our North American red-tailed hawk. When that epithet was found to be taxonomically invalid, the hawk was later renamed *swainsoni* by the French biologist Charles Lucien Bonaparte, a nephew of Napoleon Bonaparte. The Swainson's thrush and Swainson's warbler were also named in the naturalist's honor.

The Swainson's hawks crossing over Texas that I watched were on the first phase of a roughly 6,000-mile maximum migration, from nesting grounds in the western prairies in places as far north as central Alberta and Saskatchewan and toward the grasslands of Argentina. They had converged from throughout the central and northern plains to this common flightline, after having fattened up on the abundant fall grasshopper crop of their breeding grounds. From Texas southward the birds would roughly follow the Mexican Gulf coastline or follow the Pacific slope of Mexico and Central America all the way to the mainland of South America. None of the other raptors passing over Texas had such a long migratory flight ahead of them, although broad-winged hawks also were mostly headed for South America, where they winter in its tropical western regions. Broadwings greatly exceed the Swainson's hawks in overall numbers at Hazel Bazemore, which is at the eastern edge of the Swainson's hawk migration route. Little is known of what they might eat while on this long migration. However, it is unlikely that fasting could occur over the entire three-month migration period, and the birds do not lose great amounts of weight as might be expected should fasting occur. Flying during the warmer hours of daylight, when thermals or other updrafts are best developed, little if any time for daylight hunting seems to be available to them. Arrival in Argentina does not occur until about November. In that area grasshoppers and similar grassland insects provide the primary winter food.

While on their wintering grounds the birds feed almost entirely on insects, primarily grasshoppers. This predilection exposes them to toxic chemicals sprayed in agricultural areas to control grasshoppers, and at times such pesticide poisoning has resulted in massive die-offs of hawks. The spring migration back northward is a mirror image of the fall one; in Central America, for example, both migrations are largely compressed into a two-week period, although the extreme dates are spread out over about two months.

Most birds are back in their Great Plains breeding range by April, and pair-forming behavior begins immediately thereafter. Like other buteos, courtship is largely aerial and begins with the pair circling in wide arcs several hundred feet above the nest site, in a soaring "sky dance" (Fig. 19). Periodically the smaller male performs a swift and steep dive, followed by a rapid regaining of altitude, and soon thereafter a repetition of the dive. These repeated dives may end with the male landing on the tree near the nest, on a nearby tree, or sometimes even on the ground, to be joined soon by the female. Copulation may follow this spectacular performance. Most matings occur on trees or fenceposts, and most occur during the nest-building period. Long-term monogamy appears to be the rule; pairs have been found annually to reestablish previously held pair bonds for as long as ten years, although the removal of a female's mate may cause her to form a new pair bond within a few days.

On return to their breeding grounds the nesting birds' diet quickly

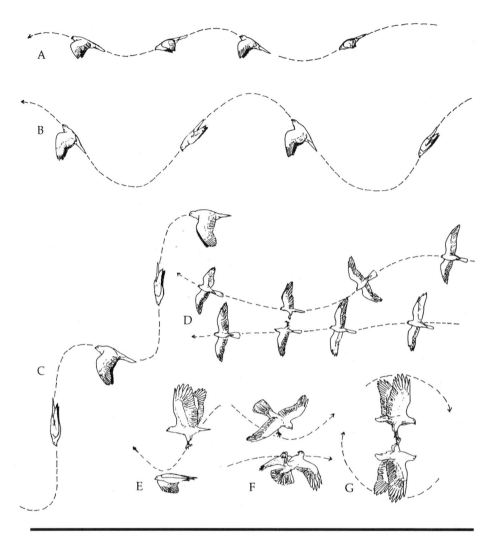

19. Aerial displays of *Buteo* hawks and related hawks and eagles, including undulating flights (A, B), steep dives (C), mutual soaring and foot-touching (D), "parachuting" (E), talon-grasping (F), and cartwheeling with locked talons (G). Not all of these displays are known for the Swainson's hawk. From Johnsgard (1990).

shifts from insects to larger vertebrate prey types. On the northern Great Plains (Alberta, Saskatchewan, North Dakota) these are likely to consist mainly of ground squirrels (unweighted average prey frequency of three studies, 49 percent), other rodents (unweighted average 31 percent), and birds (unweighted average 17 percent), ranging in size from meadowlarks to ring-necked pheasants. However, immature nonbreeders continue to feed largely on insects and forage in groups. They are unusually adept at catching large insects in the air with their talons but also may run them down on the ground.

The breeding pairs are quite defensive of their nesting sites, and as a result nests tend to be well spaced. In three Great Plains studies (Wyoming, Alberta, and South Dakota) the mean internest distances ranged from 0.88 to 1.4 miles. Red-tailed hawks are also aggressively excluded when possible, but redtails have a seasonal advantage in that they already have well-established nests by the time the Swainson's hawks arrive in spring. Ferruginous hawks have different nest-site requirements and so are less competitive with Swainson's hawks; in fact, a kind of cooperative territorial defense involving these two species was reported in one study. Nevertheless, in the Alberta aspen parklands these three buteo species have a dietary overlap of about 80 percent, and when pairs of any two species nest close together their reproductive success declines. However, overall ecological differences—the ferruginous occupying more open lands, the redtails woodlands, and the Swainson's intermediate habitats—help to provide for niche segregation.

Nest-building may begin within a week or two of arrival and generally requires about a week to complete. Eviction of other hawk species from the prior year's nest, such as red-tailed hawks, is sometimes successful, but similar attempts to dislodge great horned owls are typically failures. Nests are usually placed in solitary, often rather small trees, or at least in trees usually smaller than those used by red-tailed hawks in Nebraska. Old nests of American crows, common ravens, or black-billed magpies are sometimes also used. The female does virtually all the incubation of the usually two- or three-egg clutch, and it requires a rather long period of thirty-four to thirty-five days for hatching. Like other raptors, the young hatch in the sequence that the eggs were laid, which may result in an average two-day difference in their ages. At least in some situations, death of the younger or youngest chick is fairly common, often occurring when the brood is between two and four weeks old; this may be the result of either starvation or fratricide. At times a third individual has been seen helping at the nest; it is unknown whether such birds are young siblings of the previous year, or represent possible polygynous mating. Since the period to sexual maturity is usually at least three years, such helping by nonbreeding immatures might seem likely. A few cases of polyandrous matings have been reported.

The juveniles remain with their parents for about a month after their thirty-eight- to forty-five-day fledging period and are dependent upon them for some time. Fledging success rates seem to be highly variable. Anywhere from about 30 to 80 percent (unweighted mean of three Great Plains studies, 69 percent) of the pairs typically fledge at least one chick, and average production of fledged young varies from about one to two chicks (unweighted mean of four Great Plains studies, 1.38). At least in Saskatchewan, reproductive success seems to be closely related to relative ground squirrel availability during the breeding season. Maximum longevity, like that of other raptors, is quite long, approaching twenty years in rare instances. But lifespans are usually much less, perhaps averaging about eight years. Significant causes of mortality include killing by humans, now mainly limited to Latin America, and pesticide poisoning, again largely limited to the wintering areas.

Ferruginous Hawk

The term "ferruginous" refers to the rust-colored thigh feathers of this beautiful steppe-dwelling buteo; its earlier common name, "ferruginous rough-leg," describes its feathered lower legs, a trait also found on the related but much more widespread rough-legged hawk. The latter species is an Arctic-breeding form whose grouselike feathering might be considered a distinctly useful adaptation for thermal insulation in cold weather, but its value to the plains-breeding and somewhat migratory ferruginous hawk is less apparent. Both species also have remarkably wide gapes for buteos, which give them a slightly froglike appearance when seen from the front and which probably allow for the swallowing of rather large prey, especially rodents (Fig. 20).

One of the most memorable ferruginous hawks I ever encountered was soaring high above me while I was lying flat on my back at the very crest of Scotts Bluff National Monument, 800 feet above the surrounding high plains in western Nebraska. I was leading a group of ornithology students from our biological station, and we were gazing lazily upward into the intensely blue sky, simultaneously absorbing the sun's

20. Swainson's (*left*) and ferruginous hawks (*right*), adult heads and feet. Drawing by author.

warm rays and inhaling the sweet odors of nearby ponderosa pines. While thus pleasantly engaged, one of my university's higher administrators suddenly appeared, leaning over me, temporarily obscuring my view of the hawk, and inquired politely if this were the usual way I teach my classes. Since I already had tenure and had been at the university far longer than he, it didn't bother me.

Few Great Plains birds have greater panache (appropriately, the word originally meant wearing a decorative feather) than do ferruginous hawks. I have often wished they had been called ferruginous eagles, as then they might be more fully appreciated by the public. They are certainly as large and majestic as some of the Old World eagles, and they often nest, eaglelike, on the tops of buttes or other similarly elevated landmarks on the high plains (Fig. 21). Like the other buteos, they often spend long hours circling slowly in the sky in search of prey, and as they tilt their upperparts toward the observer, their beautiful pinkish upper tail surface and whitish "windows" at the base of their flight feathers temporarily come into view.

21. Ferruginous hawk.
Drawing by author.

In contrast to those of the Swainson's hawk, migratory movements of the ferruginous are fairly minor and probably rarely exceed 1,000 miles, or southward at maximum to the Central Valley of Mexico. But most wintering is probably done in the arid highlands of northern Mexico and in the southern Great Plains. Probably the most northerly populations migrate the farthest and the most southerly the least, if not remaining residential altogether. Also unlike the Swainson's hawk, the ferruginous hawk manifests no major seasonal dietary shifts. Throughout the year, some 80 percent (by frequency of occurrence) to 95 percent (by biomass) of the species' prey consists of mammals, with a predominance of rabbits and hares (especially in westernmost parts of the range). These dietary components are followed secondarily by ground squirrels and prairie dogs (these items are mainly taken in populations occurring east of the Continental Divide). Birds and reptiles make up increasingly tiny dietary components and insects virtually none. The eastern and western populations also differ in their habitat ecology, with short-grass and shrubsteppe plains the typical habitats of the Great Plains birds and more arid semidesert and desert habitats used westwardly. However, some population mixing does occur, and no evidence of subspeciation exists.

Hunting is done by short flights from lookout perches, ground searching and pouncing on subsurface prey, low-altitude aerial hunting, and hovering searches, the last method especially frequent during windy conditions. At least in Utah, the ground-hunting technique has been found to be the most successful approach.

With the end of winter, the birds begin moving northward into the plains, arriving ahead of the Swainson's hawks, mostly in February and March, but encountering the residential red-tailed hawks in the relatively few Great Plains habitats where these two rodent-hunting species might interact. Generally, the ferruginous hawk is limited to rather treeless plains, although low trees (such as pinyon-juniper woodland edges) and sparsely wooded habitats such as shallow riverine valleys may be used, and these additionally may offer potential tree nest sites. Nevertheless, locations with eroded buttes, knolls, low rimrock ledges, or other elevated sites are distinctly preferred, as they offer many potential nest sites having panoramic views.

Monogamy is the typical mating system, and at least some birds appear to remain associated as pairs throughout the year. At times, up to three birds have been observed at nests, suggesting the presence of occasional helpers or possible deviations from strict monogamy, but so far there is no indication that mate-switching ever occurs.

Pair bonds are apparently established or renewed near the birds' breeding locations by aerial soaring and diving maneuvers very similar to those described for the Swainson's hawk. Talon-grasping in the air, during which the interlocked birds may spiral downward some distance before separating, is also an apparent courtship display.

Throughout their range, ferruginous hawks nest on a variety of substrates; in a sample of more than 2,100 nests the most commonly used sites were trees and shrubs (49 percent), followed by cliffs (21 percent), with outcrops and human structures each constituting about 10 percent. In the Great Plains, where elevated sites are rare, a wide variety of nesting sites is typical. In Colorado, short-grass prairies are by far the most common habitat used during the breeding season (about eighty breeding bird survey blocks, or nearly half the total reports), as compared with nearly equal use of short-grass prairie and rural sites by breeding Swainson's hawks. A nest can be completed, or refurbished, in less than a week, and nests are more typically constructed of dry twigs than of herbs, twigs, and bark, as usually used by Swainson's and red-tailed hawks. Little is known of nest-site fidelity in subsequent years or of mate-retention tendencies. Nest densities tend to be quite low, often only averaging about one nest per forty square miles (or 100 square kilometers), and at maximum density about one nest per four square miles.

Like other buteos, the female does most of the incubation and brooding, while the male stands guard and hunts for both pair members as well as for their hatched chicks. Incubation lasts an estimated thirty-two to thirty-three days, the eggs hatching in the sequence in which they were laid. Clutch sizes are rather variable but in the Great Plains tend to average about three to four eggs, the actual size probably varying locally or annually with relative prey abundance. Fledging requires thirty-eight to fifty days, with the smaller males fledging substantially sooner than females. Attacks by older chicks on younger ones are infrequent, but fratricide may occur during periods of drought and associated food stress.

Two nest-success estimates (the fledging of at least one chick per nest) from Idaho and Utah were of 45 and 72 percent, but this is likely to be a quite variable statistic. The average number of fledged young produced annually per breeding pair is obviously also quite variable but usually ranges between two and three chicks. Young birds may begin to disseminate from their nesting areas as soon as a month after fledging but often remain in loosely associated groups of siblings. Like other raptors, young birds exhibit high mortality rates their first year (one estimate of 65 percent), but thereafter survival is probably fairly high and may average about 75 percent annually, although this figure seems somewhat on the conservative side. Some two-year-old birds have been known to breed, and breeding by this age group may be quite regular. It has been estimated that the species' maximum theoretical longevity is about twenty years.

Suggested Readings

Gilmer and Stewart 1983, 1984; Johnsgard 1990.

Swainson's Hawk: Blair and Schitoskey 1982; Dunkle 1977; Lehman et al. 1998; Lokemoen and Duebbert 1976; Pilz 1983; Porton 1977; Ra-

makka and Woyewodzic 1993; Snow 1974; Zelenak and Rotella 1997; Zelenak et al. 1997.

Ferruginous Hawk: Andersen 1995; Bechard and Schmutz 1995; Dechant et al. 1999d; Green and Morrison 1983; Groskorth 1995; Olendorff 1993; Roth and Marzluff 1989; Rothfels and Lein 1983; Schmutz 1984; Schmutz et al. 1980; Thurow and White 1983.

5   Dawn Dances on the Prairie: *Prairie-chickens and Sharp-tailed Grouse*

It is a melancholy thought that, after its compatriots had disappeared, the last surviving male heath hen [the Atlantic-coast race of the greater prairie-chicken] in North America faithfully returned each spring to its traditional mating ground on Martha's Vineyard, Massachusetts, where he displayed alone to an unseeing and unhearing world. . . . No one knows exactly when or how that last survivor died, and no bells tolled to mourn his passing.

—Paul Johnsgard,
The Grouse of the World

My mother was born in the early 1900s, on a farm homesteaded by her father along the Sheyenne River of southeastern North Dakota, near where the Sheyenne National Grasslands are now located. In that tall-grass environment she learned the prairie flowers and the prairie wildlife and transmitted that information and passion to me when I was still a small child. I also acquired her often tattered nature books, from which I learned many of the flowers and birds common in North Dakota grasslands. But while a child I never saw a live prairie-chicken; ring-necked pheasants had by then largely replaced prairie-chickens as easily hunted gamebirds, especially along gravelly roadsides where they appeared each early morning and late afternoon while searching for grit. Mother sometimes told me stories about having heard the prairie-chickens calling softly in the distance on early spring mornings while she was out riding her pony, but even she missed out on seeing their magical dawn dances. It wasn't until I came to Nebraska in the early 1960s that I finally had an opportunity to watch the sun bisect the eastern horizon on a cold March morning, atop a prairie-covered hill in Pawnee County. I finally realized that until then my life had been incomplete and that henceforth all Nebraska springs must be celebrated at least once in the company and presence of prairie grouse.

It required a failed trip, perhaps even two, before I discovered that I must be fully hidden in a blind at least a half-hour before sunrise, that the wind must not be blowing too strongly, and that it must not be raining, if I were to be privileged enough to witness the complete show. Even then, one could only hope that some curious fisherman from the nearby lakeshore would not hear the birds' activity and wander up the hill to see what was going on, or that a coyote or passing northern harrier wouldn't similarly break up the party. But on those occasions when the weather was just right, and the gods of chance were fully appeased, the performance began. Typically, just as it was getting light enough to see broad outlines, a few lone figures could be seen slowly and silently proceeding up the hill from varied directions, like well-camouflaged archers stealthily approaching Macbeth's castle at Dunsinane. Only a few moments later the first grouse call could be heard, a mournful but still soothing and almost dovelike series of three notes, which seemed to belong in a sacred sacrament more than in a broadcast from a nameless prairie hilltop. These haunting notes would then be answered by others, and soon the hillsides would resound with the chorus. By that time the sun would typically just be breaking the horizon, and both the players and the surrounding winter-dead grasses would progressively become illuminated by golden backlighting. By then too, if I were very lucky, a female or two might appear, cautiously making her way among and past the displaying males, seemingly carefully assessing their individual qualities. The sight of even a single female would transform the entire scene from one resembling a fairly sedate promenade to something more like a bacchanal, with the males jumping about, uttering wild whoops, and engaging in fierce beak-and-claw fights over territorial dominance.

As the sun progressively rose, the birds became progressively less exuberant, and within an hour or so after sunrise some of the peripheral walk-ons had departed, leaving only the principal actors left to squabble over territorial boundaries and increasingly to scan the skies and horizon for possible danger. Soon the morning chorus of meadowlarks would be well under way, and flocks of migrating red-winged blackbirds and small strings of ducks could often be seen peppering the morning sky. Too soon it would be time to take down my tent hurriedly and rush back to Lincoln, hopefully but not invariably arriving just soon enough to prepare adequately for my morning lecture obligations.

Greater Prairie-chicken

Few species have been so closely associated with the North American grasslands as have prairie-chickens. The Atlantic coastal race of the greater prairie-chicken, the so-called "heath-hen," was an important source of meat for the earliest of our New England immigrants, and the same is true of the early settlers moving into the eastern tall-grass prairies from Kentucky west to the Dakotas. Providentially, this interior race of prairie-chicken, the "prairie hen," thrived under the limited degree of habitat alteration brought about by these early settlers. It could sequentially exploit the grain crops they had planted for easily obtained nutrition during late summer and fall; move into heavier wooded cover during the snowy winter months where buds, seeds, and acorns were available; and then utilize native grasslands in spring and summer for nesting and brood-rearing cover.

With this combination of conditions, the prairie-chickens followed the settlers westward, until the grasslands became so completely destroyed that not enough natural cover remained to sustain them, and the population gradually waned. In one state and province after another the greater prairie-chicken declined and then disappeared, in spite of increasing concern and protection from hunting. Only in a few states did enough native prairie survive to allow the birds to find their preferred habitat combination. This was especially true in Kansas, where the rock-strewn Flint Hills in the eastern third of the state prevent effective plowing but allow grazing of the tall-grass prairies, and the Nebraska Sandhills grasslands, where the too-sandy soils have done much the same in preserving these similar grasslands. In all other states the birds have simply disappeared, or at most still barely survive in fragmented populations that are largely confined to relict prairie preserves. In eastern Texas the Attwater's prairie-chicken, a variant race of the greater prairie-chicken that has adapted to coastal prairies, likewise barely survives. It is now largely dependent for its continued survival on the regular release of hand-reared birds from captive stock. This process is foredoomed to failure because of the loss of the race's genetic diversity through inbreeding. There is also an inability of natural selection to maintain a stock that is adequately fitted for survival in the wild from a few hand-reared individuals having had no experience with natural mortality factors. Added to these problems are new ones, such as the recent appearance of fire ants, which do great damage to reproductive efforts by ground-nesting birds.

Despite these unfortunate situations, it is still possible to watch prairie-chickens displaying on crisp spring dawns in several midwestern states; it is a performance that makes one wonder why anybody would prefer to remain at home and watch televised sports. Like all the other species of grassland-adapted grouse, the birds display in competitive arenas, or leks, in which males compete over extended periods every spring of their adult lives, trying to establish favorable territories relative to all the others present. Roughly speaking, the arenas represent a rounded archery target, with the peripheral (and less experienced males) occupying the outer perimeter and having no real opportunities for mating success. The longer a male lives, and it may take three or four years for a male to work his way into the central "bull's-eye" area, the greater his chances of becoming socially dominant and attracting a female. There is thus a linear dominance/fitness hierarchy present in this social and spatial organization; more aggressively dominant males can muscle their way toward the center and by their location alone can thus be recognized by females as desirable mating partners.

Few if any copulations occur off the lek boundaries, and most evidence suggests that each female copulates only once, this single mating providing enough sperm to fertilize her entire clutch of eggs, which she will tend wholly alone. Unlike most avian territories, the lek provides neither nest sites, foraging grounds, nor any other valuable resources; it is simply nothing more than a mating station. Physical landscape features may help to make one site more valuable than another for such competitive arenas. Among prairie-chickens an elevated hill, providing panoramic visibility, and rather low-cropped grasses, which reduce the chances of a sneak attack by a ground-dwelling or low-flying predator, are both important landscape elements. Favored display sites are used year after year by the birds; there are records of some grouse leks being used for a century or more. As a result, these sites may be good places for finding arrowheads, since the Great Plains natives also frequented them for reliable spring hunting opportunities.

Individual territories on the leks of greater prairie-chickens are surprisingly small, sometimes only about twenty feet in diameter, and their margins are contested daily by aggressive calls and postural display. Sometimes the edges are also marked by actual fights that involve clawing, pecking, and wing-beating (Fig. 22E). However, most of the males' display time is spent uttering low-pitched "booming" calls while standing almost motionless in a highly stereotyped cocked-tail and drooped-wing posture (Fig. 22A). Production of these low-frequency calls is facilitated by inflation of the male's anterior esophagus and the consequent expansion of the sides of his neck into orange "air-sacs." These otherwise invisible areas of skin are temporarily exposed below erect, elongated feathers that somewhat resemble rabbit ears (Fig. 23). Although the amplitude of sound thus generated is not great, the low frequencies carry great distances, and the males' colorful throat patches and their white undertail-coverts can be seen from far away, especially under low-light conditions.

Should a female be attracted to the lek, the males' calls expand to include excited whooping notes, and the intensity and frequency of booming accelerate. Sometimes a male will prostrate himself before an approaching female (Fig. 22C), or he may briefly jump into the air in a cackling "flutter-jump" (Fig. 22D) to attract the female's attention. Usually the visiting females leave the lek shortly after sunrise, after which activity rapidly declines, and there is increased apprehensiveness among the males over possible danger from daytime predators. Then, with the slightest threat, the birds are likely to flush and flee in all directions. They may return for a brief round of activities around sunset, but females never visit the leks at that hour, so activities then are quite subdued.

Following a successful mating, each female wanders off some distance—up to a half-mile from the lek—and finds a suitable nest site, if one has not already been chosen. Nest sites typically are in grasses that provide both vertical and horizontal cover, usually between ten and thirty inches high. Studies in Missouri by Mark Ryan and others suggest that nesting will not occur in prairie areas smaller than about 160 acres. Eggs are laid on a near-daily basis, the first about four days after copulation, until a clutch of ten to twelve is completed. The incubation period of twenty-three to twenty-five days begins only with the completion or near-completion of the clutch, or sometimes a few days thereafter. The female will not return to the lek again unless she loses her first clutch; there is unlikely to be any further contact with adult males until flocks begin to re-form in fall.

Many nests fall prey to ground predators, and renesting efforts about eight to nine days after such losses are not uncommon. Rarely, a second renesting attempt may be made after failure of the first renest. The list

22. Displays of male greater and lesser prairie-chickens, including booming by greater prairie-chicken (A), gobbling by lesser prairie-chicken (B), flutter-jumping by greater prairie-chicken (C), bowing by greater prairie-chicken (D), and fighting by greater prairie-chickens (E). The trachea and esophagus of a male greater prairie-chicken are also shown (F), as are sonograms of the males' booming and gobbling calls (two-second durations, after Schroeder and Robb 1993 and Geisen 1998). Drawing by author, adapted from Johnsgard (1973; 1983).

23. Greater prairie-chicken, male calling. Drawing by author.

of known egg predators is very long and includes snakes, mammals, and birds as well as fire ants. Nesting females are also the target of many predators. Nesting success is variable but averages 44 percent (22 to 65 percent range) for Great Plains birds, somewhat less for Attwater's. Early seasonal efforts are more successful than later ones, and nests in thicker cover are more successful than those in thinner vegetation. Because of renesting efforts it is likely that about half the females will succeed in producing a brood annually, although there is also a high mortality rate among hatched chicks. Roughly speaking, in a stable population, about half the birds in the autumn flocks will be young, which corresponds to an adult mortality rate of about 45 to 50 percent. Under such conditions, average longevity among fledged young is less than two years, so relatively few males survive the three or four years needed to attain the status of a lek's alpha male or "master cock."

Lesser Prairie-chicken

The lesser prairie-chicken is not much more than an arid-adapted, slightly smaller version of the greater. Taxonomists have had a difficult time justifying its species-level status, especially since the two populations are not in geographic contact, so their possible degree of genetic and ecological isolation cannot be tested. Like that of the greater prairie-chicken, the range of the lesser has contracted greatly in recent times, but it probably always has been most closely associated with the sandsage-steppe and shinnery oak woodlands of the arid southwestern Great Plains. As such, it never enjoyed the population surge exhibited by the greater during early settlement times, since this region never became a center for growing small-grain crops. Instead, its range has simply progressively contracted, so that now it is mostly confined to the western, usually sandy, parts of Kansas, Oklahoma, and Texas and to eastern New Mexico. There are a very few early specimens known from the sandsage areas of southwestern Nebraska, suggesting that its original range may have extended that far north. Fossil records extend the species' range west to Oregon, and a possible ancestral or very similar species occurred in South Dakota.

Presently, the lesser is essentially limited to mixed bluestem and sand sagebrush or shinnery oaks, in relatively sandy soils, the shinnery oak association more typical in southern parts of its range and the sand sagebrush community in more northerly areas. Shinnery oak rangelands, with a moderate development of small-grain crops, may represent its current most optimum habitat combination. Evidently freestanding water is not needed by this form, a fact that probably distinguishes it physiologically from the greater, which is rarely found far from water.

Like the greater, the lesser prairie-chicken is essentially sedentary, and males probably rarely stray far from their traditional leks. Adults feed heavily on the acorns, leaves, and other green parts of shinnery oak during winter in southern areas, but grasshoppers are preferentially eaten whenever they are available. In early spring the males move to their leks, which usually are sparsely vegetated sites on knolls or ridges, presumably both being factors that improve visibility. In many respects the aggressive/sexual displays of males on leks are minor variations of the greater's: being smaller, the birds move and call at a faster rate; their booming (so-called "gobbling") notes are also higher and more variable in pitch (Fig. 22B). When booming, their "air sacs" are notably smaller and more circular in outline than are those of greaters, and their color is more reddish. Additionally, the yellow vascularized combs above their eyes are larger and more conspicuous than in greaters. Lessers are more prone to perform booming in an antiphonal interplay between adjacent males, as a presumed agonistic contest. Although natural hybridization between greaters and lessers is geographically impossible, controlled hybridization has shown that the hybrid males' displays and vocalizations are intermediate and that the hybrids are fertile. This fertility should not be surprising, since hybrids between greater prairie-chickens and sharp-tailed grouse are also entirely fertile.

Like greaters, male lesser prairie-chickens develop a linear hierarchy of male dominance, which radiates outward in all directions from the center of the lek. The alpha male or master cock dominates mating opportunities, with one or sometimes two centrally located males accounting for 90 percent or more of the copulations. These dominant males defend smaller territories than do those on the periphery, but they are much more strongly contested. Average territory size (33 to ca. 125 square yards) is also substantially smaller than the approximate 500 square yards typical of that of greater prairie-chickens.

A short time after the female has copulated she begins her nest, probably within only a few days. The nest site chosen tends to be less densely vegetated than those greaters choose, but the usual vegetation height is similar. Besides nesting in bunchgrasses, nesting under shrubs also occurs commonly. Nesting on north- or northeast-facing slopes is common, apparently as a mean of protection from winds and direct sunlight. As with the greater, eggs are laid on a near-daily basis, and the usual clutch consists of about ten to twelve eggs. The incubation period of twenty-four to twenty-five days is also similar, and males likewise play no role in any form of parental behavior. Seemingly, nesting success is lower than in greaters (average of ten studies, 28 percent), but renesting efforts are common following clutch failure. Predators include the same wide range of animals (birds, mammals, and reptiles) as are known to affect greaters; higher nesting success seems to be correlated with earlier seasonal clutches, nests placed in higher and denser vegetation, and those produced during wetter-than-average years. Average brood sizes are also larger in wetter years.

Typically, there is an average of about 3.5 young per adult female present in hunted fall populations, or somewhat more than a 50 percent overall ratio of immatures relative to all adults. The 45 to 47 percent incidence of adults in fall populations corresponds closely with an estimated annual adult mortality rate of 53 percent for adults that is based on banded birds. The estimated maximum longevity is about five years, which means that few birds live long enough to serve as alpha males for more than a single breeding season.

Sharp-tailed Grouse

The first sharp-tailed grouse I ever saw was in the middle of the Nebraska Sandhills; more accurately, it occurred while I was in a blind, within a national forest, within the heart of the Sandhills. This seemingly somewhat incongruous habitat description relates to the fact that a forest of conifers was planted early in this century, at the urging of Charles Bessey, in the center of one of the most treeless areas of the Great Plains. Bessey was a renowned botanist who was convinced that, since Nebraska had been largely covered by conifers during the late Pleistocene, there was no reason to believe they shouldn't grow there again, if given a proper start through seedling plantings. His unlikely predictions proved to be largely true, and a mature forest has developed amid a 20,000-square-mile area of grass-covered sand, like a Saharan oasis wholly surrounded for as far as the eye can see by Ozmandian-like dunes. The area has proven an ideal habitat for sharp-tailed grouse as well as for some prairie-chickens, the latter at almost the western edge of their Nebraska range, the sharptails near their eastern edge.

I was there in mid-April, at the peak of the grouse's display season but still early in a Nebraska spring, and my makeshift plywood blind was placed at the edge of the lek, letting in both wind and occasional snowflakes at its corners. I had heard that a hybrid grouse might also be part of the lek, in which sharptails predominated. As dawn arrived and my teeth stopped chattering, there indeed was a single hybrid male present, spending most of his time avoiding threats by males of both species and rather ineffectually trying to display during the few times he had an opportunity. The bird's displays were neither very strongly performed nor very impressive visually. He seemed to lack any of the attractive features of either parental species and never was able to penetrate anywhere close to the middle of the lek, being rebuffed by both species. Regardless of his probable fertility, it is very unlikely that females of either species would pay it much heed, should he somehow manage to catch their attention.

The Great Plains race of sharptails is one of the most grassland-oriented of this species' several races. Other races are (or historically were) found in the desert grasslands of the Southwest, the sage-dominated shrubsteppes of the Columbia Basin, at the edges and early successional stages of the boreal forest of Canada, and near the boundaries of Arctic tundra around southern Hudson's Bay and in western and central Alaska. Nearly all these populations have undergone substantial population changes in historic times, especially the more southern forms in the Great Plains, Great Basin, and Columbia Basin, where native grasslands have all but vanished. Unlike the greater prairie-chicken, the sharp-tailed grouse exhibited no great flush of population increase as grains crops invaded these grassland areas during settlement. It seems to require a greater degree of native vegetation during the breeding season and perhaps depends less upon grain and relies more upon buds and catkins of trees and shrubs for its winter survival.

Many of the basic life-history attributes of sharp-tailed grouse are very similar to those of the prairie-chickens. It is more westerly and northerly in its overall geographic range and probably evolved west of the Continental Divide while the prairie-chicken was evolving east of it. Both of these species' breeding systems closely revolve around a promiscuous mating pattern that is centered on and dependent upon a tightly organized lek, with a strict positive association between a male's relative individual dominance and its probable breeding success. Although it may be convenient to describe the species' many elaborate male displays and vocalizations as "courtship" activities, these postures and calls certainly evolved from, and are still largely concerned with, the establishment of intrasexual dominance. Successfully mating, or alpha, males are more likely to maintain central territories and have larger sperm volumes and more highly motile sperm than nonsuccessful ones, but the heterosexual signals of all participating toward females are seemingly identical. Successful males may, however, display at a higher overall frequency or intensity than others, as is known to be the case for several other arena-forming species. In the case of sharptails, birds with higher courtship rates do tend to be more successful in mating, and different rates of specific displays, such as dancing and tail-rattling, also help account for variations in mating rates.

The most common, or at least most distinctive, display of male sharptails on the lek is "dancing" (Fig. 24A). It is a highly stereotyped forward movement, the wings rigidly held out like airplane wings and the feet quickly stamping at a rate of about twenty times per second, which causes the cocked tail feathers to vibrate horizontally, their edges rubbing over the shafts of adjacent feathers and producing a snakelike rattling sound (see upper band of sonogram). This tail-rattling perhaps corresponds to the rapid opening and closing of the tail feathers during

24. Displays of male sharp-tailed grouse, including dancing (A), cooing (B), bowing (C), and running parallel (D). Sonograms of the male's cooing (*below*) and tail-rattling (*above*) are also shown (two-second total duration, after Kermott and Oring 1975). Drawing by author, adapted from Johnsgard (1983).

a prairie-chicken's display but is much more noisy, and the dance is an exaggerated version of the alternate foot-stamping-in-place by prairie-chickens. The sharptail's counterpart vocalization of booming is "cooing," (Fig. 24B, and lower band on sonogram). It is neither so loud nor quite so low pitched, about 300 to 340 Hertz (cps) versus around 270 Hertz, as the booming of greater prairie-chickens, and the air sacs are not so greatly expanded. The bright yellow comblike and highly vascularized areas of skin above each eye are fully expanded for long periods of display, although the violet-tinted air-sacs are partly inflated during most displays other than cooing. The route each male takes during each dance sequence, which lasts but a few seconds, is seemingly a random pattern of loops and turns, but there is a high degree of synchronization in the timing of these displays. Between these bouts of frenzied dancing the birds stand motionless and statuelike, perhaps listening for predators that would probably not be heard above the sound of tail-rattling. Rates of both tail-rattling and foot-stamping increase when females are present, as do sharp *chilk* and corklike calls that at least functionally seem to correspond with the whooping call of prairie-chickens. Flutter-jumping in this species is also similar to that of prairie-chickens, as is "bowing" (Fig. 24C) in the near presence of females. One male display that is lacking in prairie-chickens is parallel running (Fig. 24D), which most often occurs at the edges of two neighboring and contested territories. As with prairie-chickens, one or at most a very few males account for the great majority of matings at any single lek, and the majority of males have no opportunities at all.

Following a successful copulation, the female leaves the lek, and a female well may have visited the lek briefly for several days before mating is consummated. A single copulation serves to fertilize her entire clutch of ten to twelve or so eggs, the first of which is laid from one to three days after copulation. The nest is typically located in fairly thick vegetation, which may consist of grasses, be near or under shrubs, or even under small trees. Renesting is common following the first or even later clutch loss, and such behavior very probably requires a second visit to the lek for refertilization.

Incubation lasts twenty-one to twenty-three days, and hatching is nearly synchronous. Many nests are lost to a variety of predators, and typically nesting success rates range from about 50 to 70 percent. Often broods are reduced to about half their original size before the young become independent, and by fall it is likely that about half the population consists of the young of the year. Similarly, annual survival rates of adults rarely reach 50 percent and may be lower in heavily hunted populations. The maximum known age attained in the wild is 7.5 years.

Suggested Readings

Johnsgard, 1973, 1983.

Greater Prairie-chicken: Horak 1985; Peterson and Silvy 1996; Ryan et al. 1998; Schroeder and Braun 1992; Schroeder and Robb 1993; Sparling 1979, 1981; Svedarsky 1979; Svedarsky et al. 1997.

Lesser Prairie-chicken: Crawford and Bolen 1975; Geisen 1994a, 1994b, 1997, 1998; Horak 1985; Locke 1992; Riley et al. 1994.

Sharp-tailed Grouse: Berg 1997; Connelly et al. 1998; Gratson 1990; Gratson et al. 1991; Hillman and Jackson 1973; Kermott 1982; Mitchell and Riegert 1994; Sisson 1976; Tsuji et al. 1994.

6

Shorebird Sagas:
Long-billed Curlew,
Marbled Godwit, and
Upland Sandpiper

Both birds [curlews and whimbrels] were known as harbingers of death, and in the sense that they are birds of passage, that in the wild melodies of their calls, in the breath of vast passage and bare regions that attends them, we sense intimations of our own mortality, there is justice in the legend.

—Peter Matthiessen,
The Wind Birds

It is almost impossible to imagine a long-billed curlew as ever having been symbolic of impending death; to see one is cause to exult in one of life's visual pleasures, and to hear its wild, lonely call is enough to send shivers up and down one's back. The long-billed curlew is at once one of the largest and most breathtakingly beautiful of the world's shorebirds; only one other curlew species of eastern Asia is slightly larger. Like all curlews, both sexes of adult long-bills have wonderfully lengthened bills (up to nine inches in females, considerably less in males) that are gracefully decurved in the manner of a crescent moon; indeed the generic Latin name *Numenius* refers to that very similarity.

The annual return of the curlews to the Nebraska Sandhills each spring is an event that is just as exciting to the Sandhills ranchers as are the first songs of the returning western meadowlarks in March or the first yucca blossoms in June. Somehow, long-billed curlews and the Sandhills seem to belong together. Both have an air of wildness about them, and perhaps both can best be appreciated from a distance, as when the birds can be seen standing majestically at the crest of a dune or while they are walking slowly through a wet

Sandhills meadow in a patient search for insects. One of the treasured memories of my life came during a hot July day at Crescent Lake National Wildlife Refuge, in the western Sandhills. Then I counted at least fifty-three adult and recently fledged young curlews assembled in a single irrigated meadow, and all were foraging busily to put on fat for their early fall migration to the Pacific coast. A few weeks later not a curlew was to be seen anywhere, and the Sandhills would not hear their calls again for at least eight months.

The first long-billed curlew nest that I ever found was located on Arapaho Prairie, a preserved area of Sandhills grassland in Arthur County, western Nebraska. Arthur County is the very epitome of Sandhills country; the entire county has only a single small village (appropriately named Arthur), with a general store, a filling station, and a Protestant church that is mostly constructed of hay bales. The cattle pastures surrounding Arthur are fenced in by a few strands of barbed wire held up by wooden posts. Hundreds of these posts are crowned with discarded and upside-down cowboy boots, these serving no obvious utilitarian function except perhaps to further a strange regional egocentric affectation and to offer a convenient landing platform for upland sandpipers. Arthur's village golf course, which consists mostly of sand traps, has a small, flat area of green grass that doubles as a landing strip for small airplanes and helicopters. This is helpful if not absolutely necessary for ranchers who would much rather fly into town than drive twenty or more miles over sandy trails that threaten to swallow a car's wheels up to its axles. Windmills rather than trees serve as helpful landmarks in this relatively featureless country and often do double-duty as convenient lookout points for hungry raptors.

I knew from the worried calls of the adult male curlew I had disturbed on Arapaho Prairie that a nest must be somewhere nearby, and after flushing the female I simply sat down, trying to avoid sitting on sandburs or prickly-pear cactus, and waited impatiently. Eventually the female ended her cautious circling, set her wings, and finally landed. She then slowly and quietly made her way up a slight grassy slope. About halfway to the crest she suddenly disappeared from view, and I knew my quest was over. I set up a blind, initially some thirty feet from the nest, but gradually moved closer until I was only a few yards away. Even from that distance it would take some time after entering the blind to determine if the female was sitting or not, for her plumage blended perfectly with the sand and dead grass around her.

Long-billed Curlew

As the largest of the North American curlews, indeed the largest of all our North American shorebirds, the long-billed curlew is a very special bird. Like Cyrano's nose, its bill is so long that, instead of being a visual liability, it adds grandeur and a degree of distinction to the bird's appearance. Were it not for the intermediate-length bills of all the other curlew species it might be difficult to explain its gradual evolutionary development, and its strong curvature perhaps might seem even more problematic. Yet long and decurved bills are not uncommon among probing birds, and the curlews seem unhindered by its length and curvature when feeding on dry land. Presumably it offers some foraging advantage when probing in deep, wet sand, as often occurs on coastal wintering areas. More interesting, the bills of adult females are substantially longer than those of the somewhat smaller males (Fig. 25), a morphological pattern that also occurs in other curlews as well as in the fairly closely related but virtually straight-billed godwits, such as the marbled godwit.

Wintering areas of the population breeding in the Great Plains and wintering in Mexico or (infrequently) in Central America are not well defined, but there are substantial winter populations along the Gulf Coast from western Louisiana to the Mexican border at the mouth of the Rio Grande, where numbers are especially high. There is also a group that winters in interior Texas, mostly in the region between Midland and San Angelo. The large population that winters in central and southern California presumably is the same population that breeds west of the Continental Divide.

At least the latter wintering population feeds in tidal flats during periods of low tide and roosts in nearby but more inland marshy areas. The birds occupy muddy tidal habitats during daylight hours, using various foraging strategies. These include purely tactile clues to detect hidden and burrowing prey while they probe, standing in rather shallow water with the bill slightly open and moving its tips slowly over the substrate until a prey item can be detected and quickly grabbed and relying on strictly visual clues for detecting submerged prey. Mud crabs and various shrimp (mostly ghost shrimp and mud shrimp) are the usual coastal California prey. Later, on their breeding grounds, the birds forage either by visual pecking or probing into burrows or holes in soft ground, probably searching for insect larvae as well as adult beetles or

25. Long-billed curlew (*top*), marbled godwit (*middle*), and upland sandpiper (*bottom*). Head and bill profiles of females (*upper*) and males (*lower*) of the first two species are illustrated. Drawing by author.

26. Long-billed curlew displays, including defensive flight (A), bounding soft-kerr-kerr (SKK) flight, gliding phase (B), aggressive upright posture (C), aggressive crouch-run (D), precopulatory wing-raising by male (E), and nest-scraping display by male (F). Sonogram of *curl-ee* call (two-second duration) after Robbins, Bruun, and Zim (1983). Drawing by author, adapted from Johnsgard (1995).

other subterranean insects. Drinking of surface water is rarely if ever performed, so presumably they need not have such freestanding water within their territorial boundaries.

Soon after their spring arrival in the central and northern plains, the unpaired curlew males begin advertising for mates, but many birds arrive seemingly already paired, and they soon reclaim their previous year's territories. Territory sizes are not yet well known, but studies by Roland Redmond in Idaho suggest that males may defend collective foraging and nesting territories of about thirty-five acres. Thomas Bicak estimated that in the Nebraska Sandhills the pair advertises and defends a core area of about 2.5 acres, over which one or both pair members display regularly during the pre-egg stages of the nesting cycle.

Perhaps the most conspicuous breeding-season display is the "core-area flight display" (Bicak). It was called the "bounding soft-kerr-kerr flight" (abbreviated as the SKK flight) by Julia Fitzner, whose terminology and descriptions of the species' displays seem unusually complete. In this display the bird rapidly gains altitude, sets its somewhat bowed wings (Fig. 26B), and glides back to earth, uttering a series of soft *kerr-kerr* notes during the entire descent. Ground calling is also used, but the notes, repeated *whee* sounds, are different. During aerial territorial defense (Fig. 26A), deeper wingbeats are used, the call is a loud and distinctive *curl-eee,* and the bird or birds will repeatedly circle the intruding person or mammal, sometimes diving at them. When threatening conspecifics on the ground, an "aggressive upright" posture may be assumed (Fig. 26C) or a more intense "crouch-run" toward the intruder, with scapulars raised and the folded wings variably drooped.

An important sexually oriented display is "scraping," during which the performing bird lowers its breast to the ground and flexes its legs, kicking its feet alternately backward, as if making a nesting scrape (Fig. 26F). This is a rather common courtship display among shorebirds and some other ground-nesting species. The bird may also toss vegetation sideways, as if nest-building.

Displays performed by males only include a "courtship-run" of the male toward the female, its head held upright and the wings variably held out to the side and drooped, while the tail is held high. As the male reaches the female, the wings are raised, exposing their cinnamon-colored undersides (Fig. 26E). This posture is a copulatory invitation display and is followed immediately by "shaking," in which the male shakes his head and bill from side to side and up and down in a U-shaped pattern, ruffling the female's scapular feathers. The male's wings are still raised, and he utters a strange mixture of squeaky notes. At the peak of this display the male may attempt to mount the larger female, still holding his wings erect and adjusting them to maintain balance. The female does not crouch but spreads her wings somewhat to provide a better balancing opportunity for the male. As copulation is terminated, the female drops forward briefly, then escapes out from under the male. No postcopulatory displays are evident.

The scraping behavior that occurred earlier as a courtship display now becomes a functional method of nest-site selection and nest-building. Several different sites may be used for scraping, but eventually one is somehow chosen, and at that point scraping is replaced by vegetation-tossing. At least in southeastern Washington, where Fitzner studied the birds, landscape features such as ground slope (little or none apparently preferred) and vegetational structure, rather than specific grass species composition, seem to be important site-selection criteria. Low-stature grasses, and grasses that do not provide dense visual barriers but do offer irregular patterns of vegetation density that might complement the bird's cryptic plumage pattern, appear to serve as preferred nest sites. Sites fairly close to a conspicuous object, such as a rusty discarded can, a pile of manure, or similar protruding objects, also seem to be preferred. A minimum distance to other curlew nests of at least 300 to 500 yards may also be a significant factor in nest placement and perhaps also influences minimum population densities.

Copulations continue through the egg-laying period, and eggs are laid at about two-day intervals. Like that of many shorebirds, a four-egg clutch is virtually universal, and the eggs rather pointed ends allow them to be neatly arranged in a compact radiating or starburst pattern, with their more rounded ends directed outward. Perhaps because curlews prefer to nest in rather low vegetation, their nests are often preyed upon by visually hunting aerial predators. These include black-billed magpies, American crows and common ravens, reptiles such as bullsnakes, and mammals such as coyotes and skunks. Both sexes attempt to defend their nests against such threats from predators, and males will also regularly assist neighboring pairs in such defensive activities. Few attempts at renesting following loss of the initial clutch have been reported.

Both sexes participate in incubation, which requires about twenty-seven to twenty-eight days. Typically, the female incubates during the daylight hours, and the male at night. Changeovers are accompanied by whistled signals from the incoming bird as it lands some distance from the nest, which is then answered similarly by the sitting bird. The nest is then approached cautiously and on foot.

Following hatching of the eggs, the nest is likely to be abandoned the same day, although a late-afternoon hatch will result in the birds remaining overnight in the nest. The male typically stands guard as the female leads her chicks from the nest, typically to a higher location. Females may abandon their broods at two to three weeks of age, after which the males undertake care of the broods alone. Fledging occurs at about six weeks, but considerable overland movement may have occurred by that time. Not long after fledging, premigratory flocking begins, and soon thereafter the southward migration is under way, long before most other resident breeders have begun to leave the prairies.

Nesting success is apparently quite variable from year to year and from place to place, based on Fitzner's observations in Washington. However, in Redmond's study area in Idaho, the population remained fairly stable over a six-year period. The average clutch survival rate (hatching success) was estimated at 40 percent over a three-year period, with little apparent annual variation. The average number of young raised per female was judged to be only 0.17 to 0.40 annually, which would not seem adequate to sustain the population indefinitely. However, a quite high annual adult survival rate of 85 percent was also estimated, and it was calculated that only 58 percent of the fledged young would need to survive until their first breeding at three years to maintain this population.

Marbled Godwit

The marbled godwit was named in part for the softly variegated or "marbled" pattern of its adult breeding plumage. The godwit component evidently was derived from the Old English *god wiht*, meaning a "good thing," and presumably originally referred to its culinary appeal rather than to its aesthetic characteristics. Few would argue that the marbled godwit is a very good thing indeed: seeing a small flock flying northward overhead in early spring gives one a sense of assurance that somehow things are right in the world and offers some increased confidence in the future.

Somewhat smaller in length than the long-billed curlew, the marbled godwit similarly shows a greater dimorphism in adult bill-lengths than

27. Marbled godwit, adult in flight. Drawing by author.

in adult body mass (Fig. 27). Unlike the curlews, godwits have pale pinkish to orange (in breeding condition) at the base of their very slightly upturned bills, which again are somewhat different in the two sexes, being more brightly colored in males. The birds are about the same size and mass as whimbrels, but in plumage they more closely resemble long-billed curlews, in that adults of both species have distinctive cinnamon-colored underwing-coverts. A cinnamon-toned to isabelline color is also pervasive over most of the rest of their bodies. This color approximates that of dead grass and makes incubating birds very hard to locate in a previous year's dead-grass cover.

Wintering areas of this species are surprisingly widespread but seem to be concentrated on the California coast, plus the coastlines of Baja, Sonora, and Sinaloa. Relatively few birds winter along the Gulf Coast, a rather surprising fact considering that such a wintering area would make for an easier migration from the central plains than one crossing the Rocky Mountains. The relatively few banding recoveries thus far available allow for a clear determination of migration routes from the plains to the Pacific slope, based on information summarized by Cheri Gratto-Trevor.

Coastal mudflats or sandflats and adjoining wet savannas are preferred winter habitats. In such areas a diverse assortment of invertebrates are consumed, primarily during periods of low tide, which are located by probing as well as by visual searches. Generally while foraging the birds stand in shallow water (two to five inches deep), with their bills, or sometimes even their entire heads, submerged. Under bright moonlight conditions, some nocturnal foraging may occur, and after heavy rains more upland sites may also be exploited for earthworms. Polychaete worms (most commonly), small bivalve mollusks, crustaceans (small crabs), and earthworms are primary winter foods; insects, especially grasshoppers, aquatic pondweed tubers, leeches, and even small fish such as sticklebacks may be eaten on migration and while in breeding areas. At least in some areas during late summer and fall, tubers may be the single most important food source, especially for adults attempting to build fat reserves, but juveniles are likely to concentrate on foods having higher protein content.

Upon spring arrival at their Great Plains breeding grounds, the birds seek out relatively short and sparsely vegetated habitats with nearby wetlands of varying sizes and degrees of permanence. Native prairie grasslands and hayfields are preferred over introduced ("tame") grass cover types or idle grasslands. Grazed grassy habitats are preferred over ungrazed ones, and areas with heavier shrub cover may also be used less frequently than those lacking shrubs. Small northern populations breeding around James Bay and in Alaska may use rather different breeding habitats, especially including those having small shrubs or low trees present.

Probably soon after arrival on their breeding areas, males establish territories and begin performing "ceremonial circling flights," which may function more to attract females than to advertise breeding territories, inasmuch as nests may later be placed some distance away. During these flights the male ascends some 70 to 300 feet above ground, then circles over a wide area with slow wingbeats, calling repeatedly (Fig. 28, *above*). Finally, he glides slowly to earth or regains altitude and repeats the display. At times the male may instead dive almost vertically downward until it is within about twenty feet of earth and then land with both wings temporarily lifted above the back, briefly exposing its cinnamon undersides (Fig. 28, *lower left*). A flight of less certain function, seen only twice by Timothy Nowicki, was a "figure-8 ceremony," during which two birds performed low flights over rather large areas in a somewhat circuitous route. Expulsion chases by males toward intruding single or paired birds also occur, as do "joint flights," in which a male follows his mate in gently undulating flights about seventy feet above ground, usually in a fairly straight course.

The nest-scrape ceremony (Fig. 28, *lower right*), a squatting, rocking, and sideways plant-tossing activity, is a behavior pattern similar to that described for the long-billed curlews. It was not described by Nowicki or by Gratto-Trevor as a courtship ceremony but as a functional prenesting behavior associated with an actual nest site. It may, however, serve both roles, as it does in various shorebird species.

On their breeding grounds, the most conspicuous call of adults (Fig. 28, *top*) is a loud *ger-whit* that is uttered during the high-altitude ceremonial circling flight of territorial males, as described by Nowicki. It is also used, with little variation, during the male's nest-scraping ceremony and under other circumstances, and by both sexes when they are calling to their young.

Potential nest sites are selected by the male, and these sites are presented through nest-scraping behavior to the female, who in turn may then accept or reject them. Sites selected are often quite far from water. They also are in quite short grassy cover, usually less than six inches high, without overhead concealment and with rather slight horizontal screening immediately around the nest. Sites selected are similar in attributes to those listed as constituting general breeding habitat. Forbs are typically in low frequency near nests, and shrubs are absent. Unlike long-billed curlews, marbled godwits seem to have no tendency to nest anywhere near rocks, bushes, or other protruding objects.

Nearly always the female lays four eggs, at one- to three-day intervals. Clutches of more than four eggs are rare and perhaps are always the result of two birds laying in the same nest. Renesting rates following clutch losses have been documented as beginning three to eight days after clutch loss, but this will most likely depend on the female's stage

28. Male marbled godwit displays, including ceremonial circling flight (*above*) wing-up (*lower left*), and scraping (*lower right*). Drawing by author; sonogram of *ger-whit* call (duration two seconds) after Gratto-Trevor (in press).

of incubation. If the nest is lost early in the breeding season, at least half the females seem to attempt to renest. Incubation may begin sometime prior to the laying of the last egg, and it is shared by both sexes. As do curlews, males seem to incubate through the night and females during the day, with changeovers occurring during the evening. The incubation period is twenty-three to twenty-six days.

Since these birds nest in remarkably exposed sites, their susceptibility to predation is high. Nesting success rates determined by Gratto-

Trevor in Alberta averaged 59 percent over a four-year period, but when adjusted for estimates of nests lost prior to discovery the rates are substantially lower, from 11 to 67 percent yearly. The same was true in a study in the Prairie Potholes region of the Dakotas, Montana, and Manitoba, where an adjusted 40 percent nest success rate was estimated. Most nest losses are from predation rather than desertion, and in the Prairie Potholes study all the identified nest predators were mammals. As a result of such losses, annual productivity seems rather small. In the case of Gratto-Trevor's three-year study, only 18 percent of the females succeeded in fledging at least one chick, and the average productivity was only 0.25 young fledged per female per year. This low rate of annual recruitment seems to be counterbalanced by a high annual adult survival rate of at least 87 percent (observed among wintering birds in northern California). Furthermore, a single banded individual is known to have reached an age of at least twenty-nine years, one of the most remarkable longevity records for any wild shorebird in North America.

Soon after the brood's twenty-six to thirty-day fledging period, or even before, the female typically leaves the male in charge; and not long after the broods have become independent, flocking prior to fall migration begins. Failed breeders or nonbreeders assemble and leave soonest, with some birds beginning to arrive on the California coast as early as August. These presumed nonbreeders or failed breeders are followed by successful breeders and finally by juveniles, which begin to migrate south several weeks after breeding adults. The juveniles typically arrive on California wintering areas in December. Their route is not known, but the lowest and thus easiest available route for them over the Continental Divide would be to use the gap between the Northern and Central Rockies in west-central Wyoming.

Upland Sandpiper

William Bartram (1739–1823), a botanist and an artist, was the son of another famous American botanist, John Bartram. In his later years (1812–1823) William Bartram also became the director of the Philadelphia Botanic Garden. In 1831 the upland sandpiper's generic name *Bartramia* was established posthumously in Bartram's honor by the French biologist René Lesson. This species has therefore sometimes also been known as "Bartram's sandpiper," although it seems unlikely that Bartram ever saw one during his entire lifetime.

Until fairly recently, the accepted English name for this species was the upland plover, presumably because of its short, ploverlike bill, its relatively large eyes, and its tendency to favor grassy uplands and meadows rather than marshy shorelines. Yet in all other anatomical and behavioral respects this elegant shorebird has much more in common with the curlew group than with the typical plovers, such as the mountain plover and killdeer. And, like curlews and godwits, after landing it often holds both wings upright for a moment before folding them daintily into its flank feathers; in fact, the upland sandpiper seems to make a fetish of this particularly endearing trait.

Few ornithologists have seen and studied upland sandpipers on their wintering areas of southern South America, but the habitats they use and the foods they consume are likely to differ but little from those they use in North American areas. In any case, almost this entire phase of their life history needs to be filled in by future observers. Early writers such as William H. Hudson wrote of the birds arriving on the Argentine pampas as early as September and then spreading out over the vast areas that once were native grasslands. The upland sandpiper has historically been considered a table delicacy in Argentina, replacing the Eskimo curlew after that species became rare and finally apparently extinct. The birds remain there until February and March, with the northward migration getting under way in mid-March and continuing into early April. By March the earlier migrants are arriving in Texas and Louisiana, and the primary flow of northward movement seems to occur between the Rocky Mountains and the Mississippi Valley.

Many birds arrive on their breeding areas already paired, so perhaps courtship begins during the spring northward migration. Less probably pair bonds are retained throughout migration and the entire time they are on their South American wintering areas. In a Wisconsin study, Irvine Ailes found that five of fifteen birds that he had banded as adults the previous year returned to his study area. Two of them returned already paired with their previous year's partner, and two returned with new mates. The fifth bird returned without his prior mate, and he was unsuccessful in attracting a new one during the summer. Two of sixty birds banded as chicks the previous year also returned, suggesting that perhaps some yearling birds attempt to nest. Possibly many others remain on the wintering grounds or in intermediate locations throughout their first year.

Although eastern Colorado is the western edge of the species' Great

Plains breeding range, the birds are seen there most often on tall-grass–sandsage habitats, followed progressively less often by croplands, midgrass prairies, and short-grass prairies. Several other habitat types are also used rather sparingly, judging from records summarized in the *Colorado Breeding Bird Atlas*. Elsewhere, as in Wisconsin and Vermont, the combination of large expanses of relatively short grasses and level or slightly undulating topography seem to be the criteria selected by the birds. Hay meadows, large pastures, agricultural lands that include stubble, moderately grazed pastures, and similar habitats are used during the breeding season. The presence of even a few shrubs or trees reduces an area's attractiveness to the birds. Likewise, lightly grazed or ungrazed areas in the midgrass prairies are favored over grazed ones, and even slight grazing tends to reduce nesting success. Areas much smaller than 500 acres are unlikely to attract breeding upland sandpipers.

By late April or early May the birds are back on their breeding areas, and territorial establishment begins immediately. Its most conspicuous hallmark is the male's utterance of its "long whistle," a sort of prolonged "wolf whistle" that is preceded by a whistled or somewhat throaty chatter (Fig. 29). This same vocalization is also performed under various circumstances by females. A more common vocalization is a bubbling, prolonged series of *quip-ip-ip-ip* notes that are uttered throughout the breeding season by both sexes and in a variety of circumstances.

Territoriality is advertised by a high circling flight (Fig. 29, *above*) and also in low flights barely ten feet above the ground, during which the male calls repeatedly and flies using a "flutter-stroke" that consists of very rapid but shallow wingbeats (Fig. 29, *below*). The strokes are mostly confined to the lower plane of the body, the wingtips scarcely rising above the midpoint of the body at the top of each stroke and the outer parts of the wings seemingly curved downward. This flutter-stroke phase is followed by a prolonged glide. Females may also perform flight displays above the pair's territory.

Territories tend to be somewhat clustered, the birds nesting in a loosely colonial manner. They include nesting, foraging, and "loafing" sites. Studies by Daniel Bowen indicate that upland sandpipers nesting in groups had a higher average nesting success rate than those outside of such colonies, where the nesting success matched that of other prairie-nesting species. Nest sites are selected that typically are in open grasslands, with standing grasses from about six to ten inches high. Sites in areas where the grass is more than twenty inches tall seem to be

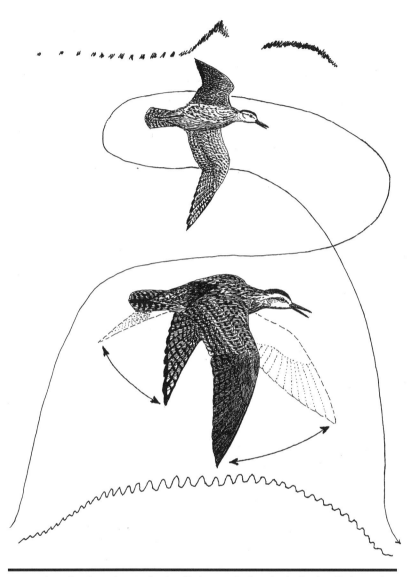

29. Male upland sandpiper display flights, including high display flight with calling (*above*) and low flutter-flight (*below*). Undulating lower line indicates deep wingbeats during flutter-flight. Vocalization diagram (subjective interpretation, duration ca. four seconds) based on description by Buss and Hawkins (1939). Drawing by author.

30. Upland sandpiper, incubating adult. Drawing by author.

avoided, although in rare cases nest cover up to nearly thirty inches has been observed. Often sites are chosen that provide a canopy of grasses, obscuring the nest from overhead view. Sometimes a nest will be placed fairly close to a fencepost, which often serves as a convenient lookout site; more rarely it will be situated at the base of a shrub or small tree.

Eggs are laid at the average rate of one per day or at slightly longer mean intervals. Nearly all completed clutches consist of four eggs; rarely have five eggs been found in a nest. There is no evidence of polygyny in this species; on a few occasions when trios of birds have been found, the extra bird has proven to be a male. Incubation begins with the laying of the last or the penultimate egg and requires an average of twenty-four days. It is performed mostly by the female, but the male always remains nearby, alerting his mate to the first sign of danger by using the long whistle while circling overhead. The female usually utters the short whistle when she is flushed from the nest. Crows, skunks, and minks are known to be serious nest predators, with additional losses sustained by mowing, grazing, and similar human-caused activities. The incidence of renesting following nest failure is still unknown, but hatching dates in a North Dakota population studied by Kenneth Higgins and Leo Kirsch had a markedly bimodal distribution, the two peaks about twenty-five days apart, suggesting that such renesting is not rare. A similar but less pronounced second hatching peak was found by Ailes in Wisconsin.

The nesting success rates of upland sandpipers appear to be typical of shorebirds. In a Wisconsin study by Irvin Buss and Arthur Hawkins, 34 percent of forty-seven nests were failures, mostly owing to trampling by cattle and egg predation by crows. In Ailes's Wisconsin study, a higher nesting success rate of 85 percent (but for a small sample of thirteen nests) was determined; and in the North Dakota study involving 172 nests, the nesting success rate was estimated at 67 percent (Fig. 30).

There is a fledging period of about thirty to thirty-four days in this species, during which time the young may wander some distance with their parents, foraging on grasshoppers, crickets, and other insects. A wide variety of insects is eaten by both adults and young, although waste grain may also be consumed by migrating birds. The birds are also attracted to cattle dung, where they catch insects that are attracted as well.

Whoever invented the word "grace" must have seen the wing-folding of the plover [upland sandpiper].

—Aldo Leopold,
Sand County Almanac

Upland sandpipers begin to leave their breeding areas in August, or about two months after the initial hatching peak. In Wisconsin, the birds are present on their breeding grounds for a total of slightly more than 100 days, or little more than some Arctic-breeding shorebirds.

Suggested Readings

Johnsgard 1981.

Long-billed Curlew: Allen 1980; Cochrane 1983; Fitzner 1978; Forsythe 1970, 1972; King 1978; McCallum et al. 1977; Pampush and Anthony 1993; Redmond 1984, 1986; Redmond and Jenni 1986; Sugden 1933.

Marbled Godwit: Colwell and Oring 1990; Dechant et al. 1999h; Gratto-Trevor, in press; Guay 1968; Higgins et al. 1969, 1979; Nowicki 1973; Ryan 1982.

Upland Sandpiper: Ailes 1980; Ailes and Toepfer 1977; Bicak 1977; Bowen 1976; Bowen and Kruse 1993; Buss and Hawkins 1939; Colwell and Oring 1990; Dorio and Grove 1979; Higgins and Kirsh 1975; Higgins et al. 1969, 1979; Kaiser 1979; Kirsch and Higgins 1976; Lindmeier 1960; Skinner 1974; Swanson 1996; White 1983.

7   # High Drama on the High Plains: *Prairie Falcons, Mountain Plovers, and Prairie Dogs*

One does not sell the earth on which people walk.

—Tashunca-Uitco (Crazy Horse)

The first wild prairie falcon that I ever saw was in the Pine Ridge country of northwestern Nebraska, a land that, like the nearby Black Hills, has been long lived upon by the Oglala Sioux. But it is also the blood-stained land where the Sioux's greatest hero, Crazy Horse, was murdered while being held a captive by the U.S. Cavalry, and where Wounded Knee became a household word for genocide long before Rwanda, Somalia, or Bosnia entered our collective consciousness. It is moreover a land where the descendants of Crazy Horse still live out miserable lives, in one of the most poverty-stricken areas of America. They were forced into a region of arid plains and badlands that no settlers wanted, following the U.S. Army's successful conclusion of the Indian Wars, and from which the bison, the Indians' keystone survival species, had been eliminated. However, the adjacent forested and beautiful Black Hills, lands that long had been held sacred to the Sioux and Cheyenne, were taken from them. The discovery of gold in the Black Hills in the mid-1800s, and the subsequent intrusion of whites into this region, was one of the initial causes of the Sioux uprising. It also set the stage for the last great battles of the Indian Wars, culminating in Gen. George Custer's most famous, if fatal, encounter on the short-grass plains near the Little Bighorn.

One of the Black Hills' granite peaks has since been chiseled and blasted away to resemble the faces of four of white America's greatest national heroes, and a national all-season playground for the wealthy has been developed. But the prairie falcons don't seem to mind any of this; vulnerable prairie dogs and abundant ground squirrels still populate the open grasslands, and even today there are some vertical cliff faces suitable for nesting that rock climbers haven't yet discovered and that snowmobiles and ATVs can't readily approach.

There are few avian calls more exciting than the challenging scream of a prairie falcon; it puts the American bald eagle's weak whistle to shame. Add to this the irregular geometry of an eroded rimrock landscape, a sky without apparent limits, the whisper of a cooling wind over bending grass, and the smell of sagebrush—the spell is complete. When I was doing fieldwork for a book on the natural history of Jackson Hole and the Tetons, one of my greatest pleasures came on those days that I could relax and spend hours watching a pair of nesting prairie falcons. Their aerie was about ten feet below the lip of a vertical cliff face that was several hundred feet high, where a shallow recess allowed the female protection from the elements and from most of its potential predators. A pair of common ravens nested fairly nearby in a vertical crevice of the same cliff. Yet should either of the adult ravens or any of their recently fledged young venture too close to the falcon nest it would immediately be met by fierce aerial attacks from the ever-watchful male, who usually stood watch on a small windswept and gnarled lodgepole pine growing at the very crest of the cliff. From his roost there was an unobstructed view over the broad, sage-covered valley, and any ground squirrel foolish enough to stray very far from its burrow would not live long enough to learn from or regret its mistake. Coyotes often hunted

About the brink of a precipice a dozen falcons are at play. It is courting time and the birds are showing off. . . . The rock walls resound with boisterous music, and the observer feels as though he were witnessing the play of elemental forces— riotous, exultant, unrestrained, the very passion of freedom and conquest.

—William Dawson,
The Birds of California

the same valley floor for ground squirrels but posed no threat to the falcons. Black bears were not infrequent, and rarely, or so I was told by a local old-time resident, a lone wolverine would lope casually across the valley floor.

Prairie Falcon

Perhaps the prairie falcon and mountain plover should exchange common names; mountain falcon and prairie plover would fit each far better. Both species have their primary ranges in arid short-grass or shrub-steppe environments, where a considerable amount of bare ground offers the mountain plover a place to walk easily about in search of surface insects and where small mammals and birds cannot easily hide from the falcon. If the peregrine can be thought of as a high-altitude dive bomber, then the prairie falcon is more like a low-altitude sneak-attack weapon. It often courses only a few feet above the ground cover, allowing little time for a potential prey to see it far enough in advance to be able to plan an effective escape strategy. Birds are often caught in flight by full-speed chases (Fig. 31). Whereas the mountain plover is quite content to live in the flattest possible environment, the prairie falcon prefers buttes, badlands, or rimrock for its immediate surroundings. The *Colorado Breeding Bird Atlas* data indicate that cliffs, followed by short-grass prairie, are by far the two most frequently used habitat types of the prairie falcon in that state. In contrast, short-grass prairie is virtually

31. Prairie falcon chasing a mountain plover. Drawing by author.

the only habitat type used by mountain plovers, with croplands and barren ground sites of very secondary significance.

If a traveler is heading west across the central plains states, the sight of a prairie falcon will convince him that he now indeed is in the west. Some eastward drifting of birds to the Missouri Valley or even beyond may occur during winter, but this is more likely to be peregrine territory. Winter movements are not so much a true north-south migration as they are wanderings, although a few birds may travel as far south as Mexico's Central Valley. The birds seem to congregate during winter in a relatively few favored hunting localities, such as in Nebraska's Niobrara Valley, in the vicinity of Great Bend, Kansas, along the Arkansas and San Luis Rivers, and in the Kiowa and Pawnee National Grasslands. Even higher concentrations occur locally in northwestern Utah and in the California-Nevada border region, but these probably support birds breeding well to the west of the Great Plains. It is generally believed that Canadian birds breeding east of a line approximating the Saskatchewan-Alberta border winter in areas west of the Rockies and that those breeding to the east of that zone winter in the Great Plains.

In these wintering areas, open-country environments are used for visual hunting. During the winter period the birds feed opportunistically on whatever is seasonally available. Ground squirrels are hibernating, so the birds are likely to shift to small birds, especially horned larks and meadowlarks. Indeed, large populations of wintering horned larks may provide a special attraction to prairie falcons. Driving through the Pawnee National Grasslands in October, one may see thousands of horned larks working the fields and gradually moving south, along with smaller flocks of migrating mountain bluebirds and occasional longspurs. With great luck, one may see a prairie falcon take off from a fencepost, rise 100 feet or more, and then bear down on these birds, causing them to flush and scatter in wild panic.

Such birds are likely to be captured during unrestrained aerial chases, but the prairie falcon uses other techniques when hunting for rodents. Probably the most common search-and-attack method is a low-altitude approach, flying barely above the vegetation and following the contours of the land, thus keeping below the visual detection range, or protective "radar screen," of the prey. At times searching will also be done from higher altitudes, with actual attacks taking the form of low-angle stoops. Steeper and swifter descents, such as those used regularly by peregrines, are sometimes also employed but not nearly so frequently.

Adult prairie falcons are only about 80 percent as heavy as adult pere-grines and may not attain the peregrine's maximum speed during stoops. Just as within that species, adult females weigh 30 to 40 percent more than males, so some species- and sexually related differences in prey-catching possibilities exist.

During the long nonbreeding period, pairs do not attempt to remain together. However, limited information suggests that birds tend to win-ter in the same areas from year to year, with immatures moving south-ward earlier in fall and returning north later in spring. Although prob-ably many birds remain sexually inactive their first year, or at least cannot obtain nesting territories in competition with older birds, there are good records of first-year females nesting successfully, and this situ-ation may be especially true in expanding or recovering populations.

With the return flight of adults to their breeding grounds, either sex may arrive first. Pairs evidently find one another and reestablish old pair bonds, or males begin to search for new mates by finding an available nest site and starting to advertise above and around it. Only a fairly small area around the site is actually defended; this may include a semicircu-lar (if on a cliff face) or a more circular zone extending about 400 yards from the nest and about 100 yards above it.

Aerial prenesting displays may involve mutual soaring by the pair above the nesting area and also expulsion of intruders from the nest-ing vicinity, although foraging areas well away from the nest sites may be shared by neighboring pairs. Patrolling behavior by the male, con-sisting of flights from one edge of the territory to a perch at the other edge and then back again, begin well before egg-laying. These flights peak about ten days before incubation and resume again when the eggs hatch. Other aerial displays of prairie falcons are not yet well described, but most observations suggest that pair-bonding postures are very simi-lar if not identical to those of the well-studied peregrine. The accom-panying sketches are thus based on that species' social behavior (Fig. 32). Like that of other falcons, most courtship is centered on the nesting ledge. Displays mostly consist of rather stereotyped posturing associ-ated with investigations of potential nest sites and food-begging or cop-ulation-solicitation behaviors of the female toward the male. One com-mon early display is the "head-low bow," in which both birds hold their heads low, beaks oriented somewhat away from each other and with their body feathers sleeked, apparently showing their mutual nonag-gressive intentions.

s32. Prairie falcon pair-forming displays, including head-low bowing (A), prey presentation by a perched male (B), hitched-wing precopulatory display of male (C), aerial begging by female (D), begging by perched female, and copulation sequence (F–G). Drawing by author, based mainly on peregrine studies.

Female prairie falcons tend to be unusually aggressive and may attack males during early stages of pair formation. Females also perform nest-scraping movements at the nest site, and the male may approach her with his body held in a horizontal posture and with a somewhat swaggering gait. He may also fly repeatedly to and from the ledge to attract her attention. The two birds may gently nibble one another's beaks while they are standing on the nesting ledge. Feeding of prey by the male to the female is an important aspect of courtship and often precedes copulation. A distinctive "hitched-wing" posture is used by both sexes to indicate a readiness to copulate, with the folded wings held high above the body and their heads somewhat lowered. This same posture is used by the male as a postcopulatory display. Prior to laying, the birds may copulate as many as four times per hour, but the average is only about four per day over the fifty days prior to egg-laying, or a total of nearly 200 copulations.

Although nests are most often placed on horizontal recesses in cliffs that also provide some vertical overhang, nests on buildings, in caves, and in trees have also been described. Old stick nests made by eagles or ravens are sometimes used; no materials are carried in by the birds themselves. South-facing exposures are favored, as are sites above the midpoint of the cliff. Sites with well-developed overhangs, providing shade from the afternoon sun, may be used in locations where summer heat or strong winds can be a potential problem.

Copulation by the pair may begin as early as fifty days or more before egg-laying begins and peaks about four weeks prior to that time, suggesting its possibly important role in pair-bonding. The eggs are laid at intervals of about two days, with clutches typically of five eggs. Smaller clutches are not uncommon, and clutches of six or even more rarely have been reported. It is very possible that the female's condition, as reflected by relative prey availability, is a primary determinant of clutch size. Springs having cold, inclement weather, perhaps affecting hunting opportunities, can also result in lower clutches.

Incubation begins with the laying of the first egg, and the female does all the nocturnal incubation as well as most during the day. Hatching occurs over a seemingly broad range in the wild, but under conditions of captivity requires an average of 33.5 days. In spite of their quite inaccessible nest sites, some clutches are lost to predators or other factors. Renesting has been reported, although it is evidently rare. The female also does all the nighttime brooding and nearly all the daytime brooding, with the male providing essentially all the food during the first week after hatching. Thereafter, the female begins to spend more time foraging and less brooding, so that when the young are approaching fledging she may bring in nearly half the food. Fledging occurs at an average of thirty-eight days following hatching, but a similar period of time following fledging is spent while they are wholly dependent on their parents for food. Even after this dependency period, the young birds remain within the pair's territory until they begin fall dispersal at about two months of age or more. Some of the young continue to associate with siblings during and after this dispersal period.

Nesting success is evidently fairly high in this species, with long-term studies and data from short-term observations suggesting that about 70 to 75 percent of the nesting efforts succeed in rearing one or more chicks to fledging, and about 2.8 young are fledged per successful nest. Nesting success is closely correlated with relative abundance of principal prey species, typically ground squirrels, with spring weather sometimes also influencing it. First-year survival rates of juveniles are quite low, as is common in raptors, and may range from about 15 to 35 percent. However, annual survival rates of adults are seemingly fairly high, from about 65 to 80 percent. With the latter survival rate, the probable life expectancy could be as high as about fifteen years. It is unlikely that such great longevities are typical, however, and perhaps a four- or five-year period of effective reproduction would be more likely.

Mountain Plover

Mountain plovers, short-grass prairie, and prairie dogs simply once belonged together, as did the bison and the pronghorn. Grazing by these native ungulates kept the short and medium-length grasses even shorter and provided improved opportunities for the plovers' visual hunting of grasshoppers or other grassland insects. Prior to winter, the birds would migrate into the even more arid lands of the Chihuahuan and Sonoran Deserts and the Central Valley of California, where grazing by other native ungulates helped maintain this short-grass environment.

Still today the plovers migrate annually to wintering grounds in the southern Great Plains, northern Mexico, and the interior valleys of California. The Mexican winter distribution remains poorly known, and current information suggests that California is the primary wintering area, even though breeding is confined to areas east of the Continental

Divide. Thus, migrations tend to be largely east-west rather than north-south, with the birds passing above both the Rocky Mountains and the Sierra Nevadas each spring and fall. Much of the migration may be undertaken at night, but few details are available.

Arrival on their wintering ground occurs by early November, where the birds spread out over grazed or burned annual grasslands or similarly grazed or burned agricultural lands. Whether on wintering areas or breeding grounds, they once gravitated to barren or nearly barren locations, such as prairie dog mounds and bison wallows. Now similarly denuded sites such as water tanks where cattle have destroyed the vegetation, roadbeds, or recently plowed fields are used. There grasshoppers are generally abundant, as are other terrestrial insects such as beetles, ants, and crickets. These are captured visually, usually after short runs. Like some other ground-feeding birds, the plovers may quickly patter the ground surface with one foot, evidently to help expose and frighten possible prey. Few items other than insects are eaten, and evidently the birds do not require freestanding water to obtain their metabolic fluid needs. Like other plovers these birds have relatively large eyes and probably can see prey under rather dim light conditions.

With the spring migration, the birds begin returning to the short-grass high plains, which occur at elevations of about 2,000 to 6,000 feet. Spring arrival between early March and mid-April is fairly typical. A similarly early fall departure is also typical, this often occurring in July or early August, or soon after the young fledge. In areas where prairie dog towns still survive, their colonies are highly attractive breeding-season habitats, especially in localities where the grass is otherwise moderately high and dense. Semidesert sites with scattered low sagebrush, yuccas, cacti, or salt-tolerant forbs and shrubs are sometimes also used, but great horizontal visibility appears to be of prime importance to this species during all seasons.

Only a few days after their arrival on the breeding ground, the males begin to establish nesting territories. These tend to be surprisingly large for such small birds, averaging about forty acres each in the case of three individually marked Colorado males. As might be expected from such large territories, their edges are ill-defined, and substantial edge overlap may occur. One of the major displays used by males to advertise territory is the "falling-leaf" display, so named by William Graul. In this display the male ascends about fifteen to thirty feet. He then raises his wings to form a V-shape over the back and floats back to earth in a side-

33. Mountain plover, male bowing (*below*) and flight-song (*above*) displays. Undulating line indicates flapping phase of display flight. Sonogram (two-second duration) after Knopf (1996a). Drawing by author, display postures adapted from sketches by Graul (1973).

ways rocking motion, much like a falling leaf might do (Fig. 33, *above*). During this downward glide he utters a loud, repeated call (see sonogram), of *wee-wee-wee,* whistling notes. These individual notes are repeated up to fifteen times, at the rate of about seven notes per second. The same call is uttered while the bird is on the ground and involved in aggressive encounters, and rarely (as after copulation) the female utters the same note. Several other notes are used during aggressive encounters, in sexual situations, and in parental-offspring interactions.

Another possibly important but seemingly rare flight display is the "butterfly flight." It is an aerial display that is common in many shorebirds and is characterized by the bird flying high above his territory, using slow and deep wingbeats. Aggressive encounters on the ground with intruding birds include horizontal threat postures directed toward the opponent and running in parallel. The latter display probably is most often performed at the edges of adjoining and contested territories, as is true of the closely corresponding display in sharp-tailed grouse.

Specifically sexually oriented postures include the exhibition of a potential nest site by nest-scraping behavior (see curlew and godwit accounts, chapter 6). In a related bowing display (Fig. 33, *lower right*), the male stands above the nest scrape and lowers his head while tilting his bill downward. He simultaneously lifts and somewhat spreads his tail, exposing its upper surface to the female's view. He also expands his throat, closes his eyes, and utters a low mooing call. The female (*lower left*) may pay little or no attention initially, or she may perform the same display in response to the male.

Copulation is preceded by the male approaching and performing rapid foot movements in an upright posture, and uttering *chert* calls as he moves from side to side behind her. If the female crouches, the male mounts. He may remain balanced on her back for astonishingly long periods, reportedly anywhere from less than a minute to more than thirteen minutes before copulation is finally achieved.

Nests are typically placed on barren substrates, sometimes near piles of cow manure or sometimes beside vehicle tracks or ruts. However, most frequently the immediate surroundings exhibit less dense and lower vegetation than is typical of nearby locations and often consist of recently disturbed substrates, such as newly plowed land.

The eggs are laid at the average rate of one per thirty-four to forty-eight hours and thus are not deposited on a predictable daily or alternate-day basis. Somewhat surprisingly, three eggs rather than four constitute the usual clutch, this unusually small clutch perhaps being an adaptation to living in an arid environment where resources are scarce.

Incubation is performed by both sexes and lasts about twenty-nine days, but the relative role of the two sexes in incubation is still not established. During hot daytime hours it may be more important to shade the eggs to prevent overheating than to keep them warm, but during the cool nights bodily heat may need to be applied. The greatest amount of parental attention is paid during very hot days. Egg losses may result from predation, flooding, hail damage, and perhaps from heat exposure, although this last factor has not yet been documented for undisturbed nests.

Hatching is virtually simultaneous, and if it occurs early in the morning the nest will be abandoned that day. A late afternoon hatch, or inclement weather, will cause the birds to remain on the nest overnight. Fledging occurs about thirty-three to thirty-six days after hatching, with at least one adult tending the brood through the entire fledging period. It has been reported that the female may leave her brood in the care of the male before it is fully independent and begin laying and tending a second clutch alone, which might increase the annual rate of reproductive success somewhat. This ability to produce a second clutch after successfully breeding seems rather surprising in view of the small three-egg clutch apparently typical of the species.

Soon after fledging, both the young and the adults gather and begin to leave the breeding grounds. Nesting success on the Pawnee National Grasslands of Colorado was found to vary from about 26 to 65 percent during different years or in different studies, and the number of young hatched per successful nest varied from 0.26 to 1.4. Considering all nesting attempts, an average of only 0.17 to 0.74 fledged young per nesting effort are believed to survive long enough to undertake their fall migration. This very low annual recruitment rate is perhaps a reflection of the difficult environment in which the birds breed.

It is believed that only a single year is required to attain reproductive maturity. There is as yet no information on average adult annual survival rates or estimates of longevity, but both would have to be quite high if the population is to maintain itself, given the species' apparently low rate of reproductive success.

Suggested Readings

Prairie Falcon: Allen 1987; Anderson and Squires 1997; Johnsgard 1990; Maher 1982; Marzluff et al. 1997; Platt 1981; Runde 1987; Squires et al. 1993; Steenhof 1998; Steenhof et al. 1999; Wrege and Cade 1977.

Mountain Plover: Dechant et al. 1998; Graul 1973, 1975; Graul and Webster 1976; Johnsgard 1981; Knopf 1996a, 1998; McCafferey et al. 1994; Olson-Edge 1987; Parrish et al. 1993; Shackford 1991; Shackford et al. 1999.

8   Meadows and Marshes:
Northern Harrier,
Wilson's Phalarope, and
Franklin's Gull

When I was still attending high school in North Dakota's Red River Valley, I would take every opportunity that I could to borrow the family car every sunny weekend day between late March and early May. I would also pack a hot thermos, hip boots, and my 1930s-vintage Kine Exakta 35-mm camera with its antiquated and uncoated 180-mm Zeiss lens. Then I would drive the thirty or so miles over rutted and snow-lined roads south to the vicinity of Lake Traverse. This shallow glacial-formed lake is located in extreme northeastern South Dakota, at the southern outlet of glacial Lake Agassiz, and it marks the approximate headwaters of both the Bois des Sioux and Minnesota Rivers. From this modest if not invisible east-west continental divide, the Minnesota River flows southeast, eventually joining the Mississippi and reaching the Gulf of Mexico. However, the Bois des Sioux flows north to join Minnesota's Ottertail River and thus to form the Red River of the North, their combined waters ultimately reaching the Arctic Ocean. Amid lush prairie marshes punctuating rolling glacial moraines near the village of White Rock, I could surround myself with a galaxy of migrating waterfowl and shorebirds.

Often, while hiding in water knee-deep among the thick phragmites and cattails, great blizzards of snow geese would pass above me, often so closely that I would instinctively duck my head but still feel the breezes made by their wings. Male northern harriers, which always seemed to arrive each spring a few weeks in advance of the brown-clad females, would materialize as silent silver shadows, gliding just above the marshy vegetation (Fig. 34). Later in the spring, ebony-headed Franklin's gulls would scream noisily overhead, swirling about as wildly as confetti in a whirlwind. On rare occasions, ethereal and impossibly long-necked western grebes would pass gracefully by on the water, their soft voices tinkling like distant silver chimes, their intensely crimson eyes resembling lasers.

Many years later, I picked up an incapacitated but still feisty adult western grebe along the shoreline of a prairie marsh in western Nebraska. One of its feet was missing; the remaining bloody stump suggested to me that it probably had been recently amputated by a hungry snapping turtle. I wondered how much longer the bird could survive, as it would not be able to dive efficiently and catch elusive prey underwater. Yet after looking into its flashing and defiant eyes I was unwilling to end its life, and so I carefully returned the bird to its element. Perhaps a passing prairie falcon or the northern harrier that was nesting nearby could finish the story; I simply couldn't bear to do it myself. Later, in the very same area, I saw a peregrine come blazing down out of the sky like a bolt of lightning, passing within ten feet of my car's roof and scattering the frantic shorebirds and ducks everywhere along its flight path. Very few things go completely to waste in nature, and I doubt that this grebe did.

Northern Harrier

It seems not quite fair to claim the northern harrier as a North American grasslands bird; I have seen this species coursing gracefully over the lowlands and upland moors of Scotland and northern England, where it is called the hen harrier. A similar species of harrier confusingly called the marsh harrier also occurs in Britain, at least in southern England. It was probably for such reasons that the common English name "northern harrier" was adopted a decade or more ago in preference to "marsh hawk," its traditional North American name. Somehow "marsh hawk" seemed most appropriately descriptive of this bird. Its new name "har-

34. Northern harrier, adult male in flight. Drawing by author.

rier" refers not to the birds' possible capture of hares (which would be extremely unlikely) but to the harrying behavior these birds exhibit toward their prey. It is true that the species is generally distinctly northern in its North American breeding distribution, but I have seen their nests in central Nebraska, and there are local breeding records south as far as the Gulf Coast. Probably the happiest choice for its name is the Latin one: *Circus* refers to the undulating or even almost looping (thus "circular") flights of territorial males in early spring as they define their territories, and *cyaneus* describes the somewhat bluish tint to the adult male's gray plumage, which contrasts with its darker, "dipped-in-ink" wingtips (Fig. 34).

More than any other large hawk of the central plains, the adult northern harrier exhibits strong plumage dimorphism of the sexes as well as moderate dimorphism in body mass. Females are not only larger than males by about 40 to 50 percent but are also a rich chocolate brown on their upperparts, perhaps allowing them to blend in with their dead-grass nesting environment. Juveniles are basically the same color dorsally as females for their first year but are a much richer cinnamon-rufous on their underparts. Both juveniles and adults of both sexes have white rump patches that, together with their long tails and wings, provide for easy identification. Their long wings allow the birds to glide at rather slow speeds. They maintain their aerial stability by adopting a distinct upward dihedral in their wing positioning, in the same manner as do gliding turkey vultures. Another usual feature of harriers is their development of somewhat owl-like facial disks (Fig. 35). These feathers, together with unusually well-developed hearing, allow the birds to detect the movements of even small rodents such as mice and home in accurately on their sometimes unseen locations.

Throughout the winter months harriers concentrate on catching small rodents, especially microtene voles, but supplement these foods with mice, shrews, rabbits, and passerine birds. More northerly wintering birds are more prone to take mostly voles; toward the south there is an increasing dependence on other rodents and on passerine birds, especially meadowlarks and similar-sized avian prey. Unlike prairie falcons, which also often capture meadowlarks, harriers do not capture such birds during prolonged chases but are more likely to grab them unawares while they are perched or hiding among grasses. During summer the prey spectrum broadens and especially is likely to include older nestlings and recently fledged or at least somewhat ambulatory birds. A typical prey item is tiny relative to the harrier's body mass and on average weighs only about two ounces, which is closer in size to a northern cardinal (another fairly common prey species) than a meadowlark. Rarely prey as large as about two pounds may be taken. The birds have quite long tarsi, somewhat like those of barn owls, but have fairly weak toes and talons, at least as compared to those of buteo hawks. Like those of barn owls, their long tarsi might be useful for reaching down into tall grass to grab prey. The success rate of attacks on birds is lower than that

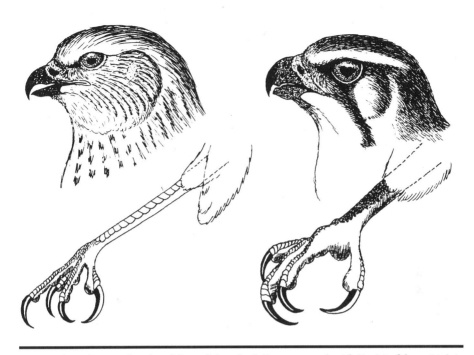

35. Northern harrier, head and feet of female (*left*), compared with Prairie falcon (*right*). The location of the harrier's external ear is also shown (*dotted line*). Drawing by author.

on mammals, and vole-hunting over snow cover is more successful than hunts done in the absence of snow.

Prey is captured using varied strategies, including gliding or powered low-altitude flights over fairly long distances, shorter quartering flights, and flights that follow vegetational edges, such as fencerows. Pounces may be preceded by hovering, quick turns or by direct attacks without change of speed or direction. Early morning and evening hunts are commonplace, but no true nocturnal hunting in the manner of owls seems to have been reported. Under favorable foraging conditions the birds may cache excess prey for later consumption, at least during the breeding season. Not surprisingly, females tend to take larger prey than do males during the breeding season, based on sizes of items that are brought back to the nest.

Wintering by this species extends surprisingly far southward, with birds seen occasionally in Panama, and more rarely individuals reach northern South America. However, the majority of Great Plains birds seem to winter in the southern states and Mexico. Peak numbers in the Great Plains occur in various parts of the southern plains, such as along the Pecos River of western Texas, along the lower Rio Grande, the Red River Valley along the common boundaries of Texas and Oklahoma, and along the Arkansas River in Kansas. Many of these concentrations are located near wildlife refuges, and there the birds are prone to specialize on wounded waterfowl. During the winter, foraging individuals may cover about 100 miles per day, mostly within localized hunting territories up to a square mile in area. Females exclude the smaller males from such territories. It seems likely that young birds winter farther south than adults, and females perhaps winter north of males, based on their relative body masses and consequent probable cold tolerance. Yet in spring males precede females as to their arrival times on northern nesting grounds, probably because of the importance of establishing good breeding territories as early as possible.

By March or April birds will have arrived on their breeding areas of the northern plains, and males soon begin advertising their territories. The birds seek out relatively large areas of thick grasslands, especially low prairies, lightly grazed meadows, and nearly dry marshes with thick edges of emergent vegetation. Less often they choose drier upland prairies or even croplands, but wetter environments are more frequently used than dryland habitats.

With the arrival of females on the breeding grounds, usually a week or more after the males, territorial and courtship interactions begin. There seems to be little or no mate retention from year to year, and at least in some areas there is a slight predominance of females in the adult population, which may be a contributory factor in the tendency toward polygyny exhibited by this species. Males begin territorial advertising and female attraction by performing "sky-dancing," which consists of a series of frequently repeated U-shaped aerial maneuvers, ascending and descending from between 30 and 300 feet above the ground, as the bird tracks over a course of up to a half-mile in linear distance. Some chattering calls may occur at the zenith of each arc. At the end of the flight the male may descend to earth and disappear at a point that may serve to indicate a potential nest location. Interested females will follow the male and perhaps investigate the site themselves. Evidently those males that perform such displays most vigorously are able to attract females most effectively, and such birds may acquire a harem of from two to five females. However, many males acquire but a single mate, and there is also some evidence that subadult yearling males are likely to attract only subadult females. Breeding territory sizes are seemingly highly variable in area, and perhaps such variation is a reflection of the relative food resources within the territories as well as presumably indicating variations in individual male fitness.

Males defend their territory against intruders by lowering their legs as they fly above other males, or the two birds may also grasp one another's talons. Males also escort others out of their territories but respond to new females and thus prospective new mates by sky-dancing. Aerial food-transfers to mates are common early in the mating period, the female flying up from the ground and flipping upside down briefly to catch food in the air as the male above drops it. Later, as the female is occupied with egg-laying, ground transfers of foods are more likely. Food-passing behavior also frequently precedes copulation, which usually occurs on the ground rather than in elevated sites.

Either sex may select the nest site. Often males may initiate nest-building; such behavior may cause the female to take over and finish the nest. Males also may gather materials from some distance away and transfer them to females in an aerial exchange similar to food exchanges or may pass them to her at the site itself.

Nests may be placed in a rather wide assortment of sites, including the edges of freshwater marshes, wet or damp marsh meadows, dry upland grasslands, or even in cultivated fields. The primary criteria seem to consist of thick and heavy vegetation, with a possible preference for wet sites over dry ones, presumably because of reduced probabilities of predation by terrestrial predators or human disturbance. Materials continue to be added to the nest through incubation and even after hatching; this may be especially important in wet sites, where there is danger of nest submergence below water level.

Eggs are laid at the rate of usual two-day intervals but sometimes less frequently. Clutch sizes are typically from four to six eggs but as many as twelve have been reported. Any clutch of more than six would have to be regarded as exceptional, and smaller-than-normal clutches are more likely to be produced by supplementary mates, who are not fed so assiduously as is the primary mate. Undoubtedly food availability at the time of egg-laying must be a primary determinant of clutch size, as it is in many raptors. At least among larger clutches, the first-laid eggs in a clutch are likely to be females, and later eggs in the series tend to be males. This rather remarkable if not inexplicable trait may help to account for an unbalanced sex ratio among adults that favors females. First-hatched young in raptors are more likely to survive than those from eggs laid later, because of the ability of older chicks to compete more effectively for limited food supplies. However, siblicide among the broodmates is very rare, although should a chick die in the nest it may be consumed by its siblings or its mother.

Growth rate differences between the sexes appear fairly soon among nest-mates, and newly fledged females may weigh as much as one-third more than males of about the same age. Until the chicks are about two weeks old the male provides the food for his mate (or mates) and the growing chicks. Supplemental female mates begin hunting on their own sooner than does the male's primary mate, presumably because they are provisioned less often.

Fledging occurs at about one month, the smaller males attaining flight ability slightly sooner than females. Males also leave the vicinity of the nest sooner than females by a few days, the collective average being about sixty days.

As with other raptors, annual reproductive success is controlled by prey availability and associated male provisioning rates; early nests (those of primary female mates) are also more productive than later ones produced by supplemental mates. Considering all nests collectively, 3.1 chicks hatch on average from successful nests, and a fledging success of about 1.8 chicks fledged per initiated nest is typical. Relative nest concealment, the presence of forb (but not shrub) cover, and greater levels of ground moisture or immediate wet surroundings may contribute to improved breeding success. Although polygynous mating improves overall male productivity, the converse is true for females, primarily because of lower provisioning rates by polygynous males.

Wilson's Phalarope

Alexander Wilson (1766–1813) is the generally accepted father of American ornithology. Wilson was born in Scotland, but in 1792 he immigrated to the United States, where he worked first as surveyor and later as a schoolteacher. Under the influence of William Bartram (see the upland sandpiper section, chapter 6), he conceived the idea of what was to become the first great published work on the birds of North America, which he wrote and illustrated. The first of a projected series of ten volumes of his *American Ornithology* was published in 1808, but the eighth volume was still at the printer's when Wilson died in 1813. Alexander Wilson's work thus anticipated the even larger and far more sumptuously illustrated monograph on North American birds that was published by John J. Audubon a few decades later. Wilson also contributed far more to our technical knowledge of American birds than did Audubon or any of their predecessors. The Wilson's storm-petrel, Wilson's plover, and Wilson's warbler were also named in his honor.

The Wilson's phalarope was first discovered on its South American wintering grounds in 1819, not on its Great Plains breeding grounds. All three of the phalaropes are north-temperate to high-Arctic breeders, but all also undergo long, sometimes transequatorial, migrations. The three species also have partially webbed feet, but the Wilson's has the longest toes and the least amount of webbing between them (Fig. 36). This adaptation seems to serve phalaropes equally well on land, in small wetlands, and even on the open ocean, where few other shorebirds venture. The Wilson's phalarope also has the longest and most delicate bill, and like the two others it feeds mostly while swimming rather than while wading. It delicately touches the tip of its bill to the water's surface, thus letting capillary action draw tiny, plankton-sized organisms into its mouth (Fig. 37A).

36. Heads and feet of adult female Wilson's phalarope (*left*) and mountain plover (*right*). Drawing by author.

37. Wilson's phalarope behavior, including male foraging (A), female's low-head threat (B), and copulation sequence (C–G). Drawing after photos by author. The sonogram of female's courtship call (duration 0.25 second) is after Colwell and Jehl (1994).

The Wilson's phalarope, uniquely among the species considered in this book, is remarkable in that it has been proven to exhibit sequential polyandry. Among the world's three phalarope species, this was the last one for which polyandry was proven. Yet, like the other two, it exhibits all the traits one would expect in a polyandrous species. These include reversed sexual dimorphism (females are both larger and, in breeding plumage, more brightly patterned than males), female establishment of territory and subsequent advertising for male mates, and total male care of the eggs and chicks. The removal of female responsibility from all parental duties sets the ecological stage for potential polyandry, and the fairly long breeding season in the northern plains provides enough time to find, mate with, and turn over a second clutch to another willing male.

Like the other phalaropes, the Wilson's engages in long-distance, transequatorial migrations. The other two species are likely to spend their nonbreeding periods in pelagic environments, but the Wilson's heads for Central Andean saline lakes in the high, cold and arid Peruvian, Bolivian, and northern Chilean and Argentine altiplano, a tundra-like environment not far below the permanent snowline. Probably it feeds there in much the same way, and on the same kinds of nearly microscopic foods, as it does in North America, although little is known of this phase of its life history. It is known that, before undertaking this long fall migration, the birds congregate after breeding on hypersaline lakes of the American West, where they undergo their postbreeding molt and take on fat. From there the adults apparently take a nonstop, overseas route above the Pacific Ocean. Juveniles evidently take an overland route southward through Mexico and Central America to South America.

The return migration to the North American breeding grounds is also overland, although it is possible that first-year birds oversummer in South America, since they don't breed until their second year, and it is seemingly fairly common for shorebirds that migrate transequatorially to remain in the southern hemisphere through their first year of life. The spring migration northward moves forward through the central plains, with areas such as the Cheyenne Bottoms wetlands receiving massive numbers of birds, and similar shallow, alkaline wetlands of the western Nebraska Sandhills are also heavily used. Some birds stop to breed in these Kansan and Nebraskan marshes, but the majority continue onward to nest in the northern plains states and prairie provinces, especially in North Dakota, Montana, Saskatchewan, and Alberta.

Phalaropes arrive on their breeding grounds of the central and northern plains in late April or early May. At Crescent Lake National Wildlife Refuge in western Nebraska they quickly congregate at a single hypersaline lake, Border Lake, while often ignoring other nearby and relatively freshwater habitats. Brine flies are abundant at that lake, and probably little else is consumed, judging from personal observations. In other locations brine shrimp are also eaten regularly, but there is little diversity otherwise in their diets.

Females quickly begin courtship activities, but no exclusive territories are established, and the birds remain quite gregarious throughout the breeding season. Low, growling *wa* notes that seem to function as courtship calls are commonly uttered at this time by females; these notes carry rather far in spite of their low amplitude. Females extend their necks vertically when calling thus, either while in flight or on the ground, presumably to increase resonance capabilities of low-frequency sound components. Other calls of even lower average frequency are also produced, such as a *purr* call that occurs in both sexes during aggressive encounters, while they extend the neck forward in a low-threat display (Fig. 37B). A froglike *chug* call is uttered by females when they are close to males.

Pair-forming actually begins during spring migration, and courtship continues through the nesting period. Females may pursue the males in aerial chases and also will defend males that they have diverted from the attentions of other females. Once pair bonds have been established the birds may remain closely associated, with either sex following the other. Copulation behavior may be initiated by either sex but most frequently is started by females. It can occur in shallow water, in water of swimming depth, or on dry land. Preliminary posturing is quite subtle and may easily go unrecognized by inexperienced observers. In one case that I personally observed and photographed (Fig. 37C–G), the male stood for some time very close to and facing a female. She finally responded with an erect, swollen-neck posture, apparently calling. The distance was too great to distinguish the type of call being uttered, presumably the *chug* call. The male then quickly flew up on the female's back, and copulation followed so rapidly that I obtained only a single exposure of it. The male then dismounted, and no obviously ritualized posturing occurred between them immediately thereafter.

38. Wilson's phalarope, female swimming. Drawing by author.

Pair-bonding is of rather short duration, lasting some seven to ten days from initial pairing to the completion of a clutch of four eggs. Then, the female will desert her male almost immediately, or up to two weeks thereafter, and begin to court other males. However, once the male begins incubating her clutch, she may defend him from the attention of other females. There is no evidence that females ever participate in either incubation or brooding behavior.

Females lay their eggs at the rate of one per day, in a nest scrape that they presumably select but which is lined with grasses by the male over the egg-laying period. Sites are selected that are in relatively tall and dense vegetation and usually fairly close to water. Because of the thickness of cover selected, nests are difficult for humans to locate. The almost invariable clutch size is of four eggs, but occasionally larger clutches have been found, certainly the work of more than one female. Very rarely parasitism by brown-headed cowbirds has been reported, but such efforts are doomed to failure since no parental feeding is performed by phalaropes. Incubation by the male usually begins with the

39. Chicks of upland sandpiper (*left*), Wilson's phalarope (*upper right*) and long-billed curlew (*lower right*). Drawing by author.

laying of the penultimate egg and requires an average of twenty-three days.

The chicks are as precocial as those of other shorebirds but are quite differently patterned on their dorsal surface than are those of curlews or upland sandpipers (Fig 39). Their striped back pattern is probably adaptive in hiding among dense grassy wetland vegetation; in the curlew and sandpiper chicks, their more buffy and mottled background colors seem adapted to a drier and more exposed substrate. Phalarope chicks are able to swim almost immediately after drying out, following emergence from the egg, and are tended exclusively by the male. Their fledging period is still unreported.

Females are prone to remate and renest soon after deserting their initial mate. An estimated 22 to 43 percent of females in Saskatchewan were believed to breed at least a second time. Some were found to produce as many as four clutches, with interclutch intervals of only a few days between them. As a result, it is difficult to measure annual productivity, but nesting success (nests that successfully hatch at least one chick) has been estimated in one study as about 33 percent, with about half these nests hatching all four eggs. Fledging success rates are still un-reported, but males sometimes if not often attempt to mate again and renest following initial clutch loss, and second renesting efforts have also rather rarely been reported. A high rate of return of marked birds to breeding grounds the following year suggests that adult annual survival rates are quite high, in the neighborhood of 85 to 90 percent. Such high adult survival further suggests that a longevity of eight to ten years may not be unusual for birds surviving their first year.

Franklin's Gull

Sir John Franklin (1786–1847) was a distinguished seaman, an officer of the British Navy, and the commander of several British exploratory voyages to Arctic Canada in repeated and ultimately futile efforts to try to establish a practical Arctic sea route (the so-called and greatly desired Northwest Passage) to the Pacific Ocean. The last and most disastrous of these expeditions resulted in the abandonment of the ice-bound ship and the eventual deaths by starvation of its entire crew, including Franklin himself. The western race *franklinii* of the Canadian spruce grouse, which was originally described as a distinct species, was named in Franklin's honor. Like the Wilson's phalarope, the Franklin's gull was first collected while on migration in Mexico, presumably en route to or from its wintering grounds, rather than on its breeding grounds in the northern Great Plains. Its strange Aztec-based name, *pipixcan,* is of unknown meaning.

Some ornithologists might question the inclusion of the Franklin's gull in a list of prairie birds inasmuch as, like the Wilson's phalarope, it is certainly dependent upon wetlands for its breeding. Yet it is confined to prairie wetlands of the northern plains to an even greater degree than is the phalarope, and in earlier times it was sometimes poetically, if in-appropriately, called the "prairie dove." The birds do have a wonderfully buoyant and bouncy appearance while in flight, and a flock of migrat-ing birds undulating over the hilly plains strikes one as rather dovelike and unquestionably as extremely beautiful. Although Franklin's gulls were not the same species that saved the locust-plagued crops of the Mormons in an almost biblical fashion (they were California gulls), this species just as assiduously follows farmers' plows in spring, quickly con-suming any and all insect larvae or other prey that are thus exposed.

Few if any Franklin's gulls regularly winter north of Central America, and the vast majority winter along the Pacific coastline of South America, mainly between Peru and northern Chile. Since there are few records from Colombia, it is assumed that at least most birds reach their destination via an overseas and probably nonstop Pacific route, much like the route described for the Wilson's phalarope. Unlike phalaropes, these birds remain mostly coastal during the nonbreeding period and feed opportunistically on whatever might be then available, including even garbage and offal. They arrive on their wintering areas late in the year, probably in November or December. Departure dates in spring are uncertain, but the birds begin to arrive in the central plains of North America by early April, probably having followed a more interior northward route through Central America and Mexico. At that time of year the birds are especially beautiful, with jet black heads and a somewhat rosy pink cast to their underparts, presumably from crustacean-based carotenoids that they consumed while still on their wintering grounds. They are also in a fresh breeding plumage that has followed two complete molts they have undergone since the summer before, a complex and unique molting pattern among North American gulls.

Once the birds arrive in the Great Plains on their spring migration, flocks are likely to be seen foraging in wet meadows or on newly worked agricultural fields. They also sometimes congregate on garbage dumps and landfills, where they often mix with other generalized gull foragers. Grasshoppers, earthworms, miscellaneous adult and larval insects, and seeds are all likely to be consumed; perhaps even some small rodents might be captured and eaten as well. They seem to have little fear of farmers riding about on tractors during the feeding frenzies that often accompany spring planting operations. Sometimes they also cluster along the newly mown grassy runways of small midwestern airports, where grasshoppers are easily seen and captured; more than one plane has suffered the consequences of ingesting a flock of Franklin's gulls into its propeller or its jet engine on takeoff or landing.

By late April or early May, birds are arriving on their northern breeding areas, and territorial behavior begins immediately. Some pair-bonding may begin before such arrival but becomes more intense immediately afterward. Construction of nesting platforms is the first important step for a male to achieve in this process; such a platform becomes the focal point for advertisement behavior. A base of bent-over upright stems, or a mat of floating vegetation, provides the initial framework for the nesting platform, but this will be supplemented through the nesting season as such materials become waterlogged and begin to sink. The area immediately around the platform is defended for a distance of only a few yards, although the actual territorial size, and thus possible internest distances, is variable and in some cases may be as little as less than a yard.

From this platform or other nearby points the male begins to advertise himself, primarily by uttering "long calls" (Fig. 40), a long sequence of repeated calls that start with more prolonged notes but become more rapid toward the end and often are terminated with vertical head-tossing (Fig. 40D). Perhaps most often the bird begins the sequence while in an oblique posture (Fig. 40C), with his head diagonally in line with the body and somewhat raised above the back. As the display proceeds, he is likely to assume a low oblique posture (Fig. 40F). He then terminates this sequence with one or more head-tosses, which usually mark the end of the sequence and after which the bird relaxes. Independent head-tossing may also occur. As with other gulls, a basic social display is the "upright" posture (Fig. 40B), which is usually performed toward potential opponents, in an imposing stance with neck held vertically and the bill directed toward the other individual. This posture is often used in conjunction with the long call, which may be uttered in varied postures, and with head-tossing. Another basic agonistic gull display is "choking," (Fig. 40E), in which a posture similar to the low oblique is assumed, but the neck is curved and the bill tilted downward. Repeated *woof* notes are uttered, somewhat resembling a muffled version of the long call notes. This display, as well as "gakkering"—a long series of brief notes accompanied by an erection of the head, neck, and back feathers, undulating head movements, and sometimes also wing-flapping—is common during aggressive encounters.

An important variant of the upright display is one in which the black facial mask is somewhat hidden from the rear by postural and feather-positioning changes, making the rear of the head appear somewhat fluffed (Fig. 40A). In this posture the male performs a "facing-away" display toward any females that may land nearby. This apparently submissive, or at least nonaggressive, posture is assumed by both birds simultaneously and may be held for some minutes, the birds occasionally turning their heads back to look at one another.

Females solicit courtship feeding by assuming a hunched posture and performing repeated head-tossing. She may even peck at the male's bill,

40. Franklin's gull, adult displays (after Moynihan 1958), including aggressive upright (A), intermediate upright (B), oblique with long call (C), head-tossing with long call (D), choking (E), and low oblique (F). Sonogram (duration three seconds) of long call after Burger and Gochfeld (1994).

in a manner similar to those of nestling birds wanting to be fed. The male may then regurgitate food, and copulation often follows such courtship feeding.

Since there is little evidence to indicate strong site-tenacity by birds returning to previous nesting colonies in subsequent years, there is also not much likelihood of mate fidelity from year to year. Chances of such fidelity are also decreased by the strongly colonial nature of these birds when nesting and the reduced chances of encountering a prior year's mate among the sometimes tens of thousands of other birds using the colony.

Nest sites are preferentially in substantial vegetational cover that is near open water, the latter advantage to allow for both visual displays and an escape route from predators. However, there should also be sufficient vegetational cover present below to provide an adequate nest support, preferably rooted vegetation, and also some overhead cover to offer some protection from the intense sun or from bad weather. Both sexes help build the nest and continue to tend it by adding new materials. Materials may often be stolen from unguarded nests, which is easier than cutting and tearing new green material from nearby vegetation. Although the nest tends to sink gradually as materials are waterlogged, rainfall may also cause water levels to rise and threaten flooding.

Eggs are laid at the rate of one every twenty-four to forty-eight hours, and the usual clutch is of three eggs. Both sexes incubate at about equal intensities, the onset of incubation occurring with the laying of the second egg. Apparently renesting following nest failure is rare, unless such losses occur very early in the nesting cycle. Because of the aquatic nest site, most egg predators include such aquatically adapted species as mink, but nesting adults are also susceptible to predation by great horned owls and northern harriers. Probably the majority of nest losses come from flooding, hailstorms, eggs or young chicks falling out of the nest, or exposure after the adults have been frightened from the nesting colony by predators.

Incubation requires twenty-three to twenty-six days, with the chicks hatching nearly simultaneously. They are raised on the nest platform until about twenty days, at which time they may leave the nest and aid in gathering new nest materials, but they don't actually fledge until about thirty-two to thirty-five days of age. At that point the young begin to flock on open water within the colony, and a few days later the adults and young begin to leave the colony together.

Nesting success in this species is often quite low. High periods of egg mortality occur during the egg-laying period, and there is also a period of high posthatching mortality when the chicks are quite young and subject to death from severe weather. There may also be a high mortality rate among recently fledged young. Very little information on reproductive success exists, but it would seem that only about half the breeding females manage to fledge at least one chick, and few nests succeed in rearing more than a single chick to fledging.

Suggested Readings

Northern Harrier: Hammerstrom 1986; Johnsgard 1981; Macwhirter and Bildstein 1996; Picozzi 1984; Rice 1982; Simmons 1983, 1988; Temeles 1989; Watson 1977.

Wilson's Phalarope: Bomberger 1982; Colwell 1986, 1987, 1992; Colwell and Jehl 1994; Colwell and Oring 1988; Dechant et al. 1999n; Delehanty et al. 1998; Howe 1972; Jehl 1987; Johnsgard 1990; Kagarise 1979; Murray 1983.

Franklin's gull: Burger 1972, 1974; Burger and Gochfeld 1994; Collias and Collias 1957; Guay 1968; Kopachena and Evans 1990; Moynihan 1958.

9   The Silent Hunters of Dusk: *Burrowing and Short-eared Owls*

For many, perhaps most, people, there are really only two categories of birds. There are the usual run-of-the-mill kind, and then there are owls. Owls exert some of the same strange and powerful fascinations over people as do snakes. Both are mysteriously silent, their respective talons or fangs inform one that they are obviously dangerous, and they are generally more likely to be encountered at night than during broad daylight. And yet, in contrast to the small-headed and beady-eyed snakes, the massive heads of owls, their wonderfully large and wide-set eyes, and their slow, almost magisterial bearing might cause one to assume that they must also possess great knowledge. It is no accident that Athena, Greek goddess of knowledge, often carried with her a small owl that conveniently perched on her shoulder to whisper advice to her—until recently the official generic name of the burrowing owl was *Athene.*

In many parts of the world owls are widely believed to be reliable if ominous foretellers of the future and, in some disparate cultures, to hear an owl call out at night is a certain omen of imminent death. But few rodents ever hear the death-knell of the owl before they feel its fatal talons, and there are few if any more effective nocturnal rodent hunters than the owls. In spite of all their good works from the standpoint of farmers and other rural dwellers, owls remain feared by many people and are more likely to be shot as presumed poultry killers than valued as unequaled controllers of disease-carrying and crop-eating mice and rats.

Nearly all North American owls, including the short-eared, have wings with tiny fringes on the leading edges of their flight feathers. These fringes reduce turbulence during flight in more highly nocturnal owls and help render them wholly silent while approaching mammalian prey. Like those of the two North American species of diurnal pygmy owls, the wings of burrowing owls lack this specialization.

Many owls can detect and capture their rodent prey in total darkness, aided by their complex ear anatomy and associated spectacularly fine hearing abilities. They are also aided by their enormous and highly sensitive eyes, which are richly endowed with densely packed retinal rods to facilitate maximum nighttime vision under minimum levels of illumination. In some small owls such as screech owls the weight of a single eye may equal 4 percent of the bird's total body weight, or a mass comparable in humans to the weight of our entire brain!

One of the hallmarks of evolution is variability and deviation from the norm, and thus much of what I have just written simply does not apply to burrowing owls. The rather weak talons and small beaks of burrowing owls are better equipped for capturing large insects such as beetles than for killing large rodents. Burrowing owls also have small and poorly developed facial disks surrounding their similarly rather small external ears; these traits relate to their reduced capacity for achieving highly directional sensitivity to low-amplitude sounds that may be made by mammalian prey.

Further, the eyes of burrowing owls lack a special reflective layer behind their retinas that helps reflect light back through their visual receptors of the retina to facilitate extreme low-light vision. Such reflective layers, like those present in cats and other nocturnal mammals, make their eyes appear to glow in the dark when illuminated. Although often awake at night, especially on bright moonlit nights during the breeding season, burrowing owls hunt mostly during the day and early evening, relying mainly on their vision rather than on their hearing.

Like the short-eared owl, burrowing owls have yellow instead of brown iris coloration. This eye color has nothing to do with an owl's visual sensitivity but seems to be correlated to both species' more diurnal or crepuscular and less nocturnal activity. Yellow makes a more conspicuous and thus a better signaling color than does brown under such lighting conditions.

Burrowing Owl

Few if any North American birds are so dependent upon and associated with specific mammals as the burrowing owl is with prairie dogs. It is true that the burrow of many other large mammals, such as gophers or marmots, will at times be used. At other times a natural crevice, such as sometimes occurs in rocky areas, will suffice, but it seems that the burrows of prairie dogs are "just right" in size and depth for use as nesting sites by burrowing owls. Beyond that, prairie dogs typically occupy short-grass habitats offering wonderful vistas that allow daytime scanning for both predators and potential prey. Included among such prey are scarab beetles, which feed on the dung left by prairie dogs and which in turn provide a primary source of food for the burrowing owls. The prairie dogs seem to benefit not at all from these uninvited if unobtrusive guests, but they offer no real threats either, and perhaps both benefit to some degree from one another's alarm system. Among the threats to both are coyotes and badgers. The prairie dogs' deep holes offer a fairly safe escape route from coyotes but may provide little defense from badgers, whose appearance in a colony causes general panic among birds and prairie dogs alike. No doubt snakes such as bullsnakes and rattlesnakes are also easily able to gain entrance to nest chambers, but adults and well-grown young are usually able to evade these threats through the use of alternate escape tunnels.

At least in the northern parts of their North American range, burrowing owls are fairly migratory. Relatively large winter concentrations are known to exist in central Texas, where they occur amid prairie dog colonies, and wintering populations of unknown size also extend southward all the way to southernmost Mexico and Honduras. The northern limit of usually overwintering populations is still undetermined, but even nearly all of those nesting in Oklahoma and New Mexico are believed mostly to disperse or migrate during winter. There are, however, wholly residential populations in Florida and southern California, as well as in the West Indies. The birds also occur, as many distinct geographic races, in Central and South America southward as far as Tierra del Fuego, and these southern South American populations are also migratory. Limited banding results from the Great Plains suggest that birds nesting on the northern plains winter farther south than those breeding on the central plains, thus producing a kind of leapfrog migration pattern that is also known to occur among many other variably migratory birds in North America.

When the owls return in spring to their breeding areas, which in Nebraska occurs about the end of April, they spread out over the plains in search of suitable nesting holes. Although in Florida some self-burrowing of cavities may occur, this is not so in the Great Plains, although it is likely that some additional digging or preparation of the nest cavity may be performed. It is likely that foraging behavior shifts during spring, too, from small mammals and other foods available on wintering areas when insects are lacking to an increasing reliance on insect prey. This does not mean that small mammals or other vertebrate prey is altogether ignored—I once saw a male burrowing owl dragging a dead thirteen-lined ground squirrel to a nest containing well-grown young. It is possible that the mammal had been run over by a car or otherwise disabled previously, but the carcass seemed to be intact. The female in turn took the prey and dragged it down the nesting hole.

Foraging during the breeding season certainly occurs all day long, with insects largely consumed at that time, and continues into dusk or even beyond. And on moonlit nights the birds remain active and are more likely to take small mammals at that time, in spite of their limited nocturnal visual capabilities. At least in Saskatchewan, Colorado, Wyoming, and Nebraska invertebrates are the most prevalent breeding-season prey type, although it doesn't take many small mammals or birds to tip the biomass intake balance in the direction of vertebrates. Furthermore, in Saskatchewan, South Dakota, Iowa, and Oklahoma the use of vertebrates declines and invertebrate consumption increases during the breeding season. Insects are seemingly taken at random according to their relative availability, but beetles are taken especially often, judging from the frequency of their occurrence among regurgitated pellets. Caches of both vertebrate and invertebrate prey are sometimes made; they have been found within winter burrows as well as nest burrows and sometimes are stored in burrows some distance from the actual nest site.

Soon after establishment of a potential nest burrow, male burrowing owls begin uttering their primary song, a dovelike *coo-cooo*, that serves as a territorial proclamation as well as a female-attraction signal. When thus calling, the bird bends forward and slightly expands his throat feathers (Fig. 41A–B). This tends to expand the white area of the throat, and the bird is also able to control the amount of white facial feathering that is visible directly above and below the eyes (Fig. 41C–D). This call may be performed through the night under favorable circumstances but is uttered little if at all during daylight hours. A variation of this same call is uttered by males during copulation.

Several other vocal and nonvocal sounds are produced. As with other owls, rather loud bill- or tongue-snapping noises are produced when in a defensive situation, as when cornered. Adults lower their heads, open their wings (Fig. 41F), and make these snapping sounds repeatedly, which are supplemented by rattling notes that somewhat resemble a rattlesnake's stridulation sounds. Comparable calls uttered by young birds under similar circumstances are even more rattlesnakelike and may be quite disconcerting to humans. The birds may also stand fairly tall in a threatening or defensive posture, with the wings opened laterally (Fig. 41G).

Courtship by the male includes repeated short display flights, during which he ascends, hovers briefly, descends about halfway to the ground, and then ascends again and repeats the process. Circular flights by the male over the immediate vicinity of the nest burrow have also been seen. The male presents food to courted females, sings the primary song in their presence, and both birds may perform mutual preening and billing. Prior to copulation the male reportedly approaches the female, uttering a distinctive five-note call, while the female stands quite erect. According to a different account, both sexes stand tall and erect, the white feathers of their faces maximally expanded, but with the female neither so erect nor her feathers so markedly expanded as the male's. Mutual billing (Fig. 41E), or head-scratching of the female's head by the male, may follow copulation, and the male may also continue to expose his white facial areas to the female at that time.

Nest renovation probably continues through the pair-bonding period; excavation is achieved by digging with the beak and backward kicking with the feet. The shape of the tunnel depends on the animal that originally constructed it, but it is likely to have one or more turns and perhaps a second entrance to allow for possible escape should the first be blocked or entered by a predator. Digging and renovation action result in a mound of soil accumulating near the entrance of the burrow, which makes for a convenient lookout site for the birds. Frequently, bits of dried manure of horses, cattle, or other ungulates are spread around the

41. Burrowing owl displays, including male bowing display (A), singing posture of male (B), variations in exposure of white feathers during male calling (C–D), reciprocal preening by paired birds (E), threat-call posture (F), and nest-defense posture (G). Drawing by author, mostly adapted from Johnsgard (1988), but E after photo by Rob Curtis and F after photo by author. Sonogram of male song (duration 1.0 second) after Haug et al. (1993).

entrance to the nest as well; it is generally assumed that this might be an adaptive method of masking odors. However, other nonodorous and highly visible materials are sometimes also used, such as shredded paper or other debris.

Eggs are laid by the female at the rate of about one per thirty-six hours. Clutch size, as in many owls, is quite variable and probably depends largely on prey availability at the time of nesting. From seven to nine eggs constitute a common clutch size, but as many as twelve eggs have been reported from Kansas. Incubation begins with the first egg; thus a very substantial age difference can exist among young from eggs laid early and late in the clutch sequence. The incubation period requires some twenty-eight to thirty days; and within about two weeks after hatching, young begin to try to peer out of the nest or stand beside it, especially if both adults are off gathering food. The female usually keeps her chicks out of sight while she is constantly in attendance, which occurs during the earlier phases of brooding. However, if there are several older young to be fed, she is likely to spend an increasing amount of time away from the nest.

During the incubation and long chick-rearing period the nest is under threat from many sources, of which badgers may be the most significant. Weasels and skunks may be locally important predators of eggs and young as well. Nesting success is seemingly quite variable, from as low as 33 percent to 100 percent success in rearing at least one fledgling.

42. Burrowing owl family. Drawing by author.

Average numbers of young birds fledged relative to all nesting attempts range from 1.6 to 4.2 (fig. 42), with a slightly higher range if only successful nests are considered. Presumably both weather and relative prey availability are likely to influence fledging success, but there is still little information on these topics. Average survival rates for birds in migratory populations are too poorly studied to support much faith in the data. However, in the nonmigratory Florida and southern California populations annual respective survival rates of about 60 and 80 percent for adults would seem quite believable and close to other owl survival estimates. At least one wild bird was known to have survived almost nine years, which is in line with maximum expected longevities, given such average survival rates.

Short-eared Owl

Like the northern harrier, the short-eared owl can be claimed as a North American grasslands species only by virtue of special pleading. It is widespread in Eurasian grasslands and also occurs in South America and even on the Galapagos Islands and in Hawaii. It additionally breeds in Arctic tundra but cannot be described as being unusually common anywhere. Rather, it always seems to appear unexpectedly and rather ghost-like, usually near dusk, when it can sometimes be seen quartering silently over low fields and meadows, its slow and seemingly easy wingstrokes making it appear like some gigantic and fantastic Alice-in-Wonderland moth rather than a flesh-and-blood owl.

Yet owl it is, with sharp talons, well-feathered legs, a strong beak, and an unusually expressive face, which can vary in appearance from seemingly rather docile or even quizzical to a look that is distinctly fierce and almost satanic, depending on its degree of feather erection (Fig. 43).

The short-eared owl is one of those owls that literally occupies the twilight zone, effectively operating between the daylight mode of activity typical of most hawks, pygmy owls, and even the burrowing owl, and the dark-of-night operations that are the special province of barred and barn owls. In that regard it overlaps temporally with the great horned owl, a much bigger predator that usually doesn't often stray far from wooded habitats. However, the great horned owl is a mortal enemy of short-eared owls and indeed of all owls that are smaller than itself. It is not rare to find the remains of such seemingly invulnerable birds as short-eared owls and barn owls around the roosts or nests of

43. Short-eared owl head portraits (relaxed, *upper left,* threat, *upper right*), and female with young. A side view of the head and feet, showing the location and size of the external ear conch, is also shown, as is a ventral view of the syrinx. Drawing by author, adapted from Johnsgard (1988).

great horned owls. Thus, short-eared owls rarely venture near wooded areas. Not only are great horned owls to be found there, but the similar-sized barred owls and long-eared owls may also be present and effectively able to harvest the small mammal resource.

Like most medium-sized owls, the short-eared is a small-mammal specialist, feeding largely on microtene rodents such as meadow voles over grassy meadows, in much the same manner as that employed by northern harriers. Like that species, the birds sometimes drop directly down on prey without first losing air speed, or at other times they may hover momentarily before dropping in for the kill. In spite of their fine eyesight and hearing, most capture attempts are unsuccessful, although success seemingly improves with age and experience, as typical of predators generally.

Like those of some other owls such as the barn owl, their ear openings are asymmetrically oriented on the sides of the head, facilitating both horizontal and vertical localization of sounds, and their expanded external ear area is supplemented by a flap of skin that helps direct sound into the ear canal (Fig. 43, *lower left*). Their ears are adapted for detecting rather low sound frequencies (especially around 6,000 Hertz), and similarly their syringeal membranes of the trachea produce low-frequency sounds that are ideal for long-distance communication. Their large wing expanses reduce wing-loading, allowing for slow flight and reduced flight noise. As with other owls, their frontally situated eyes allow for a broad field of stereoscopic vision. It is generally believed that owls have reduced color vision capabilities and more effective nocturnal but monochromatic vision, yet the degree or extent of color vision of this somewhat diurnal owl remains to be established.

In a comprehensive review of North American food-intake studies, Denver Holt determined that nearly 80 percent of more than 20,000 prey items in North America consisted of microtene voles such as *Microtus,* although several other families of rodents were represented. A typical daily intake may be one or two adult voles. A few birds are also taken as prey, but these are evidently mainly obtained in coastal areas. In other areas the usual incidence of birds taken relative to other prey types is under 2 percent.

As winter passes, the birds gradually move northward. Or, if food is plentiful on the wintering grounds, the birds may remain there to breed. Males coming into breeding condition begin to utter their courtship song, either from the ground or while in flight. The song is a repeated series of about thirteen to sixteen *hoo* notes on the same pitch, lasting about three seconds. Courtship flights are characterized by an ascent with rather bouncy wingstrokes and flying in rather tight circles, then hovering briefly while singing. Next may come a descending glide that includes several wing-claps, followed again by climbing and a repetition of earlier phases. The entire sky-dancing sequence may end with a spectacular descent, or "sashay flight" (Fig. 44D–E), in which the wings are

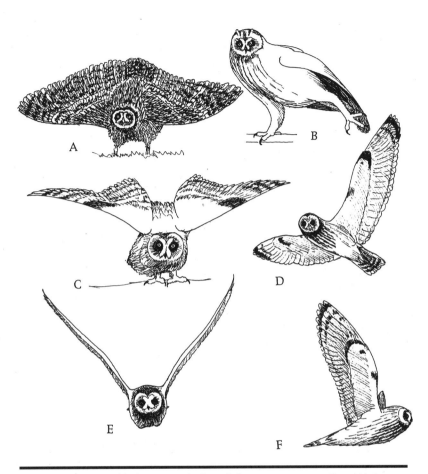

44. Short-eared owl behavior, including defensive wing-spreading (A), leg- and wing-stretching (B), double wing-stretching (C), "sashay flight" (D), and "underwing display" (E–F). Drawing by author, adapted from Clark (1975) and Johnsgard (1988).

held upward at a high angle and the bird rocks back and forth, rather like the mountain plover's falling-leaf display. "Underwing" displays are also performed in flight, the exaggerated wingstrokes exposing the lower wing surfaces (Fig. 44F). This display is apparently usually performed during territorial patrolling. Ground displays include a double wing-spreading defensive stance, with most feathers ruffled and both wings erected vertically above the back (Fig. 44A). This behavior is quite different from the bird's normal wing-stretching behavior, as performed during preening and other "comfort" activities. (Fig. 44B–C).

Pair-bonding is thought to be monogamous, although one or two cases are known in which polygyny was suspected. Pair-bonding seems to occur by the female watching the male's aerial displays and at least sometimes joining in and chasing the male. The two birds may then descend together, and copulation on the ground might ensue. It is also known that copulation may follow prey-presentation by the male. It is believed that pair bonds last only a single season, although data on this subject are still sketchy.

As with other owls, nest-building and egg-laying begin early in the year, an adaptation that allows for hatching and rearing of the chicks to occur during the spring flush of small-mammal populations. Nest sites are typically in fairly heavy grass cover, averaging about twenty inches high. They are usually on a dry substrate, such as a small knoll, and among the previous year's dead vegetation. Feathers and grasses are used for the nest lining. At times nests have been found placed over the remains of the previous year's site, suggesting that some degree of nest-site fidelity is present. However, current evidence would suggest a rather low rate of return to the same territory in succeeding years. Females lay their eggs at the approximate rate of one per day or sometimes on alternate days. Incubation begins immediately and with a clutch of usually five to eight eggs (a maximum of eleven has been reported). The intervals between the laying (and hatching) of the first and last egg in the set may approach twenty days. Incubation is by the female only and requires an average of twenty-one days. The downy, pale buffy chicks are brooded by the female alone (Fig. 43, *lower right*), and the male is kept busy bringing in enough food for the entire family.

Hatching success is of course quite variable by locality and year but often ranges from three to seven chicks per nest, averaging about 75 percent of all eggs laid. It is thought that some replacement clutches may be produced following early nest destruction. Nest predation of eggs by skunks and various corvids such as crows or ravens is known; and predation of adults by foxes, larger owls, and other raptors is also well documented. Deaths of younger or weaker broodmates by siblicide have been reported, and the number of young reared and fledged from all nests among various North American studies averages about two to four.

Little is known of postfledging mortality rates during the first year, or even of annual adult mortality rates. They are likely to be similar to those of other raptors, i.e., very high mortality the first year of life, followed by relatively low annual mortality thereafter. There is a record of a wild bird surviving nearly thirteen years in Europe.

Suggested Readings

Burrowing owl: Dechant et al. 1994; Desmond and Savidge 1995, 1996; Haug, Millsap, and Martell 1993; Hughes 1993; Murphy 1993; Pezzolesi 1994; Plumpton and Lutz 1994; Rich 1986; Schmutz et al. 1991; Thompson and Anderson 1988.

Short-eared owl: Clark 1975; Colvin and Spaulding 1983; Dechant et al. 1990; Holt 1993; Holt and Leisure 1993; Stone et al. 1994.

10

A Lark by Any Name:
Meadowlarks, Horned Lark, and Lark Sparrow

The bird [horned lark] suddenly mounts high into the air, going up silently in irregular circles, climbing nearly vertically, to such a height that he appears but a little speck in the sky, several hundred feet up. Arrived at this eminence, he spreads his wings and soars, emitting meanwhile his song, such as it is— one or two preliminary notes and then a series of squeaks and high notes with a bit of a fine trill. The whole has a jingling metallic sound like distant sleigh bells, although the squeaks remind one strongly of an old gate.

—Charles W. Townsend,
Birds of Labrador

Sometimes life on the prairie seems a contradiction in terms. At least in North Dakota there is little visible sign of prairie life between the first snowfall of October and the spring thaw, which usually begins in late March. In 1952 I organized a Christmas bird count with my undergraduate adviser and two other biology students near my hometown of Wahpeton. It was the first Christmas count ever done for Wahpeton and one of only five done in North Dakota that year, which says something about the futility of bird-watching during a North Dakota winter. In nearly nine hours of walking over snow-packed fields and through barren riverine woodlands, and more than two hours of almost fruitless driving, we saw only sixteen species, of which seven were resident woodland dwellers (three woodpeckers, black-capped chickadee, white-breasted nuthatch, brown creeper, and great horned owl). The rest included three shrub-associated migratory sparrows or boreal finches (American tree sparrow, dark-eyed junco, and common redpoll), three tundra-breeding, overwintering migrants (snowy owl, snow bunting, and Lapland longspur), and three introduced resident exotics (European starling, house sparrow, and ring-necked pheasant).

At least in that fairly typical year, not even a doughty horned lark or an optimistically overwintering meadowlark was to be found.

Western Meadowlark

Few birds gladden the hearts of prairie dwellers as does the western meadowlark. It makes its first spring appearance while snow is still on the ground, sings resolutely in the face of a March snowstorm, and huddles patiently on a fencepost during driving rainstorms. It is one of the last prairie birds to stop singing in late summer; dickcissels and western meadowlarks reliably carry on even during the hottest days of August. It also remains on its breeding grounds much longer than does the dickcissel, which wastes little time in heading for the tropics of South America as soon as its breeding responsibilities are over. Meadowlarks persist long enough to see the goldenrods ripening into glorious full bloom, the sumac leaves at wooded edges catching fire, and the Indian grass rusting to the sheen of polished copper. Some meadowlarks wait for the first snowfall before finally abandoning their breeding grounds and may even salute a crisp but sunny October morning with a well-polished song or two.

During the winter period, the highest concentrations of western meadowlarks occur in the central and southern parts of the Great Plains, with the greatest continental densities occurring in the vicinity of Kirwin National Wildlife Refuge, Kansas, and with a secondary peak in the grasslands of western Texas. Some limited wintering occurs north to South Dakota and Wyoming, depending on the severity of the weather during any particular year. These winter distributions roughly parallel the breeding-season differences between eastern and western meadowlarks, suggesting that the two species then tend to exclude one another, although with a greater apparent tendency for the western to exclude the eastern than vice versa.

In winter the birds are found in much the same habitats as are used during the breeding season. They preferentially select open, grassy-dominated fields, which now consist largely of agricultural lands rather than prairie. At this time of year weed seeds and waste grain play an important role in their diets. Annually, animal materials, mainly insects, provide the majority of foods eaten, with plant materials the remainder, especially grain. Besides searching visually for surface items, both North American meadowlark species have sharp, tapered beaks like awls that

45. Male heads of lark sparrow (A), horned lark (B), western meadowlark (C), and eastern meadowlark (D). Drawing by author.

they can insert into the soil; prying open their upper and lower mandibles, they then expose subsurface foods (Fig. 45). Grains are especially important winter foods, which as spring advances are progressively supplanted by insects. Meadowlarks have also been found to eat the eggs and nestlings of some other birds, although this would seem to be an infrequent activity at best.

Spring migration begins early, and small flocks of meadowlarks are usually to be seen moving north across fields that are still mostly snow-covered in early March. It is not known whether northernmost birds are more prone to take the longest migrations to and from southern wintering areas, leapfrogging over intermediate populations that migrate the shortest possible distances, but a few long-distance recovery records from banded Canadian birds might suggest this to be the case.

On arrival at their breeding areas, the birds spread out over grasslands of all types. They even use such marginal habitats as orchards, grassy roadside ditches, and some croplands, especially the more weedy or densely planted ones. At least in the eastern Great Plains, where sympatric overlap with eastern meadowlarks is common, the westerns can quite reliably be found in drier and higher sites; the easterns are found closer to water and in higher and denser vegetation, such as that occurring at the bottoms of hilly terrain. Yet territories of the two species are often in sight of and within easy hearing range of one another, and territorial exclusionary behavior between these species seems to be as intense as are intraspecific interactions.

In addition to their well-known primary songs, western meadowlarks also utter several other notes that to varying degrees resemble those of the eastern meadowlark (Fig. 46). The most commonly heard call is a loud, brief *chupp,* uttered by both sexes when disturbed and comparable in function and sound characteristics to the higher pitched *dzert* note of the eastern. Females utter a rapid rattlelike call and males a slower but similar "roll," especially during the earlier parts of the breeding season. Rather similar chattering calls are produced by both sexes of the eastern.

By far the most widely recognized vocalization of the western meadowlark is the male's primary or advertising song (Fig. 46, upper sonogram). It is as typical of the western plains as a coyote's yipping howl or the flight call of a long-billed curlew. This wonderful flutelike array of notes tumbling forth like water from a bucket is too rapid and variable to put easily into words, but it may have as many as eleven separate acoustic elements, all uttered in less than two seconds. The earlier notes in the sequence are more prolonged and are sung on varied but fairly uniform pitches; with the latter, more rapid ones slide quickly up and down the scale, resembling some legendary Paganini-like virtuoso simply proving how good he really is. This song is typically uttered from an elevated perch, such as a fencepost, with the breast strongly raised and the boldly patterned black and yellow feathering evident to all. Although

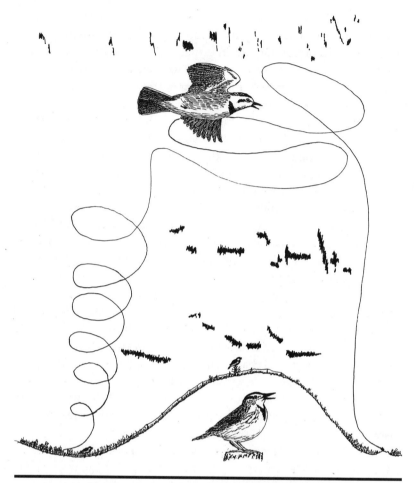

46. Horned lark flight display (*above*), and eastern (*lower left*) and western (*upper right*) meadowlarks' territorial songs. Sonograms of horned lark (1.5 second duration) after Beason (1995), of western and eastern meadowlarks (2.0-second durations) after Lanyon (1994, 1995). Drawing by author.

western meadowlarks sometimes sing in flight, their flight-song consists of a less structured warbling, preceded by a few whistles, and is mostly limited to the period of pair formation and establishment of territories.

Territories are thus proclaimed by perches-song and flight-song, beginning as soon as the birds arrive on breeding areas and sporadically even on wintering areas. Song activity increases when the females arrive, typically somewhat later than do the males. Individual males sing a variety of unique song types, usually ranging from about three to twelve. Some of these song types may be shared with other males in the local population, but no two males exhibit exactly the same repertoire. A male may repeat one of his song types several times but will switch to a different type on hearing a rival, perhaps to reduce the likelihood of this other male becoming habituated and thus less responsive to a particular rival's song type. Thus, song-switching may be important both in territorial defense and in achieving mate attraction. Males having the largest song repertoires also tend to be among the first to obtain mates and have greater reproductive success than do less gifted males, suggesting that song is an example of "honest advertising" of a male's overall quality or vigor.

Western meadowlarks tend toward polygyny in their mating systems, with successful males frequently attracting two females into their territories, and sometimes as many as three. Territories are quite varied in size individually and perhaps geographically, but at the extremes range from about three to thirty acres. These territories are quite dynamic, with their areas and shapes changing through the season, as conditions change. Moreover, those males that are unsuccessful in attracting females also are most likely to lose their territories. Eastern and western meadowlarks maintain territorial segregation wherever they overlap in range, although at least in eastern Nebraska this separation is facilitated by minor species differences in their ecological preferences. It has been reported that in such areas of sympatry, western males are larger than elsewhere, have more colorful and boldly patterned underparts, and are more prone to respond to playbacks of the songs of eastern meadowlarks than is the case in areas where the two are not in geographic contact.

Pairing by females occurs almost immediately after their arrival, presumably using clues and selecting males largely based on individual male song characteristics. Pair bonds last for as long as the female is involved with incubation or brooding. However, a male also courts other females that are attracted into his territory and guards both or all of them against stolen copulations by other nearby males. Copulation is preceded by an imposing strut by the male around the female, with his breast feathers expanded and his crown feathers erected. Such copulations occur within the male's territory and are mostly confined to the preincubation phases of reproduction.

Nests are always well-concealed structures, typically located in rather dense grass that overarches the nest scrape and hides it from overhead view. A runway or entrance tunnel usually leads into the nest and provides for ready entrance or egress without disturbing the adjoining vegetation. The female builds the nest alone, usually in about a week, or even less time in the case of later nesting efforts.

Egg-laying is done on a daily basis, until a clutch of about five eggs is completed. Incubation is done by the female alone, starting with the laying of the last egg, and requires thirteen to fourteen days. Although only the female broods the chicks, males bring food to any and all the mates he may have acquired. Fledging occurs at ten to twelve days. Throughout nearly the meadowlark's entire North American range, and certainly in the Great Plains region, the brown-headed cowbird is evidently at least locally a serious brood parasite, with as many as 22 percent of a sample of forty-one Wisconsin clutches so affected. However, its effect on fledging success by meadowlarks is still unmeasured.

Breeding success is influenced by the fact that females will renest if they lose their first clutches but do not attempt to raise more than two broods successfully per season. Clutch sizes tend to be largest early in the season, but there does not appear to be any significant difference in average brood size through the season. Yet early females are more successful than later-nesting ones, and in line with this a male's primary mate is likely to be more successful than any later secondary mates. However, there are also marked annual differences in breeding success. In Wisconsin and in Manitoba studies, seasonal fledging success averaged 2.44 and 2.30 young. Annual mortality rates are still unmeasured, mainly because of the low rate of return of marked birds to their natal areas in following years.

Eastern Meadowlark

I have always thought that the eastern meadowlark was a somewhat second-class and perhaps slightly effete or decadent species, at least compared with the western, since it didn't seem able to survive the open expanses and climatic hardships of the Great Plains. I didn't personally encounter the species until I was already in college, since the western was the only meadowlark present where I grew up in North Dakota. And after finally hearing the eastern's slurred and simpler song, I decided it didn't hold a candle to the melodious notes of the western. Probably had I grown up in the region in which only easterns occur I would have felt differently and perhaps thought that the western is too much of an acoustic show-off. In any case, we can be grateful that collectively the meadowlarks occupy virtually all the North American grasslands, and perhaps next to the city-adapted and almost semidomesticated American robin and northern cardinal are among our most widely recognized and most beloved birds.

Unlike that of the western, the wintering range of the eastern meadowlark is nearly a carbon copy of its breeding range. This is true at least in terms of its densest wintering concentrations, which extend from northeastern Texas north through Oklahoma to eastern Kansas, with secondary concentrations in Alabama and along the common border of the Carolinas. Similarly, its densest breeding concentrations extend in a nearly unbroken band from eastern Texas north through Oklahoma, eastern Kansas, and Missouri, with some lower concentrations east of the Mississippi. Wintering birds occupy essentially the same habitats as do wintering westerns, namely open grasslands, meadows, and fields, including cultivated fields, but the birds are also sometimes found in wetlands, an unlikely wintering habitat for westerns.

Easterns consume weed seeds and waste grain during the winter months, and at times they may pick over traffic-killed animals or may even resort to limited small-animal predation, in times of winter stress. As the weather improves and foraging for insects becomes more productive, the birds gradually shift their diets toward this source. The species is able to probe deeply and pry open its bill while it is below ground, in the same manner as do western meadowlarks and various other long-billed icterid relatives.

Only in the northernmost parts of the eastern's range does much seasonal migration occur, but it appears that these northern birds are prone to migrate rather long distances rather than the least possible distance. They often seem to fly to the southeastern states, but there is no clear directionality or year-to-year consistency of wintering locations.

With the onset of spring a greater array of vocalizations is apparent. The most frequent utterance by both sexes is a short and intense *dzert* note, uttered upon disturbance. When greatly excited, both sexes utter whistles, and under somewhat less intense stimulation, such as upon seeing a hawk, a chattering call, lasting up to about 1.5 seconds and having about the same pulse rate (ca. 15/second) as a sharp-tailed grouse's tail-rattling. A single *dzert* note often precedes the rattling chatter. Other calls are also uttered under various circumstances.

The male's primary song and flight song are his two major territorial advertisements and mate-attraction signals. Like that of the western's, the flight-song of the eastern is a rather unstructured assortment of whistles, warbles, and twittering notes, usually begun while the bird is still perched and lasting up to twelve seconds. The male's primary song, sung from a conspicuous perch, is shorter than that of the western (averaging about 1.25 to 1.50 seconds), usually has no more than five separate vocal elements that are not organized into two or more discrete phases, and is almost entirely composed of slurred notes having descending pitches (Fig. 46, lower sonogram).

Spring singing begins with the arrival of males on their territory and peaks during courtship. It waxes and wanes with succeeding nesting efforts and may resume again in fall for a rather brief period. Males sing from several perches within their territory, generally selecting the highest available point. Individual males sing a bewildering array of song types, so many that an accurate count is impossible. In one case fifty-two different songs were recorded from a single male in an hour, although typically a particular song type is uttered several times in succession before switching occurs. During territorial interactions and those with females the rate of song-switching is greatest. Perhaps because of such large repertoires, males show poor discrimination abilities between neighboring males and those of strangers.

In areas of sympatry with westerns, eastern meadowlarks do not discriminate differentially between the two species' song types, responding in the same way to playbacks of both. However, eastern meadowlarks having had no prior exposure to western meadowlark songs do not respond to their songs, although they will respond visually to dummies of western meadowlarks. Evidently responsibility for proper species recognition and avoidance of hybridization rests on the abilities of the females to make proper discriminatory choices. Hybrids in nature are rare, although in the Platte Valley of Nebraska they seem to be moderately common. In that region, and in the Nebraska Sandhills region, eastern meadowlarks occur as small, often isolated, populations, and perhaps mating choices for females are rather limited as a result. Hybrids are known to be viable and sexually active, although their fertility is low and this fact probably is important in maintaining an effective degree of reproductive isolation between them.

Like many other icterids such as brown-headed cowbirds (see Fig. 17) and grackles, agonistic interactions are marked by visual posturing that includes upward bill-tilting while in a rather slimmed posture. A rapid expansion and shutting of the tail feathers, exposing their lateral white patterning, and a simultaneous opening and closing of the wings are commonly performed at the same time and may be accompanied by *dzert* calls. A general fluffing-out of plumage, called "expansion posturing," is also common during territorial disputes.

Territory sizes of these species are very similar to those of the western meadowlark, usually varying from about three to five acres and, like those of the westerns, being subject to considerable change in shape and size as the season progresses. Also like that species, males attempt to attract several females into their territories, rarely attracting as many as three. Obviously not all males are successful in getting multiple mates, and perhaps half of all territorial males have to settle for a single female. Pair bonds most likely last until the female has completed her parental responsibilities or failed in a final nesting effort. Aerial chases of the female by the male are typical among paired birds and are initiated by females. Prior to copulation the male normally approaches and struts around the female with greatly expanded plumage, but with his bill pointed downward rather than upward, as would be the case in agonistic encounters. Males also guard their mates carefully, to avoid the possibility of stolen copulations by neighboring males.

Nests are selected and constructed by the female, in sites perhaps identical to those chosen by western meadowlarks. Arched canopies overhead and approach runways are similarly typical. The nest opening may be oriented away from the prevailing wind in areas of strong winds and associated rainfall. Eggs are laid on consecutive days, usually during early morning hours. The usual clutch is of four or five eggs, with early season clutches averaging somewhat larger than later ones, but those of polygynously mated females are not significantly different in size than clutches of those paired monogamously. Current evidence suggests that no more than two broods are successfully reared by a female during a single breeding season, although several clutches may be produced and lost in the course of a single season.

Over the meadowlark's entire breeding range, brown-headed cowbird brood parasitism is possible; there has been less time for the eastern meadowlark to adapt to the presence of this species than has been true for its western counterpart. Although reports of parasitism are widespread, the available data suggest that the incidence is not very high, and there is essentially no data on the effect of the cowbird on the reproductive potential of the meadowlark.

Incubation lasts thirteen to fourteen days, and the young hatch rather synchronously. Initial fledging, or at least nest departure, may occur at ten to eleven days, but prolonged flights are not possible until the young are three weeks old. Parental dependence lasts until about two weeks after initial fledging.

Reproductive success in this species is apparently quite variable from year to year, and perhaps also from place to place. Estimates of season-long fledging success rates range from about 2.5 to 3.0 young per female. Although in most species females mated polygynously to males are less likely to be successful than are monogamously mated ones, one study of eastern meadowlarks has not found this to be the case; in fact, the reverse was true.

Horned Lark

Unlike the meadowlarks, horned larks truly are larks, although their "horns" are nothing more than two small tufts of black feathers toward the back of the head. These tufts are usually inconspicuous and sometimes are virtually invisible. Both sexes exhibit these little decorations, and their relative importance in social signaling is unclear. The tufts of adult females are smaller than those of males, and they are only rarely erected, so sexual identification signaling would seem to be a likely function.

Horned larks vary greatly in plumage over their North American range, to say nothing of their South American and Old World range. Up to twenty-one subspecies in North America alone have been recognized at various times, which vary little in size but considerably in facial and body coloration. Most of these racial variants occur in the western parts of the continent, especially in grassland and desert regions. Body colors tend to match those of their soil substrate closely, and a crouching horned lark is usually almost impossible to see without careful searching.

The races found breeding on the Great Plains and central lowlands include *erythymia*, breeding in the shorter grasslands from Saskatchewan south to western Texas, *leucolaema*, breeding in even drier areas from Al-

A Lark by Any Name

berta to eastern New Mexico, and *praticola,* breeding in tall-grass prairies from Minnesota to eastern Kansas. The race that winters over much of the northern plains, south to about Oklahoma, is *alpestris,* a tundra-breeding race that tends to be more richly toned both above and below than are the generally paler plains breeders. Populations breeding in the northern plains tend to move variably southward during the coldest months, but those in the central and southern plains are increasingly residential.

Those birds that migrate out of the northern plains in winter remain as far north as practical and begin moving back with the first improving weather, the males arriving on their breeding areas first, followed soon thereafter by the females. The birds migrate diurnally in flocks, pausing to forage in snow-free fields, sometimes in the company of longspurs. At that time of year they feed almost exclusively on seeds, including grass seeds, waste grain, and feedlot grains, and extract seeds from plant stalks rising above the snow surface. Occasionally items are dug from the ground by the beak, including larvae and sometimes also newly sprouting green plants, and the birds' lengthened claws presumably might help spread out their weight over snowy or sandy surfaces. With warming weather, increasing quantities of insects are eaten by adults. During summer months, such protein-rich foods may constitute nearly half the entire adult diet, and young birds are fed insects exclusively. Yet adults continue to consume seeds throughout the summer and gradually increase their seed consumption through fall and into winter.

Birds arriving on their breeding grounds begin displaying almost immediately. In the central plains, song may begin as early as mid-January, although a March onset is more typical. Such songs usually begin with "intermittent song," consisting of an extended series of elements that begin with several spaced ascending syllables, followed by a more rapid and slurred series of notes that at first diminish and then increase in pitch. These songs are uttered while the bird glides, with his tail spread and wings outstretched (Fig. 46, *above*). A similar song type, called "recitative song," is a quite prolonged, seemingly rambling sequence of rapidly slurred notes, resembling the latter part of intermittent song and lasting up to several minutes, rarely up to eleven minutes in the race *leucolaema.* During this song the flying male performs steady wingbeats. The incidence of recitative song increases relative to intermittent song as the season progresses.

The usual pattern of song-flight display is for the bird to ascend

165

rather steeply into the wind, or in the absence of wind to ascend in wide circles, and to begin his song at a height of anywhere from about 200 to 800 feet. At that point he may spread his tail and glide on extended wings while singing, followed by a return to higher altitude and a repetition of the song. While singing thus, he faces into the wind and, depending upon wind velocity, may remain nearly motionless in the sky. At the end of this remarkable performance the bird is likely to close his wings and plummet back to earth, opening them just in time to lose airspeed and land on one of his song perches. Ground-singing also regularly occurs from such perches, especially around sunrise and sunset, whereas flight-songs are more likely to be seen near midday and again at sunset.

Male territories are fairly large and include all breeding-season needs. They vary according to population density but average about 4.0 acres in midwestern agricultural lands and are smaller in Colorado short-grass prairies (ranging about 1.75 to 3.50 acres). Similar ranges have been noted in shrubsteppe habitats. Territories tend to diminish in size as the season progresses and are abandoned when the young have fledged. Defense of the territory is mostly performed by males, but females sometimes participate, and juveniles are allowed to intrude.

Present information indicates an entirely monogamous pair bond that lasts for a single breeding season and during which two broods are usually raised; lost mates may be replaced within the same breeding season. It is also possible that, if a female's mate is lost, a male from a neighboring territory may form a temporarily polygynous pair bond and thereby also acquire a larger overall territory.

Male-to-female courtship includes courtship-feeding and also a ground display that probably serves as a copulatory invitation, during which the bird spreads his tail, droops his wings, and struts before the female while uttering chittering notes and while vibrating his wings. Females indicate a willingness to copulate with crouching, wing-drooping, and tail vibration.

Nest sites of horned larks are selected by the female, and nests may be placed anywhere within the male's large territory. Essentially bare ground is the preferred substrate; protective dorsal coloration probably matches this background situation better than a grassy environment would. A slight cavity is dug, thus lowering the sitting female's dorsal profile to nearly ground level; this is lined with grass and feathers. Interestingly, the female may place a paving of pebbles, dirt clods, or bits of dried dung immediately beside the nest cavity or initially even directly into it. These items may help keep the nest lining from blowing away while it is still under construction and later are removed from the cavity itself.

Eggs are laid at the rate of one per day. The usual clutch size seems to be rather variable and may slightly increase latitudinally. In the Midwest a clutch of three eggs is most typical. Rather rapid reinitiation of nests is common following their destruction. Incubation begins with the laying of the last or penultimate egg and is performed by the female alone, although the male remains nearby and may rarely feed her. In the hot climate of the southern plains and southwestern deserts, effective shading rather than incubation of the eggs may be required on hot days. Hatching occurs relatively simultaneously. The young have a distinctive gape pattern, with three black spots on their otherwise yellow-orange tongue and two at the tips of their pale yellow mandibles, the spots contrasting with a bright orange mouth lining. This pattern might be significant in allowing the parents to distinguish them from nestling parasitic cowbirds.

The young are fed by both parents and become mobile considerably before they actually fledge, the latter occurring at about two weeks of age. Their flight feathers continue to grow, however, until they are about four weeks old. I have seen rather nondescript-looking juvenile horned larks wandering around on grassy sand dunes in western Nebraska seemingly entirely on their own and found them difficult to identify until their parents finally came into view. Because of the larks' unusual precocity, nestling brown-headed cowbirds are sometimes left in horned lark nests to starve, after the lark chicks become mobile and able to abandon their nest. However, nest parasitism by cowbirds is relatively common and may reduce lark productivity by about half.

Nesting success has been estimated from various parts of this species' broad North American range and at the upper end seems to range from 65 percent in Illinois (twenty-four total nests) to as high as 71 percent in British Columbia (fifteen total nests). Fledging success estimates include a rearing of 2.6 young in fifteen successful Illinois nests, and 2.3 young reared per nest in thirteen successful Wyoming nests. This per-brood productivity estimate can perhaps be doubled for obtaining seasonal estimates, as two or three broods per season seem to be normal for birds nesting in temperate latitudes.

Lark Sparrow

The first "new" bird that I encountered on my initial trip to the Nebraska Sandhills in 1961 was a lark sparrow. It was sitting on a small juniper, amid scattered bunchgrasses and yuccas, singing as if it thought it were a western meadowlark and exhibiting a more colorful head pattern than I had ever seen in a grassland sparrow. Years later, my students in field ornithology classes in western Nebraska loved to have lark sparrows on their field quizzes, saying that its head pattern reminded them of someone wearing a University of Wisconsin football helmet. They weren't impressed when I called it a bimaculated plumage pattern. Somehow the interest level of undergraduates at the University of Nebraska seemed rarely to rise above the level of athletics, especially football.

Lark sparrows always seem slightly too colorful for their surroundings, which typically consist of rather open habitats, where a good deal of bare ground is present but where small trees, tall bushes, or other singing perches are available. In short, they often inhabit abandoned or "worthless" ground such as old quarries, gravel pits, and fields that have been left untended long enough to have grown up to weeds. However, they also occur in true tall-grass prairie, in scrubsteppe, and in semi-desert grasslands. In Colorado, the highest incidence of breeding ground occurrences is on short-grass prairie but with sagebrush, rural sites, and pinyon-juniper of secondary importance.

Even though they are larger than most grassland sparrows, lark sparrows are strongly migratory, wintering south to Mexico's Isthmus of Tehuantepec and even rarely breed south to the Chihuahuan and Sonoran Deserts of northern Mexico. There they occupy open grasslands and rather barren plains that have scattered trees or bushes, often in the company of clay-colored or field sparrows. In Sonora they occur in large flocks in the interior, usually in tall grass and dense weeds among rocky terrain. Wintering in the southern Great Plains is concentrated in Texas, especially in the arid mesquite-acacia and oak-juniper woodlands of central and southern Texas, where these low trees are interspersed with open ground, grasses, and weeds.

Wintering-ground foods are not specifically known, but in New Mexico, where the birds both breed and winter, seeds, grain, and other vegetable materials have been estimated to make up 73 percent of the diet. Much of this consists of waste grain and various annual weeds that are common in abandoned fields. Among its animal foods, more than half consists of grasshoppers, but weevils are also often taken. The birds forage on open ground and are especially prone to feed at the edges of dirt or gravel roads, flying up briefly as vehicles pass by and exposing to view their distinctive white tail corners.

Lark sparrows are fairly early migrants, typically arriving in Colorado and Nebraska in early April, in the Dakotas by late April, and in Montana and the Prairie Provinces in early May. Males arrive on nesting areas considerably earlier than do females and usually appear in small flocks, sometimes already singing vigorously. The song has been well described as consisting of a series of chants, composed of loud and clear syllables interspersed by emotional trills, the total song producing an overall gay and melodious effect (Fig. 47). The interspersed change-of-pace trills provide for an easy acoustic recognition of the species; its song approaches the Brewer's sparrow in its aesthetic attractiveness.

Lark sparrows are notable for the intensity with which males sing and display while establishing their territories. Actual fights between males are common, sometimes involving as many as five or even six birds simultaneously. A vertical bill-tilting may precede actual fighting, during which two males may rise almost vertically in the air as they try to strike one another with their wings. Females are initially treated in the same manner as an intruding male, with upward bill-tilting, tail-spreading, and wing-fluttering behavior. Males may also sing during rather short flights, again marked by tail-fanning and rapidly beating wings. At such times the bird may fly from songpost to songpost, singing all the while, or may circle back and land again at the place where he began.

Copulation is probably preceded by such strutting, tail-spreading, and wing-fluttering, but the male may also present the female with a small twig. This is passed to the female's bill during copulation, after which the pair may fly off together, the female still carrying the twig in her bill.

Although season-long monogamy is likely to be the usual mating system, at least one well-documented case of polygyny has been seen, in which a male tended two nests that were situated about 100 yards apart and copulated alternately with both the females.

Although in most sparrows the female seems to be the sex that selects the nest site, Donald Baepler's observations in Oklahoma suggest that the pair does so together, flying about and examining potential sites. At this time the male may carry a small twig in his bill, depositing it at what he apparently considers a suitable nest site. This behavior may occur at several different sites before the female selects one for actual use.

47. Male lark sparrow singing on juniper. Sonogram of male song (duration ca. 2.5. seconds) after Robbins, Bruun, and Zim (1983). Drawing by author.

In California, nests have been found in such unlikely sites as cliff crevices but are more frequent in evergreens such as junipers or in various hardwoods such as oaks. There the nests average about seven feet above ground. On the short-grass plains the nests may be placed on the ground itself, usually in clumps of grass or other herbaceous vegetation. In Arizona, nest-site substrates typically have about 50 percent grass cover and nearly 40 percent bare ground, with the remainder consisting of forbs and woody vegetation. Grass height is quite low at nest sites, often under five inches.

Although the birds are certainly somewhat territorial, nests may at times be placed surprisingly close to one another. Thus, nests are sometimes less than thirty yards apart, and there may even be clusters of nests within an area of about 100 yards in diameter. It is possible that at least some of these clusters are a result of undetected polygyny. Nesting also often occurs close to the nest of other species, perhaps of flycatchers such as kingbirds, which actively try to evict potential egg predators from their nesting tree and thereby indirectly also protect the nests of other nearby species.

Nest-building requires about three to four days, and the first egg is laid a day or two later. The usual clutch is of four or five eggs, which are laid on a daily basis. Only the female incubates. At least in Oklahoma, lark sparrows are sometimes parasitized fairly strongly by brown-headed cowbirds, with as many as about 45 percent of their nests thus affected. Elsewhere in the lark sparrow's broad nesting range there is much less evidence of the cowbird's being a significant threat. Lark sparrows have been known to desert their nests when confronted with a cowbird egg but also have been seen feeding young cowbirds. There may be a differential response, depending on an individual lark sparrow's prior exposure to cowbirds, or perhaps its response depends upon the stage of seasonal breeding progression.

Incubation lasts eleven to twelve days, and both sexes feed the developing young with about equal vigor. The female does most or perhaps all of the brooding. After nine to ten days the young are likely to leave the nest, even though their flying abilities are quite limited at that age.

Second broods are believed to be the norm in some parts of the lark sparrow's range, but Baepler found no definite evidence for it in Oklahoma, where the breeding season should be long enough to permit two or even three broods. However, one or more renests following the loss of an early nesting effort were documented by him.

After fledging, the birds begin to form loose flocks, even though some occasional singing may continue to occur in late summer. Fights may even break out among the birds, sometimes occurring between males and females and at other times between adults and young, or even with other species, such as field sparrows.

Suggested Readings

Bock and Bock 1987.

Western meadowlark: Aweida 1995; Dale et al. 1997; Falls and D'Agincourt 1981; Falls et al. 1988; Granfors et al. 1996; Horn and Falls 1988, 1991; Horn et al. 1993; Kinstler and Sordahl 1994; Lanyon 1956, 1957, 1994.

Eastern meadowlark: Brown 1988; D'Agincourt and Falls 1983; Falls and D'Agincourt 1981; Kinstler and Sordahl 1994; Knapton 1987, 1988; Lanyon 1956, 1957, 1995; Rotenberry and Klimstra 1970.

Horned lark: Beason 1970, 1995; Beason and Franks 1974; Boyd 1976; Greer 1988; Hurley and Franks 1976; Kershner and Bollinger 1996; Knick and Rotenberry 1995; Skinner 1974; Sutton 1927; Trost 1972.

Lark sparrow: Baepler 1968; Krueger 1981; McNair 1985; Newman 1970; Renward 1977; Swanson 1992.

11

Music over the Shrubsteppe: *McCown's and Chestnut-collared Longspurs; Lark Bunting*

A distance without limits, a horizon that did not bound the world but only suggested endless space beyond.

—Wallace Stegner,
Wolf Willow

The three species described here share one common, indeed endearing, trait. The beautifully clad males perform wonderful flight-songs in spring, during which they sing while fluttering up into the sky in a manner not unlike horned larks or Sprague's pipits but at a height where earthbound people can fully appreciate them without the aid of binoculars. Frances Mickey, describing the McCown's longspur, provides a slight notion: "The male proclaimed his right to a territory chiefly by a characteristic flight-song. In the early spring he was a persistent and exuberant singer. He mounted into the air, spread his wings and floated downward, repeating over and over the phrases of his song, *see, see, see me, see me, hear me, hear me, see.* Sometimes he did not alight after one descent, but rose immediately for another song."

McCown's Longspurs

The McCown's longspur is generally regarded as having been discovered and first scientifically named in 1851. However, it was almost certainly this species that was also seen and described four decades earlier by Capt. Meriwether Lewis in what is now

Montana, during June 1805. He observed several kinds of sparrows and (retaining Lewis's original and innovative spellings) "also a small bird which in action resembles the lark . . . this bird or that which I take to be the male rises into the air about sixty feet and supporting itself in the air with a brisk motion of the wings sings very sweetly, has several shrill short notes reather of the plaintive order which it frequently repeats and varies, after remaining stationary about a minute in his aireal station he descends obliquely occasionally pausing and accomnying his descension with a note something like *twit twit*; on the ground he is silent." This performance, as transcribed by R. G. Thwaits from the original journals of Lewis and Clark, differs but little from what I first observed a century and a half later in western Nebraska during a peerless blue-sky day in May, over remnant short-grass prairies near Scotts Bluff. The longspur's flight reminded me of those Fourth of July rockets that quickly rise into the air, explode, and then send a small cardboard cargo gently floating back to earth on a paper parachute that might be brightly patterned like an American flag.

Like many of the nineteenth-century American naturalists of his time, John P. McCown (1815–1879) was a soldier in the U.S. Army, serving mostly in the frontier country of the American West. He was stationed in Texas during the 1840s and subsequently published his field notes on the birds he saw and collected in that region. The McCown's longspur was first collected by him on its wintering grounds in the high plains of western Texas and was named in his honor in 1851 by George Lawrence.

The four species of longspurs are named for their unusually long hind claws, a feature that they share with pipits and larks and that probably is useful when walking on snow or soft sand. The longspurs, pipits, and larks also share the trait of having white markings present on their outer tail feathers, thus producing a contrasting pattern with their otherwise brown tail. This patterning is very evident when the birds are in flight but is totally hidden when the tail feathers are held shut, as is usual when the birds are walking or resting on the ground. The head patterns of longspurs in breeding plumage also are quite distinctive (Fig. 48). Apart from these features, the longspurs are fairly typical grassland- or tundra-adapted sparrows, which in winter plumage tend to spread out over the flat fields of the central plains in great flocks at the southern edges of the winter snowline, where they are able to disappear into the landscape quite magically.

48. Heads of breeding male (A) and female (B) lark bunting and of males of McCown's (C) and chestnut-collared (D) longspurs. Drawing by author.

Of the four longspurs, the McCown's is the one most closely associated with short-grass prairies; the chestnut-collared favors higher and more diverse vegetation. In croplands, short-grass prairie accounted for nearly all the breeding-season records of McCown's longspurs, with barren ground and croplands scarcely otherwise represented. They are thus common associates of horned larks and mountain plovers, especially the former, whose ecologies on the short-grass high plains are very similar, including both the foods taken and the characteristic of having elongated hind claws. During the winter these longspurs, horned larks, and Sprague's pipits similarly seek out short grasses and semidesert grasslands; the longspurs at least also use overgrazed pastures and plowed fields. The wintering range of the McCown's longspur extends from Arizona, New Mexico, and western Oklahoma across the Chihuahuan Desert of northern Mexico and south to northern Durango, where they sometimes associate with migrant or resident horned larks and wintering chestnut-collared longspurs.

During the winter period the birds are primarily seed-eaters, especially of grasses and small-seeded weeds, but with grain consumed to some extent, too. With the coming of spring there is a gradual shift to insects, especially grasshoppers, at least among females. However, males continue to eat a preponderance of seeds throughout the summer. This same sexual dichotomy of differences in choice of summer foods has also been observed in the chestnut-collared longspur and the horned lark. Probably chicks are fed exclusively on insects, mostly grasshoppers.

Longspurs are fairly early migrants, following the receding snowline northward and reaching their breeding ground of northeastern Colorado in late March or early April. Even in southern Alberta, at the northern edge of their breeding range, they are likely to be present by the end of April. Both sexes move in loose flocks, the males arriving in advance of the females by about two weeks.

By the time females have arrived, males are already on their established territories and displaying actively. Active singing continues throughout the courtship and the incubation period, some males singing even while helping tend young. Although it is most intense during early morning hours, some singing and song-flight behavior is present throughout the entire day, at least during the period of maximum display. Some singing may be done from perches on various elevated sites such as boulders or fenceposts, but most occurs during song-flights (Fig. 49, *top*). Under such conditions the song is longer and more complex than that performed when the bird is perched and usually lasts about eight to ten seconds. A rate of three such song-flights per minute may occur during the period of territorial establishment, and the bird often reaches maximum heights of about seventy-five feet.

Territories are relatively small and in various regions have been found to average from about 1.5 to 2.5 acres. They may be typified as having a preponderance of short grasses only a few inches high, plus a substantial amount (ca. 25 to 40 percent) of bare ground. Relatively barren,

49. McCown's longspur (*top*), chestnut-collared longspur (*middle*), and lark bunting (*bottom*), male flight display, including songs uttered at apex of flight. Undulating line represents flapping phase of flight. Sonograms of McCown's longspur (3.0-second duration) after With (1994), of chestnut-collared longspur (2.0-second duration) after Hill and Gould (1997), and of lark bunting (2.5-second duration) after Robbins, Bruun, and Zim (1983). Drawing by author.

heavily grazed hilltops, or hillside slopes with southern (warmer) exposures, and perhaps those with drier substrates appear to be favored. Selected sites are often those that are also favorable for egg-laying by grasshoppers. Territories are all-inclusive, but at times group flights by an entire local population have been seen in spring, during which all the birds temporarily leave their territories, fly about, then separate and return to their respective locations. The possible function of such flights, which do not seem to be mobbing responses to a predator, is still unknown.

In spite of their wonderful aerial displays, male McCown's longspurs seem to settle for monogamy. Only one possible case of polygyny has been described, and that one was debatable. It is possible that, through the aggressive actions of the mated female, no other females are allowed on a male's territory. Besides performing aerial displays, males also court individual females by standing near them and raising the nearer wing vertically, exposing its white underwing lining to her. Copulation is preceded by circling a female, singing, and performing this exposed underwing display. Pair bonds last for only a single season, which normally would include the production of a second brood, or at least an attempt in this regard. There is no evidence yet of extrapair copulations and also no positive or negative evidence on the possible reestablishment of pair bonds in subsequent years.

The nest site is selected by the female, somewhere within her mate's territory but occasionally near its edge or even beyond it. In that case the male modifies his territorial boundaries to encompass the nest site. The nest is a simple scrape, often at the base of a bunchgrass clump, a small shrub or cactus, or even cattle dung, perhaps to provide some shade or to help break up the bird's outline. Additionally, protection from prevailing winds may be a significant factor in site selection. Mid-height bunchgrasses, and *Opuntia* cacti such as prickly pear, are commonly selected for providing such cover, but sometimes the nest is placed in fully exposed situations. The sites selected are seemingly identical to those used by horned larks in similar habitats, but both lark buntings' and chestnut-collared longspurs' nests differ in that overhead grassy canopies are invariably present.

Eggs are laid at the rate of one per day, until a completed clutch of three or four eggs is attained. Three-egg and four-egg clutches seem to be about equally common, at least in the northern parts of the breeding range; three-egg clutches are usual farther south. Incubation lasts twelve days and is performed entirely by the female. Predation rates on eggs and nestlings are high and include not only the usual canid, mustelid, reptilian, and avian predators but also various rodents, such as ground squirrels and prairie dogs. However, brood parasitism by brown-headed cowbirds is almost nonexistent, probably because the longspurs breed in areas with no shrubs or trees, a situation unfavorable for cowbirds.

Fledging takes another eleven to twelve days, although the chicks are likely to leave the nest by ten days, before they can barely flutter above the ground. Following actual fledging the young are likely to remain dependent on their parents for another three weeks.

Because of the species' strong tendency to renest following clutch failure, there is a fairly high rate of ultimate nesting success. Hatching success, as measured by the percentage of eggs producing nestlings, has been estimated at around 50 to 65 percent in various studies and the average brood size in successful nests at about 1.7 to 2.8 newly hatched chicks per nest. Fledging success, if measured only from successful nests, seems quite high in some studies but low in others and has ranged from about 2.7 to 3.5 chicks. Second broods may increase the seasonal production of fledged young, but only about half the females in one study attempted a second nesting, and the success of these second broods seems to be lower than for first nestings. All told, about one-quarter of the females succeed in raising a second brood, thus increasing the season chick production by about 25 percent. Overall, females can perhaps be expected to produce an average of from 1.1 to 2.0 fledged chicks per season, judging from a variety of studies.

Chestnut-collared Longspur

One of the most attractive, if not trademark, birds of the midgrass prairies of the northern plains is the chestnut-collared longspur. It occurs along with Baird's sparrows, Sprague's pipits, and the other prairie-adapted avifauna that once relied on bison for periodic grazing and maintenance of their nesting habitat. Its range largely corresponds with the historic summer range of the bison on the northern plains and, like that of the bison, its summer range has shrunk considerably in historic times, especially along its southern boundaries. These now reach the edges of western and northwestern Nebraska but once extended well into Kansas.

Like other longspurs, the chestnut-collared migrates substantially southward in winter, concentrating in the drier grasslands and semideserts in the American Southwest and the southern Great Plains, with the highest densities roughly occurring along the Pecos River, in the region between the common boundaries of New Mexico and Texas. There is a secondary wintering peak along the Red River, in the boundary region between Texas and Oklahoma. Yet it is not attracted to riverine vegetation as such and is indeed likely to remain well away from heavier wooded or shrubby cover. It may, however, be attracted to water sources in otherwise dry environments and will tolerate the presence of scattered shrubs or arborescent yuccas. Its wintering range also reaches into the deserts of interior northern Mexico as far south as Mexico's central volcanic belt. There it occurs in flocks and associates to some extent with the McCown's longspur. It is more likely to be found in somewhat higher grasses and less arid habitats, associating loosely with wintering Sprague's and American pipits as well as with the rather broadly adaptable horned lark.

Like the other longspurs, the chestnut-collared subsists on grass and weed seeds throughout the winter period, consuming little if anything else. These seeds tend to be of types that are quite small, and no studies yet indicate that cultivated grains are significant in their diet at any time. With warming weather, increasing quantities of insects are eaten by adults, at least by adult females, and this food source may represent as much as half the total diet on the breeding grounds. Like other grassland passerines, chicks are fed exclusively on an invertebrate diet that is quite diverse but that consists mostly of rather small individual items.

There is a fairly early departure by longspurs from their wintering areas, with males leaving sooner and likewise arriving on their breeding grounds in advance of females. By early April the birds are back in southern breeding areas, and the northern parts of their summer range are occupied by late April to early May. Little time is wasted by the arriving males in establishing and advertising their territories. Territories tend to be established on short-grass prairies or midgrass prairie that has recently been grazed or mowed, so that it is no more than about twelve inches high and preferably somewhat less. In an optimum habitat, territories may average about one to two acres, with larger territories (up to about ten acres) in marginal habitat. Territories are nonoverlapping and all-inclusive and furthermore tend to be somewhat clumped. Some foraging may also occur beyond the limits of defended areas, especially when adults are busy feeding their young.

Together with posturing, the primary means of territorial and sexual advertisement by males consists of singing. The primary song is fairly short (2.0 to 2.5 seconds) and may have up to ten vocal elements, including repeated ones. The latter part of the song tends to vary more than the earlier portion, but both consist of mostly down-slurred elements, sometimes transliterated as "say it loud, so loud, ul-ee-ee." Some songs are uttered from perches, and these are seemingly little if at all different from those uttered in flight. Like the McCown's, the chestnut-collared longspur male often launches himself into the air during territorial advertising display, ascending to a height of about fifty feet and singing during the fluttering upward phase as well as while briefly undulating at the apex of the flight (Fig. 49, *middle left*). Then he floats back downward, tail widely spread, feet dangling, and often singing until he lands. Or he may ascend again before landing and repeat the performance. Compared with the McCown's, the bird does not reach so great a height, sings for a shorter duration, and continues to flutter his wings during the downward phase. The males' underpart colors, and also their tail and head patterning, are quite different in the two species (see Fig. 48) and may help to complement these behavioral differences between them. Females are evidently attracted to such performances, and it might easily be imagined that such energetic activities provide a ready mechanism for exhibiting individual vigor and fitness as well as emphasizing species distinctiveness. However, hybridization between these two species has been documented, in spite of these ecological, plumage-pattern, and behavioral differences between them.

As with the McCown's longspur, there is no evidence yet of any deviation from a monogamous mating system or any good measure of the incidence of stolen copulations. However, the presence of chicks in a nest that were sired by another male has been established. Precopulatory courtship by the male consists of wing- and tail-fanning, erection of the chestnut nape feathers, and an alternation of repeated head-bowing movements and holding the head high and erect. Pair-bonding lasts through the breeding season, and among a small sample of eight individually marked pairs, four of the pairs were reunited and reestablished the following year while the other four pairs were broken ("divorced") and new mates were acquired.

Females probably choose their nest site, since they alone construct it. It is placed in fairly sparse grass but nevertheless in vegetational cover that is somewhat higher than that preferred by McCown's longspurs. Native grasslands are preferred over "tame" pasturelands, and recently grazed, mowed, or burned areas are also preferred. Typically the nest is hidden under a grass clump or at times placed beside cattle dung. It is excavated so that the back of the incubating bird is almost at ground level. At least in Alberta, nests tend to be protected by vegetation on their southern and eastern sides, presumably in response to variations in wind exposure or solar radiation.

Eggs are laid at the usual rate of one per day, with clutches of four being the most common. Egg-laying by brown-headed cowbirds is less frequent than one might speculate, and this may be the result of an early initiation of egg-laying by the longspur, before the cowbird has become very active. The seemingly low parasitism rate occurs even though longspur nests are usually not well hidden. It has been suggested that this visibility may be a benefit, by making it harder for an intruding cowbird to lay its egg undetected.

Incubation is by the female alone and requires 10.0 to 12.5 days. Both sexes bring food to the developing brood. The female likewise does nearly all the brooding, but the male participates to a slight degree. Grasshoppers and many other invertebrate types are fed to the chicks, including some spiders. The young leave the nest at nine to eleven days.

Nesting success is seemingly high, given the birds' rather exposed nests, averaging 55 percent in one study. The longspurs are persistent renesters following clutch failure. As many as four nesting efforts have been documented in a single season, specifically, a successful initial effort followed by three more attempts. A new nest is typically begun only a few days after the fledging of the first brood, and there are even a few cases of a third brood being attempted within a single season. Among successfully hatched nests, nestling success (percent of hatchlings fledged) runs about 60 to 90 percent, and overall breeding success (number of fledglings as a percent of total eggs laid) may exceed 50 percent, judging from available data. Under such circumstances, females raising a single brood are likely to fledge about 3.5 young per year; those producing two broods (nearly 20 percent of those rearing their first) average about 7.0 fledged young; and a very few females (less than 1 percent) may rear three broods, thereby fledging about 9.0 young. These figures appear to be surprisingly high, at least as compared with other ground-nesting prairie passerines.

Survival rates and estimated longevities for chestnut-collared longspurs have been based on minimum return rates of marked birds to breeding areas in subsequent years. These results suggest a minimum annual survival rate of about 66 percent for males but only about half that rate for females. The lower rate for females is likely to reflect lower site fidelity in that sex rather than such significantly lower survival rates. The greatest longevity estimate established by this means is a minimum of four years after initial banding as an adult, but longer lifespans should be possible for males, if these statistics are reliable.

Lark Bunting

The lark bunting has always posed an ecological-distributional paradox for me in western Nebraska. Near Ogallala, in the Platte Valley, I never saw them during the breeding season until several years after I started teaching summer courses at our field station. Then one spring they appeared in a single irrigated alfalfa field a few miles from camp, where they seemed to materialize miraculously in large numbers. For many succeeding years they continued to use only this single field but were always abundant there. Otherwise, I could count on seeing them only about five miles north of the village of Oshkosh, in the narrow ecological transition zone between the heavy clay soils of the North Platte Valley and the edge of the Nebraska Sandhills, where native sand-adapted grasses begin to wrest dominance from the planted milo and other irrigated crops. However, there the birds appeared so regularly, and in such a precise location, that while driving through that area I could confidently alert my naive ornithology class to begin looking for flocks of lark buntings on fences and fields in the next mile ahead and be absolutely certain that they would appear, as if on cue. In the Sandhills proper, only a mile or so farther north, the birds disappeared again, there to be ecologically replaced by horned larks.

Along with the McCown's longspur, the black-plumaged male lark bunting, with his contrasting white wing patches, provides one of the great late-spring spectacles of the short-grass prairies. From fields seemingly devoid of life, one male after another will spring into the air, singing lustily as he ascends some twenty feet or so (Fig. 49, *lower left*).

Then, still singing, he floats back down in a mothlike manner, with wings outstretched above in a steep V and, almost as rapidly as he appears, drops back down into the vegetation and disappears. There is a nearly mesmerizing sleight-of-hand component to all this, and it has a hypnotic effect on human observers. Presumably, it also does something for female lark buntings.

Lark buntings are strong migrants, abandoning their tuxedolike male summer plumages for more informal attire in winter, when they concentrate in southern Texas, especially the Big Bend region, and extend southward across northern Mexico and the Baja Peninsula. However, they rarely reach farther south than central Mexico. Their flocking tendencies of summer persist through the winter, when they aggregate in open habitats that have a good deal of bare ground present, plus some grasses and weedy vegetation. They are also attracted to roads where grain from trucks may have spilled. They are early fall migrants, often arriving in wintering areas while the adult males are still largely in their breeding plumage. There they spread out over fields and barnyards in small flocks and generally are much less tolerant of humans than while on their breeding areas.

Winter food analyses are not available, but summertime foods not surprisingly are high in invertebrate materials, especially grasshoppers. Weevils are perhaps the second most frequent type of insect prey. Plant materials include waste grain and weed seeds, mostly of small-seeded annual forbs. As usual, young birds are fed nothing but insects. Flocks of lark buntings are attracted to hordes of grasshoppers, and perhaps local annual variations in breeding numbers of the buntings might be correlated with relative grasshopper abundance.

The lark bunting is a rather late spring migrant. It arrives on its breeding grounds of eastern Colorado and western Nebraska in early May, the males by then back in their full nuptial plumage and flocks suddenly appearing almost overnight. By mid-May they have reached North Dakota, and by the end of May they are back on their breeding areas of southern Saskatchewan. In Colorado the birds immediately seek out short-grass prairies, with nearly half of all reported breeding-season bunting sites being of that habitat type and with progressively fewer reported from croplands, altered midgrass prairies, and native midgrass prairies.

Males arrive on their breeding area before females by nearly a week, and it may be nearly two weeks before the migrant flocks disperse and begin to settle in suitable nesting habitats. Over their entire range, lark buntings typically seek out grasslands of low to moderate height, with a rather small area (up to about 15 percent substrate coverage) of bare ground, and often with some scattered shrubs, such as sagebrush. Increased litter depth may also be correlated with higher numbers of birds.

If territories of any kind exist, they must be very poorly defended indeed, as singing males often occupy adjacent fenceposts without any obvious animosity between them. Apparently only during the very short, less than week-long, period that they are forming pair bonds do males attempt to defend their territories. Once they have obtained a mate, the males are perhaps kept too busy helping with incubation or brooding to spend any time defending territories. These have been estimated to be as small as 0.25 acre, or as large as about 3.0 acres, but territorial boundaries seem to be honored more in the breach than in the keeping.

Singing by such males is almost continuous for several weeks, as the birds vocalize both from perches and from the ground. The songs uttered from either position are similar (Fig. 49, sonograms). In a limited study of two males in Kansas and Colorado, Jerry and Norma Stillwell found that their songs consisted of a random assortment of several phrases, varying in both pitch and musical quality and consisting of trills, buzzes, or singles notes repeated up to ten times. The total number of phrases present in a single song may be from three to seven, and an individual bird may utter at least eleven different phrase combinations at various times. Most frequently the song begins with several *sweet* notes, not unlike those of a song sparrow, which may be followed by several chatlike single notes, then groups of trills, buzzes, or combinations of these. While in the air, the displaying bird may repeat parts of the song as if to prolong it and typically begins singing just as he is reaching the apex of his flight. The neck is stretched forward somewhat while singing, but the bill is not opened widely and the head is not tilted upward (Fig. 49).

There is no indication that the birds fight strongly over songpost ownership or otherwise engage in seriously hostile behavior to one another. Given this situation, it would seem likely that nonmonogamous mating may at least occasionally if not regularly occur, with the birds relying more on song, individual posturing, and vocalization quality to attract females rather than on hostile or territorial interactions to keep competing males away from possible or actual mates.

Nest sites are apparently chosen with some care. Important criteria include such things as adequate warmth from the morning sun but shade from the afternoon sun and ventilation from cooling south winds but protection from cold north winds. Grasses around nests are usually five to ten inches high, with relatively few shrubs but more forbs than typical of surrounding vegetation. The nest is usually built next to the base of a shrub or forb, or in a clump of grass. Nesting begins later in spring than is true of longspurs and horned larks, and the birds usually nest in both taller and moister vegetation than any of these. They also tend to feed on larger grasshopper prey and thus help partition the foraging niches of these ecologically and geographically overlapping species.

Eggs are laid on a daily basis following nest completion, and the usual clutch is of four or five eggs. Incubation lasts twelve days, and some observers have seen males participating, though others have not. Cowbird brood parasitism may be locally important, as for example in North Dakota and Montana, where a 33 percent parasitism rate (for eighteen nests) was reported, but in areas such as Kansas the effective parasitism rate may be lower, owing to nest desertion and possible ejection of the cowbird eggs by the parents.

Nest departure occurs at about eight to nine days. Second broods have been reported by at least one observer but have been questioned by others. Possibly apparent second broods were the result of renestings following early failure.

Suggested Readings

McCown's longspur: Dechant et al. 1999i; Felske 1971; Greer and Anderson 1989; Krause 1968; Mickey 1945; Ryder 1980; With 1992.

Chestnut-collared longspur: Dechant et al. 1999b; Harris 1994; Hill and Gould 1997; Moriarty 1965; Wyckoff 1986.

Lark bunting: Baldwin et al. 1969; Butterfield 1969; Creighton 1971, 1974; Davis et al. 1999; Dechant et al. 1999g; Erwin 1981; Finch et al. 1987; Huntley 1997; Pleszcynska and Hansell 1980; Sealy 1999; Shane 1974, 2000; Stillwell and Stillwell 1955; Taylor and Ashe 1976; Thompson and Sullivan 1979; Wilson 1976.

12   Furtive Sparrows in the
Grass: *Clay-colored,*
Grasshopper, and Vesper

The prairie is not a great place to be if you are a small, fragile, flying insect. Recently I walked through a late-August stand of seven-foot tall big bluestem, switchgrass, and Indian grass on the loess-covered bluffs near the Missouri River near Omaha. I let my open fingers run through the ripening grass stalks for the sheer tactile pleasure of it, gradually covering my shirt with the bright orange pollen that was thus tossed into the wind. There was not a mosquito to be seen or heard. Indeed, after a few cold late-summer nights there were few apparent insects of any kind, although the grasshoppers that I detected were no doubt busily attempting to devour the tender grass shoots almost as rapidly as they could grow. Keeping ahead of the grasses would have been a fruitless endeavor; save for a narrow foot-wide and newly mown path through the grass, it required real effort for a human to push through the endless head-high grasses, and I wondered if a bison would have even been able to see where it might be heading. Seemingly a small sparrow hiding on the ground might feel itself surrounded by redwoodlike giant grass stalks and thus uncomfortable at the prospect of suddenly encountering a predator.

Beyond the grassland's edge only a few dozen yards away, there were invisible white-breasted nuthatches yank-yanking in the woods like little toy trumpets, blue jays were periodically screaming, and black-capped chickadees were quietly minding their own business. As soon as I entered the woods the wind died down magically, and I was promptly assaulted by mosquitoes. It was a totally different, almost Oz-like experiential transformation; and suddenly hearing rather than seeing became the operative sense. There was not a single grasshopper to be seen, and the world of plant growth, insect life, and bird activity was occurring well above my head rather than below and around me. Even though it was late in the breeding season and fall migration was just starting, an occasional yellow-billed cuckoo's call echoed through the woods, and an eastern wood-pewee made some tentative and feeble attempts at song. The cuckoo remained invisible, but the wood-pewee finally showed itself on one of the dead branches of a tree, its colors blending perfectly with the bark of the branch.

Behind me, the prairie birds remained deathly quiet. The dickcissels were no doubt getting ready to depart for their long fall migration, and the generally noisy meadowlarks were being unusually silent. There was not a peep to be heard from any of the grassland sparrows. Even when they are singing lustily, the insectlike songs of clay-colored and grasshopper sparrows are anything but obvious, and when in full song the males are as likely to remain hidden as not. Vesper sparrows are also only infrequently to be seen, although they are not nearly so secretive, their voice is much louder, and their song is more beautiful than are those of the other two. The species' almost ethereal song, often uttered in the evening, is the basis for its vernacular name, "vesper."

Clay-colored Sparrow

A few sparrows seem to be perfectly named; such is the clay-colored sparrow. Its breast and dorsal background color is that of dried clay, a common substrate color of this dryland sparrow. However, its somewhat more richly toned cheeks are neatly outlined in white, making it second only to the lark sparrow in terms of the attractiveness of its head patterning among the prairie sparrows (Fig. 50). It is perhaps more accurately described as a low-shrub species than a true grassland bird, and its greatest abundance during the breeding season occurs in the ecotone between the northern prairies and the aspen parklands, but it also

50. Male heads of clay-colored (A), grasshopper (B), and vesper sparrow (C). Song sonograms respectively after Vickery (1996), Knapton (1994) (durations 1.75 seconds), and Robbins, Bruun, and Zim (1983) (duration 2.5 seconds). Drawing by author.

breeds in the low shrublands around the southern end of Hudson Bay and in the scrublands of northern Canada. Low second-growth woods, burned-over forested areas, and similar woodland transition habitats seem to be favored by these birds.

Like the northern-breeding longspurs, this sparrow is a relatively long-distance migrant, regularly wintering from the Rio Grande Valley of Texas southward throughout nearly all of Mexico to the isthmus, including drier coastal areas. Rather dry grasslands, with scattered shrubs or other low woody vegetation, are its favored winter haunt. Seeds of a wide array of weedy forb species and grasses are eaten during that season. With the arrival of spring, migrants begin to eat increasing quantities of insects, and nestlings are fed exclusively on insects, especially grasshoppers.

Spring migration is done in loose flocks. Large numbers of the birds often appear in western Nebraska during late April and early May. On some days the grasslands seem to be literally covered with actively foraging clay-colored sparrows; the next day they may be gone but another flock appears soon thereafter. There they often can be seen in the company of migrating chipping sparrows and farther west are likely to appear with migrant Brewer's sparrows. Both of these closely related species overlap on their breeding grounds to some degree with clay-colored sparrows, too, but they exhibit minor differences in habitat preferences and apparent climatic tolerances. Migration by clay-colored sparrows occurs both nocturnally and during daylight hours. The birds arrive on their breeding grounds in mid- to late May.

Upon arrival, little time is wasted by the males in territorial establishment. There is a measurable differential sex migration and an earlier arrival of males than of females by a matter of a few days. The territories of males are surprisingly small, perhaps because a good deal of foraging is done outside the territorial boundaries on seemingly "neutral" land. As a result, territories are often only 0.25 to 1.0 acre in area and tend to remain rather stable in size throughout the breeding season. Minimum territorial size may be determined by minimum internest distance, and the presence of suitable nest cover may be the single most important determinant of territorial suitability. Some degree of interspecific territoriality with chipping sparrows, Brewer's sparrows, and song sparrows has been reported, although the intensity of such territorial interactions is less than those occurring intraspecifically.

Monogamy is the only type of mating system so far documented for clay-colored sparrows; pair bonds evidently persist through an entire breeding season, but there is only very limited evidence of individual bonds being reestablished in one or more subsequent years. Territorial advertisement and mate attraction is attained by singing from various perches within the territory as well as by exclusionary behavior by resident males. The male's primary song is a somewhat insectlike buzzing, most often composed of two or three long phrases, collectively lasting about 1.5 to 2.0 seconds but sometimes consisting of several shorter notes (maximum of eight) of about the same overall duration. Typically the first note tends to ascend slightly in frequency, and the second or last may tend to descend, but these differences are rather minimal at best. The maximum sound energy occurs at about 4 kilohertz. There is no evidence of local dialect difference in songs, probably because of substantial individual variation within single populations. There is also a low correlation of song-type similarity between neighboring males, so that each male in a local population can be individually identified by his specific song characteristics. Although most males sing with a single song type, some may utter two types, and rarely one may have a three-song repertoire. From seven to nine songs per minute are commonly uttered. An individual male is likely to persist singing his specific song type or types from year to year.

Males generally sing from perches quite close to the ground and often remain close to a nesting female while singing. Nesting begins only a short time after females arrive, so pair-bonding must occur quite rapidly. Females presumably choose the nest site, which is typically located in the branches of a shrub. In Manitoba, snowberry is most commonly chosen as a nest site and is used more often than the plant's relative frequency among the vegetation would predict. This may be a result of the fact that snowberry leaves intercept most of the overhead sunlight, providing good visual protection from above. Nests built early in the breeding season tend to be placed slightly lower than later ones, when grass heights are higher. However, throughout the season nests are usually no more than about ten inches above ground but apparently never actually touch the ground. They may be placed in a grass clump only a few inches above ground, though.

Eggs are laid on a daily basis, and the normal clutch consists of four eggs. Brown-headed cowbirds are frequent exploiters of the clay-colored sparrow, with parasitism rates of as high as about 40 percent of all nests. Multiple parasitism, with as many as four cowbird eggs, has been reported. Rarely do any clay-colored sparrow young survive when they are raised with a cowbird chick.

Incubation requires ten to fourteen days, most frequently eleven to twelve days, with some participation from the male. Similarly, males may brood the hatched chicks when the female is off foraging. Nest departure may occur as early as seven days after hatching, but actual fledging does not occur until the chicks are fourteen to fifteen days old. The chicks remain with their parents for a week or more after fledging but gradually disperse and begin to assemble in grounds around favored foraging sites. Only rarely is a second brood undertaken by females.

Reproductive success data are limited. In a sample of 517 eggs followed by Richard Knapton, 285 hatched (hatching success 55.0 percent) and 221 fledged (rearing success 77.5 percent, overall breeding success

42.7 percent). An average of 1.7 chicks was fledged per nest. No good data on annual survival rates exist, but maximum known longevities are of four and five years.

Grasshopper Sparrow

If the clay-colored sparrow is well-named, then the grasshopper sparrow is even more appropriately labeled; not only does it eat almost nothing but grasshoppers during the breeding season, but also its song can scarcely be distinguished from a grasshopper's buzzlike stridulation. The bird's so-called song is higher-pitched than the similar buzzing of a clay-colored sparrow and does not seem to carry nearly so well for any great distance. Indeed, by the time I reached sixty my ability to hear it at a distance of more than about ten yards evaporated, and without that auditory clue most grasshopper sparrows are likely to go unnoticed.

Grasshopper sparrows are much like clay-colored sparrows as to their winter distribution but extend even farther south. Only in the coastal grasslands of southeastern Texas and Louisiana do they overwinter to any great extent within the United States, although scattered overwintering groups may occur farther north. From Texas the birds extend southward throughout all of Mexico except for the Yucatan Peninsula, with most wintering concentrations in grassy fields and pastures offering only scattered shrubs. Mesquite savannas and grassy pastures with scattered shrubs are the favored habitat. Some very local residential populations are also known to exist in Mexico, and indeed these also occur southwardly in Central America as far as Panama and even on into northern South America, confusing the known wintering and breeding distributions to some degree. There are also largely or entirely residential populations in Florida and the West Indies.

The grasshopper sparrow has one of the most robust bills among the small grassland sparrows (see Figs. 50B and 51), producing a sort of Roman-nosed visual effect as seen from the side. This strong bill allows the bird to crush hard seeds as well as the exoskeletons of hard-bodied insects such as beetles. The seeds eaten include many grass and small weed seeds but also those with seedcoats as large and thick as those of sunflowers. At least during fall, seeds compose about 70 percent of the diet and probably represent even more of the species' food intake during winter. By spring the predominance of the species' foods has shifted

51. Grasshopper sparrow male on dead annual sunflower stalk. Drawing by author.

in favor of insects, mostly grasshoppers, and this situation continues throughout the summer. Caterpillars and beetles are also significant parts of the summer diet.

Grasshopper sparrows begin their northward spring migration through the Great Plains rather late as compared with other sparrows, passing through the central and northern plains in mid- to late April or even into May. Males arrive on their breeding grounds a few days in advance of females. Evidently much of the migration occurs at night; and in contrast to the practice of clay-colored sparrows, for example, flocking by migrants does not occur. Thus, the first sign of birds on the breeding area is likely to be the sounds of their songs.

In the central and northern plains, the breeding habitat consists of grasslands with heights ranging from short-grass to tall-grass prairie but usually those with few shrubs present. In Nebraska, the Sandhills grasslands, with yuccas providing a shrub substitute, are rather densely occupied. In Colorado the short-grass and variously altered mixed-grass prairies of the northeast and southeast have the densest populations, with more than 80 percent of all breeding-season occurrences of the species on grasslands of some type. In the Dakotas and Kansas the midgrass to short-grass prairies are most often used; fenceposts often provide convenient songposts where shrubs are wholly lacking. Generally, lower and sparser grasses (those under ten inches high, and with 2 to 20 percent bare ground present) are favored over taller and denser ones, especially sites with a well-developed litter layer. Relative to other grassland sparrows, the birds are likely to use areas of sparser vegetation than do the Henslow's and Savannah sparrows, but denser than that of the vesper sparrow, and with fewer shrubs present than on sites favored by clay-colored sparrows. Large tracts of grasslands are favored over smaller ones.

Males establish territories that correspond closely with this general habitat description. They are of moderate size for grassland sparrows, averaging in various studies anywhere from about two to three acres. Some very small territories have been found in some mainland areas outside the Great Plains on both coasts and also on some offshore coastal islands.

Territories appear to be rather fluid in size and shape, owing to seasonal changes in the breeding population of males. It is thought that monogamy is the normal mating system, but the birds are still little studied in this regard, and occasional undetected polygyny is possible. Courtship behavior also is still only poorly known, and copulatory behavior remains undescribed.

Females place their nests in well-hidden sites; even in the sparsely vegetated Nebraska Sandhills their nests are notoriously hard to locate, and finding one requires either extreme luck by nearly but not actually stepping on a nest or by dragging a heavy rope over potential nest areas. The nest is built in a matter of a few days and is invariably covered over with a canopy of interwoven grasses, so that it is completely invisible from above. Occasionally overhanging forb or shrub leaves may also serve as a canopy. A side entrance is typical, and the nest is often located at the base of a grass clump. At least in some areas there may be a consistent directional orientation of the nest opening, presumably chosen in relation to relative solar insulation or prevailing wind direction.

Eggs are laid at a daily rate until a usual clutch of four to five are present. In spite of the excellent concealment of their nests, grasshopper sparrows are occasionally parasitized by brown-headed cowbirds. The level of such parasitism is usually less than that of many grassland sparrows, attesting to the crypticity of their nest sites. In two Kansas studies, surprisingly high parasitism rates of 22 and 50 percent have been documented, although in each case the sample size was fairly low. Hatching and fledging rates of grasshopper sparrows are both adversely affected by such brood parasitism.

Incubation is by the female alone and requires eleven to thirteen days. Not only do both adults help feed the chicks, but other unrelated attendants may also participate. These helpers have been identified as adults from nearby territories that have lost their nests or chicks through predation, and as unrelated juveniles. Such assistance from nonrelated birds is tolerated by the parents so long as actual food is being brought by them. The young usually leave the nest at about nine days while still unable to fly, but nevertheless they are agile on their feet.

At least throughout the Great Plains it is believed that two broods are attempted per season. Farther south, as in Florida and the West Indies, additional nesting and brood-raising efforts are likely. Average clutch sizes tend to diminish through the season, perhaps because second clutches usually consist of only three eggs. Perhaps as many as three or four nesting efforts per season may be typical for birds losing early clutches. Estimates of minimal nesting success—measured as producing at least one fledged chick per nest—range from 35 to 52 percent in the central plains. Figures on average numbers of chicks fledged per successful nest are still very limited; one estimate of 0.8 young per successful nest was in an agricultural area with high predation rates and very low overall nest success. One Maine study suggested that about one-quarter of the fifty-three pairs studied managed to fledge one or more young of at least one brood. Apparently, very few pairs manage to fledge two broods in a season, and first-year breeders are even less likely to do so.

Vesper Sparrow

My early memories of vesper sparrows date back to childhood days in North Dakota, where the birds often could be seen flitting about in grasses and shrubs near dusty roadsides, often engaging in their favorite leisure-time activity of taking dust baths. Their white eye rings set them apart from the other dingy brownish sparrows of that area (see Fig. 50), and their uniquely white outer tail feathers flashed when they were flushed from the roadside. I never learned to associate their wonderful postsunset song with the species, this experience occurring long before the days of universal field guide availability. I thus didn't realize what I had been missing until much later in life. In Nebraska the birds appear rather fleetingly, during spring and fall migration, singing only to a limited degree on their way northward, and so again I must live largely in the absence of their vocal beauty. After the classic nature writer John Burroughs heard its wonderfully touching evensong, he discarded the species' old and descriptive but less poetic name, "bay-winged sparrow" and recommended renaming it the vesper sparrow; the name has since stuck.

Vesper sparrows are fairly migratory, rarely overwintering as far north in the central plains as Kansas. They reach their highest Great Plains abundance in the grasslands and savannalike dry woodlands of Texas, with particularly large concentrations in the Big Bend region and in the range country of southeastern Texas. From the Mexican border they extend southward through drier habitats all the way to the Isthmus of Tehuantepec, where they are found in loose flocks in brushy second growth and weedy, overgrazed grasslands. While in Mexico the birds often associate with white-crowned, lark, and Brewer's sparrows.

During the nonbreeding season vesper sparrows are effective seed-eaters; their rather heavy bill and relatively large size enables them to handle fairly large seeds (see Fig. 50). They do consume some waste grain as well as the seeds of many weeds, but analyses of winter foods are still limited. Over a broader time scale, the species' foods include about two-thirds animal materials, including many grasshoppers, plus the usual assortment of other insects common in grassy environments, the rest consisting mostly of weed seeds. The birds can survive in very arid environments and appear to be independent of any need for access to freestanding water.

Migration northward occurs on a broad front through the Great Plains but usually not in large flocks such as are seen in lark buntings and clay-colored sparrows. However, in Colorado flocks have been seen following the retreating snowline and gathering with horned larks along the snowmelt areas of roadsides. Although the hotter parts of the central and southern plains seem suitable for use by such migrants, they are avoided by breeders. These birds seek out the northern plains and, in Colorado, the mid- to higher levels of sagebrush and higher montane grasslands as they become seasonally available.

Vesper sparrows are moderately early spring migrants, passing through the central plains in late March or early April and often arriving in northern plains breeding areas by the end of the latter month. Whereas many grassland-adapted sparrows cannot tolerate agricultural fields as prairie substitutes, the vesper sparrow is quite able to make this transition. It occupies fields of corn, soybeans, grain crops, grassy waterways in row crops, fencerows, meadows, pastures, abandoned fields, ditches, and railroad rights-of-way. If there is any commonality to these diverse habitats it is that most of them are rather dry and sparsely vegetated. Lighter, more sandy soils are also seemingly preferred over heavy, claylike soils. The vegetation is also typically fairly low, with at least some bare ground present, a considerable numbers of forbs, and with only scattered shrubs or low trees. However, in montane areas sage-dominated scrublands, timberline or clear-cut forests, and even alpine areas may be used. Areas having cooler micro- and macroclimates are preferred over warmer ones, and this apparent intolerance to hot weather may account for the birds' absence as breeders in the central and southern plains, where abundant suitable habitat would seem to be available.

Once on breeding areas and when establishing territories, the personalities of these rather elusive and sometimes skulking birds change quickly. They advertise themselves and their territories with conspicuous wing-raising and tail-spreading displays, given as they strut before a female, and occasionally they also perform true song-flights. During such flights the songs the males sing last about three times as long as do perched songs and contain additional vocal elements. Perched songs usually last from about 2.5 to 4.0 seconds, with pitch changes of as much as an octave and with many paired or often-repeated notes (see Fig. 50). Additionally, the species can utter two nonharmonic notes simultaneously, a vocal trick not rare in birds but one that humans cannot emulate. Notes may be slurred or constant, and the pitch of the song components may tend to rise, fall, or otherwise vary. One transliteration is *"Too too tee tee chup-chup-chup-chup-cheat-a-little-eat-a-little chip,"* with some parts such as the *chip* and *chup* notes often omitted or the entire sequence variously altered.

Territories thus proclaimed are fairly large; in Michigan they have been estimated from 1.2 to 1.8 acres, with from eight to twelve territorial birds occupying an uncultivated field of 14.0 acres. In this area, as well as in many other habitats, the birds also use wooded edges, the males singing in higher trees bordering the woods. Other studies in central and eastern states have found estimated breeding densities of three to eighty-six pairs per 100 acres, the lowest densities occurring in agricultural fields and the highest densities in natural grasslands.

Pair-bonding is season-long, which typically means the attempted production of two broods and rarely of three, although the latter achievement is even more rarely successful. Monogamy is assumed to be the prevailing mating system. Occurrences of extrapair copulations are still unverified, but this apparently complete monogamy remains to be fully documented.

Females construct their nests in short, sparse vegetation, a situation reflecting their overall breeding season habitat preference. A positive association between nest location and percent of bare ground, as well as percentage of forbs, has also been reported, although nesting success has been negatively correlated with the amount of bare ground present around the nest. Often early nests are built under the prostrate dead stems of weeds; and especially very early nests may be completely exposed from above, only to be hidden later by the growth of fresh grass. A clod of dirt, a clump of grass, or a dead weed may also serve as a nest site. Recently burned sites, or mowed sites on which the grass has been cut to ten inches or less, are both likely nest locations.

Eggs are laid daily, and the usual clutch is of four eggs. Because of their relatively exposed nests, clutches are often exploited by brown-headed cowbirds. This may be especially true of early-season nests, which not only are more exposed but which also are produced before most other host species are laying. Vesper sparrows nesting in areas where trees are nearby are also at higher risk because of the cowbird's tendency to watch for suitable hosts while perched and hidden in such locations.

Incubation lasts eleven to thirteen days, and nest departure requires another nine to thirteen days on average, before flight is fully attained. For the first month of their lives the chicks are dependent on their parents, but if it is a first brood the female wastes little time in starting a second clutch. In one group of twenty-nine nesting pairs, fifteen pairs raised one brood, thirteen raised two, and one succeeded in raising three. There is a fairly high level of return of adults to the same area in subsequent years. In a Michigan study, eleven of twenty-four banded birds returned the year following banding, and one pair was known to be mated again in the following year. One male returned to the same nesting territories for four consecutive years. However, none of forty-five banded nestlings was seen the following year.

Suggested Readings

Clay-colored sparrow: Best and Rodenhouse 1984; Krueger 1981; Patterson and Best 1996; Perritt and Best 1989; Rodenhouse and Best 1983; Reed 1986; Swanson 1996; Whitmore 1979, 1981.

Grasshopper sparrow: Buech 1982; Dechant et al. 1999c; Fox 1961; Hill 1992; Knapton 1978, 1980, 1994; Messmer 1990; Munson 1992; Pernanen 1994; Salt 1966; Walkinshaw 1939.

Vesper sparrow: Dechant et al. 1999e; Delany and Linda 1998; Johnson and Igl 1995; Knapton 1978, 1980, 1994; Patterson and Best 1996; Smith 1963; Swanson 1996; Wells and Vickery 1994; Vickery 1996; Whitmore 1979, 1981; Wiens and Rotenberry 1979.

13 Songs of the Northern Prairies: *Sprague's Pipit, Bobolink, and Savannah and Baird's Sparrows*

Stretching out in the warm sand of the blowout, I drop into a light, unencumbered sleep, and the unending, liquid song of the Sprague's pipit comes with me. All else is quiet. History accretes upon itself, the sun advances several degrees, and we move farther into the Holocene.

—Don Gayton,
The Wheatgrass Mechanism

I have seen most of the world's great avian spectacles, including the endless streams of brant and eiders migrating along Alaska's Bering Coast, the trogons and humming-birds of the Central and South American cloud forests, the great spring congrega-tions of sandhill cranes and waterfowl in Nebraska's Platte Valley, the assemblages of unique waterfowl on Australia's billabongs, the pink clouds of flamingos above Kenya's Lake Naivasha, and turkey-sized kori bus-tards patiently stalking their insect prey among the countless migrating wildebeests of Tanzania's Serengeti. Yet one simple prairie pleasure has eluded me for more than sixty years. This is the sheer delight of lying down in a Dakota mixed-grass prairie during May, with a Sprague's pipit skylark-ing above and pasque flowers waving their feathery plumes all around me. The Dakota Sioux believed that the pasque flower sang out its beautiful song to all the other flower nations in early spring, ex-horting them to awaken and to join in its celebration of rebirth. Having such antici-pations in store makes long winter nights on the Great Plains worth tolerating.

Sprague's Pipit

Isaac Sprague (1811–1895) was a botanic draftsman who helped illustrate Asa Gray's famous *Textbook of Botany*. Sprague also accompanied J. J. Audubon during a collecting trip up the Missouri River in 1843, while Audubon was preparing his monograph on North American mammals. The pipit now bearing Sprague's name was one of three bird species (the Baird's sparrow and western meadowlark were the others) discovered by Audubon during that trip and later described by him. Audubon also found the first nest to be described for this species, a significant achievement that has only infrequently been repeated since then. The first specimen of this prairie-dependent pipit was collected in what is now west-central North Dakota, where it is relatively common. However, even Arthur C. Bent admitted overlooking it during his visits to that state while he was researching his monumental series of life histories of North American birds.

The Sprague's pipit is, at least for me, one of those near-mythical creatures, its very existence reminding me of a situation similar to that of learning late in life that you grew up only a block away from a person who was to become world famous but whom you never encountered or had then even heard of. Perhaps poor eyesight during my youth prevented me from ever seeing the bird as it sang endlessly while flying nearly beyond the view of even 20:20 vision; I will never know.

For most of the year the life and behavior of the Sprague's pipit is wrapped in mystery. Its frequencies of occurrence on Audubon Christmas counts were too few and sporadic for meaningful analysis by Terry Root. However, it appears to winter mainly around the Big Bend region of Texas and near the coast of east-central and especially extreme southeastern Texas, in regions largely coincident with the southern distribution of bluestem and similar *Andropogon* grasses. From this Texas-Mexico boundary region the species winters southward into central and eastern Mexico, extending south as far as the central volcanic belt and preferentially occupies open grassland habitats.

Nothing is known of its wintertime foods and not much more about its foods in general. A very small sample of analyzed stomachs suggests that the birds mainly eat insects, mostly grasshoppers and crickets, plus some seeds of weedy forbs. The relatively acute bill shape would also suggest a mostly insectivorous diet (Fig. 52). Young are fed only on

52. Male heads of Sprague's pipit (A), Baird's sparrow (B), Savannah sparrow (C), and bobolink (D). Drawing by author.

insects so far as is known, mainly grasshoppers, crickets, and moths. Like other pipits, its hind toe has an unusually lengthened claw (see Fig. 13).

The birds evidently migrate south through the Great Plains in October and November and begin to return in late February and March. By late April and early May they are back on their northern breeding areas. There are only three states where a bird-watcher has more than a remote chance of seeing breeding Sprague's pipits; in descending frequency they are North Dakota, Montana, and South Dakota. Similarly, in Canada three provinces support virtually all that country's breeding Sprague's pipits; again in descending order they are Alberta, Saskatchewan, and Manitoba. The species' breeding range is highly coincident with that of the Baird's sparrow, and the preceding description of relative frequencies of occurrence applies to that species just as well as to the pipit. Both of them are largely confined to northern mixed-grass prairie. Few grassland endemics have such restricted breeding ranges as do these two and thus are in such future danger of population decline and potential extinction, owing to native prairie habitat losses. In studies of native and planted grasslands of southern Saskatchewan, David Duncan and Margaret Skeel found that the Sprague's pipit was the sixth most common species detected among singing males; the Baird's sparrow was fifth. The western meadowlark was most commonly seen or heard, followed in turn by the horned lark, clay-colored sparrow, vesper sparrow, Baird's sparrow, Sprague's pipit, and chestnut-collared longspur. The pipit was less than half as commonly encountered (41 percent) as the meadowlark, and the Baird's sparrow was slightly over half as common (55 percent). Both species were detected in about one-third of the grassland samples. The pipit was most common in native prairie (32 percent frequency) and far less frequent in planted crested wheatgrass stands (13 percent frequency); the Baird's sparrow was slightly more frequently seen in the crested wheatgrass than in native prairie (65 percent versus 53 percent).

Further Saskatchewan studies by Stephen Davis and David Duncan confirmed this vegetational relationship and indicated that Sprague's pipit occurrence, as well as those of clay-colored and Savannah sparrows, shows a positive relationship to the presence of standing vegetation. In contrast, the vegetation height was the most positive correlate of occurrence by Baird's sparrows, as well as for grasshopper and Savannah sparrows. Collectively, comparing the distributions of Sprague's pipits, Baird's sparrows, and chestnut-collared longspurs in Saskatchewan, Davis, Duncan, and Skeel have observed that Sprague's pipits and longspurs are both more abundant in native grasslands and seeded pastures than in haylands or croplands, whereas Baird's sparrows occur as frequently in haylands as in native grasslands and seeded pastures. Thus, the Sprague's pipit is more likely to suffer from prairie conversion than is the Baird's sparrow.

Conversion of native prairies to crested wheatgrass has the effect of increasing the amount of bare ground, decreasing plant species diversity, decreasing litter, and reducing vegetation density near ground level. Both Baird's sparrows and Sprague's pipits respond positively to increasing degrees of sheltered habitats, regardless of specific vegetational makeup, with the Sprague's pipit occurring in higher numbers in habitats having an intermediate degree of plant cover. Similar Saskatchewan studies by Brenda Dale and others have found that Baird's sparrows and Sprague's pipits are most abundant in native grasslands, of intermediate abundance on annually mowed non-native hay, and least common on idled non-native hay. However, idled hay showed higher overall productivity of these species and other grassland sparrows than did mowed fields, presumably because of mowing-induced mortality.

Soon after arrival on their breeding grounds, male Sprague's pipits establish territories. The birds are more common on extensive grasslands than on smaller ones, suggesting area sensitivity, with a probable minimum area requirement of about 470 acres. The birds are also more prone both to brood parasitism and nest depredation on smaller sites than on larger ones. In both North Dakota and Saskatchewan there is evidence of two peaks in breeding activity and aerial display incidence, these occurring during late May and July or even into August in North Dakota, and in late May and early July in Saskatchewan. This dual pattern would suggest that females are likely at least to produce replacement clutches and in some favorable breeding years might be double brooded.

On their return to the breeding areas, males soon establish territories. Mark Robbins reported that territories tend to be concentrated along high ridges or other elevated areas having short grasses and low densities of sedges and forbs. Along one such ridge about 760 yards long, at least three territories were located one year and five in another, suggesting that the males' individual territories averaged about 500 feet in length. Male display rates tended to be highest (about seven per minute) in May, especially during morning hours, but their durations were longest (averaging about twelve to seventeen minutes) in June. The longest continuous display observed by Robbins lasted nearly three hours, with an average of 5.7 songs uttered per minute.

In the typical sequence of display, the male takes off into the wind, until a height of about 60 to 125 yards is reached. It remains within a fairly small area of less than 100 yards in diameter, flying into the wind if one is present, otherwise flying in large circles above the territory. As the song begins, the tail is spread and the wings are extended almost horizontally, and a long glide occurs. Flapping resumes only with the completion of the song, which lasts 2.5 to 3.0 seconds. The song has up to twelve syllables of repeated, jingling, and metallic *tsee* notes, these sometimes being described as resembling a set of tiny sleighbells. These notes are highly modulated in frequency but are centered at about five kilohertz, and their pitch somewhat descends gradually toward the end of the song (Fig. 53, *above*). Between song bouts the bird makes a series of about thirty wingbeats, varying somewhat with wing intensity, and then repeats the song. At the end of such a series, the bird partially closes or lifts its wings, dropping rather rapidly to the ground. It opens its wings just before alighting and flies in a short, undulating path before disappearing in the grass.

The nest site selected by the female is typically at the base of a grass tussock, partly to completely domed over from above. These sites also tend to be in dense, relatively tall grasses, having a low amount of bare ground and a low density of forbs. A favorite cover plant in Saskatchewan is wheatgrass, but there is little evidence for specific plant preference, except perhaps that grasses providing good overhead cover are selected. Such cover not only reduces nest visibility from above but may also help retard heat loss at night. Besides having an overhead canopy, the nest often has a partly or completely covered-over entrance runway, which is often sharply curved and may be as long as six inches. Studies by Glenn Sutter indicated that no directionality of nest-entrance orientation is apparent.

The usual clutch is of four to five eggs, which are incubated for an average of about fourteen days and are brooded for another eight to twelve days. Although the nests are extremely well concealed, they sometimes fall prey to brood parasitism by brown-headed cowbirds. Apparently most of the incubation and brooding is done by the female. However, the male may take charge of the newly fledged chicks, thus

53. Male Sprague's pipit and bobolink flight displays, including pipit song at apex of song-flight (*above*), rapid descent (*right*), and bobolink's flutter-flight (*middle*). Lines indicate typical flight pattern; larger undulations of bobolink flight line indicate deepest flutter-flight wingbeats. Sprague's pipit sonogram after Robbins 1998 (three-second duration). Bobolink song sonogram (four-second duration) after Martin and Gavin (1995). Drawing by author.

freeing the female to begin another nesting cycle. In three instances of proven renestings studied by Sutter and others, the intervals between loss of one nest and the start of a new one were ten to fifteen days, and one female began a new nest twenty-one days after fledging her first brood. This is considerably longer than comparable intervals between first and second nestings reported for the horned lark or Baird's sparrow, suggesting that parental care of fledged pipit young may last longer than is typical in these two grassland species. Seven of fifteen monitored birds succeeded in raising some chicks to fledging age.

Of seventeen pipit nests that were studied by Stephen Davis and Spencer Sealy, three were parasitized by cowbirds and about half were lost to predation. An average of 1.36 pipits was fledged from fourteen unparasitized nests; none was fledged from three parasitized nests. Considering only seven unparasitized and successfully hatched nests, 2.71 pipits were fledged per nest.

Bobolink

Like the dickcissel, the bobolink's common name is based on a rather loose interpretation of the male's song. It approximates the bubbling, often repeated jumble of notes uttered by the territorial male in his song-flight, classically and poetically transliterated as "bob-o'-link, bob-o'-link, spink, spank, spink." Its Latin name translates as "long-clawed rice-eater," which is a pretty accurate description, especially of its foraging ecology during spring and fall migration in the American South. Its fondness for rice has been disastrous for the species. Uncounted thousands of these "ricebirds" were shot yearly on rice plantations from before the turn of the century and until they received federal protection under the Migratory Bird Treaty. This slaughter occurred when great migrating flocks descended in late August on the southern states' rice fields and gorged themselves, in preparation for the long trans-Caribbean flight southward or having just returned from such a flight in spring, exhausted and ravenously hungry. The species' rather long hind claws are useful in clinging to the rice stems, and its strong sparrowlike beak is well adapted for crushing grass and other small, hard seeds (see Fig. 52). Even during the breeding season nearly half the food intake consists of weed or grain seeds or other plant materials, representing a surprisingly high percentage of vegetative foods. However, like those of the other grassland passerines, nestlings are fed exclusively on invertebrates such as insects.

The majority of the fall migrants that eat ripening rice and other grain crops continue their migration from the tip of Florida south to stopover points in Cuba and Jamaica, where they also feed on available seeds and then continue over a direct sea route to northern South America. Some fall migrants fly a more eastward route from Florida, passing through over Puerto Rico and the Lesser Antilles, and a relatively small proportion follows a mainland route though Central America. Their ultimate wintering area is the Pantanal region of northern Argentina, plus adjacent parts of Brazil and Paraguay, where they arrive late in the year. There they also feed on rice, small grain, and similar plant materials and have remained a major pest in rice fields to the present time. Birds from the westernmost parts of the species' range may winter in western South America, and this route probably accounts for the species being commonly seen in the Galapagos Islands, about 600 miles to the west of Ecuador.

The species' remarkably long migration route, up to 10,000 miles each way, involves considerable overwater navigation, well beyond any possible visual landmarks. Recent studies suggest that magnetically based locational clues, which in birds can theoretically provide latitudinal but not longitudinal input, are probably an important aspect of achieving such amazing navigational abilities. However, the anatomical-neurophysiological basis for exhibiting such capabilities for nonlandmark navigation remains a relative mystery. It is believed by some observers that the basis for magnetoreception lies in magnetically active iron-containing cells of the trigeminal and olfactory nerves and that a star-based visual navigation system takes over after the latitudinal "inclination compass" setting has been established. The birds are also sensitive to daylength changes while on their wintering grounds and thus may be limited in their southward winter range to those middle latitudes that do not reach sixteen hours of daylight during the austral midsummer months. Otherwise, they might become reproductively active prior to their spring migration northward and fail to migrate.

On their spring arrival at their breeding grounds, bobolinks seek out hayfields and grassy meadows, typically those having a mixture of grasses and forbs and preferably with moderate to high overall vegetation height, with large amounts of litter present and relatively high grass-to-legume ratios. Larger hayfields are preferred over smaller ones, and older, established fields are similarly preferred over recently seeded ones. When they use pastures or hayfields, vegetation that is not extremely thick or very sparse, or closely grazed or mowed, and that lacks a high shrub density is favored. As with the Henslow's sparrow and Savannah sparrow, an intermediate to high height-density value of vegetation seems to be a preferred habitat feature, although a few studies have shown a negative abundance correlation with this particular environmental attribute.

Male bobolinks are notable for at least two remarkable breeding traits. One is their territorial vocalizations. Males have two basic song types, each of which contains from twenty-five to fifty elements, and each has certain stereotyped components that collectively last about three to four seconds, rarely up to as long as eleven seconds. Both song types may be uttered while perched or in flight, and there seems to be no difference between them relative to either situation. Typically, the two types are uttered in random sequence during a bout of prolonged singing, but in some populations one of the two types seems to be composed of a subset of the components of the other, although their introductory portions may be different. No clear differences in function of the two types have been proven, although some ideas have been advanced, such as that one song type is more related to intrasexual communication and the other more important in intersexual functions. When countersinging in response to a broadcast tape-recording, males tend to try to match the song types being broadcast. They are less likely to respond to nonlocal songs if they have not had any prior exposure to them, but after such an experience they will respond more strongly than to local dialect songs.

Song-flights (Fig. 53, *below*) are performed with the head held low, the tail somewhat depressed, the rump feathers fluffed, and the white shoulder feathers raised. These flights are often nearly circular above the male's territory, and his wings are bent deeply in flight, barely passing the horizontal on the upstroke. Less actively displaying males, as measured by song-flight durations, are likely to father fewer offspring than are the more active ones; and those with artificially shortened wings have shorter display flights and are also less successful in attracting mates than would otherwise be expected.

The second feature of bobolinks that is remarkable is their tendency for polygyny. Bobolinks were one of the first North American birds in which multiple paternity of a female's clutch was proven. Territorial males that control abundant resources such as food or unusually attractive vegetative characteristics may attract and mate with more than one female, most frequently two, but rarely as many as four. Extrapair copulations may also result in a female's laying eggs that were fertilized by more than one male. Most frequently, such copulations occur when older females are paired to younger males.

Pair formation is quite synchronous within local populations, but after his second day of courting one female, a male will begin trying to attract others. Both sexes help defend the nest, using diversionary "broken-wing" or "rodent-run" tactics toward humans or other mammalian predators. Following nest failures, females regularly renest, and at least in some populations a second nesting effort may be undertaken, even following the successful fledging of the first brood.

Nesting success among bobolinks seems to be fairly high. Brood parasitism by brown-headed cowbirds is generally rather low although it may be quite variable by locality or site. It may affect from fewer than 5 percent of the nests to as many as 43 percent, the higher parasitism rates evidently associated with nesting sites located near wooded edges. Initial nesting efforts have higher average fledging success rate than do later renests (56 percent versus 39 percent in one New York study). The estimated average number of young fledged annually have ranged from a maximum of 2.5 young in a New York study to 2.1 in a Wisconsin study. Adverse weather and flooding appear to be the most significant factors affecting breeding success. Second broods appear to add little to overall success, but nest helpers, who help feed dependent chicks, might at times contribute to a female's breeding success. Such helpers perhaps represent an unmated offspring of the previous year or an unrelated male that may have helped sire some of the female's young.

Savannah Sparrow

The common or vernacular name "Savannah" sparrow does not refer to this species' preferred habitat but instead is derived from Savannah, Georgia, where it occurs only in winter and where it was collected by Alexander Wilson. However, the species name *sandwichensis* refers confusingly to a bay on Unalaska Island, in the tundra-covered Aleutians, the sparrow's type locality and part of this species' very large breeding range. Among the sparrows discussed in this book, the Savannah has the broadest breeding range, and because of its substantial geographic variation and capabilities for local specialization it has adapted to a wide array of open-country habitats. These range from Arctic tundra in the north to as far south as the cool upland grasslands in the volcanic belt of central Mexico. They include sedge bogs in boreal forests; tall-grass, shorter mixed-grass, and coastal prairies; hay meadows, pastures, and salt marshes. The Savannah sparrow may thus be considered a "prairie" species as a kind of courtesy appointment; its preference for moist microhabitats and somewhat cool climates suggests that the Great Plains are not its primary environment of choice.

Winter habitats differ but little from summer ones, and in the southernmost parts of its breeding range (southern California and Mexico) the species is sedentary. Seeds make up a larger proportion of its foods during that season, but insects and other invertebrates are consumed as they become available. Animal prey are diverse; unlike most grassland sparrows the birds may feed warblerlike in trees and may even leap up to capture butterflies or other insects in flight. Caterpillars are a favorite food when easily available, as are beetles, grasshoppers, and, in coastal areas, small crustaceans. Some coastal populations with relatively large bills can crush the exoskeletons of small crabs.

The northward spring migration of Savannah sparrows begins early, the birds typically arriving on their Great Plains breeding areas during late March and April. This migration, as well as the fall one, occurs mainly at night. However, the birds appear to use three different navigational aids, including two celestial sources (solar and stellar) and also magnetic orientational capabilities. Evidently, the setting sun provides important directional input during both spring and fall; this daily reinforcement of directional information is then applied to the birds' presumably innate abilities to use the stars as a visual nighttime compass mechanism. These visual clues in turn may help to "set" the internal "magnetic compass" that is evidently present in this well-studied species, as it is also believed to be in the bobolink. Older birds that have previously migrated exhibit better orientational abilities than younger ones, suggesting that experience and learning also play an important navigational role.

Shortly after their arrival on the breeding grounds, males, which migrate about a week in advance of females, establish territories and begin singing. Territories are highly variable both geographically and ecologically, ranging in size from as little as 0.12 acre (in New Brunswick) to 3.1 acres (in sparse Nova Scotia habitats). Territorial boundaries are dynamic, and territories tend to increase in size during the breeding season, especially if a second mate can be attracted. Large territories are more likely to attract additional females, but song rate and territory size are not positively correlated. In both sexes, more than 90 percent of surviving adults return to within about fifty yards of their previous year's territory. Inexperienced first-year males are unable to establish territories easily, unless they can find a similarly young female and can also locate an area that is not occupied by an already established pair.

The advertising songs of territorial male Savannah sparrows remind one of those of song sparrows, consisting of several spaced introductory notes that are brief and high-pitched, followed by a more complex and melodious phrase, the entire sequence lasting up to four seconds. Within the same population, different males sing variations of the same basic song. Flight-songs are not used, but males do perform flutter-flights, with their legs dangling and the tail cocked diagonally upward, and with fluttering wingbeats, serving to circumscribe their territorial boundaries and threaten other intruding males.

Territories and nest sites are generally characterized by predominantly grassy cover, with nearly no shrubs, 10 to 20 percent forbs, up to 60 percent litter cover, and a mean canopy height of about twenty to forty-five inches. Very tall, dense vegetation may be avoided, but low, dense vegetation may be a preferred combination. Areas with high densities of forbs and shrubs seem to experience lower nesting success, although shrubs and small trees often are present within the territory and may be used as singing posts. Unburned and ungrazed grasslands, with higher litter densities, are preferred for nesting, although foraging may be preferentially done in more open areas. Nesting may increase for two or more years following fire, and in some areas recently burned grasslands seem to be preferred. Sites of smaller than about 25.0 acres are used less than larger ones, and the birds are unlikely to use any sites of less than 2.5 acres for nesting.

In many populations, polygyny seems to be fairly common, although both geographic and temporal variation in its incidence seems to be the rule. In some areas, such as the Maritime Provinces, polygyny seems fairly frequent among males (at times involving up to almost 50 percent of them), but at the northern edge of the species' range monogamy may be more efficient, perhaps owing to the shortness of the available breeding season. Polygyny may occur as a result of a late-arriving yearling female, or a female whose mate has prematurely disappeared, associating herself with an already paired male; or perhaps a female may undertake a second laying cycle after fledging her young and similarly attaching herself to a nearby already paired male. There seems to be no difference in gonad volume, bodily size, or age in monogamous versus polygynous males, and a male may vary as to his mating situation in different years.

Nesting success of course varies greatly but averages higher when mammalian predators are lacking, as on some small coastal islands. Clutch sizes tend to decline in late-nesting birds and are smaller in first-year breeders than in older age groups. Brood parasitism by brown-headed cowbirds seems to be generally low, but most of the available data come from areas where the cowbird is fairly rare. Polygynous males succeed in rearing more offspring than do monogamous ones, but the opposite applies to females mated monogamously versus nonmonogamous males. Although survival to fledging seems to be quite high, anywhere from about 2 to 14 percent of the eggs produced will be represented the following year by yearling birds. Annual adult mortality thereafter is also apparently highly variable, ranging geographically or annually from about 35 to 75 percent and not differing significantly between the sexes.

Although coastal breeding populations tend to exhibit strong natal philopatry among yearling individuals, this is less apparent among young birds reared in the continental interior. However, adult birds from all regions tend to return faithfully to the same wintering areas, and they are very likely to return subsequently to virtually the same territory that they occupied in previous years.

Baird's Sparrow

Spencer F. Baird (1823–1887) was long affiliated with the Smithsonian Institution, initially serving as an assistant secretary (1850–1878), and later (1878–1887) as the institution's secretary. During this overall thirty-seven-year period many important ornithological explorations of the American West were undertaken, and several bird species were discovered. The Baird's sandpiper and Baird's sparrow were both thus discovered and named in his honor, the sandpiper being named in 1861 by Elliott Coues, America's greatest ornithologist. The Baird's sparrow was discovered in 1843 by J. J. Audubon in western North Dakota during his final field expedition up the Missouri Valley, when the Sprague's pipit was also discovered.

The Baird's sparrow is one of the few dozen or so bird species that many North American bird-watchers would consider giving up their eyeteeth to see. It is not as large as an upland sandpiper, as colorful as a longspur or lark bunting, or as highly melodic as the vesper sparrow or western meadowlark. Its overall coloring and head pattern likewise are fairly forgettable (see Fig. 52). Like Mt. Everest, it simply is there, and so for avid birders it must be seen. "There" is the northern midgrass prairies of western and central North Dakota, eastern Montana, and the southern parts of Alberta and Saskatchewan. This is a relatively small breeding range and one that is getting smaller each year. I didn't realize how lucky I was to see the Baird's sparrow as a child; at that time it still bred locally in the Red River Valley but from which it is now virtually gone. It took a while for me to identify it, as it wasn't even shown or described in my few relatively primitive references on birds. I finally found an illustration of it in T. S. Roberts's classic *Birds of Minnesota*, which our small city library had on its permanent reserve shelf and which was my ultimate basis for judging both truth and beauty.

Not only do Baird's sparrows have a limited breeding range, but their wintering range is also rather small. Within the United States it winters mainly just along the Mexican border, from Arizona east to Texas, but only in very low numbers. Most wintering occurs in northern Mexico, mainly in Chihuahua, western Coahila, and northeastern Durango, where it mostly occurs in native grasslands and generally remains inconspicuous and out of sight unless it is flushed.

Foods of the Baird's sparrow in winter remain unstudied but are believed to consist of weed seeds. During the breeding season small insects are eaten, with grasshoppers making up the bulk of foods fed nestlings and spiders of secondary importance. Evidently dew provides an adequate source of water where standing water is not easily available.

Spring migration is apparently done at night, the birds moving either individually or perhaps in small flocks but remaining unobtrusive and generally very difficult to locate. However, they arrive in North Dakota by early May and at the northernmost parts of their Canadian breeding range by mid-June. Nowhere are the birds extremely abundant, but they are most often found in large, ungrazed, or only lightly grazed midgrass prairies, with water nearby in the form of streams or ponds. This preference for proximity to water may simply reflect association with denser and taller grass cover rather than specific moisture needs. Woody vegetation has a negative effect, although shrubs or similar tall perches may serve as singing posts. Other than native grasslands, the birds less preferentially use hayfields, seeded pastures, retired croplands, weedy fields, some grainfields, and dried wetland basins. Grasslands more than eight to ten inches high, but no more than three feet high, seem to constitute the range of acceptable heights, and there should also be a dense ground litter of residual vegetation, both for escape purposes and nest cover. It is possible that extremely dense ground cover might inhibit movement and visibility, however. Perhaps related to this is Maiken Winter's finding that in mixed-grass North Dakota prairies, higher densities occurred on areas periodically burned in the past, where litter thickness was less than in unburned prairies, and more bare soil was present.

In favored breeding habitat the density of Baird's sparrows may reach about eleven to twenty-two pairs per 100 acres, rarely up to thirty pairs, and in grazed sites as low as five pairs. Territories under dense breeding conditions are thought to average from 0.36 acre to 0.58 acre but under less crowded conditions average about 3.5 acres. There is some indication that males tend to place their territories close to one another, which could affect estimated densities in very local areas. It has been suggested that minimum area requirements for maintaining a breeding population of the species may be about 155 acres.

Male Baird's sparrows advertise their territories by singing, especially during early morning hours and when other males are also singing. The song is rather more elaborate than that of some relatives such as the grasshopper sparrow or Henslow's sparrow. It usually consists of three or four preliminary notes, followed by a longer, lower-pitched and pulsing trill, although not loud. Under good conditions it carries much farther than that of the grasshopper sparrow and may be uttered up to about eight times per minute. Rainfall inhibits song activity, but during some summers singing persists throughout the entire breeding season, probably reflecting renesting or second-clutch initiation.

Studies by Michael Green indicate that there is no apparent geographic variation in male song across the species' range, but each male will sing any one of the twelve song types that characterize the species. Green's work suggested that this species can recognize partial song playbacks and those that are broadcast with substantial fluctuations in relative amplitude, abilities he thought to be acoustically related to its grassland environment. He also suggested that the absence of geographic song variation in this species is related to the species' somewhat nomadic lifestyle.

Mating is believed to be monogamous, with laying on the Canadian breeding grounds usually not occurring until June. Nests are built on the ground, most often being placed in a depression below a tuft of narrow-leaved grass, often in a deep depression without overhead cover. In some areas nests have been found placed at the base of small shrubs, but this would not appear to be typical. The eggs are laid on a daily basis until a full clutch is completed, most often of five eggs. Late-season clutches tend to be smaller, presumably either as a result of the stresses of renesting or double brooding.

Because so few Baird's sparrow nests have ever been studied, the incidence of brown-headed cowbird parasitism is still little known. However, the studies of Stephen Davis and Spencer Sealy in Manitoba suggest that such parasitism may be quite common, with 36 percent of the seventy-four nests they studied so affected. They also reported a 32 percent parasitism rate for sixty-one Saskatchewan nests, with additional available records of an 11 percent parasitism rate for twenty-seven other Canadian nests. In their study, the presence of one or more cowbird eggs reduced average sparrow clutch size by 1.4 eggs, reduced hatching success by 0.8 chicks, and reduced overall productivity by 1.1 fledged chick per successful nest. Additionally, the birds hatched 21 percent of the cowbird eggs in their nests, a very high success rate for cowbirds. Nest predation rates were also judged to be high by Davis and Sealy (39 to 47 percent), with mammals, birds, and snakes potential sources of predation.

> *It was not prairie dwellers who invented the indifferent universe—puny you may feel and vulnerable, but not unnoticed. This is a land to mark the sparrow's fall.*
>
> —Wallace Stegner,
> *Wolf Willow*

Incubation requires eleven to twelve days, and nest departure occurs eight to eleven days later. Overall nest success was judged to be 37 percent by Davis and Sealy. One certain case of a second nesting attempt was documented, and double brooding has also been suspected but not proven in earlier studies. Because of their seminomadic tendencies, there is little indication that birds show any site fidelity, and there is no real information on mortality rates, mean longevity, or other demographic parameters.

Suggested Readings

Sprague's pipit: Bridges and Leatherman 1991; Davis et al. 1996, 1999; Dechant et al. 1999m; Harris 1933; McConnell et al. 1993; Robbins 1998, in press; Roberts 1932; Stewart 1975; Sutter 1996, 1997; Sutter et al. 1995, 1996.

Bobolink: Bakker et al. 1983; Bollinger 1998; Bollinger et al. 1990; Bollinger and Gavin 1991; Martin 1967, 1971; Martin and Gavin 1995; Martin and Robertson 1992; Trainor and Peltz 1996; Wittenberger 1976.

Savannah sparrow: Dechant et al. 1999j; Dixon 1978; Potter 1972; Powell and Collier 1998; Rogers 1998; Swanson 1996; Watts 1996; Wheelwright and Rising 1993; Whitmore 1979.

Baird's sparrow: Cartright et al. 1937; Davis and Sealy 1998; Davis et al. 1996, 1999; Dechant et al. 1999l; Green 1992; Jones et al. 1998; Mahon 1995; Sousa and McDonal 1983; Stewart 1975; Sutter et al. 1995, 1996; Winter 1994.

14 The Peripheral Seed-eaters: *Dickcissel; Henslow's, Cassin's, and Brewer's Sparrows*

The birds I heard today . . . sang as freshly as if it had been the first morning of creation.

—Henry David Thoreau

It is perhaps not without significance that we tend to think of sparrows and grass in much the same way; not only are sparrow-like birds adapted to eating grass seeds and similar small, hard seeds, but they sometimes also seem to be the only birds commonly seen in grassland. Further, they seem to reproduce almost as rapidly as grass grows and have much the same color as does dead grass during fall or winter. But grass seeds are relatively tiny food items, they are often unavailable during the breeding season, and they don't provide the high protein food sources that insects offer. In forests and woodlands, tree seeds (including nuts) tend to be larger, and at least those produced by conifers are often persistently retained on trees and thus are relatively available throughout the year. However, their efficient harvest may require special beak structures, such as crossed bills, or very heavy, crushing beaks. Thus, sparrowlike crossbills and grosbeaks are the coniferous forest counterparts of the grassland sparrows.

Some twenty years ago, John Weins and M. I. Dyer made an interesting analysis of grassland versus coniferous forest bird communities of western North America. Among six grassland communities (one

218

tall-grass, two sites each of mixed-grass and short-grass, and one shrub-steppe community), the number of breeding bird species ranged from three to five, averaging 3.5 By comparison, six montane coniferous forest communities had from seven to fifteen bird species present, averaging 11.8. Overall breeding densities of birds in the grasslands ranged from 399 to 888 individuals per square mile (unweighted average 593); in the coniferous forests the range was from 3,183 to 7,477 individuals per square mile (unweighted average 5,094).

The grassland bird community also obtained from 4 to 24 percent of its total energy intake from seed foods (unweighted average 14.3 percent); in the coniferous community the corresponding range was 16 to 43 percent (unweighted average 21 percent). Finally, the grassland birds consumed an unweighted average of 107 pounds of grass and forb seeds per square mile (41.5 kilograms per square kilometer) in a single season, but the coniferous forest community birds consumed a corresponding average of 2,679 pounds of seeds per square mile (470 kilograms per square kilometer), mainly those of conifers. Thus, the coniferous forest community had roughly three times greater breeding species diversity, had an overall avian population density nearly nine times greater, placed a greater reliance on seeds as a food source, and had a ten times greater overall seed consumption rate! It would be interesting to make a similar comparison of grassland and hardwood forest bird communities, where the food resources are considerably more diverse and probably are less continuously accessible.

Dickcissel

When I was a child in southeastern North Dakota, I never encountered the dickcissel and am convinced it then didn't occur around the vicinity of the little village where I spent my childhood. In fact, I didn't encounter the species until I moved to southeastern Nebraska twenty years later, when I was surprised to discover how abundant it was in habitats not very different from those of eastern North Dakota. I was even more surprised upon more recently visiting the small country cemetery near my hometown where my grandparents are buried and hearing dickcissels singing loudly all around me. They must have become much more common in that part of North Dakota during the three or four decades I had been away. It is known that the dickcissel sometimes undergoes major changes in local abundance from year to year; and during the

54. Male heads of Henslow's sparrow (*left*) and dickcissel (*right*). Upper sonograms (durations 1.5 seconds) after Robbins, Bruun, and Zim (1983). The lower expanded-time sonogram of the Henslow's sparrow is after Borror and Reese 1954 (duration 0.3 second). Drawing by author.

same period in the 1940s that I might well have encountered it as a child, the species was likewise known to be rare or absent from the vicinity of Des Lacs National Wildlife Refuge in north-central North Dakota. This same sort of dramatic fluctuation of dickcissel populations is especially widespread near the edge of the species' range in the eastern United States, which the dickcissel has gradually colonized during the past two centuries.

The dickcissel (Fig. 54, *right*) was so-named on the basis of its primary song, which among its many regional variations can sometimes be transliterated as *dick, dick; ciss, ciss, ciss,* the preliminary note or notes rather weak, and the following ones loud and downslurred, much like the distress call made by various quails when they are held in the hand. At least this is a fairly good interpretation of its song in eastern Nebraska. In the western parts of the state its song differs substantially, especially in the usual numbers of each of its two major elements. Thus, each year when I first encounter it there I must confirm its identity visually and relearn its local song.

The dickcissel has the longest migration of any of the sparrowlike birds of the Great Plains, largely wintering in the grasslands and grainfields of the Venezuelan llanos. Not only must the birds undertake this arduous migration twice a year, but they also are subjected to constant harassment by agricultural interests in the rice- and sorghum-growing areas of Venezuela, where they spend nearly eight months of each year. Uncounted numbers are purposely exposed to aerial-sprayed pesticides during this period, causing unknown rates of mortality and morbidity. No doubt their winter foods must also include weed seeds and wild grasses, but little specific information is available. However, their summer foods are well studied and include a majority of animal materials, and about one-third of the materials are of plant origin. Most of the latter are weed seeds, but grains such as millet are also favored. Among insects, grasshoppers, and to a lesser extent crickets, are strongly represented in their diets. Early studies suggest that a pair and their four young are likely to consume about 200 grasshoppers daily. Since each grasshopper consumes about 150 percent of its body weight in leafy materials daily, the amount of grain crop tonnage protected by dickcissels on a statewide basis is somewhat astronomical.

Dickcissels are late arrivals on the nesting areas in the central Great Plains, presumably because of their long migration route. I have never seen them during my spring ornithology classes, which terminate in early May, and the birds are more likely to arrive during the third or even final week of May. Then quite suddenly, males seem to be everywhere, and it is not unusual to see five to ten males quite uniformly spaced and perching conspicuously on fences and telephone wires in the course of a country mile.

Dickcissels seem to be extremely tolerant of habitat variations and are probably more common in altered habitats than in native grasslands. They use weedy fields, clover or alfalfa hayfields, idle grasslands and Conservation Reserve Program lands, pastures, disturbed or restored prairies, meadows, weedy rights-of-way or ditches, grain crops, and almost every other vegetational combination that is mostly herbaceous. They seem to prefer rather tall and dense herbaceous cover, without many shrubs or trees but with some available songposts in the form of utility wires, scattered trees or shrubs, or other elevated sites. Litter depth tends to be high in areas preferred by dickcissels and the incidence of bare ground comparably low. The presence of some tall forbs, either for use as nest cover or song perches, may be a significant factor in habitat choice. Generally, increased vegetation density, vegetation height, increased litter, increased grass cover, and increased forb abundance favor dickcissel use, but increased tree or sapling density and size have adverse influences.

Not only are males somewhat larger in body mass than females, but males also vary somewhat in mass themselves and strongly compete intrasexually for favorable territories. Males defending territories in native prairie are less attractive to females than those in various old fields or similar variously disturbed habitats. Females arrive on the breeding grounds about a week later than males and seem to make match choices based on territory quality as well as on male behaviors, judging from observations by Elmer Finck in Kansas. However, females do not choose males on the basis of their body mass but evaluate habitat quality, especially the overall volume of vegetation, as the primary cue for their choice. Secondarily, they seem to rely on behavioral traits, perhaps song frequency or similar indicators of individual male fitness, for making mate choices. Females do not show a significant degree of site tenacity or fidelity to prior year's mates, so males must compete anew each spring for their mates. Thus some males are successful in obtaining two females as mates while others can attract none. Although females show no apparent site fidelity, males do, and about half are likely to return to their same territory the following year.

Males sing almost continuously through the summer months, but those that are unable to attract females are prone to abandon their territories after a time and perhaps establish territories at another, possibly better, location. Thus territories tend to shift considerably through the course of a breeding season, as males jockey about for position. Territory quality in terms of foods present may be especially important for dickcissels, as the female undertakes perhaps all the food-gathering for rearing her brood and often strays well outside her mate's territorial limits in food searches.

Territories in Kansas seem to be quite small, from 1.1 to 1.4 acres in native prairies to as little as 0.3 acre in old-field habitats. Similarly, in Illinois, old-field territories typically range from 0.9 to 1.3 acres and in Oklahoma prairies from 0.6 to 1.2 acres. Some higher estimates (3.5 to 3.7 acres) of territory sizes in Iowa and Oklahoma prairies and tall pastures have been made. Dickcissels can breed on some fairly small habitat fragments, with estimates of about twenty-five acres being a typical minimum estimate. However, both breeding density and average productivity are higher in larger habitat units. Brood parasitism rates also at times tend to increase with increasing breeding densities, but not uniformly so. Increased habitat shrubbiness, increased proximity to trees, and decreased habitat fragment size are factors most likely to increase brood parasitism rates in this and other grassland species.

Female dickcissels place their nests either on the ground or near it, perhaps more often under forbs than in grasses, but at times also in the crotches of shrubs. Later nests are more likely to be in forbs than earlier ones, and most but not all studies have correlated nesting densities with forb abundance, seemingly because insects are more abundant in forb vegetation than among grasses. Additionally, forbs might provide better overhead camouflage than do grasses and better shading from midday sun. In an Illinois study by Alfred Gross and published in Bent's life histories, seventy-eight nest sites were tallied. Clover and alfalfa meadows provide the most common cover (thirty-six nests), and grassy meadows were next most common (seventeen nests). Shrubs or small trees supported ten nests, and miscellaneous, mostly weedy sites accounted for the rest.

Four eggs constitute the usual clutch, laid one per day. Incubation requires eleven to thirteen days and fledging another eleven to twelve, although the young often leave their nest prematurely, at about one week. Dickcissels fall prey to parasitism by the brown-headed cowbird at a sometimes appalling rate. Parasitism rates of as low as only 2.8 percent have been reported for 143 nests in Texas but as high as 94.7 percent for nineteen Kansas nests. Rates seem to be particularly high in areas of high cowbird density such as Kansas and Nebraska, often affecting about half the initiated dickcissel nests. The rather late breeding of the dickcissel may make it a frequent target, as well as its tendency to nest in places where convenient perching places for female cowbirds are present. John Zimmerman estimated that in Kansas, parasitism reduces dickcissel productivity by about 30 percent, with an average loss of two eggs per nest in May and declining to one in July, when cowbird egg-laying is on the decline. Together with predation, especially by snakes, the incidence of Kansas dickcissel nests that are successfully hatched is only about 15 percent. Because of a long posthatching dependency period for the young, females are evidently not double brooded, although renesting following clutch or brood loss is likely. Kenneth Steigman's work in Texas indicated that over a four-year period pairs produced an average of one fledgling per nest each season, and 24.3 percent of 624 total eggs produced young that were reared to fledging. Nearly all predation losses there were caused by snakes, and brood parasitism was very low.

Henslow's Sparrow

The Reverend John S. Henslow (1818–1861) was an English cleric who, as a geologist and botanist at Cambridge University, unknowingly helped alter the history of biological science by first befriending a young student named Charles Darwin and later recommending him for the post of naturalist on the globe-circling voyage of the British exploratory ship HMS *Beagle*. In 1860, less than a year before his death and while serving as president of the British Association of Science, Henslow also chaired the famous debate in Cambridge on Darwin's evolutionary (and revolutionary) theory of natural selection, a theory that Henslow never himself accepted. It was one of the most famous debates in the history of science, and it also made famous its two primary participants, Bishop Samuel (Soapy Sam) Wilberforce and Darwin's friend and longtime champion, Thomas H. Huxley, later to become widely known as Darwin's Bulldog.

The Henslow's sparrow was first discovered in Kentucky by John J. Audubon and somewhat surprisingly was named for this relatively obscure English cleric/professor who never visited America. Audubon had met Henslow during his travels in England, while obtaining subscriptions to his then still-forthcoming illustrated monograph on North American birds, and propitiously named the sparrow for a man whose influence on science would be far greater than either person would probably have ever imagined at the time.

Henslow's sparrow is one of those maddeningly difficult species to locate, even for those with perfect hearing. I have yet to hear a Henslow's sparrow in the field and, without that ability, the chances of ever seeing one on my own are virtually nil. I have searched likely looking fields to no avail, even those where I had been assured that

Henslow's sparrows are present. When I first came to southeastern Nebraska nearly four decades ago, Henslow's sparrows were considered state rarities, limited to the extreme southeast, but since the inception of the CRP they have become locally common and have spread considerably westward along the Platte River. Similar expansions have occurred in other states.

The winter distribution of the Henslow's sparrow is almost as baffling as its summer range. Christmas count data show a spread of records from Texas to Florida, with apparent larger numbers along the east coast of Texas, especially around Galveston Bay, along the panhandle of Florida, and around Cocoa Beach, Florida. Other winter records extend from Florida north to South Carolina. But even these relatively "dense" concentrations are extremely low. There seem to be no Mexican records, making the overall winter distribution very uncertain. In Florida the birds favor grassy areas in longleaf pine woods, as in clearings and in relatively wet, boggy sites. Wintertime foods are unstudied in detail, but from spring to fall the birds subsist mostly on animal materials (over 80 percent by volume), with grasses and weed seeds constituting the plant fraction. Grasshoppers, crickets, katydids, beetles, and various other insects make up most of the animal component.

Spring migration in this species is fairly late, the birds arriving in central and northern states during the latter part of April and early May. There are very few records of migrant birds, and only one description of a "mass migrating flight" that actually consisted of several other sparrow species in addition to the Henslow's sparrow.

The densest breeding concentrations of Henslow's sparrows in the eastern and more heavily wooded states seem to occur in Michigan and Ohio; in the central plains states probably the greatest numbers of breeding birds occur in northeastern Oklahoma, eastern Kansas, and western Missouri. Characteristics of good breeding habitat consist of grasslands with well-developed litter, a considerable amount of residual dead vegetation, and a high percentage of grass cover but with scattered forbs present that serve as songposts. Native warm-season grasses with later growth traits may sometimes be preferred over introduced cool-season species, but the evidence on this is weak. Woody vegetation may be tolerated or even selected at low levels, but again differing studies have come to opposite conclusions as to the positive or negative effects of woody plants on the distribution and abundance of breeding Henslow's sparrows.

Very soon after their spring arrival, males become territorial and begin singing. Site fidelity is present in males; in Maryland C. S. Skipper found that five males, from a total of eighty-seven banded Henslow's sparrows, returned to breed within 165 yards of where they had been captured the previous year, indicating at least some site fidelity exists. None of the banded juveniles was found to return to its natal site. Individual male territories are generally very small, typically ranging from 0.4 to 2.5 acres, but minimum habitat size may nevertheless be an important influence on breeding density. Densities tend to increase with increasing habitat size, and minimum habitat area may be about seventy-five acres to maintain. However, one Michigan field of forty acres held a population of thirty to forty males one year, and another Michigan field of 160 acres supported forty to sixty birds, according to Sydney Hyde. Perhaps the greatest breeding density ever reported was ten pairs occupying a half-acre planting of hazel and blackberry in Iowa. Possibly one method of reducing intersexual competition for food in such small territories is for the male to forage farther from the nest and at different distances from the nest, as Jerome Robins has suggested to be the case.

According to most observers, the song of a male Henslow's sparrow is seemingly a two-noted *"flee-sic"* or *"tsi-lick,"* which lasts only about 0.3 second, the elements of which are scarcely separable even on a normal-speed sonogram (Fig. 54, upper sonogram, *left*). However, sonographic analysis by Donald Borrer and Carl Reese has shown the vocalization to be much more complex than this, with six rather than two separate acoustic elements. The first generally audible syllable is actually the fourth and lowest note, and the second syllable is composed of the fifth and sixth elements, which descend slightly in pitch. This complexity is noticeable only in a markedly slowed-down version of the song (Fig. 54, lower sonogram, *left*), in which the generally descending frequencies of each of the two major song components become apparent. The song's overall range in pitch is from about ten to five kilohertz. Intervals between successive songs are very short, usually only one to five seconds.

Henslow's sparrows are presumably monogamous, although one case of an extrapair copulation was reported by Sydney Hyde, involving a female mating with a male from a nearby territory. Courtship is poorly described, but in part reportedly consists of the male carrying about a billfull of grass and either presenting it to the female with fluttering wings or taking the female on a tour of his territory, apparently pointing out suitable nesting sites.

The nest is built mainly if not entirely by the female, but with the male close at hand and sometimes carrying blades of grass about as if helping. Typically the nest is placed close to the ground, amid tall and dense vegetation and often within clumps of dead litter, although the birds have been known to nest in fields that were burned earlier that same spring. Typically the nest is loosely placed among stems of grass or surrounding dead vegetation, with no effort to weave the materials into the site. The nest is apparently never placed in or immediately adjacent to woody vegetation. Four or five days are needed to complete a nest and, if it is destroyed, a new site can be chosen and a second nest built in no more than six days.

The clutch is typically of four eggs, which are laid daily by the female, while the male perches and sings nearby. In Missouri, Maiken Winter found that clutch sizes of the Henslow's sparrow tend to decline during the season, but there are two peaks of nest initiation, one in mid-May and the second in mid-June. This second nesting peak may have resulted from renesting efforts or second broods, late initiation of nests by some females, or may simply be a result of small sample size. During the three summers of Winter's study, nesting success remained about the same and averaged higher (40 percent) for Henslow's sparrows than for dickcissels. Incubation requires eleven days, and the chicks leave the nest nine to ten days after hatching. The brooding of the young and most of the feeding is done by the female.

The nests are very well hidden, and brood parasitism by brown-headed cowbirds seems to be fairly infrequent. In northeastern Oklahoma, two of twenty-four Henslow's sparrow nests (8 percent) were found to be parasitized. In a Missouri study, Winter found the rate of cowbird parasitism to be fairly low (5.3 percent of fifty-nine nests) and substantially less than the rate (8.8 percent) she observed for dickcissels nesting in the same area or than the overall parasitism rate of 8.1 percent for all grassland birds nesting in her study area. In both Henslow's sparrows and dickcissels, brood parasitism had the effect of reducing the host clutch, lowering the number of nestlings, and reducing nesting success rates.

Cassin's Sparrow

John Cassin (1813–1869) was a naturalist and a world traveler who for twenty-six years was associated with the Philadelphia Academy of

Natural Sciences, eventually becoming a curator of that institution's bird collection. Among his publications was *Illustrations of the Birds of California, Texas, Oregon, British and Russian America,* published in 1856. During his long career he described nearly 200 species of birds, perhaps an all-time record for an American ornithologist. The Cassin's sparrow was discovered in southern Texas and was first described in 1852 by Dr. S. W. Woodhouse. The Cassin's auklet, Cassin's finch, Cassin's kingbird, and Cassin's vireo were also named in his honor, and *Cassinia,* a Delaware Valley ornithological journal, was likewise named for him.

I have never seen a Cassin's sparrow in Nebraska, but not for lack of wanting or trying. One summer a small group of singing males appeared in a sage-covered area of highlands near our biological field station and was well studied by station biologists. Unfortunately, by then I had already returned to Lincoln for the summer. I was nevertheless certain they would return the following year, so I waited impatiently until then. By the next spring some roadwork had been done in that area, and part of the sagebrush habitat that they had utilized had been badly torn up. There was no trace of Cassin's sparrows. But they are noted for their eruptive tendency to appear one year at the northern edge of their range, then only to disappear again after breeding once or twice. This one-time occurrence thus may have been a reflection of the Cassin's predictable unpredictability and not an instance of road-grader rage.

The Cassin's sparrow is a species more of the southwestern desert grasslands and mesquite woodlands than of the prairie grasslands. The heart of its breeding range lies in the Staked Plains region of western Texas and eastern New Mexico, a habitat so arid and featureless that according to local lore early explorers were forced to erect stakes as trail guidemarks to avoid getting lost. It also commonly breeds northward in the rain shadow region of eastern Colorado and western Kansas. Occasionally it also extends into the southwestern region of Nebraska and recently also has bred in the adjacent southeastern region of Wyoming.

The winter distribution of this species is less well known, as it is mostly concentrated in Mexico. Within the United States it seems to be generally confined to an area extending from southeastern Arizona eastward along the U.S.–Mexican border to the mouth of the Rio Grande, with a probable concentration in the Big Bend region. In northern and north-central Mexico it is a year-round resident south almost to the central volcanic belt, although few actual breeding records exist for Mexico. Along with several other equally dull-colored and elusive .

55. Male heads of Cassin's sparrow (*left*) and Brewer's sparrow (*right*). Duration of Cassin's sparrow song sonogram (*above*, after Borror 1971) 2.5 seconds, of Brewer's sparrow (after Robbins, Bruun, and Zim 1983) 7.0 seconds. Drawing by author.

Aimophila sparrows, it occurs there in arid to semiarid brush and in grasslands with scattered brush, yuccas, or low trees, where it and its near relatives are notable for their lack of obvious colorful fieldmarks (Fig. 55). Tall grasses, where the birds can easily hide, seem to be preferred over short and scattered plants, at least during winter. It may also move into weedy fields during the nonbreeding season. Apparently the birds do not need a source of standing water and only rarely drink even when it is available. During the winter they survive on small seeds of grasses and weeds but switch to insects as soon as they become available in spring.

These birds are so secretive for most of the year that little is known of their migration timing in most areas. However, in southeastern Arizona, where breeding has only rather recently been documented, the birds often appear conspicuously in mid-July, apparently having moved westward from breeding grounds in the southern Great Plains. At this time the birds are still in breeding condition, and the males are in full song. Pairs may even begin to build nests but apparently in most cases go no farther than that with their autumnal breeding activity. This is rather remarkable behavior for any species, since it would suggest that the birds left their breeding grounds prematurely. It may also result from the birds having encountered breeding conditions that were too dry to begin a second brood, stimulating an early fall migration. The sparrows continue to arrive in September and October and remain in Arizona through the winter. They depart again in March or April and are gone from most of the state by the first of May. However, local breeding has been documented in Arizona in recent years.

In eastern Colorado, the birds arrive as early as mid-April but remain inconspicuous until male territorial singing begins during the second half of May. At that time their behavior is suddenly transformed; instead of being nearly invisible, they are suddenly to be seen and heard everywhere, at least in their preferred short-grass plains habitat. In the *Colorado Breeding Bird Atlas* study, short-grass prairie habitats accounted for half of all breeding season observations, and sandsage shrubsteppe accounted for another 25 percent. Although the birds apparently don't require water for drinking, wet springs stimulate plant growth and insect populations, which in turn stimulate breeding activity in these birds. A very dry spring may prevent local breeding altogether or may cause the birds to move out and attempt breeding somewhere else. On the other hand, too much rain and associated too-tall grasses may also make an area temporarily unsuited for breeding. As a result, the Cassin's sparrow has a rather fluid breeding distribution, especially at the climatic boundaries of its range.

When the males arrive on their breeding areas, they seek out areas where the ground is dominated by grasses and where shrubs or scattered trees are present. In overgrazed areas where grasses are few, *Opuntia* cacti and forbs serve as substitutes. Hackberry trees and mesquites up to twenty-five feet tall are common associates of Cassin's sparrows in south-central and southern Texas, and dense, often thorny shrubs are often present. Grasses up to a foot in height and covering 50 to 75 percent of the ground surface may be close to ideal ground cover. In favorable situations territorial males may be spaced as close as about 100 yards apart.

Studies by John Schnase in south-central Texas are especially valuable in defining the breeding biology of this still little-known species. His study area was a mixture of mid-height to short grasses, with scattered or thickety mesquite trees averaging about five to ten feet tall, *Opuntia* cactus averaging 1.5 feet high, and a ground cover of about 60 percent. Most males arrived on his study area in early March, although some may have overwintered. When the first females appeared in late March, the males became much more evident, and pair-bonding was evidently completed by the latter part of April. Over a two-year period, the mean breeding density was eleven birds per 100 acres, or twelve to fifteen pairs present on his 250-acre study area.

Early-season singing by the males was weak and tentative but soon improved, although it was not coincident with the onset of flight-songs. Initially the birds sang from hidden perches, which later changed to conspicuous perches, when "song duels" by males on adjacent territories became prevalent. By the latter half of March flight-songs began, and these increased in frequency through March, until all singing comprised such flight behavior. Typically, the displaying male would fly up from an exposed perch at a rather steep angle until he reached about twenty to thirty-five feet, the song beginning before the apex of the flight and continuing throughout the rest of the flight display (Fig. 56, *above*). After reaching his high point, the male held his wings in a horizontal attitude, elevated his tail, and arched his head backward, then glided back to his original perch or, more often, to another. Sometimes the wings were fluttered during the descent phase. Most song-flights were performed in early morning, from sunrise onward, declining and terminating by noon. At maximum, about four display bouts per minute were typical. Males also began to sing again as sunset approached but terminated at dusk. Primary song continued intermittently through the summer but decreased in intensity by late April.

The typical primary song of the Cassin's sparrow has six separate phrases, collectively lasting an average of 2.5 seconds and centering at six kilohertz, but with an overall range of two to nine kilohertz. Fourteen males studied by Schnase had from two to four different song types in their repertoire, averaging 2.9. Each of the fourteen males had a unique collective repertoire and could thus be recognized in the field. Usually a male would sing two to four songs of a given type and then

56. Song-flight of male Cassin's sparrow (*above*), with typical song (duration 3.0 seconds, after Schnase 1984). Also singing male Brewer's sparrow (*below*) with "long song" sonogram (*above,* duration 13.0 seconds), plus two examples of "short songs" (duration 8.0 seconds, *below*) (after Rotenberry et al. 1999). Drawing by author.

begin another, so that his entire repertoire would be completed within a sequence of fifteen songs. Often the song will begin with one or more introductory whistles, followed by a prolonged trill lasting up to one second; and this in turn is followed by several short, clear whistles, usually of varied frequencies.

The territories of Cassin's sparrows are all-inclusive and are mostly maintained through song. After they have been established they tend to remain stable through the rest of the breeding season. In Schnase's study area all territories include some mesquite thicket (average, 28 percent) and open grasslands. Twelve males had territories averaging 6.4 acres over the two-year study period but with significant yearly variations. Females visited male territories and evidently formed pair bonds within about two weeks. Apparently the birds formed stable, monogamous pair bonds, and only one male was observed to remain unpaired each summer, out of ten to eleven males studied during the two-year period.

In Schnase's study area, egg-laying began in mid-May and continued until late July. Most initial eggs of clutches were laid in June. Although three cases of renesting were found, no evidence of second broods was detected, even though such double brooding has been suggested elsewhere. Nests were usually placed in prickly-pear cacti, but some were placed at the base of mesquites, and the rest were in other types of vegetation. All were elevated but were close to the ground. Egg-laying began only two to three days after nest completion, and eggs were deposited daily until the clutch, usually of four eggs, was complete. One closely monitored clutch had an eleven-day incubation period, the last egg hatching on day twelve. Fledging occurred the ninth day after hatching. Within two or three days after fledging, males again began skylarking, suggesting that second broods may indeed be possible if not likely, and one such male did not respond to the female's alarm calls toward older fledglings. Mating with another female for a second brood is also a possibility.

Of a total of twenty-five males studied over three summers, twenty-three obtained mates, but five of these twenty-three pairs were unsuccessful in producing any fledged chicks. However, forty chicks were produced by the eighteen successful pairs, or 2.2 fledglings per pair. Eleven eggs failed because of abandonment or simply disappeared, and three nests were parasitized by brown-headed cowbirds. Two of these nests were abandoned.

Brewer's Sparrow

Thomas M. Brewer (1814–1880) was a multicareered and multifaceted person. Although a friend of John J. Audubon, he seemingly was a friend of very few other people, owing to an abrasive personality. At various times during his life Brewer was (albeit briefly) a medical doctor, a political journalist, and eventually a publisher. Throughout his adult life he was also a passionate oologist. He published the first volume of his never-completed *North American Oology* in 1857. With Spencer Baird and Robert Ridgway, he was also a contributing author of the first volume of the *History of North American Birds,* published in 1874. The Brewer's sparrow was discovered in the Black Hills of what is now South Dakota and was named for him by John Cassin (see preceding section). The Brewer's blackbird of western North America was also named in Brewer's honor.

Brewer's sparrows may be neither very large nor at all colorful, and they have even been described by an otherwise generally politically correct ornithologist as "having no distinction whatsoever." Yet they are the species that I most closely associate with the seemingly endless sagebrush flats in Washington State's Columbia Basin, located just east of the Cascades, and with the similar sage-covered tablelands of Wyoming's Jackson Hole, lying in the comparable rain shadow of the Teton Range. Many of the sagebrush plains of Washington State were being efficiently bulldozed and planted to irrigated crops as rapidly as humanly possible when I did graduate fieldwork there in the 1950s. I have avoided returning to the Columbia Basin ever since, in fear of what I might see there now. With the destruction and disappearance of the sage, there are probably no more green-tailed towhees, sage sparrows, and all the other wonderful dryland birds that once gave life and joyous sound to that great silver-green sea of sagebrush. Of these birds it was the Brewer's sparrow that provided me with the greatest personal pleasure upon hearing its distinctive and lilting song, which was always offered in full measure in spite of its spritelike, diminutive size.

Perhaps because of its small size, the Brewer's sparrow winters quite far south, with only a few U.S. localities, such as the Big Bend region of Texas, supporting many birds. There and farther south it winters alongside and with the clay-colored sparrow. The wintering grounds of both these species continue southward through the upland grasslands and semideserts of interior northern Mexico. The Brewer's sparrow is likely to be found in somewhat more arid areas having only scattered shrubs or trees and even in actual desert habitats. There they occur in flocks and when not foraging are likely to be found in bushes, even at times singing in chorus, together with wintering white-crowned sparrows. The birds are able to survive and even thrive in the absence of free water, getting their metabolic needs from air-dried seeds alone.

On its wintering grounds the Brewer's sparrow probably is almost entirely granivorous, but little actual data exist for that season. Grass seeds and quite small weed seeds are known dietary components. Summer diets are high in arthropods, mostly those that are no more than about one-eighth of an inch in length or diameter; the Brewer's sparrow's bill length and depth are correspondingly among the smallest of the grassland sparrows (Fig. 55, *right*).

Spring migration northward is moderately early and is undertaken at night. The birds apparently move northward in small flocks, arriving in Colorado breeding areas by mid-April and with most migration there over by the end of the month. Nearly all the breeding season records are concentrated in montane sagebrush or lowland sagebrush, but with some use of tall desert shrub, montane shrublands, and various grassland types. Some of the high-country breeders there may be part of the "timberline" form of Brewer's sparrow that perhaps constitutes a still-unrecognized sibling species.

Breeding season habitats supporting dense populations additionally include shrubs, especially sagebrush, of moderate height (up to five feet), low shrub species diversity, higher forb and lower grass frequency, and relatively level ground with little duff or litter, considerable bare ground, and limited rockiness. Foraging is more likely to be done on shrubs rather than on the ground or at the bases of bunchgrasses. Most food is obtained by gleaning for arthropods at the shrub's leaves and stems, although some seeds may be obtained from the ground.

Territories are established by males immediately upon their arrival on breeding areas. They are quite variable in size but tend to be rather small, with estimates as low as 0.25 acres in central Washington, about 1.3 acres in Idaho, and 1.3 to 5.8 acres in Oregon and Nevada. Population density is probably an important determinant of territory size.

Territories are advertised by perched singing from shrubs, often the highest available one within the territory. Males produce two distinct song types (Fig. 56, *below*), the "long song" and the "short song." The long song is the longest perched utterance of any of the grassland sparrows, often lasting up to fifteen seconds and consisting of a strange canarylike mixture of trills, buzzes, and other rapidly repeated elements of varied pitches (Fig. 56, upper sonogram). It is of moderately high pitch (ca. 4,000 to 6,000 Hertz), but with each of the separate phases on the same pitch. The short song (Fig. 56, lower sonogram) lasts up to three seconds and has from one to three phases, typically buzzy trills similar in sound structure to the long song. Short songs usually start with a higher frequency trill that is followed by a slower and lower frequency trill.

The long song tends to be the one used early in the breeding season and also earlier in the day; the short song may be heard throughout the day and may even occur during migration and occasionally during winter. Short songs may also be uttered when the bird is actively foraging. However, the long song is typically sung from a tall shrub, preferably live sagebrush, and a single bout of singing may last up to ten minutes.

So far as is currently known, Brewer's sparrows form monogamous pair bonds, and no extrapair copulations have yet been reported. Courtship-feeding is known to occur during pair-bonding, but little else is known of specific pair-bonding or unique copulatory signaling. The pair bond persists through the breeding season, including any renesting efforts or second broods, but there is still no evidence of mate resumption in subsequent years. However, about 25 percent of a group of banded males returned to the same nesting habitat as used the prior year, so remating might be at least occasionally expected.

Females construct their nests in four to five days, seeking out sites in sagebrush (preferentially) or other living shrubs that are taller and denser than average and that have less than average bare ground below. Nests tend to be placed in the densest part of the bush and are at least either inches above ground and usually more than a foot above ground, with nest height tending to increase in later nesting efforts. Often the nest is placed at the middle height of the shrub supporting it. Perhaps the increasing average height of the nest later in the season reflects increasing protection from ground-based predators or gaining an increased exposure to cooling winds during the hot summer months.

Eggs are laid at the rate of one per day, and the usual clutch is of three eggs, with four not uncommon. Clutch sizes average higher in springs following wet winters, but there is not yet any evidence of lower clutch sizes later in the breeding season, as might be expected. Renesting following initial clutch loss is regular, and second broods have also been reported, but the incidence of such double brooding is still unknown. Parasitism by brown-headed cowbirds is seemingly geographically variable, ranging from none in samples from Oregon and Nevada, 5 to 13 percent in Idaho and Washington, and over 50 percent in Alberta. A collective average for these samples is 6 percent for 444 nests, the low overall rate probably reflecting the fact that cowbirds are still rather rare over most of the Brewer's sparrow's range. Parasitism usually results in a desertion of the nest by the sparrow.

Incubation requires ten to twelve days and is mostly performed by the female. Both parents help feed and brood the chicks, with females providing somewhat more food than males. Nest departure occurs at six to nine days, while the young are still flightless. Fledging occurs several days later. The birds are very hard to study by this age, and there is no information on later stages of juvenile behavior.

There seem to be considerable variation as to how many territorial males in a population obtain mates and the usual great variability of reproductive success from time to time and place to place. Estimates of the number of nests successful in producing at least one fledged chick have ranged from 1 to 85 percent and the average number of chicks fledged from 0 to 2.5. Egg and chick predation seems to be the greatest single determinant of breeding success. Increased breeding success has been positively correlated with increased precipitation the preceding winter and negatively correlated with populations of ground squirrels, which are known predators of eggs and nestlings. Shrikes and snakes have also been implicated as significant predators of adults, eggs, or chicks.

There is still no good information on mortality rates of average longevity estimates, in large part because of a seemingly very low incidence of nestlings returning to their natal site to breed the following year (none was observed among a sample of about 400 banded chicks).

Suggested Readings

Dickcissel: Basili 1997; Berry 1971; Best et al. 1997; Blankenspoor 1970; Dechant et al. 1999k; Fink 1983; Fretwell 1986; Harmeson 1974; Hurley and Franks 1976; Long et al. 1965; Meanley 1963; Overmire 1963; Schartz and Zimmerman 1971; Steigman 1993; Swanson 1996; Zimmerman 1971, 1983.

Henslow's sparrow: Clawson 1991; Dechant et al. 1999f; Hands et al.

1989; Herkert 1994b; Hyde 1939; Reinking et al. in press; Robins 1971a, 1971b; Skinner 1974; Skipper 1998; Smith 1992; Swanson 1996; Winter 1998, 1999; Zimmerman 1988.

Cassin's sparrow: Borror 1971; Hubbard 1977; Maurer et al. 1989; Schnase 1984; Williams and LeSassier 1968.

Brewer's sparrow: Bock and Bock 1992; Doyle 1997; Freeman-Gallant 1997a, 1997b; Johnson and Igl 1995; Knopf et al. 1990; Nordin et al. 1988; Pernanen 1994; Petersen and Best 1985, 1986; Rich 1978; Rogers 1998; Rotenberry and Weins 1989, 1998; Rotenberry et al. 1999; Schroeder and Sturges 1975; Weins et al. 1989, 1990.

Conclusion:
The Disappearing Prairie
and Its Declining Avifauna

The whole of the surface of these beautiful plains is clad, throughout the season of verdure, with every variety of color, from grave to gay. It is impossible to conceive a more infinite diversity, or profusion of hues or to detect the predominating tint, except the green, which forms the beautiful background, and relieves the exquisite beauty of all the others.

—Judge J. Hall

George Santayana once wrote that those who forget the past are condemned to repeat it. It is in this context and spirit that a brief reprise of some of the historical points made earlier in this book is deemed worthwhile.

A Great Plains Time-Travel Scenario

It has now been about 580 million years since the start of the Cambrian period (the first major subdivision of the Paleozoic era) and the apparent initial appearance of widespread multicellular life on earth. The rocks that were formed prior to that time are nearly all of igneous and metamorphic types, which do not exhibit the fossils that commonly are preserved in sedimentary rocks. Nevertheless, there are a few algal (stromatolite) fossils in strata from Precambrian times that push the actual known history of life on earth back about 3.5 billion years before the present, or for most of the estimated total existence of the planet, about 4.5 billion years.

The width of the central Great Plains at the latitude of Nebraska is nearly 600 miles, as measured from the Missouri River at Omaha to the Medicine Bow Range of the Central Rockies in southeastern Wyoming. More specifically, it is 545 miles on Interstate 80 from the entrance ramp near the Missouri River in Omaha to the Laramie, Wyoming, I-80 exit. It is another thirty-five miles or so west on Wyoming Highway 130 upward and out of the Great Plains to the Snowy Range Pass, making a total trip distance of about 575 miles from the Missouri River to this high subalpine pass near the Continental Divide. The change in elevation over the entire trip is almost 10,000 feet, from a starting point of about 1,000 feet above sea level at Omaha to a final elevation of nearly 10,900 feet. The present-day plant communities of this east-to-west route begin in eastern deciduous riverine hardwood forest and extend sequentially through tall-grass, mixed-grass, short-grass, sage-dominated shrubsteppe, montane coniferous forest, and finally to alpine tundra.

To get a sense of the time scale discussed in chapter 1, let each mile of this route represent 1 million years. Thus, this 575-mile trip can represent the past 575 million years of earth's history. By that criterion, a 1/2 mile would represent 500,000 years; 1/10 mile, 100,000 years; 1/100 mile (52 feet), 10,000 years; 1/1,000 mile (5.2 feet), 1,000 years; and 6 inches, 100 years.

As we join I-80 in Omaha, we are at the beginning portion (Cambrian period) of the Paleozoic era, some 570 million years ago, when what is now the Great Plains was submerged in a great inland sea, and the above-water portions of ancestral North America were part of a large supercontinent that included much of today's Old World. The animals present in the waters above what would eventually become the Great Plains were mostly corals, sponges, and mollusks, plus a few primitive fishes such as sharks. Evidence of this early life can be found in limestone outcrops such as those occurring along some creeks and rivers in southeastern Nebraska and eastern Kansas.

As we drive the seventy miles from Omaha to the vicinity of Seward, we have covered 70 million years, bringing us to a mere 500 million years ago, and we are entering the Devonian period. We must drive all the way to Hershey, Nebraska (near North Platte), some 240 million years ago, before the last remnants of the Permian Sea have retreated and left us on relatively dry land. To reach the great Age of Dinosaurs, we must enter the Jurassic period of the mid-Mesozoic era. This period began some 210 million years ago, and in order to span it we must reach Ogallala, the horizontal distance representing over 60 million years and encompassing the peak of the dinosaurs' long reign. There is only a fragmentary fossil record of dinosaurs in Nebraska, but there are abundant dinosaur fossils in Wyoming, which by then was situated well above water. Its western regions were also gradually buckling and faulting as the Rocky Mountains were rising. In Europe, the crow-sized *Archaeopteryx*, a primitive bird with a long, flexible tail and wings bearing clawed fingers at its wrists, was taking flight, and early shrewlike mammals were scurrying about on the forest floors. Both groups would remain generally subordinate to larger and more powerful reptiles for another 100 million years. But eventually brains would outlast brawn.

The last great portion of the Mesozoic, the Cretaceous period, lasted more than 70 million years, representing the seventy-plus miles from about Sydney, Nebraska, to Burns, Wyoming. It was a time when the Great Plains were again covered by the shallow seas of the Interior Western Seaway. Streamlined plesiosaurs swiftly paddled through the subtropical waters, as did mosasaurs, both catching and eating squids, sharks, and primitive bony fishes. Overhead, pterosaurs were similarly on the lookout for small prey or carrion. Also present were a few sharply toothed and rather small-brained birds. Occupying the shoreline shallows were large fish-eating and loonlike divers called *Hesperornis,* while gliding above the water surface ternlike *Ichthyornis* industriously searched the waves for smaller prey.

Finally, near Burns, about fifteen miles west of the Wyoming-Nebraska border, we have reached the end of the nearly 200-million-year Mesozoic era. The dinosaurs, mosasaurs, and plesiosaurs have now quite suddenly disappeared. Early families of mammals are becoming quite abundant, having replaced nearly all the predominantly reptilian fauna that were perhaps eliminated during climatic changes brought on by the collision of the earth with an enormous asteroid at the end of the Mesozoic. Many of the modern orders of birds are also appearing in the skies, replacing the pterosaurs of earlier time. This important turning point in earth's history, occurring 65 million years ago, also represents the start of the first geologic subdivision of the Age of Mammals, the Paleocene epoch of the Cenozoic era. During this time the land that would eventually represent Nebraska and eastern Wyoming was still covered by broad-leaved subtropical forests, but high mountain ranges were rising in eastern Wyoming, including both the Medicine Bow and Laramie Ranges not far to the west.

Driving between Cheyenne and Laramie we pass through the roughly 45 million years of the Eocene and Oligocene epochs and are encountering cooler and drier landscapes, as wind- and water-carried erosion materials from the mountain ranges to the west gradually are filling and raising the western plains. We are progressively surrounded first by savannalike mixtures of trees and grasses and then finally by true grasslands. Many browsing and grazing mammals are present, including rhinos, primitive horses, and many other ungulates. Elephant-sized and curiously horned titanotheres occasionally lumber across the upland hilltops. As we approach Laramie, volcanic activity in the mountains of western Wyoming is spreading beds of lava over the Yellowstone Plateau and sending clouds of smoke and volcanic dust eastward, filling some of the lower Wyoming basins.

It isn't until we approach the village of Centennial, about twenty miles and 20 million years from our destination, that the landscape and animal life begin to resemble the grassy plains we know today. Grazing mammals of the Miocene epoch such as horses, rhinos, camels, and grass-eating rodents are to be seen, as well as a few carnivorous dogs and cats that prey on these abundant grazers. The first elephant herds appear on the horizon only fourteen miles from our journey's end; these include mastodons, four-tuskers, and several other early elephant types.

With about ten miles to go, clouds of volcanic dust from western volcanoes settle on the roads, choking the herds of grazing mammals and providing the basis for the present-day Ashfall Fossil Beds State Historical Park in Nebraska. The familiar sounds of sandhill cranes calling overhead could nevertheless be heard shortly before the deathly silence. Then, about nine miles from our destination, the ground is jolted as the Teton Range begins a sudden and spectacular rise just beyond our horizon to the west. Some five miles from the pass the whole countryside around is again jolted and is rather rapidly uplifted several thousand feet, owing to warping action of the earth's mantle. Increased erosion begins to carve out new valleys and buttes from these highlands, depositing still more sediments in Nebraska.

Just two miles from the end of our road, or a little more than 2 million years ago, we are passing through cool coniferous forests, and the first of several glaciers are sweeping southward out of Canada and down the crests of the Rocky Mountains. They bring with them many enormous mammals from the Arctic, such as mammoths, Arctic-adapted bears, giant camels, large beavers, and giant predatory cats.

The first Native Americans probably reached North America by walking across the Bering Strait land bridge of lowland tundra that connected North America and Asia during the late Pleistocene epoch. This human immigration occurred some 12,000 to 15,000 years ago, or about seventy-five feet from the end of our trip. We are approaching the Libby Flats Observation Point, at 10,847 feet, and are now surrounded at subalpine treeline, with alpine tundra on the highest slopes a few hundred feet above us. Ironically, we are actually stopping on half-billion-year-old rocks of Cambrian age, with nearby fossilized algal stromatolites, dating back in time to our approximate starting point. On the foothills and plains below there are two kinds of bison grazing in vast herds. They include a giant bison species that would become extinct at the end of the final glaciation, or about 10,000 years ago, and a smaller one that is the direct ancestor of the modern bison.

America wasn't "discovered" by Europeans until about five centuries ago, or only about three feet from the end of our road. At that time the river and stream valleys of the eastern Great Plains were inhabited by prehistoric village farmers, and the human population there was apparently surprisingly high. Yet this culture rather mysteriously disappeared about 500 years ago, to be replaced with the much more familiar and historically documented Native American groups such as the Pawnees, Sioux, Cheyennes, Arapahos, and many others. The Great Plains were mostly settled by Europeans little more than a century ago, or about seven inches from our destination, and the tall-grass prairies of the eastern plains were at least 96 percent destroyed during this tiny segment of time.

About six inches before our car comes to a complete stop the first barbed-wire fences begin to appear (1874), and within a decade all the bison will have disappeared from the plains. At the same time the bison-dependent Native Americans living freely on the high plains have also been virtually extinguished. Homesteaders are starting to appear, stimulated by federal actions to occupy and to try to irrigate the high plains through the Desert Land Act of 1877. Many settlers would quickly go broke during the droughts of the 1880s and 1890s. In 1916 the federal Stock-raising Act would similarly give settlers 640 acres of land each, to try to encourage the developing livestock industry. Most of these settlers would likewise go bankrupt and be forced to abandon their land during the drought and the Great Depression of the 1930s.

The people who are alive today represent only a few inches of our total known history of life on earth, and yet in the last 100 years the world's human population has increased threefold. The oil fields and vast coal beds below the Wyoming plains have largely been stripped of their resources during this same period. Cattle have replaced bison, and the prairie dog has disappeared or become endangered through much of its range. European starlings and similarly introduced house sparrows now occupy woodpecker-chiseled cavities that were once used by native bluebirds and chickadees. Annual grasses such as cheatgrass, as well as other introduced Old World weeds like Russian thistle, have largely replaced the sweet grama grasses that originally nourished the native grazers of this enormous grassland ecosystem.

> *One's native land is the most important thing on earth. Above all it is made holy by the ancestors, who pass it on.*
>
> —Louis Tiel

The Prairie and Its Avifauna Today

It is a curious fact of human nature that undulating lines are more interesting, and jagged lines more visually exciting, than straight lines. That simple truism is perhaps why there are far more books that have been published on the beauty of deserts, and especially of mountain ranges, than have ever been written on the plants, animals, and ecology of the plains and prairies. Unless one has been born and raised on the prairies, a painting by Mark Rothko, showing a broad horizontal red streak boldly crossing an otherwise unicolored and dark background, does not immediately strike the average viewer as representing a magnificent prairie sunset.

The exact area of native grasslands that once covered North America in prehistoric times is somewhat uncertain, but P. L. Sims has judged that there were about 0.2 million square miles (50 million hectares) of grasslands in Canada and some 1.1 million square miles (300 million hectares) in the United States. These collectively represent about 1.3 million square miles (3.4 million square kilometers), making it comparable in area to the steppes of central Asia, the only other native grassland in the world of similar size. The total area of North America is 9.3 million square miles; thus grasslands probably originally made up about 15 percent of its land area.

It was estimated by Dennis Farney that the tall-grass prairie component of the American grasslands once covered about 400,000 square miles. David Wilcove judged a lower figure for tall-grass prairies (231,000 square miles), plus a combined original area of mixed-grass and short-grass prairies totaling about 625,000 square miles. Using these several estimates, it seems likely that about 1 million square miles of native grasslands once occupied the interior of North America. In Wilcove's estimation, perhaps something approaching 4 percent of the original tall-grass prairies and about 25 percent of the mixed-grass and short-grass prairies still exist, in varying degrees of degradation. R. F. Noss and others have estimated that 99 percent of the tall-grass prairies east of the Mississippi and 85 percent west of it have been destroyed. A somewhat larger percentage of the original short-grass prairies still exists, even if they are badly degraded, judging from figures summarized by Fred Samson and Fritz Knopf.

Few of America's major ecosystems have been so important to our postcolonial history as have our grasslands, and yet few have been so effectively and ruthlessly demolished. The grasslands once nourished uncountable herds of bison; they later fed our more carefully counted herds of domesticated cattle and throughout this century have provided the biological basis for most of our agricultural productivity. Yet, in contrast to Canada, the United States has not yet seen fit to establish a Grasslands National Park. Such a park perhaps might help raise Americans' consciousness levels as to the interconnectedness of living things and the value of taxonomic diversity in promoting stable environments. This reluctance to produce a national grasslands park is perhaps in part understandable because mountains, coastlines, and even deserts look better than do prairies on picture postcards, but it also reflects the fact that grassland soils are the most fertile on earth. Landowners, having eventually discovered this, now are loath to give the prairie lands back willingly so that the government can raise bison and antelope. Instead, corn is grown on these lands at a cost greater than the price for which it can be sold, and the surplus is bought by the federal government at inflated and subsidized prices. The corn is then stored in expensive warehouses

The prairie, whose enameled plains that lie beneath me in distance soften into sweetness, like an essence, whose thousand velvet-covered hills . . . go tossing and leaping down with steep or graceful declivities to the river's edge . . . this prairie, where Heaven sheds its purest light and lends its richest tints.

—George Catlin,
North American Indians

or if necessary on the ground itself until some use can be found for it, most probably to fatten more cattle that will be slaughtered and subsequently trimmed of their excess fat so they don't cause Americans to become even more obese. It is sometimes difficult to find the logic in this.

In an effort to rank the midwestern species of migrant landbirds as to their degree of threatened decline, Frank Thompson and others used several criteria. On those bases, the twelve grassland species considered to be most in need of management attention were (in descending order): Baird's sparrow, dickcissel, mountain plover, bobolink, long-billed curlew, grasshopper sparrow, clay-colored sparrow, lark bunting, upland sandpiper, burrowing owl, Swainson's hawk, and lark sparrow. Four of these species (dickcissel, bobolink, upland sandpiper, and Swainson's hawk) are long-distance Neotropical migrants wintering entirely in and at least partly dependent upon South American grasslands. At least seven of these species (Baird's sparrow, dickcissel, bobolink, grasshopper sparrow, clay-colored sparrow, lark bunting, and lark sparrow) are probably being seriously impacted by brood parasitism of the brown-headed cowbird. The remaining three grassland species (mountain plover, long-billed curlew, and burrowing owl) require fairly large areas of grassland (or grassland-dependent associates such as prairie dogs) for breeding. Similar large areas of continuous habitat, amounting to hundreds of acres or even several square miles, are also needed by the prairie grouse for adequate flock maintenance and social stimulation during arena behavior. Similar-sized or even larger areas are needed by the larger grassland raptors for achieving their minimum home-range and foraging requirements. It is difficult enough to try to understand the minimum ecological requirements of a single prairie-dependent

> *The prairie is an intricately constructed community. The climax vegetation is the outcome of thousands of years of sorting and modifications of species and adaptations to soil and climate. Prairie is much more than land covered with grass. It is a slowly evolved, highly complex, organic entity, centuries old. Once destroyed, it can never be replaced by man.*
>
> —John Weaver,
> *North American Prairie*

species; it is probably impossible to measure it for an entire grassland avifauna.

Current Grassland Bird Populations

There are many possible ways to try to understand the current population attributes of North America's grassland avifauna. As part of these efforts in quantification, various geographic and physiographic terms relating to subdivisions of the Great Plains and central lowlands have been devised and variously accepted by different authorities. One useful method is to define these regions in terms of their physiography alone (Fig. 57), a method that is easily understood by geographers and geologists and that has often been used by the U.S. Fish and Wildlife Service (now the National Biological Service, at least in part). Another more recent and ecologically sensitive method, proposed by Robert Bailey, is to subdivide the North American regions into geographic elements that combine geophysiographic considerations with climatic-vegetational units. The resulting largest such units are called "eco-regions," and within these are progressively smaller landscape components, down to the level of local sites. This latter approach has been increasingly accepted recently and has been seemingly adopted by both the National Biological Service and the Nature Conservancy (Fig. 58; see also appendix A).

A good insight into the role of specific grassland ecological subtypes in influencing the distributions and relative abundance of grassland bird species in the Great Plains is gained by analyzing the available data according to grassland height types. Two such analyses are provided, showing clearly the associations of most of the prairie birds with particular grassland categories (see Tables 7 and 8). It would seem that the most characteristic species of tall-grass habitats are the dickcissel, eastern meadowlark, Henslow's sparrow, and greater prairie-chicken. The clay-colored sparrow, marbled godwit, sharp-tailed grouse, Baird's sparrow, Wilson's phalarope, chestnut-collared longspur, and Sprague's pipit appear to be good indicator species of mixed-grass prairie; and the McCown's longspur, mountain plover, burrowing owl, lark bunting, and ferruginous hawk are most characteristic of short-grass prairies (see Table 7). Adding information from the smaller data-sets in Table 8, the long-billed curlew can be identified as a mid-grass correlate and the Brewer's sparrow a distinctive short-grass and sagebrush form.

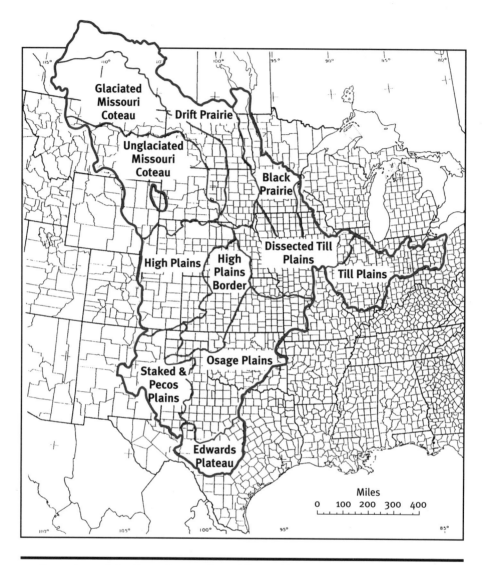

Glaciated
Missouri
Coteau

Drift Prairie

Unglaciated
Missouri
Coteau

Black
Prairie

Dissected Till
Plains

High Plains

High
Plains
Border

Till Plains

Osage Plains

Staked &
Pecos
Plains

Edwards
Plateau

Miles

0   100 200 300 400

57. Ecoregions of the Great Plains. Adapted from Bailey (1995).

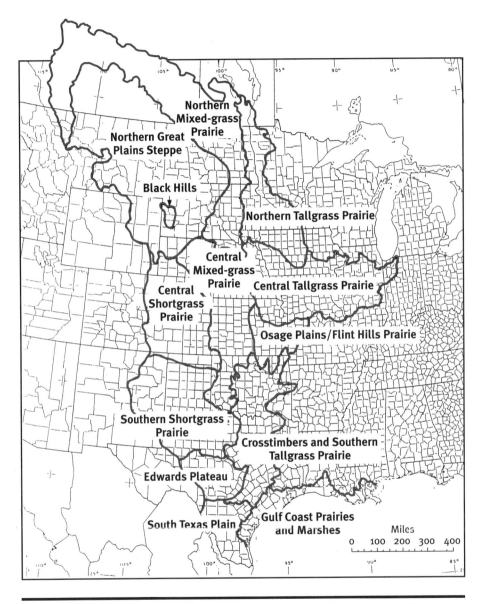

Northern Mixed-grass Prairie

Northern Great Plains Steppe

Black Hills

Northern Tallgrass Prairie

Central Mixed-grass Prairie

Central Tallgrass Prairie

Central Shortgrass Prairie

Osage Plains/Flint Hills Prairie

Southern Shortgrass Prairie

Crosstimbers and Southern Tallgrass Prairie

Edwards Plateau

South Texas Plain

Gulf Coast Prairies and Marshes

Miles

0   100   200   300   400

58. Physiographic subregions of the Great Plains and central lowlands, as defined in breeding bird surveys of the U.S. Fish and Wildlife Service.

Table Seven Relative Frequencies of Occurrence of Grassland Species in Selected Breeding Bird Censuses, 1972–1996

	Tall-grass Sites (n = 52)	Mixed-grass Sites (n = 120)	Short-grass Sites (n = 9)
Dickcissel	83%	1%	—
Eastern meadowlark	50	8	—
Grasshopper sparrow	61	58	22%
Savannah sparrow	31	32	—
Western meadowlark	36	93	33
Upland sandpiper	21	46	—
Bobolink	21	55	—
Clay-colored sparrow	—	70	—
Marbled godwit	—	11	—
Henslow's sparrow	8	—	—
Greater prairie-chicken	6	—	—
Northern harrier	4	—	—
Vesper sparrow	4	3	—
Horned lark	2	7	78
McCown's longspur	—	—	44
Mountain plover	—	—	44
Burrowing owl	—	—	22
Lark bunting	2	2	11
Ferruginous hawk	—	—	11
Chestnut-collared longspur	2	6	—
Lark sparrow	2	1	—
Sharp-tailed grouse	—	7	—
Baird's sparrow	—	5	—
Wilson's phalarope	—	4	—
Sprague's pipit	—	2	—
Short-eared owl	—	1	—

Note: Organized sequentially from tall-grass species to short-grass species and from high-frequency to low-frequency species within grassland types. Some grassland endemics as identified by Johnsgard (1979) were not encountered in any of these censuses and are thus excluded.

Table Eight Reported Densities of Breeding Birds in Seven International Biological Program (IBP) Grassland Sites

	Tall-grass Sites (1)	Mixed-grass Sites (1)	Short-grass Sites (2)	Other grasslands (3)[a]
Grassland species				
Eastern meadowlark	88.3			
Dickcissel	80.9			
Upland sandpiper	9.5	0–14.1		
Grasshopper sparrow	71.4	3.8–19.4	17–19.4	0–73.7
Horned lark		48.7–130.7	56.8–196.7	0–18.1
Western meadowlark		17.6–73.1	0–70.6, 0–63.5	
Chestnut-collared longspur		0–4.7	0–24.7	
Long-billed curlew		0–15.8		
Lark bunting			1.9–136.0	
Mountain plover			0–37.1	
Brewer's sparrow			0–71.7	
McCown's longspur			0–81.5	
Vesper sparrow				0–53.8
Other species				
Common nighthawk			0–6.6	
Mourning dove			Present	
American robin				0–21.1
Ash-throated flycatcher				0–7.5
Loggerhead shrike				0–4.7
Western kingbird				0–3.8
Scaled quail				0–1.9
Mountain bluebird				Present
Northern mockingbird				Present
Total Species	4	6	14	13

Source: Data from Weins (1973). Figures in parentheses indicate number of sites studied per grassland type; the mixed-grass site had two plots, the short-grass sites had ten. Densities are shown in estimated birds per square kilometer.

[a] Includes one site each of desert grassland, mountain grassland, and Palouse grassland.

The grasshopper sparrow, horned lark, and western meadowlark appear to be broadly adapted forms occurring in several grassland types; the Savannah sparrow and bobolink are somewhat less so. Numbers for the lark sparrow and short-eared owl are too low to suggest any strong prairie affiliation. Several species don't appear on either list, including the Franklin's gull, a wetland-dependent species. There are also two raptors missing from Table 8, the meadow- and wetland-adapted northern harrier and the Swainson's hawk of the short-grass high plains; both species have inherently low and largely prey-based population densities. Finally, the arid-adapted and shrubsteppe-associated Cassin's sparrow also failed to appear on either list.

Some sites having fairly long multiyear "runs" of bird survey data have been selected, to try to provide an index to relative species diversity in tall-grass, mixed-grass, and short-grass habitats as well as to identify those species having a high incidence of regular occurrence in each of these habitat types (see Table 9). Dickcissels, eastern meadowlarks, and grasshopper sparrows are perhaps the most consistently present species in tall-grass prairies; western meadowlarks and grasshopper sparrows would seem to be the most typical breeders in mixed-grass habitats. Horned larks and McCown's longspurs occupy that position in the single short-grass area that was tabulated. Not surprisingly, tall-grass sites typically had the highest average diversity of breeding bird species, followed in turn by mixed-grass and short-grass types.

Another way of looking at varied distribution and abundance patterns of grassland birds is to analyze them by geographic-political areas, i.e., by states and provinces (Table 10). Judging from the available published data, South Dakota supports the highest number of species representing the grassland avifauna as defined here (twenty-nine of thirty-three species) and also has substantially the highest overall breeding density of grassland birds. The grasslands of Texas represent the largest single geographic component of the original Great Plains grassland ecosystem, but both in species diversity and cumulative density that state falls toward the bottom of the list. As shown earlier (Fig. 16), the highest species density of grassland endemics is geographically centered in Montana and the Dakotas, and many of the most characteristic grassland birds have breeding ranges that do not extend as far south as the southern plains.

Looking at the data from the broadest possible perspective, including bird surveys from throughout the United States and Canada, prob-

Table Nine   Species Diversities and Breeding Densities of Birds in Various Great Plains Grassland Types, Based on Breeding Bird Survey Data

	Breeding Species	Total Density (males/40 ac.)	High-frequency Grassland Endemics[a]
Saskatchewan			
Mixed-grass	7–12	212–230	Chestnut-collared longspur (3/3)
(3-yr. ave.)	(9.3)	(221)	Western meadowlark (3/3)
			Baird's sparrow (3/3)
North Dakota			
Mixed-grass #1	9–24	92–380	Western meadowlark (19/19)
(19-year ave.)	(16.6)	(218)	Clay-colored sparrow (19/19)
Mixed-grass #2	5–14	32–197	Western meadowlark (17/19)
(19-year ave.)	(9.8)	(125)	Clay-colored sparrow (10/19)
Mixed-grass #3	3–12	7–246	Western meadowlark (19/19)
(19-year ave.)	(6.7)	(82)	Grasshopper sparrow (16/19)
Mixed-grass #4	5–14	49–230	Upland sandpiper (17/19)
(19-year ave.)	(9.0)	(115)	Western meadowlark (15/19)
Mixed-grass #5	3–15	22–435	Western meadowlark (16/19)
(19-year ave.)	(8.5)	(119)	Grasshopper sparrow (13/19)
Iowa			
Tall-grass #1	12–18	127–256	Grasshopper sparrow (7/7)
(7-year ave.)	(14.4)	(239)	Dickcissel (7/7)
Tall-grass #2	13–21	175–215	Western meadowlark (7/7)
(7-year ave.)	(16.7)	(187)	Dickcissel (7/7)
Tall-grass #3	19–25	200–266	Grasshopper sparrow (7/7)
(7-year ave.)	(20.5)	(239)	Dickcissel (7/7)
Kansas			
Tall-grass	4–7	247–376	Eastern meadowlark (5/5)
(5-year ave.)	(4.8)	(287)	Dickcissel (5/5)
Mixed-grass	19–28	170–320	Eastern meadowlark (5/5)
(7-year ave.)	(24.3)	(242)	Dickcissel (6/7)
Colorado			
Short-grass	3–4	115–131	Horned lark (4/4)
(4-year ave.)	(3.7)	(121)	McCown's longspur (4/4)
Unweighted means by grassland type			
Short-grass (1 site)	3.7	121	
Mixed-grass (7 sites)	12.0	160	
Tall-grass (4 sites)	14.1	228	

[a] Relative frequency of annual occurrence is shown in parentheses for those grassland endemics most regularly present. Data are from selected surveys between 1962 and 1984 as published in *American Birds* and from 1989 to 1996 as published in the *Journal of Field Ornithology*. The mixed-grass ("sand prairie") site in Kansas is a relict prairie on dune sand that includes wetlands and woody vegetation, which may account for its unusually high species diversity.

Table Ten   Species Diversities and Breeding Densities of Grassland Bird Species by State and Province

State or Province (sq. mi.)[a]	Total Breeding spp.[b]	Cumulative Densities[c]
South Dakota (65,600, 6.9%)	29 (3)	493.6 (100%)
Montana (110,000, 11.6%)	27 (1)	289.9 (58.6%)
North Dakota (63,700, 6.7%)	27 (7)	299.2 (60.5%)
Wyoming (34,700, 3.65%)	27 (1)	195.5 (39.5%)
Nebraska (69,500, 7.3%)	26 (–)	258.0 (52.3%)
Alberta (50,200, 5.3%)	26 (4)	194.2 (39.3%)
Saskatchewan (63,700, 6.7%)	24 (5)	297.5 (60.2%)
Colorado (42,450, 4.5%)	23 (–)	311.8 (63.3%)
Kansas (73,350, 7.7%)	23 (2)	376.5 (76.3%)
Manitoba (38,600, 4.5%)	21 (–)	156.0 (31.6%)
New Mexico (42,450, 4.5%)	19 (2)	164.1 (33.3%)
Minnesota (25,100, 2.6%)	18 (–)	97.7 (19.8%)
Oklahoma (34,750, 3.65%)	16 (1)	161.6 (32.9%)
Iowa (23,150, 2.4%)	15 (–)	192.7 (39.1%)
Texas (173,700, 18.3%)	14 (1)	131.0 (26.5%)
Missouri (17,375, 1.8%)	13 (1)	139.1 (28.2%)
Illinois (23,150, 2.4%)	13 (–)	133.3 (27.0%)

[a] Parenthetic numbers indicate area of state or province (in square miles) estimated to be once occupied by native grasslands, followed by that area expressed as a percentage of the total estimated original Great Plains grasslands (ca. 961,000 sq. mi.).

[b] Numbers indicate total breeding grassland endemics present, followed (in parentheses) by the number of those species having maximum reported overall densities in that state or province within the Great Plains region during 1965 to 1979 breeding bird surveys.

[c] Cumulative densities are sums of densities for all grassland species occurring in numbers allowing quantitative estimates during 1965 to 1979 breeding bird surveys. Parenthetic percentages show these cumulative densities relative to South Dakota, the state having the highest overall cumulative densities of grassland species (based on data of Robbins et al. [1986]).

ably provides the best means of estimating the overall population status and relative abundance of our grassland birds (see Table 11). Although the information in Table 11 is based on a comprehensive summary that covered only the first fifteen years of the breeding bird survey program, it nevertheless gives a reasonable baseline indication of the grassland bird avifauna as it existed during the 1960s and 1970s. Clearly, the two meadowlarks and horned lark are the preeminent grassland bird species,

Table Eleven   Breeding Bird Survey Data for Grassland Bird Species,
United States and Canada, 1965 to 1979

	Cumulative Birds per Route[a]	Maximum Reported Density/Distribution[b]
Western meadowlark	1,408.6	253.7 (SD)/33
Horned lark	948.8	108.5 (SK)/51
Eastern meadowlark	914.3	67.3 (OK)/44
Lark bunting	441.1	102.5 (SD)/16
Dickcissel	349.1	59.7 (KS)/32
Savannah sparrow	247.1	28.7 (WI)/43
Vesper sparrow	210.5	19.9 (MT)/46
Grasshopper sparrow	160.5	21.1 (SD)/50
Chestnut-collared longspur	125.6	33.4 (ND)/9
Clay-colored sparrow	96.9	29.9 (SK)/15
Lark sparrow	82.4	21.6 (TX)/34
Brewer's sparrow	80.0	17.6 (WY)/18
Cassin's sparrow	72.3	28.6 (NM)/8
Franklin's gull	71.4	28.0 (AB)/14
Upland sandpiper	39.9	14.7 (ND)/32
McCown's longspur	18.0	14.9 (UT)/7
Long-billed curlew	16.5	3.5 (UT)/20
Bobolink	16.3	19.2 (NB)/26
Northern harrier	14.6	1.9 (SK)/45
Wilson's phalarope	13.1	3.5 (SK)/20
Marbled godwit	12.7	4.9 (AB)/9
Baird's sparrow	11.8	6.9 (ND)/8
Swainson's hawk	11.6	1.6 (AB)/22
Burrowing owl	8.1	1.8 (KS)/19
Sharp-tailed grouse	4.1	1.5 (ND)/11
Sprague's pipit	4.1	1.9 (ND)/7
Short-eared owl	3.5	0.7 (AB)/24
Mountain plover	2.5	1.3 (NM)/5
Henslow's sparrow	2.0	0.6 (MI)/19
Ferruginous hawk	2.0	0.4 (ND)/19
Greater prairie-chicken	1 7	0.6 (MO)/6
Prairie falcon	0.7	0.2 (NV)/12
Lesser prairie-chicken	–	(none reported)

Source: Data based on summary by Robbins et al. (1986).

[a] Cumulative route totals are for all surveys in states and provinces where the species was recorded in quantified levels.

[b] Mean birds per route seen in state or province (in parentheses) having the maximum average birds per route within Great Plains region. Number shown after slash indicates species' overall breeding "distribution" (the total number of states and provinces where the species was reported, including those with only trace numbers, during the fifteen-year survey period summarized here).

followed by the lark bunting in the west and the dickcissel in the east. Of the thirteen most abundant grassland birds, sparrowlike species constitute ten and these larks the others. As we approach the bottom of the list, from the Swainson's hawk onward, we encounter increasing numbers of species that are now variously regarded as vulnerable or threatened, at least on a state or provincial level. They include nearly all the raptors and the grassland grouse, plus a pipit and a sparrow. The lesser prairie-chicken never appeared on the survey throughout the period of data coverage.

Finally, it is important to consider what may be the most significant data: statistical estimates of recent population changes in the grassland avifauna throughout almost the entire roughly three-decade period that the breeding bird survey has been in existence (Table 12). Using statistics provided by the website of the Patuxent Wildlife Research Center, it is possible to judge which of these species, regardless of their relative overall abundance, are in a state of serious decline and thus in need of special concern and attention. The only species that has exhibited highly significant population increases throughout both the entire 1966–1995 period as well as the more recent 1980–1996 subcomponent is the ferruginous hawk. Species that have exhibited highly significant declines over both durational periods are the horned lark, Brewer's sparrow, lark sparrow, bobolink, and eastern meadowlark. Species that had highly significant declines when analyzed over the entire survey period, but failed to attain that level of statistical certainty for the more recent sampling period, are the Sprague's pipit, dickcissel, Cassin's sparrow, and vesper sparrow. One species, the grasshopper sparrow, showed a highly significant decline over only the more recent of the two sampling periods. Of the thirty-two species, only the ferruginous hawk

The sea, the woods, the mountains, all suffer in comparison with the prairie. . . . The prairie has a stronger hold on the senses. Its sublimity arises from its unbounded extent, its barren monotony and desolation, its still, unmoved, calm, stern, almost self-confident grandeur, its stranger power of deception, its want of echo, and, in fine, its power of throwing a man back upon himself.

—Albert Pike

Table Twelve   Overall Annual Population Trends of Grassland Bird Species

	1966–1996 Trend	1980–1996 Trend
Northern harrier	−0.6	−1.4
Swainson's hawk	+0.8	+0.6
Ferruginous hawk	+5.2***	+7.2***
Prairie falcon	+0.3	+1.6
Greater prairie-chicken	+0.48	+6.0
Sharp-tailed grouse	+0.3	+1.8
Mountain plover	−2.7**	+3.7
Long-billed curlew	−1.4	−2.0
Upland sandpiper	+1.3***	−0.9
Marbled godwit	+0.3	+1.1
Wilson's phalarope	−1.6**	−1.7
Franklin's gull	+3.4	+15.4
Burrowing owl	+0.7	+2.5
Short-eared owl	−2.8	−0.8
Horned lark	−1.3***	−2.0***
Sprague's pipit	−4.7***	−4.5**
Dickcissel	−1.6***	+0.4
Cassin's sparrow	−2.5***	−0.2
Clay-colored sparrow	−1.1***	−0.5
Brewer's sparrow	−3.7***	−3.0***
Vesper sparrow	−0.8***	+0.1
Lark sparrow	−3.2***	−4.8***
Lark bunting	−0.9	−0.2
Savannah sparrow	−0.6**	−0.2
Grasshopper sparrow	−3.6	−2.1***
Baird's sparrow	−1.6	−1.1
Henslow's sparrow	−8.8	−10.4
McCown's longspur	+1.1	+2.7
Chestnut-collared longspur	−0.1	−1.1
Bobolink	−1.6***	−3.8***
Eastern meadowlark	−2.6***	−3.0***
Western meadowlark	−0.6	−0.3

Source: Based on data of Sauer et al. (1997). Asterisks indicate increasingly higher levels of statistical significance (* = $p < 0.10$, ** = $p < 0.05$, *** = $p < 0.01$) among apparently improving (+) or declining (−) populations of each species, based on breeding bird surveys in the United States and Canada done during the indicated time intervals. For the entire time period, highly significant ($p = < 0.01$) increases occurred in two species and highly significant declines in ten species. Less significant declines occurred in three additional species.

exhibited highly significant population increases during both sampling periods. This still relatively rare high plains species has clearly improved its status in recent decades and is no longer considered threatened in some regions. The upland sandpiper showed a similar increase for the overall survey period, but not for its more recent component.

It would appear that the great majority of the grassland birds are in some degree of population decline; only the ferruginous hawk and perhaps the upland sandpiper are improving in status. Indeed, no single ecological group of North American birds has so consistently exhibited population declines during the second half of this century than have the grassland birds, not even the Neotropical migrant birds that have received so much press attention since their declines were first documented. Unlike swans, which were once widely believed to sing sadly before they died, the prairies and their associated birds simply, gradually, and silently disappear.

Someone once wrote, and it could only have been Aldo Leopold, that in its biomass a ruffed grouse makes up only a minuscule part of the forest, but to remove it is to remove much of the life from the forest. Similarly, a horned lark or a Sprague's pipit represents an almost immeasurably tiny part of the prairie ecosystem, but a prairie without the song of a horned lark or a Sprague's pipit overhead is no prairie at all. And a place with no prairies at all is not a place that will stir the heart.

Suggested Readings

Askins 1993; Bailey 1995; Blackwelder 1909; Blankespoor 1980; Blankespoor and Krause 1982; DeGraff and Tilgman 1980; Engel et al. 1999; Gollop 1978; Graber and Graber 1963; Herkert 1991a, b, 1994a, b, 1995; Herkert and Glass 1999; Hagen and Johnston 1992; Hurley and Franks 1976; Ingl and Johnson 1997; Johnson 1972–1974; Johnson and Schwartz 1993a, 1993b; Knopf 1994, 1996b; Knopf and Samson 1996; Lauber 1991; Manning 1998; McNicholl 1988; Noss et al. 1995; Omerik 1987; Peterjohn and Sauer 1999; Price et al. 1995a; Risser et al. 1981; Samson and Knopf 1994; Sims 1988; Sodhi 1992; Terborgh 1989; Thompson 1995; Thompson et al. 1993; Vankat 1979; Vickery and Herkert 1999; Vickery et al. 1994; Wilcove 1999; Wilson and Belcher 1989.

Appendix A:
Major Grassland Preserves
in the Great Plains

In this list of more than 100 preserved native grassland sites I have attempted to include all the national wildlife refuges, national monuments, national parks, and national grasslands in the Great Plains that have substantial areas of native grass vegetation, as well as many state, county, and privately owned grassland preserves, especially those in excess of 1,000 acres (400 hectares). Some of the Nature Conservancy preserves (but very few of those listed here) may require permission for entry, and admission is charged at some state parks and federally owned sites. Areas (in acres) are indicated, and approximate locations in each state or province are abbreviated: central = C, north-central = NC, northeast = NE, east-central = EC, southeast = SE, south-central = SC, southwest = SW, west-central = WC, northwest = NW, north-central = NC. Phone numbers and/or addresses for obtaining more detailed information are provided for nearly all sites. The nearest city (or site headquarters in some cases) is indicated for all sites, and county locations are indicated for many. Most state highway maps indicate exact locations for the federal preserves and state-owned sites such as state parks, but city-, county- or privately owned sites may be harder to locate. Detailed locality information and complete bird lists for many of these locations, including nearly all the national wildlife refuges, may be found in the reference book by Jones (1990). Refuge checklists for the national wildlife refuges are also available online at the Northern Prairie Wildlife Research Center's website:<www.npwrc.usgs.gov/resource/othrdata/chekbird/chekbird/htm>.

Every national park (N.P.), national wildlife refuge (N.W.R.), national monument (N.M.), national grassland (N.G.), and wetland management district (W.M.D.) has been described, and most were mapped by the National Geographic Society (Crump 1984). Many of the state-managed state recreation areas (S.R.A.), scientific and natural areas (S.N.A.), wildlife areas (W.A.), wildlife conservation areas (W.C.A.), or wildlife management areas (W.M.A.) can be located most easily by contacting the appropriate state conservation agency. Most of the larger tall-grass prairie preserves listed here were described earlier by Madson (1993). He also listed many other smaller preserves, mostly those of the Nature Conservancy (T.N.C.) totaling more than fifty sites. Directions for reaching these T.N.C. and other nonstate or nonfederal tall-grass prairie preserves were also provided by Madson. Twenty of the short-grass prairie sites listed here were also described by Allen (1967).

So far as is known, all sites with available printed bird lists are identified, giving species totals whenever possible. Lists of summer grassland birds for thirty-six national wildlife refuges or other major bird preserves have been summarized in appendix B.

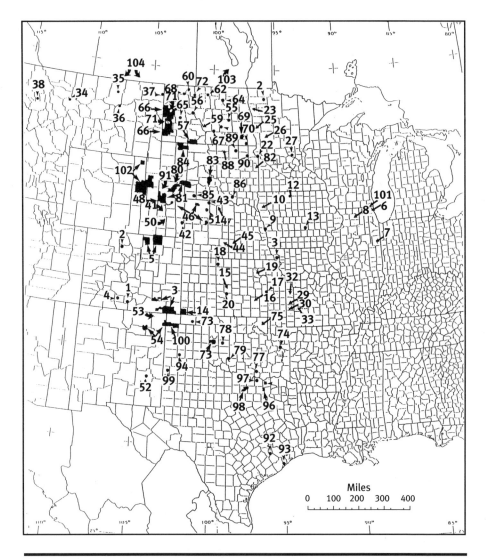

Map of protected sites having significant grassland habitats, comprising (1) national wildlife refuges, including the National Wildlife Range and National Bison Range (*small dots with arrowheads*); (2) national grasslands and national forests (*solid black, with larger straight arrows*); (3) national parks and national monuments (*curved arrows*); and (4) county-, state-, or privately owned (mostly by the Nature Conservancy) sites (*straight, narrow arrows*). Numbers correspond to those used in appendix A. A few sites, mainly widely scattered ones such as federal wetland management districts, are individually numbered in the appendix but not mapped. Some sites contain more than one unit and have multiple arrows.

Comprehensive summer bird lists as well as short descriptions for forty-four bird-watching sites in the Great Plains states were also provided by Johnsgard (1979). Additionally, many bird checklists for refuges and preserves are available on the Northern Prairie Research Station's website:http://www.npwrc.usgs.gov/resource/othrdata/chekbird/chekbird.htm.

Colorado

1. Alamosa N.W.R. 10,356 ac., SC. Bird list (list combined with Monte Vista N.W.R.) available (183 spp., 70 nesters). See appendix B. Ph. 303/236-7920. Box 1148, Alamosa CO 81101. Montane grasslands (7,500–8,000 feet elevation) and riverbottom wetlands.

2. Arapaho N.W.R. 18,253 ac., NC. Bird list available (150 spp., 69 nesters). See appendix B. Ph. 303/723-8202. Box 457, Walden, CO 80480. Sagebrush shrubsteppe and moist meadows in a glacial montane basin (North Park) with many streams forming the Illinois River.

3. Comanche N.G. 419,000 ac., SE. Bird list available (345 spp., 72 nesters, including Cimarron N.G., KS). Ph. 303/523-6591. P.O. Box 127, Springfield CO 81073. Short-grass and midgrass prairie.

4. Monte Vista N.W.R. 14,188 ac., SC. Bird list (combined with Alamosa N.W.R.) available (183 spp., 70 nesters). See appendix B. Ph. 719/589-4021. Box 1148, Alamosa, CO 81101. Montane grasslands (7,500–8,000 feet elevation) and mountain-fed streams, plus farmlands and ca. 200 small wetlands areas.

5. Pawnee N.G. 193,000 ac., federally owned; ca. 500,000 additional ac. in privately owned ranchland. NE. Bird list available (284 spp., nester total unreported). Ph. 303/353-5004. 660 "O" St., Greeley, CO 80631-3033. Short-grass high plains.

Illinois

6. Illinois Beach State Park. 829 ac., NE. Ph. 708/662-4828. Near Zion. Wet and dry tall-grass sandy prairie.

7. Iroquois County Conservation Area. 1,700 ac., NE. Ph. 815/435-2218. Near Beaverville. Tall-grass prairie on black soil. Not far away is Goose Lake Prairie Nature Preserve (1,513 ac.) Ph. 815/9423-2899. Near Morris, Grundy Co. Mesic and wet prairie and wetlands. Owned by IL Dept. of Conservation. There are also some small remnant prairies in Iroquois (Louda Prairie), Ford (Prospect Prairie), Vermillion (Windfall Field), and Will (Grant Creek Prairie) Counties. Anderson (1970) discussed the distribution of historic prairies in Illinois. A massive prairie restoration effort is under way at the 40,000-acre Joliet Arsenal, near Joliet (NE), where the Midewin National Tall-grass Prairie will eventually be established. For more information on Illinois prairie sites call the Illinois Department of Conservation (ph. 217/785-8774).

8. Nachua Grasslands (T.N.C.). 1,000 ac., NC. Ph. 312/346-8166. Near Rochelle. Tall-grass prairie. The Nature Conservancy also has several other prairie sites, including Markham Prairie (300 acres NE, near Kedzie, at the south end of Lake Michigan). The conservancy is also managing a 300-acre area within the greater Chicago area, the Indian Boundary Prairies. Contact the T.N.C. Field Office, 8 S. Michigan Ave., #900, Chicago, IL 60603.

Indiana

Indiana lies near the eastern limits of the central lowlands, in the "prairie peninsula" region that once supported extensive grasslands during the xerothermic period. Madson (1993) listed three small Indiana preserves containing prairie remnants, the largest being Hoosier Prairie Nature Preserve (439 acres, NW), near Griffith, Lake County, and owned by the Indiana Department of Natural Resources (317/232-4052). The Nature Conservancy is currently engaged in restoring a 7,200-acre Kankakee Sands prairie and wetlands habitat (ph. 317/923-7547, or contact T.N.C. Field Office, 1330 W. 38th St., Indianapolis, IN 46208).

Iowa

9. DeSoto N.W.R. 7,823 ac., SW. Ph. 712/642-4121. Bird list available (240 spp., 81 nesters). Ph. 712/642-4121. Rt. 1, Box 14, Missouri Valley, IA 51555. Riverine forest and adjoining grasslands (mostly planted) around an oxbow lake.

10. Five Ridge Prairie. 789 ac., WC. Ph. 712/947-4270. Near Sioux City. Woodlands and prairie on loess hills. Purchased by T.N.C., owned by Plymouth Co. Cons. Board. Nearby is Broken Kettle Grassland (1,187 ac.), owned by T.N.C. and the largest parcel of prairie left in Iowa. For tours, contact preserve office (ph. 712/568-2596), or Iowa's Conservancy Headquarters (ph. 515/244/5044). Mutel (1989) lists nearly fifty other public-use areas in the Loess Hills region between NW Iowa and NW Missouri. These include Loess Hills Wildlife Area, Turin Loess Hills Nature Preserve, and Sylvan Runkel Preserve (collectively ca. 3,500 acres, WC, ph. 712/423-2426), all in Monona County, near Turin. Contact Monona County Conservation Board, Box 209, Onawa, IA 51040. There is also Loess Hills Pioneer State Forest (17,190 acres, under acquisition, WC), in Harrison County, and administered by the Iowa Department of Natural Resources. Ph. 712/423-2400. Mixed-grass prairie and hardwood forest on loess bluffs. A list of 103 probable nesting Loess Hills bird species, including seven grassland endemics, was provided by Mutel (1989). The entire Loess Hills region is part of a Scenic Byway system, with maps available through the state's Welcome Centers (ph. 712/642-2114). The loess hills prairies of Nebraska were described by Nagel (1998). Not far to the east is Cayler Prairie State Preserve (640 acres, near Spirit Lake), now being restored to tall-grass prairie by the Iowa Natural Heritage Foundation (Insurance Exchange Bldg., Suite 444, 505 Fifth Ave., Des Moines, IA 50309, ph. 515/288-1846). This foundation has also published a book, *Iowa's Wild Places,* by Carl Kurtz. A list of state-owned preserves was published by the Iowa State Preserves Board in 1978. Other useful sources of information on Iowa prairie preserves are provided by Roosa (1984), Wolf (1991) and Fleckenstein (1993).

11. T.N.C Preserves. Total of nineteen preserves, including seven small prairies. Contact T.N.C. Field Office, 108 Third St., #300, Des Moines, IA 50309 (ph. 515/244-5044).

12. Union Slough N.W.R. 2,200 ac., NC. Bird list available (217 spp., 96 nesters). Ph. 515/928-2523. Rt. 1, Box 32B, Titonka, IA 50480. Upland prairie (ca. 600 ac.), croplands, and marshes, with riparian woods along Buffalo Creek and Union Slough.

13. Walnut Creek N.W.R. 8,654 ac., SC. Bird list in preparation; 69 spp. on breeding bird count surveys. Ph. 515/994-3400. P.O. Box 399, Prairie City, IA 50228. Near Prairie City. Restored and reconstructed prairie, managed partly for bison.

Kansas

14. Cimarron N.G. 108,175 ac., SW. Bird list (includes Comanche N.G. spp.) available (345 spp., 72 nesters); see Cable, Seltman, and Cook (1997) for an annotated list. See appendix B. Ph. 316/697-4621. 737 Villymaca, Elkhart, KS 67950. Short-grass plains and sandsage steppe, restored since the 1930s droughts.

15. Cheyenne Bottoms Waterfowl Management Area. 18,000 ac., C. Bird list available (319 spp., 104 nesters). Ph. 316/665-0231. Rt. 1, Great Bend, KS 67530. Marshes and moist midgrass prairie, managed for shorebirds and waterfowl. Once part of a vast 40,000-acre marsh and wet meadow, the water levels are now controlled by dikes, using water from the Arkansas River. See Zimmerman (1993).

16. El Dorado State Park. 8,000 ac., SE. Ph. 316/321-7180. Near El Dorado. Remnants of tall-grass prairie. Other prairies on private land occur between El Dorado, Elmdale, and Cottonwood Falls. The Nature Conservancy has acquired 2,818 acres south of the Cottonwood River, near Cassoday on the Butler-Greenwood County line. This area is not regularly open to the public, but tours can be arranged by calling the Nature Conservancy office in Topeka, ph. 913/233-4400. The conservancy has also recently acquired 16,320 acres in western Kansas, the Smoky Valley Ranch, in Logan County. This area contains short-grass prairie, chalk bluffs, rocky ravines, and so on. It was visited by O. C. Marsh on his famous fossil-hunting expeditions. Access is twenty-five miles south of Oakley and Interstate 70. It too is not yet open to the public, but plans are being made to provide future public access. Contact TNC office, Box HP, SE Quincy, #301, Topeka, KS 66612.

The Tall-grass Prairie National Preserve (ca. 11,000 acres) is located north of Cottonwood Falls in the heart of the Flint Hills. This was recently created (1997), and only part of it is open to the public. Most of it is still being used for cattle grazing and is intensively grazed. Short-grass prairie birds like horned larks and migrating Sprague's pipits are most probable right now. Contact information: Tall-grass Prairie National Preserve, PO Box 585, Cottonwood Falls, KS 66845 (ph. 316/273-6034), or visit their website at the URL: http://www.nps.gov/tapr/home.htm.

Zimmerman and Patti (1987) described thirteen tall-grass prairie sites, eight sandsage prairies, nine mixed sandsage and short-grass prairies, and twelve midgrass prairies as being desirable for bird-watching in Kansas. State-owned areas in the Flint Hills larger than 1,000 acres include Berentz/Dick Wildlife Area, 1,360 acres, and Elk City W.A., 12,240 acres, near Independence, Montgomery County (SE); Fall River W.A., 8,392 acres, near Eureka, Greenwood County (SE); John Redmond W.A., 1,472 acres, near Burlington, Coffey County (EC); Melvern W.A., 9,407 acres, near Lebo, Osage County (EC); Perry W.A., 10,984 acres, near Valley Falls, Jefferson County (NE); Toronto W.A., 4,766 acres, and Woodson W.A., 3,065 acres, both near Toronto, Woodson County (SE). Areas in excess of 500 acres include Eisenhower S.P., 620 acres, near Lyndon, Osage County (EC); and Nemaha W.A., 710 acres, near Seneca, Nemaha County (NE). Contact Kansas Wildlife and Parks, 900 SW Jackson St., Topeka, KS 66612 (ph. 785/296-2281). One preserved area in sandsage grassland is Sandhills State Park, 800 acres, near Hutchinson, Reno County (C) (ph. 316/321-7180).

17. Flint Hills N.W.R. 18,463 ac., EC. Bird list available (285 spp., 88 nesters). See appendix B. Ph. 316/392-5553. Box 128, Hartford, KS 66854. Tall-grass and mixed-grass prairie, hardwood forests, and shallow wetlands, as well as part of John Redmond Reservoir.

18. Kirwin. N.W.R. 10,778 ac., NC. Bird list available (191 spp., 46 nesters). See appendix B. Ph. 913/543-6673. Kirwin, KS 67644. Midgrass prairie and hardwoods surrounding the 5,000 ac. Kirwin Reservoir.

19. Konza Prairie. 8,616 ac., NE. Ph. 913/272-5115. Near Manhattan. Major research grassland (tall grass and midgrass), originally purchased by T.N.C. and under long-term study by Kansas State University Div. of Biology. Fourteen miles of hiking trails are open daily from dawn until dusk, weather and trail conditions permitting. The trails begin at the parking area near the main entrance. Pets are not permitted. Group tours of Konza are available only by appointment. See Zimmerman (1993) and Reichman (1987); Zimmerman (1985) provided an annotated bird list that was updated (including 207 species) in his 1993 book. For information on other T.N.C. holdings in Kansas, contact their Field Office, 820 S.E. Quincy, #301, Topeka, KS 66612 (ph. 913/233-4400).

20. Quivira N.W.R. 21,820 ac., C. Bird list available (252 spp., 88 nesters). See appendix B. Ph. 316/486-2393. Box G, Stafford, KS 67578. Mature hardwoods, sandhill grasslands, rangeland, farmland, and alkaline marshes. Permission to enter some areas may be required.

Minnesota

21. Agassiz N.W.R. 61,449 ac., NW. Bird list available (248 spp., 142 nesters). See appendix B. Ph. 218/449-4115. Middle River, MN 56737. Mainly hardwood forests and willow brushlands, some meadows, marshes, and tamarack bogs. Little or no actual prairie is present, but much farmland is reverting to scrubby woods and provides habitat for some prairie ecotone species.

22. Big Stone N.W.R. 10,795 ac., WC. Bird list available (237 spp., 107 nesters). See appendix B. Ph. 612/839-3700. 25 NW 2d St., Ortonville, MN 56278. Glacial till with marshes and prairies, at the southern tip of the Lake Agassiz basin. The marsh (4,000 acres) was formed by impounding the Minnesota River, which is the southern outlet channel of glacial Lake Agassiz. Prairie and Victory W.M.A.s (675 acres, Minnesota Dept. of Natural Resources [DNR]) are nearby and are blacksoil prairies over glacial till.

23. Bluestem Prairie (T.N.C.). 3,258 ac., NW. Ph. 616/331-0750. Near Glyndon (Clay Co.). Tall-grass prairie on blacksoil at the edge of Lake Agassiz. See T.N.C. list below.

24. Minnesota Wetlands Complex (three W.M.D.s, totaling 169,000 ac.), WC. Ph. 208/739-2291. Morris, Fergus Falls, and Litchfield. Rt. 1., Box 76, Fergus Falls, MN 56537. Areas of marshes and grasslands managed for waterfowl production. McKinney-Hellickson W.P.A. (1,365 acres, Becker County) contains over 800 acres of prairie.

25. Pankratz Memorial Prairie (T.N.C.), 1,935 ac., and Agassiz Dunes (T.N.C.), 674 ac., NW. Ph. 616/331-0750. Near Harold, Polk Co. (Pankratz Prairie), and Fertile, Polk, and Norman Counties (Agassiz Dunes). Low prairie (with a fen and sedge meadow), and a mosaic of oak savanna and sand prairie in a dune area, respectively. See also TNC list, no. 28.

26. R. and M. Elliott S.N.A. (T.N.C.). 529 ac., WC. Ph. 616/331-0750. Near Lawndale. Tall-grass prairie.

27. Sherbourne N.W.R. 30,479 ac., EC. Bird list available (213 spp., 113 nesters). Ph. 612/389-3323. Rt. 2, Zimmerman, MN 55398. Oak savanna, prairie grassland, wet meadows, and varied aquatic habitats, including a natural lake (Rice Lake) and impoundments.

28. T.N.C. Preserves. Total of thirty-four preserves, including about twenty prairies in addition to those listed previously. These include Ordway Prairie (582 acres, WC, Pope

County, near Brooten), Foxhome and Ketteldrummer Prairies (ca. 200 acres each, WC, near Fergus Falls, Ottertail County), and Western Prairie North (476 acres, also near Fergus Falls). In Clay County (WC) there is Margaherita Preserve Audubon Prairie (480 acres), and the Felton Prairie complex of Bluestem Prairie S.N.A. and three other S.N.A.s totaling 3,648 acres (see above and below). Wilken County (WC) sites include Town Hall Prairie (200 acres), Anna Gronseth Prairie (1,221 acres), and Western Prairie S.N.A. (320 acres). Plover Prairie (435 acres, WC near Ortonville, Big Stone County), Chippewa Prairie, 1,600 acres, SW near Appleton, Milan County) and Hole-in-the-Mountain Prairie (299 acres, SW, near Lake Benton, Lincoln County) are farther south. Ph. 612/245-2648 or 612/331-0750, or contact T.N.C. Field Office, 1313 Fifth St. S.E., #320, Minneapolis, MN 55414. Chapman et al. (1998) described twenty-six prairie sites in the Red River Valley of Minnesota, including nearly all of these.

The conservancy is currently (1999) acquiring 9,748 acres of tall-grass prairie and aspen parkland in extreme northwestern Minnesota (Grunig lands), most of which will be managed as a nature preserve. Several areas of mixed tall-grass prairie and aspen parkland are also now preserved by state or private agencies in Kittson County (ca. 59,000 acres public, 63,000 acres private, NW).

State-managed wildlife management areas or scientific and natural areas having significant prairies in northwestern Minnesota (Kittson County) include Caribou W.M.A. and Beaches W.M.A. (17,914 acres, near Lake Bronson), plus Skull Lake W.M.A. (7,480 acres) and Twin Lakes W.M.A. (8,780 acres, near Karlstad). Others are farther south in Polk County (Pembina Trail Preserve S.N.A., 2,044 acres, Pankratz Prairie, 775 acres, and Malmberg Prairie S.N.A., 80 acres, all near Crookston). Nearby in Mahnoman County are Agassiz Dunes S.N.A. (417 acres, near Fertile), and Waubon W.M.A. (640 acres NW, near Waubon). In Norman County (WC) are Frenchman's Bluff S.N.A. (51 acres), Sandpiper Prairie S.N.A. (160 acres), Prairie Smoke Dunes S.N.A. (780 acres), and Agassiz Dunes S.N.A. (4,535 acres). In the west-central region is the Felton Prairie complex of three smaller S.N.A.s (Bicentennial Prairie, Blazing Star Prairie, and Shrike Unit) and Bluestem Prairie S.N.A. (3,258 acres, near Glyndon), all in Clay County. Prairie and Victory W.M.A.s, totaling 675 acres WC, are near Ortonville, Big Stone County. In the southwestern region are Prairie Marshes W.M.A. (277 acres, near Lynd, Lyon County) and Expandier W.M.A. (560 acres, near Wyndom, Cottonwood County). The federally owned Pipestone N.M. (283 acres, near Pipestone, Pipestone County) also has some tall-grass prairie.

State parks (SPs) with notable prairies include Blue Mounds SP (1,995 acres, SW, Rock County, near Luverne), Glacial Lakes SP (1,345 acres, WC, Pope County, near Starbuck), and Buffalo River SP (1,240 acres, NW, Clay County, near Glyndon), also managed by the DNR. See Chapman, Ziegenhagen, and Fischer (1998) for a description of tall-grass prairies in the Red River Valley. A total of forty areas containing native prairie in Minnesota were fully described and mapped by Wendt (1984), and 120 preserves in Minnesota were similarly described and mapped by Henderson and Lambrecht (1997). Most of these are managed by the Minnesota DNR (Box 6, Centennial Office Bldg., St. Paul, MN 55155).

Missouri

29. Osage Prairie Conservation Area (C.A.) (T.N.C. and MO Dept. Cons.). 1,467 ac., SW. Ph. 314/751-4115 or 314/968-1105. Near Nevada, Vernon Co. Tall-grass prairie and oak woods. Greater prairie-chicken flock; also Henslow's sparrow.

30. Prairie State Park. 3,702 ac., SW. Ph. 417/843-6711. Near Liberal, Barton Co. Upland tall-grass prairie. Managed by the Missouri Dept. of Conservation. For more information on Missouri prairies, contact the Department of Conservation, P.O. Box 180, Jefferson City, MO 65102 (Ph. 573/751-4115), which has available detailed listings and descriptions of seventy-two public-access prairie sites in Missouri (Davit 1999). Larger sites not here separately listed include (1) Pawnee Prairie C.A. (MO Dept. Cons.) and Pawnee Prairie Preserve (T.N.C.), 900 acres (NW), Harrison County, near Hatfield; (2) Cordgrass Bottoms Natural Area and Locust Creek Prairie (MO Dept. Cons.), 880 acres (NW), both in Pershing State Park, Linn County, near Laclede; (3) Lonesome Prairie C.A. (MO Dept. Cons.), 627 acres (WC), Benton County, near Cole Camp; (4) Marmoton River Bottoms Wet Prairie (T.N.C.), 609 acres (WC), Vernon County, near Nevada; (5) Buffalo Wallow Prairie C.A. (MO Dept. Cons.), 1,113 acres (SW), and Clear Creek C.A. (MO Dept. Cons.), 762 acres (SW), both in Barton County, near Sheldon; (6) Bushwhacker Prairie (MO Dept. Cons.), 6,665 acres (SW), Vernon County, near Bronaugh; (7) Stony Point Prairie C.A. (MO Dept. Cons.), 640 acres (SW), Dade County, near Golden City; and (8) Diamond Grove Prairie Natural Area (MO Dept. Cons.), 611 acres (SW), Newton County, near Diamond. The Missouri Prairie Foundation (P.O. Box 200, Columbia, MO 65205, ph. 1-888-843-6739) also owns thirteen prairies ranging in size up to 376 acres. The Nature Conservancy Field Office is at 2800 S. Brentwood Blvd., St. Louis, MO 63144 (ph. 314/968-1105). See also Nelson (1985) for a description of Missouri's terrestrial communities.

31. Squaw Creek N.W.R. 6,887 ac., NW. Bird list available (268 spp., 104 nesters). See appendix B. Ph. 816/442-3187. Box 101, Mound City, MO 64470. Extensive marshlands (about half the total refuge area), with wet prairies; upland prairies and oak woods on nearby loess hills.

32. Taberville Prairie Conservation Area and National Natural Landmark (MO Dept. Cons.). 1,680 ac., SW. Ph. 314/751-4115. Near Appleton, St. Clair Co. Upland tall-grass prairie. Includes a greater prairie-chicken population.

33. Wah'-Kon-Tah Prairie (T.N.C. and MO Dept. Cons). 2,858 ac., WC. Ph. 314/968-1105. Near El Dorado Springs, St. Clair and Cedar Counties. Tall-grass prairie on uplands, and hardwood-covered valleys; the largest tall-grass prairie east of Oklahoma. Supports greater prairie-chickens, Henslow's sparrows, and other tall-grass prairie endemics.

Montana

34. Benton Lake N.W.R. 12,383 ac., C. Bird list available (167 spp., 59 nesters). See appendix B. Ph. 406/727-7400. Box 450, Black Eagle, MT 59414. Diked lake (Benton Lake) surrounded by rolling prairie grasslands and cultivated crops. Freezout Lake W.M.A. is fairly close, near Fairfield, and has some grasslands around the lake.

35. Bowdoin N.W.R. 15,437 ac., NC. Bird list available (206 spp., 102 nesters). See appendix B. Ph. 402/654-2863. Box J, Malta, MT 59538. Upland prairie and marshes around partly diked and alkaline Lake Bowdoin (ca. 4,300 ac.).

36. Charles M. Russell Natl. Wildlife Range. 1,094,000 ac., NE. Bird list available (252 spp., 98 nesters). See appendix B. Ph. 406/538-8706. Box 110, Lewistown, MT 59457. Shortgrass upland prairie, shoreline hardwoods around Fort Peck reservoir, and associated wetlands. To the southeast, near Glendive, is Makoshika State Park, and still farther

south, near Eklaka, is Medicine Rocks State Park. Both are mostly eroded sandstone cliffs but both include short-grass prairie. Contact Montana Fish, Wildlife and Parks Dept., 1420 E. 6th St., Helena, MT 59620 (ph. 406-444-2535). There is also prairie on the Nature Conservancy's Pine Butte Preserve (20,000 acres, NW), near Choteau. Permission to enter required. Contact the preserve at Pine Butte Guest Ranch, HC58 Box 34C, Choteau, MT 59422 (ph. 406/466-2377), or T.N.C. field office, Last Chance Gulch and 6th, P.O. Box 258, Helena, MT (ph. 406/443-0303). There is a new 60,000-acre prairie preserve owned by the Nature Conservancy in southern Phillips County, the Matador Ranch, supporting black-footed ferrets, prairie dogs, swift foxes, mountain plovers, and other rare mixed-grass and short-grass species.

37. Medicine Lake N.W.R. 31,457 ac., NE. Bird list available (219 spp., 96 nesters). See appendix B. Ph. 406/789-2305. Medicine Lake, MT 59247. Short-grass upland prairies, brushy areas, marshes, and impounded Medicine Lake.

38. National Bison Range. 18,542 ac., WC. Bird list available (268 spp., 104 nesters). See appendix B. Ph. 406/644-2211. Moiese, MT 59824. Short-grass plains at 4,500 feet elevation and scattered woods, managed for bison, elk, deer, and other large mammals.

39. Ninepipe N.W.R. 2,000+ ac., WC. Bird list (combined with Pablo N.W.R.) available (188 spp., 74 nesters). See appendix B. Ph. 406/644-2211. South of Ronan, just south of Bison Range. C/o Natl. Bison Range, Moiese, MT 59824. Upland prairie, marshes, and other Flathead Valley wetlands associated with irrigation.

40. Pablo N.W.R. 2,500+ ac., WC. North of Ronan, just south of Bison Range. See Ninepipe N.W.R. Similar to and near Ninepipe N.W.R., and also with irrigation-based wetlands (ca. 2,500 wetland ac.).

Nebraska

41. Agate Fossil Beds N.M. 2,700 ac., NW. Ph. 308/436-4340. P.O. Box 427. Gering, NE, 69341. Short-grass plains with rich Cenozoic fossil deposits. No bird list.

42. Crescent Lake N.W.R. 45,818 ac., WC. Bird list available (279 spp., 86 nesters). See appendix B, ph. 308/762-4893. Star Rt., Ellsworth, NE 69340. Sandhills grasslands and dozens of small, mostly alkaline shallow lakes and marshes.

43. Fort Niobrara N.W.R. 19,124 ac., NC. Bird list available (201 spp., 76 nesters). See appendix B, ph. 402/376-3789. Hidden Timber Rt., Valentine, NE 69201. Riverine woods, grassy uplands, and sandhills prairie, managed for bison, elk, and longhorn cattle.

44. Lillian Annette Rowe Sanctuary (Natl. Audubon Soc.). 2,200 ac., C. Ph. 308/468-5282. Rt. 2, Box 146, Gibbon, NE 68840. Riverine forest, wet meadows, and moist tall-grass prairie. No bird list is yet available for the sanctuary, but a complete list of breeding birds of the central Platte Valley exists, and more than 140 species have been reported (Faanes and Lingle, 1995).

45. Mormon Island Whooping Crane Meadows Preserve. 2,500 ac., SC. Ph. 308/384-4633. Near Alda. A nature center is located near the Alda interstate exchange. Riverine forest, wet meadows, and moist tall-grass prairie. The ecology of this section of the Platte River was described by Johnsgard (1984). No published bird list (but see no. 44); 212 species had been recorded on the preserve through early 1989 (Faanes and Lingle 1995). Prairie restoration is under way.

46. Nebraska National Forest. Three rather widely separated units totaling 360,000 ac.: the Bessey District, 90,448 ac., C; the Samuel McKelvie District, 115,700 ac., NC; and

the Pine Ridge District, 52,000 ac., NW. Bird list available (ca. 250 spp., 36 nesters). Ph. 308/432-3367, 308/432-4475 (Pine Ridge), or 308/533-2257 (Bessey). Headquarters: 270 Pine St., Chadron, NE 69337. The Pine Ridge unit is largely native ponderosa pines, with some grasslands, but the Bessey and McKelvie Districts consist of Sandhills prairie, with extensive conifer plantings of native and exotic pines in the Bessey unit. Significant mixed pine–grasslands areas in the Pine Ridge include Gilbert-Baker (W.M.A.), 2,337 acres, near Harrison, Sioux County (ph. 308/762-5605), Fort Robinson State Park (22,000 acres) (ph. 308/665-2900), Peterson W.M.A., 2,640 acres (ph. 308/762-5605), and Soldier Creek Wilderness (9,600 acres) (ph. 308/432-4475), all near Crawford, Sioux County. Sioux County Ranch and Guadalcanal Memorial Prairie is a working ranch near Harrison, with 5,000 acres of mostly short-grass prairie, one of several prairie sites that are owned and managed by the Plains Prairie Resource Institute, Aurora, NE (ph. 402/694-5535). One area of special geological importance, with midgrass prairies, is Ashfall Fossil Beds State Historical Park (NE), 360 acres, in Antelope County, near Royal. Contact Park Mgr., P.O. Box 66, Royal, NE 68773.

Twenty Nebraska Sandhills prairie preserves or similar areas and their associated floras and faunas were described and mapped by Johnsgard (1995). The most important of these are Valentine and Crescent Lake National Wildlife refuges, but several state parks, state recreation areas, and wildlife management areas also exist in the Sandhills. Sharp-tailed grouse and greater prairie-chickens are both fairly common in the Sandhills, as are long-billed curlews and upland sandpipers.

Tall-grass prairies supporting greater prairie-chickens also exist in southeastern Nebraska at Pawnee Prairie W.M.A., 1,021 acres, and Burchard Lake State Park, 560 acres, both near Burchard, Pawnee County. Prairie areas near Lincoln include Nine-mile Prairie (260 acres), Twin Lakes W.M.A. (1,370 acres), and Audubon Society's Spring Creek Prairie (610 acres, ph. 402/797-2301). Several smaller tall-grass prairies in this southeastern region are managed by Lincoln's Audubon Society (ph. 402/486-4846), including Wildcat Creek Prairie, near Virginia; Dieken Prairie, near Unadilla; Kasl Prairie, near Crete; and Bentzinger Prairie, near Syracuse. For information on all state-owned grassland areas, including state parks, state recreation areas, and wildlife management areas, contact Parks Div., Nebraska Game and Parks Comm., Box 30370, Lincoln, NE 68503 (ph. 800/826-PARK). Over 400 Nebraska birding sites (mostly grasslands) with public access were described by Johnsgard (in press); sixty-eight Nebraska birding sites were listed by Knue (1997), and Lingle (1994) described twenty-two birding sites in seven Platte River counties. Nagel (1998) has described Nebraska's loess hills prairies.

47. Niobrara Valley Preserve (T.N.C.). 56,000 ac., NC. Ph. 402/722-4440. Near Springview. Keya Paha Co. Riparian transition zone between western ponderosa pine and eastern hardwood floodplain forest, with adjoining sandhills prairie uplands. Partly managed for bison. No complete bird list yet, but a list of 105 summering bird species and presumptive breeders has been published (Brogie and Mossman 1983). For other T.N.C. holdings in Nebraska, which include a Sandhills fen and many wetlands, contact their field office, 1722 St. Mary's Ave., Omaha NE 68102 (ph. 402/342-0282).

48. Oglala N.G. 94,344 ac., NW. Bird list of 302 pp. (covering all of Pine Ridge area) available from U.S. Forest Service, 270 Pine St., Chadron, NE 69337. Ph. 308/432-3367 or 308/432-4475. Short-grass prairie and eroded badlands (including Toadstool Geological Park, a highly eroded badland area).

49. Rainwater Basin W.M.D. Two units, totaling 15,000 ac., SC. Bird list available (256 spp., 102 nesters). See appendix B. Ph. 308/236-5015. Near Hastings and Holdrege. Box 1786, Kearney, NE 68847. Shallow, temporary wetlands surrounded by grasslands and agricultural land. Some of these are being restored to prairie.

50. Scotts Bluff N.M. 2,988 ac., WC. Ph. 308/436-4340. P.O. Box 427, Gering, NE 69341. Conifer-covered bluffs surrounded by short-grass uplands. No bird list.

51. Valentine N.W.R. 71,516 ac., NC. Bird list available (233 spp., 95 nesters). See appendix B. Ph. 402/376-3789. C/o Ft. Niobrara N.W.R., Hidden Timber Rt., Valentine, NE 69201. Marshes, dozens of shallow and usually alkaline lakes, wet meadows, and sandhills prairie.

New Mexico

52. Bitter Lake N.W.R. 23,000 ac., EC. Bird list available (282 spp., 654 nesters). Ph. 505/622-6755. Box 7, Roswell, NM 88201 Shrubsteppe uplands and alkaline marshes, as well as ca. fifteen miles of river bottomland.

53. Capulin Mountain N.M. 775 ac., NE. Bird list available (104 spp.). Ph. 505/278-2201. Capulin, NM 88414. Upland short-grass plains and scrubby woodland around an extinct volcano.

54. Kiowa N.G. 136,505 ac., NE. Bird list available (226 spp., sixty residents or summer residents). Ph. 505/374-9652. 16 N. 2d St., Clayton, NM 88415. Short-grass upland plains. For Rita Blanca N.G. account, see Texas.

North Dakota

55. Arrowwood N.W.R. 15,934 ac., EC. Bird list available (246 spp., 105 nesters). See appendix B. Ph. 701/285-3341. R.R. 1, Pingree, ND 58476. Upland mixed-grass prairies with several small lakes and a large marsh caused by damming the James River. Nearby Chase Lake N.W.R. (375 acres) is administered here, too.

56. Audubon N.W.R. 14,735 ac., C. Bird list available (205 spp., 85 nesters). See appendix B. Ph. 701/442-5474. R.R. 1, Coleharbor, ND 58531. Upland prairies and marshes adjoining a large impoundment.

57. Cedar River N.G. 6,237 ac., SC. Ph. 605/374-3592. P.O. Box 390, Lemmon, SD 57638. Short-grass and mixed-grass prairie.

58. Crosby W.M.D. 85,819 ac., NW. Ph. 701/965-6488. Box 148, Crosby, ND 58730. Prairie wetlands managed for waterfowl.

59. Cross Ranch Nature Preserve (T.N.C.). 6,000 ac., C. Ph. 701/794-8741. Near Bismarck. Mixed-grass upland prairie and floodplain. For information on other T.N.C. holdings, contact their field office, 2000 Schafer St., #8, Bismarck, ND 58501 (ph. 701/222-8464). These include Brown Ranch (1,531 acres) and Pigeon Point Reserve in Ransom County, Davis Ranch in Sheridan County, J. E. Williams Memorial Preserve in McLean County, and Cross Ranch in Oliver County.

60. Des Lacs N.W.R. 18,881 ac., NC. Bird list (combined Souris Loop refuges) available (266 spp., 147 nesters). See appendix B. Ph. 701/965-6488. Box 578, Kenmare, ND 58746. Prairie (ca. 7,000-10,000 ac.), brushland, marshes. and several small river-dependent lakes.

61. Devils Lake W.M.D. 197,555 ac., NE. Ph. 701/965-6488. 218 W. 4th St., Devil's Lake, ND 58301. Wetlands managed for waterfowl.

62. J. Clark Salyer N.W.R. 58,693 ac., NC. Bird list (combined Souris Loop refuges) available (266 spp., 147 nesters). See appendix B. Ph. 701/768-2548. U.S.F.W.S., Upham, ND 58789. Midgrass prairie, wet meadows, woods, and wetlands, the wetlands formed by damming the Souris River.

63. Kulm W.M.D. 42,352 ac., SE. Ph. 701/647-2866. Box E, Kulm, ND 58456. Wetlands managed for waterfowl.

64. Lake Alice N.W.R. 10,772 ac., NE. Ph. 701/662-8611. Box 908, Devil's Lake, ND 58301. Lake surrounded by prairie and shoreline hardwoods.

65. Lake Ilo N.W.R. 3,737 ac., WC. Bird list available (205 spp., 83 nesters). See appendix B. Ph. 701/548-4467. Near Dunn Center. U.S.F.W.S., c/o Des Lacs N.W.R., Kenmare, ND 58746. Lake surrounded by prairie and shoreline hardwoods.

66. Little Missouri N.G. 1,027,852 ac., WC. Ph. 701/225-5152. Rt. 3, Box 131-B, Dickinson, ND 58601. Short-grass plains and eroded badlands; the largest area of federally protected short-grass plains in the nation.

67. Long Lake N.W.R. 22,300 ac., SC. Bird list available (203 spp., 78 nesters). See appendix B. Ph. 701/387-4397. R.R. 1, Moffit, ND 58560. Upland prairie, a shallow lake (Long Lake, ca. 16,000 ac.), marshes, and cultivated lands.

68. Lostwood N.W.R. 26,747 ac., NW. Bird list (combined Souris Loop refuges) available (266 spp., 147 nesters). See appendix B. Ph. 701/848-2722. R.R. 2., Box 98, Kenmore, ND 58746. Upland prairie, aspen groveland, and alkaline lakes and marshes or prairie potholes. Prairie covers nearly 80 percent of the refuge, or 22,500 acres. Sprague's pipit and Baird's sparrows are common, as are most other grassland endemics of the northern plains.

69. Sheyenne N.G. 70,180 ac., SE. Ph. 701/683-4342. Sheyenne Ranger District, P.O. Box 946, 701 Main St., Lisbon, ND 58054. Sandhills tall-grass prairie and riverine hardwoods on a sandy glacial-age delta of the Sheyenne River; the largest area of federally owned tall-grass prairie in the U.S.A. Nearby are the Mirror Pool North and Mirror Pool Swamp state natural areas (471 acres) just north of the Sheyenne River, of fens, swamps, deciduous forest, and choppy dunes, and Pigeon Point Preserve (560 acres), of spring-fed wetlands. For information contact the Nature Conservancy, 2000 Schafer St., Suite B, Bismarck, ND (701/222-8464). Chapman et al. (1998) described these Sheyenne Delta prairie sites.

70. Tewaukon N.W.R. 8,444 ac., SE. Bird list available (236 spp., 98 nesters). See appendix B. Ph. 701/724-3598. R.R. 1, Cayuga, ND 58013. Prairie, cropland, marshes, and riverine wetlands on glacial till.

71. Theodore Roosevelt N. P. 70,416 ac., WC. Bird list available (170 spp., 58 nesters). See appendix B. Ph. 701/623-4466. P.O. Box 7, Medora, ND 58645. Eroded badlands, short-grass plains, and shrubsteppe.

72. Upper Souris N.W.R. 32,000 ac., NC. Bird list (combined Souris Loop refuges) available (266 spp., 147 nesters). See appendix B. Ph. 701/845-3466. R.R. 1, Foxholme, ND 58738. Midgrass prairie, woods, and wetlands.

Ohio

Like Indiana, Ohio is far to the east of the Great Plains grasslands and has not supported extensive prairies for thousands of years. Three very small relict Ohio prairies were listed by Madson (1993; 1995). Thompson (1994) described over 300 birding sites in the state, many of which include small areas of native grasslands. A list of state-owned preserves was published by the Ohio Department of Natural Resources in 1978. Contact Ohio Div. of Wildlife, Fountain Sq., Bldg. C-4, Columbus, OH 43224 (ph. 614/532-3223). The Nature Conservancy has a sixty-page guide to their twenty preserves in Ohio. These include some small prairies, such as Lynx Prairie, near Lynx (SC). Four of these preserves are public access, and three have bird lists. Contact T.N.C., Ohio Field Office, 1504 W. 1st Ave., Columbus, OH 43212 (ph. 614/486-6789).

Oklahoma

73. Black Kettle N.G. 32,000 ac., WC. Ph. 580/497-2143. P.O. Box 266, Cheyenne, OK 73628. Midgrass and tall-grass prairie and upland woods. For Rita Blanca N.G. account, see Texas. Not far northwest and near Guymon is Optima N.W.R. 4,333 ac. Bird list available (246 spp., 106 nesters). See appendix B. Ph. 580/664-2205. R.R. 1, Box 68, Butler, OK 73625. Short-grass and midgrass prairie, sage-dominated shrubsteppe, and hardwoods adjoining Optima Reservoir on the Beaver River.

74. Sequoyah N.W.R. 20,800 ac., EC. Bird list available (250 spp., 96 nesters). Ph. 918/773-5251. Rt. 1, Box 18A, Vian, OK 74962. Adjoins Kerr Reservoir, at the confluence of the Canadian and Arkansas Rivers. Grasslands, hardwoods, wetlands, and open water. To the south, within the Ouachita National Forest, (200,000 acres, ph. 918/653-2991) is the Winding Stair Mountain National Recreational Area of more than 70,000 acres, which includes some wilderness areas, wildlife areas, and preserved botanic areas.

75. Tall-grass Prairie Preserve (T.N.C.). 44,503 ac., NC. Ph. 918/287-4803 (preserve headquarters) or 918/585-1117 (T.N.C. field office). Near Pawhuska, Osage Co. Tall-grass prairie and about 1,000 reintroduced bison; the largest area of preserved tall-grass prairie in the United States. Over 700 plant species have been identified. A bird list for the tall-grass prairie area and wooded Osage Hills has nearly 300 species, of which ninety-seven are known nesters and eight are grassland endemics (contact OK Dept. Conserv., 1801 N. Lincoln Blvd., Oklahoma City, OK 73105). The Osage Hills prairies were described by Smith (1996). Nearby is the Prairie National Wild Horse Preserve, 18,000 acres (ph. 918/333-5575).

76. Other Nature Conservancy sites. A short-grass preserve (Black Mesa Preserve) of 1,600 acres is located at Black Mesa, Cimarron County (NW). Ph. 918/585-1117. Black Mesa State Park (ph. 405/521-2409) is contiguous and also includes short-grass prairie. The Pontotoc Ridge Nature Preserve (2,900 acres), Pontotoc County (SC), near Ada (ph. 405/580-2224), includes tall-grass and short-grass prairies as well as bottomland forest, located at the eastern edge of the Arbuckle Uplift. Other smaller T.N.C. preserves in Oklahoma include remnant prairies, for information, contact their field office, 23 West Fourth, #200, Tulsa, OK 74103 (ph. 918/585-1117).

77. Tishomingo N.W.R. 16,464 ac., SC. Bird list available (243 spp., 81 nesters). Ph. 580/371-3402. Rt. 1., Box 152, Tishomingo, OK 73460. Grasslands, wetlands, oak-hickory woods, and cultivated lands, adjoining Lake Texoma Reservoir of the Red River.

78. Washita N.W.R. 8,200 ac., WC. Bird list available (220 spp., 67 nesters). See appendix B. Ph. 580-664-2205. Rt., 1., Box 68, Butler, OK 73625. Grasslands (mostly short-grass prairie), wetlands, woods, and cultivated lands adjoining Foss Reservoir of the Washita River.

79. Wichita Mountains N.W.R. 59,020 ac., SW. Bird list available (212 spp., 61 nesters). Ph. 580-429-3222. Rt. 1., Box 448, Indiahoma, OK 73552. Grassy and oak-covered uplands

up to 700 feet high (the eroded remnants of 500-million-year-old mountains) and more than 100 small wetlands, mostly impoundments. Excellent tall-grass prairie remnants. Managed partly for bison, elk, and longhorn cattle.

South Dakota

80. Badlands N.P. 243,302 ac., SW. Bird list available (208 spp., no nester total). Ph. 605/433-5361. P.O. Box 6, Interior, SD 57750. Eroded high plains with short-grass prairie and shrubsteppe.

81. Buffalo Gap N.G. 591,771 ac., SW. Bird list available (197 spp., no nester total). Ph. 605/279-2125 or 605/745-4107. P.O. Box 425, U.S.F.S., 708 Main St., Wall, SD 57790, or U.S.F.S., 209 N. River, Hot Springs, SD. 57747. Short-grass and midgrass prairie. For Oglala N.G., see Nebraska listing.

82. Crystal Springs Prairie (T.N.C.). 1,920 ac., NE. Ph. 701/222-8464. Near Clear Lake. Tall-grass prairie.

83. Fort Pierre N.G. 115,996 ac., C. Ph. 605/224-5517. P.O. Box 417, 124 S. Euclid Ave., Pierre, SD 57501. Short-grass and midgrass prairie.

84. Grand River N.G. 156,000 ac., NW. Ph. 605/374-3592. P.O. Box 390, Lemmon, SD 57638. Short-grass and midgrass prairie.

85. Lacreek N.W.R. 16,250 ac., SC. Bird list available (213 spp., 93 nesters). See appendix B. Ph. 605/685-6508. Star Rt. 3, Martin, SD 57551. Sandhills grasslands (including ca. 4,000 ac. of mixed-grass prairie) and wetlands, in the Little White River Valley.

86. Lake Andes N.W.R. 5,942 ac., SE. Bird list available (214 spp., 85 nesters). See appendix B. Ph. 605/487-7603. R.R. 1, Box 77, Lake Andes, SD 57356. Tall-grass prairie, woods, and wetlands.

87. Madison W.M.D. 25,000 ac., EC. Ph. 605/256-2974. Box 48, Madison, SD 57042. Prairie wetlands managed for waterfowl.

88. Samuel H. Ordway Jr. Memorial Prairie Preserve (T.N.C.). 7,800 ac., NE. Ph. 605/439-3475 or 701/222-8464. Near Leola. Tall-grass prairies and wetlands, the largest tall-grass prairie in South Dakota. For information on other South Dakota holdings of T.N.C., contact their field office, 1000 West Ave. North, Sioux Falls, SD 57104 (ph. 605/331-0619). The Adams Nature Preserve, 1,500 acres, SE, in the extreme southeastern Missouri Valley is the largest state-owned natural area, with grasslands and wooded bottomlands, and includes seven miles of trails. Ph. 605/773-3391, Div. of Parks & Recreation, 523 E. Capitol Ave., Pierre, SD 57501. Many state parks also have relict grassland fragments.

89. Sand Lake N.W.R. 231,451 ac., NE. Bird list available (239 spp., 111 nesters). See appendix B. Ph. 605/885-6320. R.R. 1, Columbia, SD 57433. Tall-grass prairie and woods bordering the James River, two lakes, and several marshes, the total water area ca. 11,000 ac.

90. Waubay N.W.R. 4,650 ac., NE. Bird list available (244 spp., 109 nesters). See appendix B. Ph. 605/947-4521. Box 79, Waubay, SD 57273. Tall-grass prairie and dozens of glacial-formed wetland potholes on rolling upland till.

91. Wind Cave National Park, 28,056 ac., and adjacent Custer State Park. Bird list, including Black Hills National Forest, available (186 spp., no nester total). Short-grass prairie and coniferous forest. Write U.S.Forest Service, Hot Springs, SD 57747 (ph. 605/745-4600). Although Wind Cave N.P. is mostly forested, the adjacent Custer State

Park (ca. 73,000 acres, ph. 605/255-4515) immediately to the north is mostly short-grass prairie. It is managed for bison and other large ungulates but also has some wetland habitats, including four small lakes and several streams.

Texas

92. Attwater Prairie-chicken N.W.R. 8,000 ac., SE. Bird list available (266 spp., over 70 breeders or probable breeders). Ph. 409/234-5940. Box 518, Eagle Lake, TX 77434. Coastal tall-grass prairie managed for a highly endangered race of greater prairie-chicken (now virtually extinct; eighteen birds present in summer 1999, plus twenty-eight in a Galveston County T.N.C. preserve). About 4,000 acres of tall-grass coastal prairie are present; the rest is mostly hardwoods and croplands. Smaller areas of remnant or restored coastal prairie are also present at Mad Island Marsh (7,048 acres, SE, Matagora County), Anhuac N.W.R. (24,356 acres, SE), near Anhuac (ph. 409/267-3337); and Brazos Bend State Park (4,900 acres, SE), south of Houston (Texas Dept. of Tourism, ph. 512/462-9191 or 1/800-888-8839).

93. Brazoria N.W.R. 40,854 ac., SE. Bird list available (272 spp., 71 nesters). Ph. 409/849-7771. 1216 N. Velasco, PO Drawer 1088, Angleton, TX 77515. Coastal prairie. San Barnard N.W.R. (24,500 acres) is nearby in Brazoria County. Bird list available. Ph. 409/849-6062.

94. Buffalo Lake N.W.R. 7,664 ac., NW. Bird list available (246 spp., 42 nesters). See appendix B. Ph. 806/499-3383. Box 228, Umbarger, TX 79091. Short-grass plains and alkaline wetlands; Buffalo Lake is a shallow, alkaline, and sometimes dry playa lake.

95. Black Kettle N.G. 31,000 ac., NC. See Oklahoma account for description.

96. Caddo N.G. 17,796 ac., NE. Ph. 817/627-5475. P.O. Box 507, Decatur, TX 76234. Upland mixed prairie and hardwoods. Nearby is Gene Howe W.M.A., which has a population of lesser prairie-chickens.

97. Hagerman N.W.R. 11,319 ac., NE. Bird list available (272 spp., 86 nesters). See appendix B. Ph. 214/786-2826. Rt. 3, Box 123, Sherman, TX 75090. Grasslands, hardwoods, and marshes associated with Lake Texoma. To the south in Collin County is Parkhill Prairie Reserve (436 acres), a county-owned preserve (ph. 214/548-4653 or 548-4619). Several small Nature Conservancy reserves of tall-grass prairie also occur in northeastern Texas, including Tridens Prairie, Clymer Meadow (311 acres), County Line Prairie, Mathews Prairie, and Leonhardt Prairie. For information, see Madson (1993; 1995) or contact T.N.C., P.O. Box 1440, San Antonio, TX 78295-1440 (ph. 210/224-8774). The grasslands associated with the now canceled super conducting super collider have been proposed by T.N.C. as a 12,000-acre preserve in Ellis County, near Waxahatchie.

98. Lyndon B. Johnson N.G. 20,320 ac., NE. Ph. 817/627-5475. P.O. Box 507, Decatur, TX 76234. Grasslands and hardwoods.

99. Muleshoe N.W.R. 5,809 ac., NW. Bird list available (243 spp., 59 nesters). See appendix B. Ph. 806/946-3341. Box 549, Muleshoe, TX 79347. Sandy short-grass and semi-desert grasslands and alkaline wetlands, with alkaline, often temporary, playa lakes.

100. Rita Blanca N.G. 77,413 ac., NW. Ph. 806/362-4254. Box 38, Texline, TX 79807. Short-grass and midgrass prairies. Also in the NW are Copper Breaks S.P. (Hardemann County); Matador W.M.A. (28,000 acres) near Crowell, in Ford County; and Caprock Canyon S.P. (13,906 acres) in Briscoe County, near Quitague. All have some arid grasslands present.

Wisconsin

101. Chiwaukee Prairie (T.N.C.). 580 ac., SE. Ph. 608/251-8140. Near Kenosha. Tall-grass prairie. Another important Wisconsin Prairie is Avoca Prairie–Savanna (1,885 acres). Near Avoca (ph. 608/251-8180). One-third of 206 acres is Kettle Moraine Fen and Low Prairie, near Eagle. The Wisconsin Department of Natural Resources provided a list of scientific sites in the state in 1978. For information on these and other state-owned sites, contact Wisc. Bureau of Endangered Resources, Wisc. Dept. of Natural Resources, 101 S. Webster St., Madison, WI 53702 (ph. 608/266-7012). The Nature Conservancy has published a directory to forty-two preserves, including several small prairies (*The Places We Save*). It is available from T.N.C. Field Office, P.O. Box 1642, Madison, WI 73703 (ph. 608/251-8140).

Wyoming

102. Thunder Basin N.G. 572,319 ac., NE. Ph. 307/358-4690. 809 9th St., Douglas, WY 82633. (Bird list of 231 species, breeder list unreliable). Short-grass and shrubsteppe (mostly the latter) plains, the largest area of protected prairie in Wyoming, and with the largest herd of pronghorn antelope in the state. The mountain plover, upland sandpiper, long-billed curlew, and both longspurs are common. Nearby Bureau of Land Management (BLM) lands to the east increase the effective area of native vegetation, and much of central Wyoming is also sage-dominated shrubsteppe under BLM jurisdiction.

Canadian Grassland Sites

Government-owned grassland preserves in western Canada are managed by the Western and Northern Office of the Canadian Wildlife Service, Rm. 1000, 9942-108 St., Edmonton, AB T5K 2J5. Bird research is conducted in the Prairie Migratory Bird Research Centre, 115 Perimeter Rd., Saskatoon, SK S7N OX4OX4 (ph. 306/975-4089). The national headquarters of the Nature Conservancy is in Suite 1704, 2180 Yonge St., Toronto, ON M4S 2E1.

Manitoba

103. Manitoba Tall-grass Prairie Preserve (Rural Municipalities of Stuartburn). Prairie remnants totalling ca. 5,000 ac. near Tolstoi and Gardenton. Nearby is the Gardenton Community Pasture, of nearly 12,000 acres. There are also prairie preserves in the Rural Municipalities of Woodlands (Lake Francis W.M.A., 16,000 acres) and Rockwood (Oak Hammock W.M.A., 280 acres). Chapman et al. (1998) have described these tall-grass/aspen parkland sites. Contact the Nature Conservancy, Canada, 298 Garry St., Winnipeg MB R3C (ph. 204/942-6156) or Critical Wildlife Program, Manitoba DNR, Box 24, 200 Salteaux Crescent, Winnipeg, MB R3J-3W3 (ph. 204/945-7750). Riding Mountain National Park (736,000 acres, SW) is mostly forested with conifers and aspens but has some areas of mixed-grass prairie ("fescue prairie"). Contact park headquarters at Wasagaming, MB ROJ 2HO (ph. 204/8487-2811). Likewise, Turtle Mountain Provincial Park (SW) is largely aspen parkland but has some grasslands. Contact Dept. of Natural Resources, Box 24, 1495 St. James St., Winnipeg, MB R3H 0W9, or Turtle Mountain Conservation District, Box 508, Deloraine, MN ROM OMO.

Saskatchewan

104. Grasslands N.P. 233,100 ac., SW. Bird list available (177 spp., nesting species unreported). P.O. Box 150, Val Marie, Sask. SON 2TO (ph. 306/298-2257). Southeast of Val Marie (75 mi. north of Malta, MT), in two blocks. The West Block can only be reached from Wood Mountain. Probably Canada's largest area of protected grasslands, mostly of intermediate height. The East Block also contains badlands topography and short-grass prairie. Fairly near (about 100 miles north of Havre, MT) is Cypress Hills Interprovincial Park, straddling the Saskatchewan-Alberta border (collective total ca. 85,000 acres). A transitional region of aspens, conifers, mixed-grass prairie, and fescue prairie, a mixed-grass variant. Its bird list (Godfrey 1950) includes over 200 species. Contact Cypress Hills Park, Box 850, Maple Creek, SON INO (ph. 306/662-4471). Last Mountain Lake National Wildlife Area (ca. 40,000 acres), north of Regina, is about 50 percent prairie and is an important migratory and breeding area for ducks (thirteen nesters), shorebirds (nine nesters), and songbirds (forty-three nesters, including Baird's sparrow). Nearby is Stalwart National Wildlife Area (2,700 acres, near Stalwart) of marshes, meadows, and short-grass prairie. Old Wive's Lake (103,635 acres), near Moose Jaw, also has considerable prairie. Native prairies in the aspen parkland zone are typically dominated by fescue grasses and are richer in species than are the mixed-grass prairies, but their avifaunas are very similar. In this aspen transition zone are Greenwater Provincial Park (SE, near Chelan), Duck Mountain Provincial Park (SE, near Kamsack), and Moose Mountain Provincial Park (SE, 99,000 acres, near Carlyle), all of which are mostly wooded. Park information is available from the Saskatchewan Parks, Recreation, and Culture, 3211 Albert St., Regina, SA S4S 5W6 (ph. 306/787-2700). One may also write Tourism Saskatchewan, 2103 11th Ave., Regina, SA S4P 3V7 (ph. 306/565-2300) or visit the Parks Canada internet website: <http//parkscanada.pch.gc.ca>.One may also write the Canadian Wildlife Service, P.O. Box 280, Simpson, SA SOG 4MO (ph. 306/836-2010). The regional website of the Canadian Wildlife Service <www.mb.ec.gc.ca> provides maps and detailed information on national wildlife areas and migratory bird sanctuaries throughout the prairie regions of western Canada.

105. Prairie National Wildlife Areas. Scattered group of twenty-seven units, totaling 7,247 ac., the largest being Stalwart (see no. 106) and Webb (1,055 ac., near Shaunavan). Prairie wetlands managed for waterfowl. For information, contact the Canadian Wildlife Service's Migratory Bird Research Centre (address above) or Environment Canada, Twin Atria Bldg., 2d Floor, 4999 98th Ave., Edmonton, AB T6B 2X3, ph. 403/468-8075.

Alberta

106. Cypress Hills Interprovincial Park (see no. 104). The Alberta prairies within the Cypress Hills region are somewhat more mesic than are those of Saskatchewan, but both are known locally as fescue grassland. For information, contact the superintendent, c/o General Delivery, Elkwater, AB TOJ ICo (ph. 403/893-3777). Short-grass prairie is preserved in Writing-on-Stone Provincial Park (SC, 4,500 acres), near Milk River. About sixty bird species are nesters. For information, write Box 297, Milk River, AB TOK IMP (ph. 403/647-2364). There is also native prairie at Dinosaur Provincial Park (SE, 18,000 acres), north of Brooks. The park's bird list includes 140 species, about half of which are nesters. Contact the park superintendent, Box 60, Patricia, AB TOT 2KO (ph.

403/378-4587). The Suffield Canadian Forces Base (660,000 acres, northeast of Brooks) is a vast area of protected grassland but is off-limits to the public. An area of about 113,000 acres at the east end has been designated as Suffield National Wildlife Area and supports many grassland birds. Public access may be prohibited. For general information on preserved prairie areas and sanctuaries in western Canada, contact the Canadian Wildlife Service (address above) or the Alberta Fish and Wildlife Division, Main Floor, North Tower, Petroleum Plaza, 9945 108th St., Edmonton, AB T5J 2Z4 (ph. 403/442-2605).

Appendix B:
Summer Status of
Endemic Grassland Birds
in Selected Areas

National wildlife refuges = N.W.R.; national parks = N.P.; national grasslands = N.G.

Colorado
1. Alamosa N.W.R.
2. Arapaho and Monte Vista N.W.R. 3.

Kansas
1. Cimarron N.G.
2. Flint Hills N.W.R.
3. Kirwin N.W.R.
4. Quivira N.W.R.

Minnesota
1. Agassiz N.W.R.
2. Big Stone N.W.R.

Missouri
1. Squaw Creek N.W.R.

Montana
1. Benton Lake N.W.R.
2. Bowdoin N.W.R.
3. Charles M. Russel N.W.R.
4. Medicine Lake N.W.R.
5. National Bison Range
6. Ninepipe N.W.R.

Nebraska
1. Crescent Lake N.W.R.
2. Fort Niobrara N.W.R.
3. Oglala N.G.
4. Rainwater Basin Wetland Management District
5. Valentine N.W.R.

North Dakota
1. Arrowwood N.W.R.
2. Audubon N.W.R.
3. Souris Loop N.W.R. group (includes Lostwood, Des Lacs, J. Clark Salyer, and Upper Souris)
4. Lake Ilo N.W.R.
5. Long Lake N.W.R.
6. Tewaukon N.W.R.
7. Theodore Roosevelt N.P.

Okalahoma
1. Optima N.W.R.
2. Washita N.W.R.

South Dakota
1. Lacreek N.W.R.
2. Lake Andes N.W.R.
3. Sand Lake N.W.R.
4. Waubay N.W.R.

Texas
1. Buffalo Lake N.W.R.
2. Hagerman N.W.R.
3. Muleshoe N.W.R.

Saskatchewan
1. Grasslands N.P.

State or province	Colorado		Kansas				Minnesota		Mo.	Montana						Nebraska		
Refuge	1	2	1	2	3	4	1	2	1	1	2	3	4	5	6	1	2	3
Northern harrier	C	C	C	U	o	C	C	C	O	C	A	C	C	c	c	U	c	c
Swainson's hawk	C	o	C	o	C	C		U		o	C	c	C	r	O	U	u	u
Ferruginous hawk	r		U		r	r				r	U	U	O	r	o	o		u
Prairie falcon	u	o	r		u	O	r			u	o	U	u	o	o	r	o	o
Greater prairie-chicken				C			r										U	
Lesser prairie-chicken		U				O												
Sharp-tailed grouse										O						C	C	c
Mountain plover	r																	c
Upland sandpiper		C	u	A			O	U	O	C	O	C	C	r	u	C	C	C
Marbled godwit		u					U	O	o	U	A	u	C	r	r	r	u	u
Long-billed curlew		u	C						r	U	D	U	C	C	U	C	C	c
Wilson's phalarope	C	O		A		C	U	U	o	C	A	c	C	C	U	C	O	u
Franklin's gull	U	O					A	C		A	A	C	a		o	A	A	c
Burrowing owl	O	C	C	C	O	C	O		O	O	O	C	U	O		O	O	
Short-eared owl	O	u	r	C	C	C	U	u	U	C	C	C	C	C	U	U	o	
Horned lark	C	u	A	C	C	U	U	U	U	C	C	A	A	o	O	A	A	c
Sprague's pipit										C								
Dickcissel	r		C	C	O	A	C	C	C			c	r			R	C	
Cassin's sparrow	A																	
Clay-colored sparrow	R	o			o					C	r	C	A	A	U			u
Brewer's sparrow	U	U			c					C	C	c	U	u		r		u
Vesper sparrow	C	U	r	C	c		U	C	O	U	U	C	C	A	U	R	A	c
Lark sparrow	o	O	A	C	o	C			O	o		A	C	u	u	C	A	c
Lark bunting	C	C	A		o	c			U	C						C	c	c
Savannah sparrow	C	C				u	r	O	A	A	A	A	C	A	C	r	U	
Grasshopper sparrow	r		A	C		u	r		U	U	C	u	C	u	C	A	A	u
Baird's sparrow									U	U	O		U			A		
Henslow's sparrow									R	A	R					U		
McCown's longspur	A		r						U	C	C	c	A	r	o	A	C	u
Chestnut-collared longspur										u	u	c	C					
Bobolink	u					U	C	U		R	u		A		o	C	U	u
Eastern meadowlark	A	U	A	O	O	C	C	C	U	C	A	A	A	A	C	C	U	u
Western meadowlark	A		A	A	A	A	C	C	O	A	A	A	A	A	C	A	A	c
Total summer species	17	12	20	12	13	15	13	14	16	21	25	23	25	15	14	23	20	22

Note: A/a = abundant, C/c = common, U/u = uncommon, O/o = occasional, R/r = rare, the capital letters indicating proven breeding status.

State or province	Nebr. (cont'd)		North Dakota							Okla.		South Dakota				Texas			Sask.
Refuge	4	5	1	2	3	4	5	6	7	1	2	1	2	3	4	1	2	3	1
Northern harrier	C	C	C	U	C	U	C	C	C	O	U	U	C	C	C	O	U	r	
Swainson's hawk	U	U	C	o	U	U	C	C	u	o	C	U	O	C	U	C	C	U	
Ferruginous hawk	r		r	O	r		o	r		r		o		o	r		U		
Prairie falcon		U	r			r	o		U	O		u	O	o	r	r	r		
Greater prairie- chicken		U								O									
Lesser prairie- chicken											r								
Sharp-tailed grouse		A	C	C	C	C	A	C	C						R				
Mountain plover													O			o	R	r	
Upland sandpiper	U	C	C	C	C	C	C	C	U	r	C	C	O	U	C	o			
Marbled godwit			U	C	U	C	c	o		O	o	U	u	C	C	c			
Long-billed curlew	U	u	U	C	C	C	C	U	o	R	o	U		C	U	o			r
Wilson's phalarope		C	U	c	C	c	C	c		r	o	U	u	C	C	o	o		o
Franklin's gull	r	o	r		O		r		U	O	u	O	a	A	R	c	a		
Burrowing owl	U	O	u	U	U	U	U	U	o	O	r	U	o	U	u	C	C		
Short-eared owl	U	c	u	C	C	C	U	O	o	O		C	o	U	R	r			
Horned lark	C	C	C	C	C	C	U	C	C	C	U	C	c	U	C	A	A	u	u
Sprague's pipit			U	O	U	O	O	u			A	U	U	U	U				
Dickcissel	C	C		O	R	O	O	u			o					u	A		
Cassin's sparrow									c	O						c			
Clay-colored sparrow		C	C	U	A	U	C	U	c	O		U	u	U	C	r			
Brewer's sparrow																u		U	U
Vesper sparrow	C	C	U	o	U	O	U	U	C	r	c	U	o	U	C	c			
Lark sparrow	C	C	U	o	O	o	O	U	c	C	c	U	u	U	R	c	C	C	C
Lark bunting	C	C	C	C	A	C	u	O	r		U	C	u	O	R	c	A		
Savannah sparrow		o	U	C	C	C	U	U	c		u		C	C	U	r	o	U	U
Grasshopper sparrow	C	C	C	C	C	C	U	U	r		o	C	U	U	U	u	u	U	
Baird's sparrow						U	r	r											
Henslow's sparrow																			
McCown's longspur	c		C	C	C	C	C		u			C	U	U	O	u			
Chestnut-collared longspur			C	U	C	U	C	C	r		C	U	A	O	C	r			
Bobolink	O	O	U	C	C	C	C	C			C	C	C	U	O			A	A
Eastern meadowlark	O	C	C	U	A	U	A				C	U	C	C	C	C			
Western meadowlark	C	C	C	A	A	A	A	C	R	A	C	A	A	C	C	A	A		
Total summer species	15	21	24	24	23	23	21	20	20	17	18	22	22	20	21	18	16	10	

Note: A/a = abundant, C/c = common, U/u = uncommon, O/o = occasional, R/r = rare, the capital letters indicating proven breeding status.

Appendix C:
Birds and Plants
Mentioned in the Text

Birds
American crow *Corvus brachyrhynchos*
American pipit *Anthus rubescens*
American redstart *Setophaga ruticilla*
American robin *Turdus migratorius*
Baird's sandpiper *Calidris bairdii*
Baird's sparrow *Ammodramus bairdii*
Baltimore oriole *Icterus galbula*
Barn owl *Tyto alba*
Barred owl *Strix varia*
Black grouse *Tetrao tetrix*
Black-and-white warbler *Mniotilta varia*
Black-billed magpie *Pica pica*
Black-capped chickadee *Poecile atricapillus*
Black-headed grosbeak *Pheucticus melanocephala*
Blue jay *Cyanocitta cristata*
Bobolink *Dolichonyx orizivorus*
Brant *Branta bernicla*
Brewer's blackbird *Euphagus cyanocephalus*
Brewer's sparrow *Spizella breweri*
Broad-winged hawk *Buteo platypterus*
Bullock's oriole *Icterus bullockii*
Burrowing owl *Athene cunicularia*
California gull *Larus californicus*
Cassin's auklet *Ptychoramphus aleuticus*
Cassin's finch *Carpodacus cassinii*
Cassin's kingbird *Tyrannus vociferans*
Cassin's sparrow *Aimophila cassinii*
Cassin's vireo *Vireo cassinii*
Chestnut-collared longspur *Calcarius ornatus*
Chickadees *Poecile* spp.
Chipping sparrow *Spizella passerina*
Clay-colored sparrow *Spizella pallida*
Common buzzard *Buteo buteo*

Common poor-will *Phalaenoptilus nuttallii*
Common raven *Corvus corax*
Dickcissel *Spiza americana*
Eastern meadowlark *Sturnella magna*
Eastern wood-pewee *Contopus virens*
Eiders *Somateria* spp.
Eskimo curlew *Numenius borealis*
European starling *Sturnus vulgaris*
Ferruginous hawk *Buteo regalis*
Flamingos *Phoenocopterus* spp.
Franklin's gull *Larus pipixcan*
Grasshopper sparrow *Ammodramus savannarum*
Great horned owl *Bubo virginianus*
Greater prairie-chicken *Tympanuchus cupido*
Green-tailed towhee *Pipilo chlorurus*
Henslow's sparrow *Ammodramus henslowii*
Horned lark *Eremophila alpestris*
Indigo bunting *Passerina cyanea*
Kori bustard *Ardeotis kori*
Lark bunting *Calamospiza melanocorys*
Lark sparrow *Chondestes grammacus*
Lazuli bunting *Passerina amoena*
LeConte's sparrow *Ammodramus leconteii*
Lesser prairie-chicken *Tympanuchus pallidocinctus*
Long-billed curlew *Numenius americanus*
Marbled godwit *Limosa fedoa*
McCown's longspur *Calcarius mccownii*
Mississippi kite *Ictinia mississippiensis*
Mountain plover *Charadrius montanus*
Northern cardinal *Cardinalis cardinalis*
Northern flicker *Colaptes auritus*
Northern harrier *Circus cyaneus*
Osprey *Pandion haliaetus*
Peregrine *Falco peregrinus*

Prairie falcon *Falco mexicanus*
Pygmy owls *Glaucidium* spp.
Ring-necked pheasant *Phasianus colchicus*
Rose-breasted grosbeak *Pheucticus ludovicianus*
Rough-legged hawk *Buteo lagopus*
Sage grouse *Centrocercus urophasianus*
Sage sparrow *Amphispiza belli*
Sage thrasher *Oreoscoptes montanus*
Sandhill crane *Grus canadensis*
Savannah sparrow *Passerculus sandwichensis*
Sedge wren *Cistothorus platensis*
Sharp-tailed grouse *Tympanuchus phasianellus*
Short-eared owl *Asio flammeus*
Song sparrow *Melospiza melodia*
Sprague's pipit *Anthus spragueii*
Spruce grouse *Falcipennis canadensis*
Swainson's hawk *Buteo swainsoni*
Swainson's thrush *Catharus ustulatus*
Swainson's warbler *Limnothlypis swainsoni*
Turkey vulture *Cathartes aura*
Upland sandpiper *Bartramia longicauda*
Vesper sparrow *Pooecetes gramineus*
Western meadowlark *Sturnella neglecta*
Western wood-pewee *Contopus sordidulus*
Whimbrel *Numenius phaeopus*
White-breasted nuthatch *Sitta carolinensis*
White-crowned sparrow *Zonotrichia leucophrys*
White-throated sparrow *Zonotrichia albicollis*
Wilson's phalarope *Phalaropus tricolor*
Wilson's plover *Charadrius wilsonia*
Wilson's storm-petrel *Oceanites oceanicus*
Wilson's warbler *Wilsonia pusilla*
Yellow-billed cuckoo *Coccyzus americanus*
Yellow-breasted chat *Icteria virens*

Plants
Aspens *Populus* spp.
Big bluestem *Andropogon gerardi*
Big sage *Artemisia tridentata*
Blackberries *Rubus* spp.
Black grama *Bouteloua eriopoda*
Blue grama *Bouteloua gracilis*
Bluestems *Andropogon* spp.
Buffalo grass *Buchloe dactyloides*
Bur oak *Quercus macrocarpa*
Cat-tail *Typha latifolia*

Cheatgrass (or downy brome) *Bromus tectorum*
Compass plant *Silphium laciniatum*
Crested wheatgrass *Agropyron cristatum*
Cutleaf ironplant *Haplopappus spinulosus*
Downy brome (or cheatgrass) *Bromus tectorum*
Fescues *Festuca* spp.
Globemallow *Sphaeralcea coccinea*
Grama grasses *Bouteloua* spp.
Hairy grama *Bouteloua hirsuta*
Hazel *Corylus americana*
Indian grass *Sorghastrum nutans*
Junegrass *Koeleria cristata*
Junipers (or red cedars) *Juniperus* spp.
Little bluestem *Andropogon scoparius*
Longleaf pine *Pinus palustris*
Lodgepole pine *Pinus contorta*
Magnolias *Magnolias* spp.
Maples *Acer* spp.
Mesquite *Prosopsis* spp.
Narrowleaf four-o'clock *Mirabilis linearis*
Oaks *Quercus* spp.
Panic grasses *Panicum* spp.
Pasque flower *Anemone patens*
Phragmites (or common reed) *Phragmites communis*
Pines *Pinus* spp.
Ponderosa pine *Pinus ponderosa*
Prairie false boneset *Kuhnia eupatorioides*
Prickly-pear cactus *Opuntia macrorhiza*
Russian thistle *Salsola iberica*
Sagebrush *Artemisia* spp.
Sand bluestem *Andropogon hallii*
Sandbur *Cenchrus longispinus*
Sandsage (or sand sagebrush) *Artemisia filifolia*
Shinnery oak *Quercus harvardi*
Side-oats grama *Bouteloua curtipendula*
Skeletonweed *Lygodesmia juncea*
Snowberry *Symphoricarpos alba*
Sunflowers *Helianthus* spp.
Sycamores *Plantanus* spp.
Western ragweed *Ambrosia psilotachya*
Western wheatgrass *Agropyron spicata*
Wild alfalfa *Psoralea tenuiflora*
Willows *Salix* spp.
Yuccas *Yucca* spp.

Glossary

The glossary includes some terms that, if not actually used in the text, are important to understand in conjunction with its ideas or with those of the suggested readings.

Adaptation   An evolved structural, behavioral, or physiological trait that increases an organism's individual fitness (its individual ability to survive and reproduce).

Advertising behavior   The social behaviors (signals or "displays") of an animal of either sex that may serve to identify and announce (visually and / or acoustically in birds) its species, sex, relative reproductive capacity, individual social status, and overall vigor.

Agonistic   The entire dominance / submissive behavioral spectrum, comprising a response gradient ranging from attack to escape, including intermediate ambivalent states.

Allelopathy   The deposition or secretion of substances detrimental to other plants of their own or other species in the vicinity, thus reducing interindividual competition. The leaf-fall of some trees and shrubs that are high in salts and the germinating seeds of certain plants are examples. *See also* dominant.

Allopatric   Populations of one or more species that are wholly geographically isolated from one another, at least during breeding. "Allospecies" are those allopatric populations that appear to have attained species-level distinction. *See also* parapatric *and* sympatric.

Altricial   Referring to the condition of being hatched in a relatively undeveloped stage, usually blind and without locomotory abilities. *See also* nidicolous.

Arborescent   Treelike.

Association   A specific type of biotic community, usually named for one or more plant species or genera that consistently occur as climax dominants within that community. *See also* climax community, dominant.

Avifauna   The collective bird life of a particular locality or region.

Awn   A long bristle, associated with the seed coverings or leaf tips of some grasses.

Billabong   In Australia, an oxbow lake.

Bimaculated   Doubly spotted or marked.

Binomial   Comprising two terms, such as using the combination of a generic (genus) and specific (species) name to identify an organism, which is the basis for binomial biological nomenclature. *See also* nomenclature.

Biome   A major regional ecosystem, including both the plants and animals. Comparable to an "ecoregion" if defined mainly by landscape geography rather than floristically. *See also* ecoregion *and* formation.

Boreal forests   Northern forests, especially the coniferous forests of Canada.

Brood   As a verb, to cover and apply heat to hatched young (incubation is the same behavior, when applied to eggs). Also refers (as a noun) to a group of young typically tended by a single female or pair.

Brood parasitism   The behavior of a species in which females lay their eggs in the nests of their own species (intraspecific brood parasitism) or in those of others (interspecific brood parasitism).

Bunchgrasses   Perennial grasses that grow and expand laterally through stolons or rhizomes, forming distinct, discontinuous clumps rather than the relatively continuous ground cover typical of sod-forming grasses. Bunchgrass prairie is typical of the wheatgrass-dominated Palouse prairie grasslands of the Pacific Northwest. *See also* sod-forming grasses.

Calls   Term descriptive of avian vocalizations that are acoustically simple and are often innately uttered and perceived, the production of which is not usually limited by age, sex, or season. *See also* songs *and* vocalizations.

Cambrian period   The first major interval of the Paleozoic era, lasting from about 570–590 to 505 million years ago. *See also* Paleozoic era *and* Precambrian.

Carotenoids   Red to yellow pigments derived from plant or animal materials and often present in bird feathers.

Celestial navigation   The hypothesis that migratory birds use visual clues from the sun (solar navigation) or stars (stellar navigation) in achieving simple directional or bicoordinate navigational abilities that are independent of learned landmarks.

Cenozoic era   The geologic era encompassing the past 65 million years, the so-called Age of Mammals. It has traditionally been divided into the (older) Tertiary and (newer) Quaternary periods (q.v.). Recently the more equally chronologically subdivided Paleogene and Neogene periods (q.v.) have been proposed instead.

Climax community   A stable aggregation of locally interacting species that theoretically is no longer undergoing ecological succession and is unlikely to alter significantly until the climate changes or outside forces are brought to bear. Typically it is characterized or identified by its dominant species. *See also* community, dominant, ecoregion, *and* formation.

Clutch   A complete set of eggs (one or more), normally laid by a single female and incubated simultaneously.

Community   In ecology, an interacting group of plants, animals, and microorganisms situated in a specific location. *See also* ecosystem, habitat.

Congeneric   Belonging to the same genus.

Conservation Reserve Program (CRP)   A 1985 federal cooperative program that helped convert privately owned marginal and eroding croplands to perennial grasslands for a period of at least ten years.

Conspecific   Belonging to the same species.

Cool-season grasses   Grasses adapted for growing in cooler climates and requiring more water than warm-season grasses. Also called C_3 grasses because of the 3-carbon molecule stage that is temporarily present during photosynthesis.

Coteau   From the French *coteau,* a sloping or hilly area associated with glacial moraines, such as the Missouri Coteau.

Crepuscular   Associated with dawn and dusk, occurring between diurnal (daytime) and nocturnal (nighttime) activity patterns.

Cretaceous period   The geologic interval that extended from about 146 million years ago to 65 million years ago, ending the Mesozoic era. *See also* Mesozoic era.

Dichromatism   The presence of two distinct and genetically controlled plumage patterns or colors among adults of a species' population. *See also* dimorphism, which is sometimes used synonymously.

Dihedral   Angled above (or below) the horizontal.

Dimorphism   The presence of two distinct forms ("morphs") that differ absolutely or statistically among at least the adults of a species' population. Sex-related plumage/softpart color or pattern differences are better described as sexual dichromatism, a subcategory of sexual dimorphism. *See also* dichromatism.

Display   An evolved and variably stereotyped (ritualized) behavior that communicates information within or between species. *See also* advertising behavior, ritualization, *and* territoriality.

Dominant   In ecology, descriptive of plant taxa that exert the strongest ecological effects (control of energy flow) within a community. They may maintain this dominance through sheer biomass, by controlling nutrient or water availability, maximizing interception of available sunlight, having pathogenic (allelopathic) effects on other species (or other individuals of its own species) in the immediate vicinity, or possibly through other controlling influences. *See also* allelopathy *and* community.

Drift   Glacially transported and deposited materials, either unsorted by size (till), or size-sorted (stratified drift). Not to be confused with genetic drift. *See also* glacial erratics, moraine, *and* till.

Ear conch   The enlarged outer ear area of owls, variously specialized for receiving faint sounds.

Ecoregions   Areas having similar climates, geomorphology, and potential natural vegetation composed of clusters of interacting landscapes. *See also* biome, formation, *and* landscape.

Ecosystem   An interacting group of plants, animals, microorganisms, and their physical environment, of no specific size.

Ecotone   An ecologic transition zone that physically connects two different biotic communities. Ecotones may be very broad or extremely narrow and relatively stable or dynamically changing through time.

Edge species   A species that is more common in or most characteristic of ecotone communities, such as forest-edge species. "Edge effect" refers to the fact that edge habitats often exhibit high species diversity, supporting species typical of both the adjoining habitat types and sometimes supporting unique edge-adapted species as well. Edge effects may also modify the incidence of nest predation or brood parasitism, owing to edge-related behavioral traits of the predators or parasites.

Endangered   Descriptive of taxa existing in such small numbers as to be in direct danger of extinction without human intervention. *See also* threatened.

Endemic   Descriptive of taxa that are both native to and limited to a specific area, habitat, or region. (Most of the species described in this book are not, strictly speaking, pure Great Plains grassland endemics but may also occur in grassy areas outside the region.) *See also* indigenous.

Eocene epoch   A major early subdivision of the Cenozoic period, extending from about 58–60 to 34–37 million years ago. *See also* Cenozoic era.

Eolian (or aeolian)   Shaped, carried, or influenced by wind, such as loessal soils. *See also* loess.

Epigamic   Sexual, as in epigamic signals.

Evolution   Any gradual change. Biological or organic evolution results from changing gene frequencies in successive generations associated with biological adaptations, typically through natural selection. *See also* natural selection.

Evolutionary lag   A failure in attaining rapid evolutionary response of a population to changing environmental conditions, such as the inability of many songbird species to cope effectively with brood parasitism by cowbirds within the latter's recently acquired range.

Extinct   A taxon that no longer exists anywhere. *See also* extirpated.

Extirpated   A taxon that has been eliminated from some part of its range but still exists elsewhere. *See also* extinct.

Fecundity   The number of offspring fledged per year (annual fecundity) or in an individual's lifetime (overall fecundity). Avian fecundity is influenced by such factors as age at maturity, clutch size, number of broods per season, reproductive success variables (nesting, hatching, and fledging success rates), and longevity. *See also* fledging success, hatching success, *and* nesting success.

Fen   A wetland characterized by having a boglike substrate of organic matter (peat or marl) but, unlike typical bogs, having favorable plant nutrition levels (especially calcium availability) and much greater organic productivity. Prairie fens are largely confined to glaciated areas and are relatively rare.

Fidelity   A tendency of an individual to return for breeding to a prior nest site (nest-site fidelity or tenacity), a prior year's mate (mate fidelity), or the individual's area of rearing (natal fidelity or philopatry).

Fire-influenced species   Any of several groups of species affected by fire. *Fire-dependent* species include those whose continued existence in a community depends on the periodic occurrence of fire. *Fire-tolerant* species may survive but not depend on fires for their continued presence. *Fire-sensitive* species may decline or eventually even disappear with the periodic occurrence of fires.

Fledging   The initial acquisition of flight by a bird. The period from hatching to fledging is called the fledging period, which often corresponds to the nestling period or is slightly longer. *See also* nestling.

Fledging success   The percentage of hatched young that are successfully fledged, usually as calculated from all initiated nests or from all successfully hatched nests. Also sometimes called nestling success. *See also* fecundity *and* hatching success.

Fledgling   A newly fledged juvenile bird. *See also* juvenile.

Floret   A small flower, especially of grasses.

Forest   A general term for a community dominated by rather tall-stature trees, in which the height of the trees is much greater than the average distance between them. *See also* savanna, woodlands.

Form   A convenient term having no special taxonomic significance but usually referring to a species or well-differentiated subspecies, especially one whose exact taxonomic status may be in doubt. *See also* species.

Formation   In ecology, a major type of plant community (or "biome," if the animals are included) that extends over broad regions that collectively share similar climates, soils, and biological succession patterns and that have similar life forms of dominant plants at their eventually stable or "climax" vegetational stage. Formations usually include several subcategories of plant "associations," based on their specific climax dominants. Examples of climax plant formations include tundra, temperate deciduous forest, temperate coniferous forest, savanna, desert scrub, and perennial grasslands of varying stature types (e.g., bunchgrass, short grass, midgrass, and tall grass). *See also* climax community *and* community.

Fragmentation ecology   The study of the effects of spatial splitting and subdivision of a species or community through, for example, deforestation, and the resultant production of "metapopulations." *See also* metapopulations.

Fratricide   The killing of a nestmate, usually the younger or weaker member or members of a brood. Also called siblicide or Cainism.

Gallery forest   Narrow riverine forests that follow waterways out into otherwise nonforested habitats. *See also* riparian, savanna, *and* woodlands.

Genus (adj., generic; pl., genera)   A (literally) "general" Latin or latinized name that is applied to one or more closely related species of plants or animals. If a genus has only a single included species, it is called "monotypic"; otherwise it is polytypic. The genus is the first (and always capitalized and italicized) component of a species' two-part "binomial" or scientific name. *See also* species.

Glacial erratics   Large rocks and boulders that have been glacially transported and randomly deposited over the landscape, having a composition different from that of the bedrock below. *See also* drift, moraine.

Great Plains   The nonmountainous region of interior North America lying east of the Rocky Mountains and west of the central lowlands of the Mississippi and lower Missouri drainages. The Great Plains and central lowlands merge imperceptibly; "central plains" is a convenient nontechnical term encompassing both.

Groveland   A mostly nonforested community but with scattered forestlike clusters of trees, especially groves (clones) of aspens, common in the grassland-forest ecotone area of southern Canada. *See also* parkland.

Guild   A group of species that exploits the same class of environmental characteristics (such as food types) in a similar way, whether or not they are closely related.

Habitat   The ecological situation in which a species survives; its natural "address" as opposed to its ecological profession (its niche). Also, its predictive occurrence in a specific location (community). *See also* community, ecosystem, niche.

Halophytic plants   Salt-tolerant plants.

Hatching success   The percentage of eggs laid that hatch successfully. *See also* fecundity, nesting success, *and* fledging success.

Hectare (ha)   A metrically defined area (10,000 square meters), equal to 2.47 acres. A square mile contains 259 hectares.

Hertz (Hz)   A unit of frequency equal to one cycle per second (cps); kilohertz (kHz) units equal 1,000 cps.

Hesperornis   A fossil genus (meaning "western bird') of toothed, flightless, and fish-eating birds, discovered in late Cretaceous-age strata of western Kansas.

Holocene epoch   The roughly 12,000-year interval extending from the end of the last (Wisconsinian) glaciation to the present time. *See also* Pleistocene epoch.

Home range   The entire area used by an individual, pair, or family over a specified period. *See also* territory.

Hypsithermal period (*hyps-* and *therme* from the Greek, meaning high heat)   The period, from ca. 7,000 to 1,000 B.C., of relatively warm climates in the northern hemisphere following the last glaciation. Sometimes also called the altithermal interval. *See also* xerothermic period.

Hypsodont   "High-toothed," in reference to the elongated and flattened teeth of horses and other grazers. These teeth continue growing and replacing abraded enamel, thus effectively enabling them to grind grasses rich in silica.

Ichthyornis ("fish-bird")   A fossil genus of gull- or ternlike birds with toothed jaws, originally discovered in Cretaceous strata of Kansas.

Icterid   A member of the family Icteridae, including blackbirds, grackles, meadowlarks, cowbirds, and so on.

Incubation   The parental application of body heat to eggs. *See also* brooding.

Indigenous   Descriptive of taxa that are native to, but not necessarily limited to, a particular area or region. *See also* endemic.

Innate   Pertaining to genetically transmitted traits, especially behavioral ones.

Insectivorous   Having a diet composed mostly of insects and other arthropods.

Intercalary meristem   Plant tissues at the base of grass leaves and stems that are capable of cell division.

Intergeneric   Pertaining to interactions between genera.

Interspecific   Pertaining to interactions between species.

Intraspecific   Pertaining to interactions within species.

Iridium   An element in the platinum group that is very rare on earth but more common in meteors and asteroids. An anomalous high concentration that occurs worldwide in a thin rock layer at the Cretaceous-Tertiary (K-T) boundary is often cited as evidence of a major meteorite or comet impact 65 million years ago that may have led to the extinction of the dinosaurs.

Isohyet   A line connecting points of equal amounts of precipitation on a map.

Isolating mechanisms   Genetically carried ("intrinsic") and evolved traits (such as species-specific behavioral signals, anatomical differences, and ecological or temporal breeding restrictions) that serve to prevent the exchange of genes between individuals of different species, and thus avoiding the production of viable hybrids. These include various premating mechanisms (temporal, ecological, behavioral, or anatomical differences that serve to prevent attempted matings) as well as diverse postmating mechanisms (genetic mechanisms occurring after such matings, such as gametic mortality, embryonic mortality, hybrid inviability, hybrid sterility or subfertility, and hybrid adaptive inferiority). *See also* reproductive isolation.

Jurassic period   The second major period of the Mesozoic era, following the Triassic period. It lasted from about 210 to 145 million years ago, or the beginning of the Cretaceous period, and marked the peak of dinosaur abundance and diversity. *See also* Cretaceous *and* Triassic periods.

Juvenal The feathers acquired during the nestling period, which are carried for a variable time after fledging (initial flight).

Juvenile The stage in a bird's life during which it carries feathers predominantly of the juvenal plumage and during which it fledges. *See also* juvenal.

Kettle A name applied to a group of hawks aggregated in a migrating group, especially when they are rotating collectively in a thermal.

Landscape A relatively large area within an ecoregion in which clusters of interacting vegetative communities (sites or patches) occur repetitively. *See also* ecoregions, patch.

Larimide orogeny The period of mountain-building in the central Rocky Mountains (named for the Laramie Range), beginning during the late Mesozoic and extending into early Cenozoic times.

Latin name The (usually) two-part (generic plus specific) Latin or latinized name given a species when it is first officially described (specifically, from the time of Linnaeus onward), and by which it thereafter is technically known and properly identified, thus the species' "scientific name." *See also* genus, species, *and* vernacular name.

Lek A Scandinavian word (originally meaning to flirt, in a playful manner), now used for describing a site at which communal display occurs among males of various arena-displaying and polygynous birds in competition for mating rights. Grassland examples include the North American prairie grouse and also the closely related Scandinavian black grouse, the classic lek-forming species. As a verb, "lekking" is sometimes also used to refer to the collective social display behavior of the participating males.

Litter Dead and decaying vegetable matter accumulated at the ground surface. *See also* thatch.

Loess (or loessal) soils Silty soils that have been transported and deposited by wind. These soils show little or no vertical stratification and are easily eroded. The word is of German origin, meaning "loose," and is pronounced "luss." *See also* eolian, till.

Magnetic inclination compass A hypothesis that some long-distance migratory birds such as bobolinks can detect their latitudinal location on the earth based on the degree of deviation of the plane of magnetic attraction from a horizontal axis (as occurs at the equator) to a vertical one (as is true at the magnetic poles). *See also* celestial navigation.

Mastodons Extinct elephants that differed from mammoths and modern elephants in having high-crowned teeth adapted for browsing and for living in forests rather than in grassland habitats.

Mating A descriptive, nontechnical term often loosely applied either to initial pair-bonding or copulation. Pairing is a more precise term for referring to the first meaning, at least among those bird species that individually pair-bond, and copulation is an appropriate and self-evident term for the second meaning. *See also* pair-bonding.

Meristem An area of plant cell division and growth, found at the bases and internodes of grass stems and leaves (basal or intercalary meristems).

Mesic A habitat with a moderate level of soil moisture (or other general environmental conditions, such as temperature extremes) between extremes of xeric (dry) and wet (hydric). *See also* xeric.

Mesozoic era The so-called Age of Dinosaurs, extending from about 225 to 65 million years ago, or to the start of the Cenozoic era. *See* Cenozoic era *and* Paleozoic era.

Metapopulations   Spatially subdivided populations having local, noninteracting sub-populations that are in some significant danger of becoming extinct. *See also* fragmentation ecology.

Microtene voles   A taxonomic group of rodents, including those of the genus *Microtus,* common in grasslands.

Miocene epoch   The interval within the Tertiary period (and the associated geologic strata deposited during that interval), from the end of the preceding Oligocene epoch (23.3 million years ago) to the start of the Pliocene epoch (5.2 million years ago). *See also* Oligocene *and* Pliocene epochs.

Mixed-grass (or midgrass) prairie   Perennial grasslands that are dominated by grasses of intermediate heights (often from 1.5 to 3.0 feet tall at maturity), or between those typically found in tall-grass and short-grass prairies and having some species from these two respectively more mesic and xeric types present to varying degrees. Mixed-grass prairies usually occur in areas of limited precipitation, situated geographically between tall-grass and short-grass prairies, where typically there is too little soil moisture to support tall-grass prairie but where there is more than is needed to support short-grass prairies. The fescue-dominated grasslands of southern Canada's aspen parkland borders, and especially in the region around the Cypress Hills, are a major variant of the mixed-grass prairie type and are often called "fescue prairies." *See also* short-grass prairie and tall-grass prairie.

Molt   The periodic sequential loss and replacement of feathers, thus producing a new plumage.

Monogamous   A pair-bonding system characterized by a single male and female remaining together for part or all of a breeding season or sometimes indefinitely.

Monophyletic   Having a single ancestral origin. *See also* polyphyletic.

Moraine   Gently rolling landscapes of glacial drift deposits, laid down at a glacier's lateral or terminal margins   *See also* drift *and* till.

Morph   An example of any of the phenotypic variants that occur in cases of sexual or nonsexual morphism (e.g., dimorphism, dichromatism). *See also* dimorphism.

Mosasaurs   Now-extinct marine lizards of the Mesozoic era, with very large heads and large, muscular tails used for propulsion.

Mustelid   A member of the family Mustelidae, including weasels and minks.

Natal plumage   The initial feather covering of a newly hatched bird, often downy in most birds.

Natural selection   In a broad sense, the long-term changes in gene frequencies and associated traits in populations, resulting from differential survival and reproduction of the fittest individuals within such interbreeding populations. Also applied by Charles Darwin in a more restricted sense to refer only to those traits associated with differential survival in nature, with "sexual selection" used to designate differential reproduction effects influencing only a single sex. *See also* sexual selection.

Neogene period   A recently named subdivision of the Cenozoic era. It followed the Paleogene period and lasted from 24 million years ago to the present, encompassing the Miocene, Pliocene, Pleistocene, and Holocene epochs. *See also* Paleogene period.

Neotropical migrants   Those migratory birds that winter in the Neotropic Region, i.e., from Mexico and Central America southward. Some of these are additionally transequatorial migrants, wintering south of the equator.

Nesting success   The percentage of initiated nests that succeed in fledging one or more young. *See also* fecundity, fledging success, hatching success, and nestling success.

Nestling   A recently hatched bird still confined to the nest. *See also* fledgling.

Nestling success   The percentage of hatched chicks that produce fledged young, sometimes also called fledging success. *See also* fecundity, fledging success, *and* hatching success.

Niche   The behavioral, morphological, and physiological adaptations of a species to its habitat, also sometimes defined from an environmental standpoint, such as the range of ecological conditions under which a species potentially exists (fundamental niche), best survives (preferred niche), or actually survives (realized niche). *See also* habitat.

Nidicolous   Those bird species whose young are hatched in a helpless condition, are reared in the nest, and need prolonged parental brooding and feeding. *See also* altricial *and* nestling.

Nomenclature   The process of naming objects. Binomial biological nomenclature provides a standardized two-part Latin or latinized name, the generic (general) name or genus, followed by a specific epithet. *See also* binomial *and* taxonomy.

Nuptial plumage   The definitive breeding plumage of adult birds, typically acquired by a prenuptial molt of variable extent. Now generally termed "alternative plumage" in North America.

Oligocene epoch   The interval within the Tertiary period (and the associated geologic strata deposited during that interval), extending from the end of the Eocene epoch (35 to 37 million years ago) to the start of the Miocene epoch (23.3 million years ago). *See also* Cenozoic era.

Oologist   A collector and student of bird eggs.

Orogeny   The process of mountain-building.

Orographic   Mountain-related, such as orographic precipitation. See also rain shadow.

Pair-bonding   The establishment of a (usually) monogamous and variably prolonged social bond between two individuals, typically for facilitating reproduction.

Pairing behavior   The epigamic behaviors related to mate choice and associated pair formation (pair-forming signals) and to pair-bond maintenance (pair-bonding signals). Sometimes called "courtship," but this term has undesirable human connotations. *See also* mating.

Paleogene period   A recently named subdivision of the Cenozoic era lasting from 65 to 24 million years ago and encompassing the Paleocene, Eocene, and Oligocene epochs. *See also* Neogene period.

Paleozoic era   The geologic era of "ancient life," beginning about 570 million years ago, at the start of the Cambrian period, and lasting until the beginning of the Mesozoic era, about 225 million years ago. *See also* Precambrian period *and* Mesozoic era.

Palouse prairie   The perennial grasslands of the Pacific Northwest (including the Palouse River Valley and adjoining regions of Washington, Oregon, and Idaho) that originally supported native bunchgrass prairie.

Parapatric   Populations that come into limited or sometimes extensive contact with one another along some portion of their common borders but do not actually overlap during the breeding season. Parapatric distributions are suggestive of competing, noninterbreeding populations, thus of two separate species. *See also* allopatric *and* sympatric.

Parkland   A mostly forested community, with scattered nonforested meadowlike areas, or "parks," present in the forest matrix. Common in the Rocky Mountain coniferous forests and also used to describe aspen forests in southern Canada, where scattered open areas of grassland occur in contact with aspens. Aspen parklands there are essentially a dynamic ecotone zone between boreal forest and prairie, with frequent fires and ungulate browsing favoring the grasses, but infrequent fires (which stimulate aspen sucker development) and decreased browsing favoring the aspens. *See also* groveland.

Passerine   Descriptive of members of the avian order Passeriformes; popularly also called perching birds (because of their long hind toes) or songbirds (because of their complex vocal organs). However, some species (such as crows and ravens) do not sing in the usually understood sense of this word.

Patch   In landscape ecology, a self-contained and rather uniform example of a habitat type that is variable in size but is geographically circumscribed as a single unit and that constitutes part of a more diverse landscape. A specific patch may constitute a local site. *See also* landscape.

Penultimate   The next-to-last item in a sequence.

Philopatry   The tendency of an individual bird to return to a particular location. Natal philopatry refers to a return to one's place of hatching and rearing. *See also* site tenacity.

Phylogeny   The evolutionary history or pathway of descent of an organism or group of organisms. Morphological phylogenetics are based on structural similarities, molecular phylogenetics on genetic (often nucleic acid or protein-based) traits. *See also* monophyletic *and* polyphyletic.

Plains   A nontechnical descriptive term for a flatland, especially a nonforested flatland. Derived from the Latin *planus,* meaning flat or clear. The high plains of western North America are the arid Great Plains uplands east of the Rocky Mountains that support native short-grass and shrubsteppe vegetation.

Playa lake   An ephemeral, shallow lake in a desertlike basin, typically depending upon irregular rains for its continued existence. *See also* pluvial lake.

Pleistocene epoch   The interval extending from about 1.77 million years ago (the end of the Pliocene epoch) to 12,000 years ago (the start of the current Holocene epoch). Popularly referred to as the Ice Age, this epoch includes part or all of four major glacial periods (and their associated interglacial intervals), of which the Nebraskan glaciation (ca. 2 to 1.75 million years ago) was the earliest and the Wisconsinian glaciation (ca. 150,000 to 15,000 years ago) the most recent. The Kansan (ca. 1.4 to 0.9 million years ago) and Illinoian (ca. 0.55 to 0.35 million years ago) glaciations were of intermediate age, and like the others were named after their southernmost extensions.

Plesiosaurs   Carnivorous and now extinct marine reptiles of the Mesozoic era, having flipperlike legs and necks of greatly variable length.

Pliocene epoch   The interval (and associated geologic strata deposited during that interval) extending from the end of the preceding Miocene epoch (5.2 million years ago) to the start of the Pleistocene epoch (about 1.6 to 1.8 million years ago).

Pluvial lake   A now-extinct lake that was formed during an earlier time from higher rainfall or glacial melting. *See also* playa lake.

Polyandry   A nonmonogamous mating system, in which a female may temporarily associate and copulate with two or more males, typically laying a clutch of eggs for each of them to incubate and rear. *See also* promiscuity.

Polygyny   A nonmonogamous mating system, in which a male may temporarily associate and copulate with two or more females, either simultaneously (harem polygyny) or successively (serial polygyny). *See also* promiscuity.

Polyphyletic   Descriptive of assemblages of organisms believed to have been derived phyletically from two or more ancestral groups, thus an artificial (but perhaps convenient) assemblage in an evolutionary sense. *See also* monophyletic.

Population source and population sink   Populations that exhibit a net population increase and those that undergo a net population loss over time.

Prairie   A native plant community dominated by perennial grasses. Prairies may be broadly classified by the relative stature of their particular dominant grass taxa (tall grass, midgrass, or short grass), or by the characteristic form of these grasses (e.g., bunchgrasses or sod-forming grasses). More specifically they are described by their dominant species or genera. Prairie soils are usually rich in organic matter, calcium, and other inorganic nutrients. Derived from the Old French *praerie,* a meadow. *See also* steppe *and* short-grass prairie.

Precambrian   Refers to that time in the Earth's history occurring before the Cambrian period, or at least 570 million years ago. *See also* Cambrian period *and* Paleozoic era.

Promiscuity   A mating system in which at least one sex (rarely both) has multiple sexual partners, in the absence of actual pair-bonding. *See also* polyandry *and* polygyny.

Quaternary period   The last 1.6 million years of the earth's history, including the Pleistocene and Holocene epochs. *See also* Holocene epoch, Neogene period, *and* Pleistocene epoch.

Rain shadow   The relatively dry area on the leeward side of a mountain that is drier because of moisture falling on the mountain's windward side ("orographic precipitation") and because air warms as it descends from a mountain top and thus is able to retain more moisture. *See also* orographic.

Refugium   An area where some species can survive during unfavorable environmental conditions.

Reproductive isolation   The impossibility of two populations interbreeding, owing either to preventive environmental barriers (extrinsic isolating factors) or genetic restrictions (inherent isolating mechanisms). *See also* isolating mechanisms.

Riparian   Associated with the shorelines. Gallery forests are a common type of riverine community in grassland habitats. *See also* gallery forest.

Ritualization   The evolutionary modification of a behavior into a social signal serving an intra- or interspecific communication function, or a "display."

Sandsage prairie   Prairies developed over sandy substrates, having an abundance of sand sagebrush and various other sand-adapted species.

Savanna   A Spanish term (but originally derived from the West Indian *zabana*) for describing tropical grasslands that often had scattered trees; now commonly used to describe any grassland community within which scattered trees occur. In typical savannas the distance between the trees is much greater than the average width of the individual tree canopies. *See also* woodlands.

Seral   Refers to chronologically transitional or "successional" species or stages in community development. *See also* succession, climax community.

Sexual selection   A type of natural selection in which the evolution and maintenance of traits of one sex result from the social interactions that produce differential individual reproductive success. These include both competitive interactions among members of the same sex (intrasexual or agonistic selection) and those occurring between the sexes and involving differential rates of sexual attraction (intersexual or epigamic selection). *See also* natural selection.

Short-grass prairie   A grassland (sometimes called "steppe grassland") dominated by short-stature (well under three feet tall at maturity) perennial grasses, such as various species of grama grass and buffalo grass. Perhaps more properly called "steppe" (q.v.), which is a short-grass ecosystem having much bare soil evident and arid-adapted woody shrubs variably present. When such shrubs are codominant with the grasses, "shrubsteppe" (q.v.) is a useful descriptive term. Short-grass prairies occur in areas too arid to support midgrass prairie but with more available moisture than those climates typically supporting semidesert, or even more xeric desert scrub vegetation. *See also* mixed-grass prairie, steppe, tall-grass prairie.

Shrubsteppe   A semiarid plant community that is variably codominated by shrubs—typically various species of sagebrush in western North America—and low-stature grasses (often bunchgrasses) and usually with much bare soil present between the plants. Sometimes described as "cool desert" or semidesert vegetation. In the absence (or removal by fire or other agencies) of the shrubs, this habitat type grades into short-grass steppe, or (with overgrazing) is taken over by annual exotic grasses such as downy brome. Where xerophytic trees such as mesquite are present, shrubsteppe may also grade into semidesert savanna.

Site fidelity (or site tenacity)   The social attachment of an individual to a specific site (nest site, territory, and so on) in successive seasons or years. *See also* philopatry.

Skylarking   A prolonged flight-song display, often performed at great height, as by true larks.

Sod-forming grasses   Perennial grasses that grow and establish root systems tending to bind the soil substrate in a continuous sod rather than growing in a discontinuous, clumplike, manner. *See also* bunchgrasses.

Songs   The vocalizations of birds that tend to be acoustically complex, prolonged, and are often sex-specific as well as individually unique. They frequently are uttered only at particular seasons and may have both intra- and intersexual signal value, including territorial advertisement and sexual attraction. Primary songs are typically the most complex and common such vocalizations; secondary songs are variously simpler and may have other, nonadvertising functions, such as interpair communications. *See also* calls *and* vocalizations.

Spatial scale   Measurements of abundance or species richness based on a series of units of differing sizes or spatial traits, such as patch and landscape characteristics. *See also* ecoregion, landscape, *and* patch.

Species   A "kind" of organism, or, more technically, a population whose members share the same isolating mechanism and thus are reproductively isolated from all other populations but are potentially capable of breeding freely among themselves. The term is unchanged in the plural and also used as the nomenclatural category below that of the genus and above that of the subspecies (abbreviated *sp.,* plural *spp.*). It occurs as the second (specific) component of a binomial Latin or latinized name (after the generic name), and is never capitalized in that context. *See also* Latin name *and* genus.

Steppe   A traditional Russian-based term for native short-grass communities, especially the vast semiarid areas of grass-covered plains in south-central Asia. Comparable to the popular usage of "plains" in North America. *See also* plains, short-grass prairie, shrubsteppe.

Stomata   The air pores in leaves, through which gas exchange occurs and water vapor is lost through transpiration.

Stromatolite   Fossil algae from the Cambrian era, among the oldest known plant fossils, and so-named on the basis of their distinctive mounded shape.

Subspecies   A geographically defined and recognizable (by morphology or sometimes even behavior) subdivision of a species. Subspecies species (abbreviated *ssp.,* plural *sspp.*) designations follow the species' epithet in a scientific name, constituting the last component of a thus three-part name or a trinomial. The race that shares its name with the species is the first-described, or nominate, subspecies.

Succession   The series of gradual plant and animal changes that occur in biotic communities over time, as relatively temporary (successional or seral) taxa are sequentially replaced by others that are able to persist and reproduce for a more prolonged or even indefinite period (so-called "climax" species). *See also* climax, community, *and* seral.

Superspecies   An assemblage of two or more essentially allopatric populations that are very closely related and might potentially represent biological subspecies; however, the test of reproductive isolation is lacking owing to their allopatric distributions. *See also* allopatry.

Sympatric   Populations that overlap at least in part, especially during the breeding season. By definition, sympatrically breeding but noninterbreeding populations are never considered the same species. *See also* allopatric, parapatric, *and* reproductive isolation.

Syrinx (adj., syringeal; plural, syringes)   The vocal organ of birds at the posterior end of the trachea. Syringeally produced sounds are called songs or calls, depending upon their complexity. Vocalizations may be amplified or resonated by nonsyringeal structures, such as the tracheal tube or (in male grouse) by inflated portions of the esophagus ("air sacs"). Nonsyringeal sounds or noises (such as foot-stamping, feather-rustling, and wing-clapping) are called mechanical sounds. *See also* vocalizations.

Systematics   In biology, the organization of plants and animal groups in a sequential and hierarchical manner that attempts to reflect their evolutionary relationships. *See also* nomenclature *and* taxonomy.

Tall-grass (or "true") prairie   Perennial grasslands that are dominated by tall-stature grasses, often at least six feet high at maturity, such as various species of bluestems. These species do most of their growing in the warmest part of the summer and thus are often called "warm-season" grasses. These grasslands typically occur in areas that are more mesic than those supporting lesser-stature grasses (midgrass or mixed-grass prairies) but are still too arid—or too frequently burned—to support forests. The "prairie peninsula" at the eastern end of the tall-grass prairie in the Ohio River Valley was once such a fire-controlled prairie that has now largely reverted to forest (where it hasn't been converted to farmland). *See also* short-grass prairie *and* mixed-grass prairie.

Taxon (pl. taxa)   A group of organisms constituting a particular category of biological classification or taxonomic group, such as the sparrow genus *Spizella*.

Taxonomy   A system of naming and describing groups of organisms (taxa), and organizing them in ways that reflect perceived phyletic relationships. *See also* nomenclature, systematics.

Territoriality   The advertisement and agonistic behaviors associated with territorial establishment and defense. *See also* advertising behavior *and* display.

Territory   An area having resources that are defended or controlled by an animal against others of its species (intraspecific territories), or less often against those of other species (interspecific territories). *See also* advertising behavior *and* home range.

Tertiary period   The first of the two major subdivisions of the Cenozoic era, beginning about 65 million years ago (at the end of the Cretaceous period) and lasting until about 1.8 million years ago (the start of the Quaternary period). *See also* Paleogene *and* Neogene periods.

Thatch   Standing dead grass or similar herbaceous material. *See also* litter.

Threatened   Descriptive of taxa that have declined and exist in small numbers but are not yet so rare as to be classified as endangered. Somewhat similar to "vulnerable," or "declining," which are terms used by some conservation agencies to refer to taxa in potential need of conservation measures in order to prevent a threatened or endangered status. States, provinces, and federal agencies may also establish their own criteria for such listings, as do many private conservation organizations. *See also* endangered.

Till   Unsorted glacial drift. *See also* drift.

Titanothere   Very large, horned mammals ("titanic beasts") of the early Cenozoic era that were vegetarians and ancestors of such odd-toed modern ungulates as rhinos.

Trachea   The windpipe of birds. *See also* syrinx.

Trait   A measurable phenotypic attribute (behavioral, structural, physiological), especially one that is at least in part genetically controlled.

Triassic period   The first major geologic period of the Mesozoic era, lasting from about 245 to 210 million years ago, or the start of the Jurassic period. *See also* Jurassic period *and* Mesozoic era.

Tundra   A Russian-based word (borrowed originally from Finnish) for those lands occurring either north of (Arctic tundra) or altitudinally above (alpine tundra) the treeline, in which permafrost is common and perennial herbaceous plants are dominant, but woody plants are rare and greatly stunted.

Ungulate   A hoofed mammal, either even-toed (e.g., deer and antelope) or odd-toed (e.g., horses and rhinos).

Variable area-sensitivity hypothesis   A hypothesis stating that the relationship between the probability of a species' occurrence within any single local patch depends on the landscape in which the patch is embedded. *See also* landscape, patch.

Vernacular name   The "common" or English-language name of an organism (usually a species), as opposed to its scientific or Latin name.

Vocalizations   Utterances, including both songs and calls, generated (at least in birds) by the syrinx and sometimes modulated or resonated by nonsyringeal structures, such as the trachea or oral cavity. Nonvocal sound sources include hissing, bill-clapping, and feather-generated noises. *See also* calls *and* songs.

Warm-season grasses Grasses adapted to grow during warmer periods having greater water stress; also called C_4 grasses because their photosynthetic pathway involves an intermediate 4-carbon molecule stage. *See also* cool-season grasses.

Woodlands A usually semiarid community type characterized by a mixture of small trees and nonwoody vegetation, often grasses or semiarid shrubs. Although the trees may be small, they are sometimes spaced so closely that the open distance between their canopies may be little more than the trees' average canopy diameter. Unlike forest trees, those of woodlands usually have relatively short trunks and more widespread canopies. Sometimes they are also called encinal or chaparral (both Spanish terms for oaks), such as the arid oak woodlands of the Southwest. In typical forests the trees are both much taller and more closely spaced. The term "woodlands" is also often more loosely used to refer to any community dominated by trees. *See also* forest, groveland, parkland, savanna.

Xeric Desertlike or drought-adapted; e.g., "xerophilic" vegetation of deserts. *See also* mesic.

Xerothermic period (or interval) The period of maximum dryness following the last glaciation, at about 3,000 B.C.; i.e., the driest part of the hypsithermal period. The xerothermic period followed a warm but moist "climatic optimum" period about 6,000 B.C. *See also* hypsithermal period.

References

Ailes, I. W. 1980. Breeding biology and habitat use of the upland sandpiper in central Wisconsin. *Passenger Pigeon* 42:53–63.

Ailes, I. W., and J. E. Toepfer. 1977. Home range and daily movement of radio-tagged upland sandpipers in central Wisconsin. *Inland Bird Banding News* 49:203–12.

Aldrich, J. 1966. Life areas of North America. Poster 102. U.S. Dept. Int., Bur. Sport Fisheries and Wildlife, Washington, DC.

Allen, D. 1967. *The Life of Prairies and Plains.* New York: McGraw Hill. 232 pp.

Allen, G. T. 1987. Prairie falcon aerie site characteristics and aerie use in North Dakota. *Condor* 89:187–90.

Allen, J. N. 1980. The ecology and behavior of the long-billed curlew in southeastern Washington. American Ornithologists' Union (AOU), *Wildlife Monograph* 73:1–64.

American Ornithologists' Union. 1998. *Check-list of North American Birds.* 7th ed. Washington, DC: AOU. 829 pp.

Andersen, D. E. 1995. Productivity, food habits, and behavior of Swainson's hawks breeding in southeast Colorado. *J. Raptor Res.* 29:158–65.

Anderson, R. C. 1970. Prairies in the Prairie State. *Trans. Ill. Acad. of Science* 63(2):214–21.

Anderson, S. H., and J. R. Squires. 1997. *The Prairie Falcon.* Austin: University of Texas Press. 171 pp.

Andrews, R., and R. Righter. 1992. *Colorado Birds: A Reference to Their Distribution and Habitat.* Denver: Denver Mus. Nat. Hist. 480 pp.

Andrle, R. F., and J. R. Carroll. 1988. *The Atlas of Breeding Birds in New York State.* Ithaca, NY: Cornell University Press. 551 pp.

Anstey, D., S. K. Davis, D. C. Duncan, and M. Skeet. 1995. Distribution and habitat requirements of eight grassland songbird species in southern Saskatchewan. Regina, SA: Saskatchewan Wetland Conservation Corporation. 11 pp.

Arnold, T. W., and K. F. Higgins. 1986. Effects of shrub coverage on birds on North Dakota mixed-grass prairies. *Can. Field-Nat.* 100:10–14.

Askins, R. A. 1993. Population trends in grassland, shrubland and forest birds in eastern North America. *Current Ornithol.* 11:11–34.

———. 1999. History of grassland birds in eastern North America. In *Ecology and Conservation of Grassland Birds of the Western Hemisphere,* ed. P. D. Vickery and J. R. Herkert, 60–71. Cooper Ornithological Society, Studies in Avian Biology no. 19. 299 pp.

Aweida, M. K. 1995. Repertoires, territory size and mate attraction in western meadowlarks. *Condor* 97:1080–83.

Axelrod, D. I. 1985. Rise of the grassland biome, central North America. *Bot. Rev.* 51:163–201.

Baepler, D. H. 1968. Lark sparrow. In Life histories of North American cardinals, gros-beaks, buntings, towhees, finches, sparrows, and allies, ed. A C. Bent, 886–902. Part Two. *U.S. Natl. Mus. Bull.* 237, Washington, DC.

Bailey, R. G. 1995. *Description of the Ecoregions of the United States.* 2d. ed. Misc. Publ. no. 1391 (rev.). Washington, DC: USDA Forest Service. 198 pp., with separate map.

———. 1996. *Ecosystem Geography.* New York: Springer-Verlag. 204 pp.

Baker, D. L., and F. S. Guthery. 1990. Effects of continuous grazing on habitat and den-sity of ground-foraging birds in South Texas. *J. Range Manage.* 43:2–5.

Bakker, A., K. Withrow, and N. S. Thompson. 1983. Levels of organization in the song of the bobolink (Icteridae: Dolichonyxinae). *J. Tierpsychol.* 62:104–14.

Baldwin, P. H., J. D. Butterfield, P. D. Creighton, and R. Shook. 1969. Summer ecology of the lark bunting. U.S. IBP Grassland Biome Tech. Rep., 29. Colorado State Uni-versity, Fort Collins.

Barbour, M. C., and W. D. Billings, eds. 1988. *North American Terrestrial Vegetation.* Cam-bridge, UK and New York: Cambridge University Press. 434 pp.

Basili, G. D. 1997. Continent-scale ecology and conservation of dickcissels. Ph.D. diss., University of Wisconsin, Madison.

Basore, N. S., L. B. Best, and J. B. Wooley. 1986. Bird nesting in Iowa no-till and tilled cropland. *J. Wildl. Manage.* 50:19–28.

Beason, R. C. 1970. The annual cycle of the prairie horned lark in west-central Illinois. Master's thesis, Western Illinois University, Macomb.

———. 1995. Horned lark (*Eremophila alpestris*). In *The Birds of North America,* ed. A. Poole and F. Gill, no. 195. Philadelphia: Birds of North America.

Beason, R. C., and E. C. Franks. 1974. Breeding behavior of the horned lark. *Auk* 91:65–74.

Bechard, M. J., and J. K. Schmutz. 1995. Ferruginous hawk (*Buteo regalis*). In *The Birds of North America,* ed. A. Poole and F. Gill, no. 172. Philadelphia: Birds of North America.

Bedard, J., and G. LaPoint. 1984. The Savannah sparrow territorial system: Can habitat features be related to breeding success? *Can. J. Zool.* 1819:28.

Bennett, A. T. D., and I. C. Cuthill. 1994. Ultraviolet vision in birds: What is its function? *Vision Res.* 34:1471–78.

Bent, A. C. 1927. Life histories of North American shore birds. Part 1. *U.S. Natl. Mus. Bull.* 142, Washington, DC. 420 pp.

———. 1929. Life histories of North American shore birds. Part 2. *U.S. Natl. Mus. Bull.* 146, Washington, DC. 412 pp.

———. 1932. Life histories of North American gallinaceous birds. *U.S. Natl. Mus. Bull.* 162, Washington, DC. 490 pp.

———. 1937. Life histories of North American birds of prey. Part 1. *U.S. Natl. Mus. Bull.* 167, Washington, DC. 409 pp.

———. 1938. Life histories of North American birds of prey. Part 2. *U.S. Natl. Mus. Bull.* 170, Washington, DC. 482 pp.

———. 1942. Life histories of North American flycatchers, larks, swallows, and their allies. *U.S. Natl. Mus. Bull.* 179, Washington, DC. 555 pp.

———. 1950. Life histories of North American wagtails, shrikes, vireos, and their al-lies. *U.S. Natl. Mus. Bull.* 197, Washington, DC. 411 pp.

———. 1958. Life histories of North American blackbirds, orioles, tanagers, and allies. *U.S. Natl. Mus. Bull.* 211, Washington, DC.

————. 1968. Life histories of North American cardinals, grosbeaks, buntings, towhees, finches, sparrows, and allies. *U.S. Natl. Mus. Bull.* 237, Washington, DC. 1889 pp.

Berg, W. E. 1997. The sharp-tailed grouse in Minnesota. *Minn. Wildl. Rep.* no. 10. 17 pp.

Berger, A. 1951. The cowbird and certain host species in Michigan. *Wilson Bull.* 63:26–34.

Berry, G. A. 1971. The nesting biology of the dickcissel in north central Oklahoma. Master's thesis, Oklahoma State University, Stillwater. 27 pp.

Best, L. B., H. Campa III, K. E. Kemp, R. J. Robel, M. R. Ryan, J. A. Savidge, H. P. Weeks Jr., and S. R. Winterstein. 1997. Bird abundance and nesting in CRP fields and cropland in the Midwest: A regional approach. *Wildl. Soc. Bull.* 25:864–77.

Best, L. B., and N. L. Rodenhouse. 1984. Territory preferences of vesper sparrows in cropland. *Wilson Bull.* 96:72–82.

Bicak, T. K. 1977. Some eco-ethological aspects of a breeding population of long-billed curlews (*Numenius americanus*) in Nebraska. Master's thesis, University of Nebraska, Omaha. 42 pp.

Blackstone, D. L. 1971. Traveler's Guide to the Geology of Wyoming. Laramie: Wyoming Geological Survey.

Blackwelder, E. 1909. Cenozoic history of the Laramie region, Wyoming. *J. of Geol.* 17:429–44.

Blair, C. L., and F. Schitoskey Jr. 1982. Breeding biology and diet of the ferruginous hawk in South Dakota. *Wilson Bull.* 94:46–54.

Blankespoor, G. W. 1970. The significance of nest and nest site microclimate for the dickcissel, *Spiza americana*. Ph.D. diss., Kansas State University, Manhattan. 184 pp.

————. 1980. Prairie restoration: Effect on nongame birds. *J. Wildl. Manage.* 44:667–72.

Blankespoor, G. W., and H. Krause. 1982. The birds of Minnehaha County, South Dakota, then (1907–1916) and now (1971–1975). *Am. Birds* 36:22–27.

Bock, C. E., and J. H. Bock. 1987. Avian occupancy following fire in a Montana shrubsteppe. *Prairie Nat.* 19:153–58. (Includes western meadowlark, chestnut-collared longspur, and grasshopper, lark, and Brewer's sparrows.)

————. 1992. Response of birds to wildfire in native versus exotic Arizona grassland. *Southwest Nat.* 37:73–81. (Includes eastern meadowlark, horned lark, and Cassin's, lark, grasshopper, and vesper sparrows.)

Bock, C. E., V. A. Saab, T. D. Rich, and D. S. Dobkin. 1993. Effects of livestock grazing on Neotropical migratory landbirds in western North America. In *Status and Management of Neotropical Migratory Birds*, ed. D. M. Finch and P. W. Stangel, 296–309. USDA Forest Service, Rocky Mtn. Forest and Range. Exp. Station, Gen. Tech. Rept. RM-229. Fort Collins, CO. 422 pp.

Bollinger, E. K. 1988. Breeding dispersion and reproductive success of bobolinks in an agricultural landscape. Ph.D. diss., Cornell University, Ithaca, NY. See *Diss. Abstr. Int. B. Sci. Eng.* 49(12):5181 (1989).

Bollinger, E. K., P. B. Bollinger, and T. A. Gavin. 1990. Effects of hay cropping on eastern populations of the bobolink. *Wildl. Soc. Bull.* 18:142–50.

Bollinger, E. K., and T. A. Gavin. 1989. The effects of site quality on breeding-site fidelity in bobolinks. *Auk* 106:584–94.

————. 1991. Patterns of extra-pair fertilizations in bobolinks. *Behav. Ecol. Sociobiol.* 29:1–7.

Bomberger, M. F. 1982. Aspects of the breeding biology of Wilson's phalarope in western Nebraska. Master's thesis, University of Nebraska, Lincoln. 102 pp.

Borror, D. J. 1971. Songs of *Aimophila* sparrows occurring in the United States. *Wilson Bull.* 83:132–511.

Borror, D. J., and C. R. Reese. 1954. Analytical studies of Henslow's sparrow songs. *Wilson Bull.* 66:243–52.

Bowen, B. S., and A. D. Kruse. 1993. Effects of grazing on nesting by upland sandpipers in southcentral North Dakota. *J. Wildl. Mgmt.* 57:291–301.

Bowen, D. E. Jr. 1976. Coloniality, reproductive success, and habitat interactions in upland sandpipers (*Bartramia longicauda*). Ph.D. diss., Kansas State University, Manhattan. See *Diss. Abstr. Int. B. Sci. Eng.* 37(7):3240 (1977).

Boyd, R. L. 1976. Behavioral biology and energy expenditure in a horned lark population. Ph.D. diss., Colorado State University, Fort Collins. See *Diss. Abstr. Int. B. Sci. Eng.* 37(12):5947 (1977).

Brauning, D. W. 1992. *Atlas of Breeding Birds in Pennsylvania.* Pittsburgh: University of Pittsburgh Press. 484 pp.

Brewer, R., G. A. McPeek, and R. J. Adams Jr. 1991. *The Atlas of Breeding Birds of Michigan.* East Lansing: Michigan State University Press. 594 pp.

Bridges, D., and D. A. Leatherman. 1991. Sprague's pipits and some associated bird species in extreme northeastern Colorado. *Colorado Field Ornithol. J.* 25:115–18.

Brogie, M. A., and M. J. Mossman. 1983. Spring and summer birds of the Niobrara Valley Preserve area, Nebraska: An annotated checklist. *Nebr. Bird Rev.* 51:44–51.

Brown, S. L. 1988. The maintenance and consequences of polygyny in eastern meadowlarks (*Sturnella magna*). Ph.D. diss., Purdue University, West Lafayette, IN. 158 pp. See *Diss. Abstr. Int. B. Sci. Eng.* 49(10):4132 (1989).

Buech, R. R. 1982. Nesting ecology and cowbird parasitism of clay-colored, chipping and field sparrows in a Christmas tree plantation. *J. Field Ornithol.* 53:363–69.

Burger, J. 1972. Breeding adaptations of Franklin's gull (*Larus pipixcan*) to a marsh habitat. Ph.D. diss., University of Minnesota, Minneapolis. 237 pp. See *Diss. Abstr. Int. B. Sci. Eng.* 33(6), 1972.

———. 1974. Breeding adaptations of Franklin's gull (*Larus pipixcan*) to a marsh habitat. *Anim. Behav.* 22:521–67.

Burger, J., and M. Gochfeld. 1994. Franklin's gull (*Larus pipixcan*). In *The Birds of North America*, ed. A. Poole and F. Gill, no. 2116. Philadelphia: Birds of North America.

Burkhardt, D. 1989. UV vision: A bird's eye view of feathers. *J. Comp. Physiol.* (A):164:787–96.

Buss, I. O., and A. S. Hawkins, 1939. The upland plover at Faville Grove, Wisconsin. *Wilson Bull.* 51:202–20.

Butterfield, J. D. 1969. Nest-site requirements of the lark bunting in Colorado. Master's thesis, Colorado State University, Fort Collins.

Cable, T. T., S. Seltman, and K. J. Cook. 1997. *Birds of Cimarron National Grassland.* Rocky Mtn. Range and Exp. Station, Gen. Tech. Rep. RM-GTR-281. Fort Collins, CO. 108 pp.

Cadman, M. D., P. F. J. Eagles, and F. M. Helleiner. 1987. *Atlas of the Breeding Birds of Ontario.* Waterloo, ON: University of Waterloo Press.

Cartright, B. W., T. M. Shortt, and R. D. Harris. 1937. Baird's sparrow. *Trans. Roy. Canadian Inst.* 21:153–97.

Castrale, J. S. 1983. Selection of song perches by sagebrush-grassland birds. *Wilson Bull.*

95:647–55. (Includes vesper and Brewer's sparrows, horned lark, and western meadowlark.)

Catlin, G. 1876. *North American Indians.* 2 vols. London: Chatto and Windus.

Chapman, K. A., M. K. Ziegenhagen, and A. Fischer. 1998. *Valley of Grass: Tallgrass Prairie and Parkland in the Red River Valley.* St. Cloud, MN: North Star Press.

Choate, E. A. 1985. *The Dictionary of American Bird Names.* Rev. ed. Harvard, MA: Harvard Common Press. 226 pp.

Clark, R. J. 1975. A field study of the short-eared owl *Asio flammeus* Pontoppidan in North America. *Wildl. Monogr.* 47:1–67.

Clawson, R. L. 1991. Henslow's sparrow habitat site fidelity and reproduction in Missouri. Fed. Aid. Perf. Rep., Missouri Dept. Conserv., Proj. W-14-R-45. 18 pp.

Cochrane, J. F. 1983. Long-billed curlew habitat and land-use relationships in western Wyoming. Master's thesis, University of Wyoming, Laramie. 136 pp.

Cody, M. L. 1968. On the methods of resource division in grassland bird communities. *Amer. Nat.* 102:107–47. (Includes western meadowlark, Sprague's pipit, bobolink, horned lark, clay-colored, vesper, Savannah, grasshopper, and Baird's sparrows.)

———. 1985. Habitat selection in grassland and open-country birds. In *Habitat Selection in Birds,* ed. M. L. Cody, 191–226. Orlando, FL: Academic Press.

Collias, E. C., and N. E. Collias. 1957. The response of chicks of the Franklin's gull to parental bill color. *Auk* 74:371–75.

Collins, S. L., and L. L. Wallace, eds. 1990. *Fire in the North American Tallgrass Prairies.* Norman: University of Oklahoma Press.

Colvin, B. A., and Spaulding, S. R. 1983. Winter foraging behavior of short-eared owls (*Asio flammeus*) in Ohio. *Am. Midl. Nat.* 110:124–28.

Colwell, M. A. 1986. The first documented case of polyandry for Wilson's phalarope (*Phalaropus tricolor*). *Auk* 103:611–12.

———. 1987. Breeding biology, intrasexual competition and philopatry in Wilson's phalarope (*Phalaropus tricolor*). Ph.D. diss., University of North Dakota, Grand Forks. 138 pp. See *Diss., Abstr. Int. B. Sci. Eng.* 48(8):2231 (1988).

———. 1992. Wilson's phalarope nest success is not influenced by vegetation concealment. *Condor* 94:767–72.

Colwell, M. A., and J. R. Jehl Jr. 1994. Wilson's phalarope (*Phalaropus lobatus*). In *The Birds of North America,* ed. A. Poole and F. Gill, no. 83. Philadelphia: Birds of North America.

Colwell, M. A., and L. W. Oring. 1988a. Breeding biology of Wilson's phalarope in south-central Saskatchewan. *Wilson Bull.* 100:567–82.

———. 1988b. Sex ratios and intrasexual competition for mates in a sex-role reversed shorebird, the Wilson's phalarope (*Phalaropus tricolor*). *Behav. Ecol. Sociobiol.* 22:165–73.

———. 1990. Nest-site characteristics of prairie shorebirds. *Can. J. Zool.* 68:297–302

Connelly, J. W., M. W. Gratson, and K. P. Reese. 1998. Sharp-tailed grouse (*Tympanuchus phasianellus*). In *The Birds of North America,* ed. A. Poole and F. Gill, no. 354. Philadelphia: Birds of North America.

Coupland, R. T. 1958. The effects of fluctuations in weather upon the grasslands of the Great Plains. *Bot. Rev.* 24:274–317.

Crawford, J. A., and E. G. Bolen. 1975. Spring lek activity of the lesser prairie chicken in west Texas. *Auk* 92:808–10.

Creighton, P. D. 1971. Nesting of the lark bunting in north-central Colorado. Grassland Biome, U.S. Int. Biol. Prog. Tech. Rep. no. 29. Denver, CO.

———. 1974. Habitat exploitation by an avian ground-foraging guild. Ph.D. diss., Colorado State University, Fort Collins. 154 pp. See *Diss. Abstr. Int. B. Sci. Eng.* 35(3), 1974.

Crump, D. J., ed. 1984. *A Guide to our Federal Lands.* Washington, DC: Natl. Geog. Soc. 220 pp.

Cully, J. F., and H. L. Michaels. 2000. Henslow's sparrow habitat associations on Kansas tallgrass prairie. *Wilson Bull.* 112:115–23.

Cushman, R. C., and S. R. Jones. 1988. *The Shortgrass Prairie.* Boulder, CO: Pruett.

D'Agincourt, L. G., and J. B. Falls. 1983. Variation of repertoire use in the eastern meadowlark, *Sturnella magna. Can. J. Zool.* 61:1086–93.

Dale, B. C. 1983. Habitat relationships of seven species of passerine birds at Last Mountain Lake, Saskatchewan. Master's thesis, University of Regina, SA. 119 pp.

———. 1984. Birds of grazed and ungrazed grasslands in Saskatchewan. *Blue Jay* 42:102–4. (Includes horned lark, western meadowlark, Sprague's pipit, chestnut-collared longspur, and clay-colored, vesper, Savannah, and Baird's sparrows.)

Dale, B. C., P. A. Martin, and P. S. Taylor. 1997. Effects of hay management on grassland songbirds in Saskatchewan. *Wildl. Soc. Bull.* 25:616–26.

Darwin, C. 1960. Notebooks on Transmutation of Species. *Bull. of the Brit. Mus. (Nat. Hist.), Historical Series* 2, Brit. Mus. (Nat. Hist.), London.

Daubenmire, R. K. 1968. Ecology of fire in grasslands. *Adv. Ecol. Res.* 5:209–66.

Davis, S. K. 1994. Cowbird parasitism, predation, and host selection in fragmented grassland of southeastern Manitoba. Master's thesis, University of Manitoba, Winnipeg.

Davis, S. K., and D. C. Duncan. In press. Grassland songbird abundance in native and crested wheatgrass pastures of southern Saskatchewan. *Studies in Avian Biology* 19:211–18. (Includes Sprague's pipit, chestnut-collared longspur, horned lark, western meadowlark, and vesper, Baird's, and Savannah sparrows.)

Davis, S. K., D. C. Duncan, and M. A. Skeel. 1996. Baird's sparrow: Status resolved. *Blue Jay* 54:185–91. (Data also on chestnut-collared longspur, horned lark, Sprague's pipit, western meadowlark, and clay-colored sparrow.)

———. 1999. Distribution and habitat associations of three endemic grassland songbirds in southern Saskatchewan. *Wilson Bull.* 111:389–96. (Sprague's pipit, Baird's sparrow, and chestnut-collared longspur.)

Davis, S. K., and S. G. Sealy. 1998. Nesting biology of the Baird's sparrow in southwestern Manitoba. *Wilson Bull.* 110:262–70.

———. 2000. Cowbird parasitism and predation in grassland fragments of southwestern Manitoba. In *The Biology and Management of Cowbirds and their Hosts,* ed. J. N. M. Smith, T. L. Cook, S. I. Rothstein, S. K. Robinson, and S. G. Sealy. Austin: University of Texas Press.

Davit, C. 1999, ed. *Public Prairies of Missouri.* Missouri Dept. of Conserv., Jefferson City.

Dawson, W. L. 1923. *The Birds of California.* 3 vols. San Diego, CA: South Moulton Company.

Dechant, D. J., M. L. Sondreal, D. H. Johnson, L. D. Igl, C. M. Goldade, M. P. Nenneman and B. R. Euliss. 1998 (rev. 1999). Effects of management practices on grassland birds: Mountain plover. Northern Prairie Wildlife Research Center, Jamestown, ND.

11 pp. (This and the following references by Dechant et al. are also on line. URL=<http://www.npwrc.usgov/resource/literatr/grassbird>.)

——. 1999a. Effects of management practices on grassland birds: Burrowing owl. Northern Prairie Wildlife Research Center, Jamestown, ND. 31 pp.

——. 1999b. Effects of management practices on grassland birds: Chestnut-collared longspur. Northern Prairie Wildlife Research Center, Jamestown, ND. 12 pp.

——. 1999c. Effects of management practices on grassland birds: Clay-colored sparrow. Northern Prairie Wildlife Research Center, Jamestown, ND. 15 pp.

——. 1999d. Effects of management practices on grassland birds: Ferruginous hawk. Northern Prairie Wildlife Research Center, Jamestown, ND. 20 pp.

——. 1999e. Effects of management practices on grassland birds: Grasshopper sparrow. Northern Prairie Wildlife Research Center, Jamestown, ND. 20 pp.

——. 1999f. Effects of management practices on grassland birds: Henslow's sparrow. Northern Prairie Wildlife Research Center, Jamestown, ND. 14 pp.

——. 1999g. Effects of management practices on grassland birds: Lark bunting. Northern Prairie Wildlife Research Center, Jamestown, ND. 15 pp.

——. 1999h. Effects of management practices on grassland birds: Marbled godwit. Northern Prairie Wildlife Research Center, Jamestown, ND. 8 pp.

——. 1999i. Effects of management practices on grassland birds: McCown's longspur. Northern Prairie Wildlife Research Center, Jamestown, ND. 11 pp.

——. 1999j. Effects of management practices on grassland birds: Savannah sparrow. Northern Prairie Wildlife Research Center, Jamestown, ND. 23 pp.

——. 1999k. Effects of management practices on grassland birds: Dickcissel. Northern Prairie Wildlife Research Center, Jamestown, ND. 27 pp.

——. 1999l. Effects of management practices on grassland birds: Baird's sparrow. Northern Prairie Wildlife Research Center, Jamestown, ND. 15 pp.

——. 1999m. Effects of management practices on grassland birds: Sprague's pipit. Northern Prairie Wildlife Research Center, Jamestown, ND. 10 pp.

——. 1999n. Effects of management practices on grassland birds: Wilson's phalarope. Northern Prairie Wildlife Research Center, Jamestown, ND. 13 pp.

——. 1999o. Effects of management practices on grassland birds: Short-eared owl. Northern Prairie Wildlife Research Center, Jamestown, ND. 9 pp.

DeGraaf, R. M., V. E. Scott, R. H. Hamre, L. Ernst, and S. H. Anderson. 1991. *Forest and Rangeland Birds of the United States.* Agriculture Handbook no. 688, Washington, DC: USDA. 625 pp.

DeGraaf, R. M., and N. G. Tilghman, eds. 1980. *Workshop Proceedings: Management of Western Forests and Grasslands for Nongame Birds.* USDA, Forest Service, Intermountain Forest and Range Exp. Station, Tech. Rept. INT-86. Ogden, UT. 535 pp.

Delany, M. F., and S. B. Linda. 1998. Characteristics of Florida grasshopper sparrow nests. *Wilson Bull.* 110:136–39.

Delehanty, D. J., and L. W. Oring. 1993. Effects of clutch size on incubation persistence in male Wilson's phalarope (*Phalaropus tricolor*). *Auk* 110:521–28.

Delehanty, D. J., R. C. Fleischer, M. A. Colwell, and L. W. Oring. 1998. Sex-role reversal and the absence of extra-pair fertilization in Wilson's phalaropes. *Anim. Behav.* 55:995–1002.

Desmond, M. J., and J. A. Savidge. 1995. Spatial patterns of burrowing owl (*Speotyto cunicularia*) nests within black-tailed prairie dog (*Cynomys ludovicianus*) towns. *Can. J. Zool.* 73: 1375–79.

———. 1996. Factors influencing burrowing owl (*Speotyto cunicularia*) nest densities and numbers in western Nebraska. *Am. Midl. Nat.* 136:143–48.

Dinsmore, J. J., T. H. Kent, D. Koenig, P. C. Petersen, and D. M. Roosa. 1984. *Iowa Birds.* Ames: Iowa State University Press. 356 pp.

Dixon, C. L. 1978. Breeding biology of the Savannah sparrow on Kent Island. *Auk* 95:255–46.

Dobkin, D. S. 1994. *Conservation and Management of Neotropical Migrant Landbirds in the Northern Rockies and Great Plains.* Moscow: University of Idaho Press. (Includes Swainson's and ferruginous hawks, prairie falcon, mountain plover, upland sandpiper, marbled godwit, burrowing and short-eared owls, horned lark, Sprague's pipit, clay-colored, Brewer's, vesper, lark, Savannah, Baird's, and grasshopper sparrows, lark bunting, McCown's and chestnut-collared longspurs, bobolink and western meadowlark.)

Dorio, J. C., and A. H. Grove. 1979. Nesting and brood rearing habitat of the upland sandpiper. *J. Minn. Acad. Sci.* 45:8–11.

Doyle, T. L. 1997. The timberline sparrow, *Spizella* (*breweri*) *taverneri*, in Alaska, with notes on breeding habitat and vocalizations. *West. Birds* 28:1–12.

Dunkle, F. W. 1977. Swainson's hawks on the Laramie Plains, Wyoming. *Auk* 94:65–71.

Elliott, P. F. 1978. Cowbird parasitism in the Kansas tallgrass prairie. *Auk* 95:161–67.

Ellis, J., C. Jones, D. L. Genter, J. Reichel, B. Spettigue, and D. Sullivan. 1996. *P. D. Skaar's Montana Bird Distribution.* 5th ed. Special Publ. no. 3, Montana Natural Heritage Program, Helena.

England, A. S., M. J. Bechard, and C. S. Houston. 1997. Swainson's hawk (*Buteo swainsoni*). In *The Birds of North America,* ed. A. Poole and F. Gill, no. 265. Philadelphia: Birds of North America.

Engle, D. M., T. L. Criner, J. C. Boren, R. E. Masters, and M. S. Gregory. 1999. Response of breeding birds in the Great Plains to low density urban sprawl. *Great Plains Res.* 9:55–73.

Ensign, J. T. 1983. Nest site selection, productivity and food habits of ferruginous hawks in southeastern Montana. Master's thesis, Montana State University, Bozeman.

Erdoes, R., and A. Ortiz. 1984. *American Indian Myths and Legends.* New York: Pantheon Books. 527 pp.

Erwin, W. E. 1981. Environmental influences on song-flight in lark buntings: Behavioral adaptations for communication. Master's thesis, University of Colorado, Boulder.

Faanes, C. E., and G. R. Lingle. 1995. Breeding birds of the Platte Valley of Nebraska. Northern Prairie Wildlife Research Center Home Page, Jamestown, ND. URL=<http://www.npwrc.usgs.gov/resources/distr/birds/platte/platte(version 16JUL97)>.

Falls, J. B., and L. G. d'Agincourt. 1981. A comparison of neighbor-stranger discrimination in eastern and western meadowlarks. *Can. J. Zool.* 59:2380–85.

———. 1982. Why do meadowlarks switch song types? *Can. J. Zool.* 60:3400–3408.

Falls, J. B., A. G. Horn, and T. E. Dickinson. 1988. How western meadowlarks classify their songs: evidence from song matching. *Anim. Behav.* 36:579–85.

Farney, D. 1980. The tallgrass prairie: Can it be saved? *Natl. Geog. Mag.* (Jan.):37–61.

Felske, B. E. 1971. The population dynamics and productivity of McCown's longspur at Matador, Saskatchewan. Master's thesis, University of Saskatchewan, Saskatoon.

Finch, D. M. 1992. *Threatened, endangered, and vulnerable species of terrestrial vertebrates in the Rocky Mountain Region.* USDA Forest Service, Rocky Mtn. Forest and Range Exp. Station. Gen. Tech. Rept. RM-215. Fort Collins, CO. 38 pp. (Includes ferruginous hawk, sharp-tailed grouse, greater and lesser prairie-chickens, mountain plover, upland sandpiper, long-billed curlew, lark bunting, and Baird's sparrow.)

Finch, D. M., S. H. Anderson, and W. A. Hubert. 1987. Habitat suitability index models: Lark bunting. U.S. Fish and Wildlife Serv., Biol. Rep. 82 (10.137). Washington, DC. 16 pp.

Finch, D. M., and P. W. Stangel, eds. 1993. *Status and management of neotropical migratory birds.* USDA Forest Service, Rocky Mtn. Forest and Range. Exp. Station, Gen. Tech. Rept. RM-229. Fort Collins, CO. 422 pp.

Fink, E. J. 1983. Male behavior, territory quality and female choice in the dickcissel (*Spiza americana*). Ph.D. diss., Kansas State University, Manhattan. 79 pp. See *Diss. Abstr. Int. B. Sci. Eng.* 44(5):1322 (1984).

Fitzner, J. N. 1978. The ecology and behavior of the long-billed curlew (*Numenius americanus*) in southeastern Washington. Ph.D. diss., Washington State University, Pullman. 201 pp. See *Diss. Abstr. Int. B. Sci. Eng.* 39(8):3667.

Fleckenstein, J. 1993. Iowa's state preserves system. *Iowa Conservationist* 52(1):32–41.

Fleischer, R. C. 1986. Brood parasitism of brown-headed cowbirds in a simple host community in eastern Kansas. *Kans. Ornithol. Soc. Bull.* 37:21–29.

Forsythe, D. M. 1970. Vocalizations of the long-billed curlew. *Condor* 72:213–24.

———. 1972. Observations on the nesting biology of the long-billed curlew. *Great Basin Nat.* 32:88–90.

Fox, G. A. 1961. A contribution to the life history of the clay-colored sparrow. *Auk* 78:220–24.

Frawley, B. J. 1989. The dynamics of nongame bird breeding ecology in Iowa alfalfa fields. Master's thesis, Iowa State University, Ames.

Freeman-Gallant, C. R. 1997a. Extra-pair paternity in monogamous and polygynous Savannah sparrows, *Passerculus sandwichensis. Anim. Behav.* 53:397–404.

———. 1997b. Parentage and paternal care: Consequences of intersexual selection in Savannah sparrows? *Behav. Ecol. Sociobiol.* 40:395–400.

Fretwell, S. 1986. Distribution and abundance of the dickcissel. In *Current Ornithology,* ed. R. F. Johson, vol. 4, 211–41. New York: Plenum Press.

Friedmann, H. 1963. Host relations of the parasitic cowbirds. *Bull. U.S. Natl. Mus.* 233:1–273.

Friedmann, H., and L. F. Kiff. 1985. The parasitic cowbirds and their hosts. *Proc. West. Found. Vert. Zool.* 2:225–302.

Friedmann, H., L. F. Kiff, and S. I. Rothstein. 1977. A further contribution to knowledge of the host relations of the parasitic cowbirds. *Smithsonian Contrib. Zool.* 235:1–75.

Gayton, D. 1990. *The Wheatgrass mechanism: Science and imagination in the western Canadian landscape.* Saskatoon, SA: Fifth House Publishers.

George, T. L., A. C. Folwer, R. L. Knight, and L. C. McEwen. 1992. Impacts of a severe drought on grassland birds of western North Dakota. *Ecol. Appl.* 2:275–84.

Gerstel, A. T., and J. C. Bednarz. 1999. Competition and resource use by two sympatric raptors. *Condor* 101:557–65. (Compares Swainson's and Harris's hawks).

Gibson, D. J., and L. C. Hulbert. 1987. Effects of fire, topography and year-to-year climate variation on species composition in tallgrass prairie. *Vegetatio* 72:175–85.

Giesen, K. M, 1994a. Breeding range and population status of lesser prairie-chickens in Colorado. *Prairie Nat.* 26:175–82.

———. 1994b. Movements and nesting habitat of lesser prairie-chicken hens in Colorado. *Southwest. Nat.* 39:96–98.

———. 1997. Seasonal movements, home ranges, and habitat use by Columbian sharp-tailed grouse in Colorado. *Colo. Div. Wildl. Spec. Rep.* no. 72. 16 pp.

———. 1998. Lesser prairie-chicken (*Tympanuchus pallidicinctus*). In *The Birds of North America,* ed A. Poole and F. Gill, no. 364. Philadelphia: Birds of North America.

Gilmer, D. S., and R. E. Stewart. 1983. Ferruginous hawk populations and habitat use in North Dakota. *J. Wildl. Manage.* 47:146–57.

———. 1984. Swainson's hawk nesting ecology in North Dakota. *Condor* 86:12–18.

Godfrey, W. E. 1950. Birds of the Cypress Hills and Flotten Lake region, Saskatchewan. *Nat. Mus. Canada Bull.* 120:1–96.

Goertz, J. W. 1977. Additional records of brown-headed cowbird parasitism in Louisiana. *Auk* 94:386–96.

Gollop, J. B. 1978. Changes in songbird populations since the mid-1940s in the Prairie Provinces. In *Nature and Change on the Canadian Prairies,* ed. W. A. Davis, 78–103. Can. Plains Proceedings, Can. Plains Res. Centre, University of Regina, Regina, SA.

Goriup, P., ed. 1988. *Ecology and conservation of grassland birds.* ICBP Technical Publication no. 7. International Council for Bird Preservation, Cambridge, UK. 250 pp.

Graber, R. R., and J. W. Graber. 1963. A comparative study of bird populations in Illinois, 1906–1909 and 1956–1958. *Ill. Nat. Hist. Surv. Bull.* 28:468–69. (Includes upland sandpiper, horned lark, bobolink, meadowlarks, dickcissel, and Savannah, grasshopper, vesper, and lark sparrows.)

Graham, A. 1999. *Late Cretaceous and Cenozoic history of North American vegetation north of Mexico.* New York: Oxford University Press.

Granfors, D. A., K. E. Church, and L. M. Smith. 1996. Eastern meadowlarks nesting in rangelands and conservation reserve program fields in Kansas. *J. Field Ornithol.* 67:222–35.

Gratson, M. W. 1990. Sexual selection on sharp-tailed grouse leks. Ph.D. diss., University of Victoria, Victoria, BC. See *Diss. Abstr. Int. B. Sci. Eng.* 52(1):105 (1991).

Gratson, M. W., G. K. Gratson, and A. T. Bergerud. 1991. Male dominance and copulation disruption does not explain variance in male mating success on sharp-tailed grouse (*Tympanuchus phasianellus*) leks. *Behaviour* 118:187–213.

Gratto-Trevor, C. 2000. Use of managed and natural wetlands by upland breeding shorebirds in southern Alberta. In *Proceedings of the Fifth Prairie Conservation and Endangered Species Conference,* 20–22 Feb. 1998, Saskatoon, SA.

———. 2000. Marbled godwit (*Limosa fedoa*). In *The Birds of North America,* ed. A. Poole and F. Gill. Philadelphia: no. 492. Birds of North America.

Graul, W. D. 1973. Adaptive aspects of the mountain plover social system. *Living Bird* 12:69–94.

———. 1975. Breeding biology of the mountain plover. *Wilson Bull.* 87: 6–31.

Graul, W. D., and L. Webster. 1976. Breeding status of the mountain plover. *Condor* 78:265–67.

Green, G. A., and M. L. Morrison. 1983. Nest-site characteristics of sympatric ferruginous and Swainson's hawks. *Murrelet* 64:20–22.

Green, M. T. 1992. Adaptations of Baird's sparrows (*Ammodramus bairdii*) to grasslands: Acoustic communication and nomadism. Ph.D. diss., University of North Carolina, Chapel Hill.

Greer, R. D. 1988. Effects of habitat structure and productivity on grassland birds. Ph.D. diss., University of Wyoming, Laramie. 137 pp. See *Diss. Abstr. Int. B. Sci. Eng.* 49(10):4188 (1989).

Greer, R. D., and S. H. Anderson. 1989. Relationships between population demography of McCown's longspurs and habitat resources. *Condor* 91:609–19.

Groskorth, L. C. 1995. Nest-site selection by the Swainson's hawk on the Regina plain, Saskatchewan. *Can. J. Zool.* 73:1887–90.

Gruson, E. S. 1972. *Words for Birds.* New York: Quadrangle Books.

Guay, J. W. 1968. The breeding biology of Franklin's gull (*Larus pipixcan*). Ph.D. diss., University of Alberta, Edmonton, AB.

Hagen, J. M. III, and D. W. Johnston, eds. 1992. *Ecology and conservation of Neotropical migrant landbirds.* Washington, DC: Smithsonian Institution Press.

Haley, J. E., ed. 1969. *Albert Pike's journeys in the prairie, 1831–1832.* Panhandle-Plains Historical Society.

Hammerstrom, F. 1986. *Harrier: Hawk of the Marshes.* Washington, DC: Smithsonian Institution Press.

Hands, H. M., R. D. Drobney, and M. R. Ryan. 1989. Status of the Henslow's sparrow in the northcentral United States. U.S. Fish and Wildl. Serv., Missouri Coop. Wildl. Unit. 12 pp.

Harmeson, J. P. 1974. Breeding ecology of the dickcissel. *Auk* 91:348–59.

Harris, R. D. 1933. Observations on a nest of Sprague's pipit (*Anthus spragueii*). *Can. Field-Nat.* 47:91–95.

————. 1944. The chestnut-collared longspur in Manitoba. *Wilson Bull.* 56:105–15.

Hatch, S. A. 1983. Nestling growth relationships of brown-headed cowbirds and dickcissels. *Wilson Bull.* 95:669–71.

Haug, E. A., B. A. Millsap, and M. S. Martell. 1993. Burrowing owl (*Athene cunicularia*). In *The Birds of North America,* ed. A. Poole and F. Gill, no. 61. Philadelphia: Birds of North America.

Henderson, C. L., and A. L. Lambrecht. 1997. *Traveler's guide to wildlife in Minnesota.* St. Paul: Minn. Dept. of Nat. Resources.

Hergenrader, G. L. 1962. The incidence of nest parasitism by the brown-headed cowbird (*Molothrus ater*) on roadside nesting birds in Nebraska. *Auk* 79:85–88.

Herkert, J. R. 1991a. An ecological study of the breeding birds of grassland habitats within Illinois. Ph.D. diss., University of Illinois, Urbana. See *Diss. Abstr. Int. B. Sci. Eng.* 52(7):3396 (1992). (Includes upland sandpiper, eastern meadowlark, grasshopper, Savannah, and Henslow's sparrows, and dickcissel.)

————. 1991b. Prairie birds of Illinois: Population response to two centuries of habitat changes. *Ill. Nat. Hist. Surv. Bull.* 34:393–99.

———. 1994a. The effect of habitat fragmentation on midwestern grassland bird communities. *Ecol. Appl.* 4:461–71.

———. 1994b. Status and habitat selection of the Henslow's sparrow in Illinois. *Wilson Bull.* 106:35–45.

———. 1995. An analysis of midwestern breeding bird population trends, 1966–1993. *Amer. Mild. Nat.* 134:41–50.

Herkert, J. R., and W. D. Glass. 1999. Henslow's sparrow response to prescribed fire in an Illinois prairie remnant. In *Ecology and Conservation of Grassland Birds of the Western Hemisphere*, ed P. D. Vickery and J. R. Herkert, 160–64. Cooper Ornithological Society, Studies in Avian Biology no. 19. 299 pp.

Herkert, J. R., D. W. Sample, and R. E. Warner. 1995. Management of midwestern grassland landscapes for the conservation of migratory birds. In *Management of midwestern landscapes for the conservation of Neotropical migratory birds*, ed. F. R. Thompson III, 89–116. USDI, North Central Forest Experiment Station Bulletin, Gen. Tech. Rep. NC-187. Detroit, MI.

Hicks, L. E. 1934. A summary of cowbird host species in Ohio. *Auk* 51:385–86.

Higgins, K. F., H. R. Duebbert, and R. B. Oetting. 1969. Nesting of the upland plover on the Missouri Coteau. *Prairie Nat.* 1:45–48.

Higgins, K. F., and L. M. Kirsh. 1975. Some aspects of the breeding biology of the upland sandpiper in North Dakota. *Wilson Bull.* 87:96–101.

Higgins, K. F., L. M. Kirsh, M. R. Ryan, and R. B. Renken. 1979. Some ecological aspects of marbled godwits and willets in North Dakota. *Prairie Nat.* 11:115–18.

Higgins, K. F., A. D. Kruse, and J. L. Piel. 1986. Effects of fire in the northern Great Plains. *South Dak. State Agric. Ext. Circ.* EC 761. Brookings, SD.

Hill, D. P. 1992. An experimental study of nest desertion by the clay-colored sparrow (*Spizella pallida*) in response to cowbird parasitism. Master's thesis, University of Manitoba, Winnipeg, MB, 76 pp. See *Masters Abstr. Int.* 31(4):1656 (1993).

Hill, D. P., and L. K. Gould. 1997. Chestnut-collared longspur (*Calcarius ornatus*). In *The Birds of North America*, ed. A. Poole and F. Gill, no. 288. Philadelphia: Birds of North America.

Hill, R. A. 1976. Host-parasite relationships of the brown-headed cowbird in a prairie habitat of west-central Kansas. *Wilson Bull.* 88:555–65.

Hill, R. A., and S. G. Sealy. 1994. Desertion of nests parasitized by cowbirds: Have clay-colored sparrows evolved an anti-parasite defense? *Anim. Behav.* 48:1063–70.

Hillman, C. N., and W. W. Jackson. 1976. The sharp-tailed grouse in South Dakota. SD Dept. of Game, Fish and Parks, Tech. Bull. 364 pp.

Holt, D. W. 1993. Trophic niche of Nearctic short-eared owls. *Wilson Bull.* 105:497–503.

Holt, D. W., and S. M. Leisure. 1993. Short-eared owl (*Asio flammeus*). In *The Birds of North America*, ed. A. Poole and F. Gill, no. 62. Philadelphia: Birds of North America.

Horak, G. J. 1985. Kansas prairie chickens. *Kans. Fish and Game Comm. Wildl. Bull.* no. 3:1–65.

Horn, A. G., T. E. Dickinson, and J. B. Falls. 1993. Male quality and song repertoires in western meadowlarks (*Sturnella neglecta*). *Can. J. Zool.* 71:1059–61.

Horn, A. G., and J. B. Falls. 1988. Structure of western meadowlark (*Sturnella neglecta*) song repertoires. *Can. J. Zool.* 66:284–88.

———. 1991. Song switching in mate attraction and territory defense by western meadowlarks (*Sturnella neglecta*). *Ethology* 87:262–68.

Howe, M. A. 1972. Pair bond formation and maintenance in Wilson's phalarope, *Phalaropus tricolor*. Ph.D. diss., University of Minnesota, Minneapolis. See *Diss. Abstr. Int. B. Sci. Eng.* 33(5):2410 (1973).

Hubbard, J. P. 1977. The status of Cassin's sparrow in New Mexico and adjacent states. *Am. Birds* 31:933–41.

Huber, G. E., and A. A. Steuter. 1984. Vegetation profile and grassland bird response to spring burning. *Prairie Nat.* 16:55–61.

Hughes, A. J. 1993. Breeding density and habitat preference of the burrowing owl in northeastern Colorado. Master's thesis, Colorado State University, Ft. Collins.

Huntley, C. W. 1997. Another factor that reduces brown-headed cowbird parasitism at lark bunting nests. *J. Colo. Field Ornithol.* 31:17–18.

Hurley, R. J., and E. C. Franks. 1976. Changes in the breeding ranges of two grassland birds. *Auk* 92:108–15. (Discusses dickcissel and horned lark.)

Hyde, A. J. 1939. The life history of Henslow's sparrow, *Passerherbulus henslowii*. Mus. of Zoology *Misc. Publ.* no. 41. Ann Arbor: University of Michigan Press.

Igl, L. D., and D. H. Johnson. 1997. Changes in breeding bird populations in North Dakota, 1967–1992, 1993. *Auk* 114:74–92.

Ingalls, J. J. 1872. Blue grass. *Kansas Magazine* 2 (3):270–77.

Iowa State Preserves Board. 1978. *A Directory of State Preserves*. Des Moines: Iowa Dept. of Nat. Resources.

Jackson, L. S., C. A. Thompson, and J. J. Dinsmore. 1996. *The Iowa Breeding Bird Atlas*. Iowa City: University of Iowa Press.

Jacobs, B., and J. D. Wilson. 1997. *Missouri Breeding Bird Atlas, 1986–1992*. Natural Hist. Ser., no. 6. Jefferson City: Missouri Dept. Conserv.

Jehl, J. R. Jr. 1987. A historical explanation for polyandry in Wilson's phalarope. *Auk* 104:555–56.

Joern, A., and K. Keeler, eds. 1995. *The changing prairie: North American grasslands*. New York: Oxford University Press.

Johnsgard, P. A. 1973. *Grouse and quails of North America*. Lincoln: University of Nebraska Press. 553 pp.

———. 1979. *Birds of the Great Plains: Breeding species and their distribution*. Lincoln: University of Nebraska Press. 539 pp.

———. 1981. *The plovers, sandpipers and snipes of the world*. Lincoln: University of Nebraska Press. 493 pp.

———. 1983. *The grouse of the world*. Lincoln: University of Nebraska Press. 412 pp.

———. 1986. *Birds of the Rocky Mountains, with particular reference to national parks in the northern Rocky Mountain region*. Boulder: Colorado Associated University Press. 504 pp.

———. 1988. *North American owls: Biology and natural history*. Washington, DC: Smithsonian Institution Press. 295 pp.

———. 1990. *Hawks, eagles and falcons of North America: Biology and natural history*. Washington, DC: Smithsonian Institution Press. 403 pp.

———. 1995. *This fragile land: A natural history of the Nebraska sandhills*. Lincoln: University of Nebraska Press. 256 pp.

———. 1997. *The avian brood parasites: Deception at the nest*. New York: Oxford University Press. 409 pp.

————. In press. *The Nature of Nebraska.* Lincoln: University of Nebraska Press.

Johnson, D. H. 1972–74. Breeding bird populations of selected grasslands in east-central North Dakota. *Am. Birds* 26:970–75; 27:989–90; 28:1030–31.

————. 1995. Management of northern prairies and wetlands for the conservation of Neotropical migratory birds. In *Management of midwestern landscapes for the conservation of Neotropical migratory birds,* ed. F. R. Thompson III, USDI, North Central Forest Experiment Station Bulletin, Gen. Tech. Rep. NC-187. Detroit.

————. 1996. Effects of fire on bird populations in mixed-grass prairie. In *Ecology and conservation of Great Plains vertebrates,* ed. F. L. Knopf and F. B. Samson, 181–206. Ecological Studies, vol. 125. New York: Springer. (Discusses marbled godwit, upland sandpiper, western meadowlark, bobolink, and Savannah, grasshopper, Baird's, and clay-colored sparrows.)

Johnson, D. H., and Igl, L. D. 1995. Contributions of the conservation reserve program to populations of breeding birds in North Dakota. *Wilson Bull.* 107:709–18.

Johnson, D. H., and M. D. Schwartz. 1993a. The Conservation Reserve Program and grassland birds. *Conservation Biol.* 7:934–37.

————. 1993b. The Conservation Reserve Program: Habitat for grassland birds. *Great Plains Res.* 3:273–95.

Johnson, R. G., and S. A. Temple. 1986. Assessing habitat quality for birds nesting in fragmented tallgrass prairies. In *Modeling habitat relationships of terrestrial vertebrates,* ed. J. Verner, M. L. Morrison, and C. J. Ralph, 245–49. Madison: University of Wisconsin Press.

————. 1990. Nest predation and brood parasitism of tallgrass prairie birds. *J. Wildl. Manage.* 54:106–11.

Jones, J. O. 1990. *Where the birds are: A guide to all 50 states and Canada.* New York: Wm. Morrow. 400 pp.

Jones, S. L., M. T. Green, and G. R. Geupel. 1998. Rare, little-known and declining North American breeders. A closer look: Baird's sparrow. *Birding* 30:108–16.

Kagarise, C. 1979. Breeding biology of Wilson's phalarope in North Dakota. *Bird-Banding.* 50:12–22.

Kahl, R. B., T. S. Baskett, and J. N. Burroughs. 1985. Characteristics of summer habitat of selected nongame birds in Missouri. University of Missouri, Columbia. *Agric. Exp. Station Bull.* 1056:1–155.

Kaiser, P. K. 1979. Upland sandpiper nesting in southeastern South Dakota. *Proc. S.D. Acad. Sci.* 58:59–68.

Kantrud, H. A. 1981. Grazing intensity effects on the breeding avifauna of North Dakota grasslands. *Can. Field.–Nat.* 95:404–17.

————. 1982. Maps of distribution and abundance of selected species of birds on uncultivated native upland grasslands and shrubsteppe in the northern Great Plains. U.S. Fish and Wildlife Serv., FWS/OBS-82/31. Washington, DC. 31 pp. (Includes long-billed curlew, upland sandpiper, horned lark, Sprague's pipit, bobolink, western meadowlark, lark bunting, Savannah, grasshopper, Baird's, vesper, clay-colored, and Brewer's sparrows, and McCown's and chestnut-collared longspurs.)

Kantrud, H. A., and K. F. Higgins. 1992. Nest and nest-site characteristics of some ground-nesting, non-passerine birds of northern grasslands. *Prairie Nat.* 24:69–84. (Includes northern harrier, sharp-tailed grouse, upland sandpiper, marbled godwit, Wilson's phalarope, and short-eared owl.)

Kantrud, H. A., and R. L. Kologiski. 1982. Effects of soil and grazing on breeding birds of uncultivated upland grasslands of the northern Great Plains. USDI, Fish and Wildl. Serv. Res. Rept. no. 15.

———. 1983. Avian associations of the northern Great Plains grasslands. *J. Biogeography* 10:331–50.

Kendeigh, S. C. 1974. *Ecology, with special reference to animals and man.* Englewood Cliffs, NJ: Prentice Hall.

Kermott, L. H. III. 1982. Breeding behavior in the sharp-tailed grouse. Ph.D. diss., University of Minnesota, Minneapolis. 140 pp. See *Diss. Abstr. Int. B. Sci. Eng.* 43(8):2436 (1983).

Kermott, L. H. III, and L. W. Oring. 1975. Acoustical communication of male sharp-tailed grouse (*Pedioecetes phasianellus*) on a North Dakota dancing ground. *Animal Behaviour* 23:375–86.

Kershner, E. L., and Bollinger, E. K. 1996. Reproductive success of grassland birds at east-central Illinois airports. *Am. Midl. Nat.* 136:358–66. (Includes eastern meadowlark, horned lark, Savannah sparrow, and grasshopper sparrow.)

King, R. 1978. Population status, breeding ecology and habitat requirements of the long-billed curlew. Master's thesis, Colorado State University, Fort Collins.

Kingery, H. E., ed. 1998. *Colorado breeding bird atlas.* Denver: Colorado Bird Atlas Partnership and Colorado Division of Wildlife. 636 pp.

Kinstler, K. A., and T. A. Sordahl. 1994. A comparison of perch use by vocalizing eastern and western meadowlarks. *Prairie Nat.* 26:195–200.

Kirsch, L. M., H. F. Duebbert, and A. D. Kruse. 1978. Grazing and haying effects on habitats of upland nesting birds. *Trans. N. A. Wildl. Nat. Res. Conf.* 43:486–97.

Kirsch, L. M., and K. F. Higgins. 1976. Upland sandpiper nesting and management in North Dakota. *Wildl. Society Bull.* 4:16–20.

———. 1972. Prairie fires and wildlife. *Proc. Tall Timbers Fire Ecol. Conf.* 12:289–303.

Knapp, A. K., J. M. Briggs, D. C. Hartnett, and S. L. Collins, eds. 1998. *Grassland dynamics: Long-term ecological research in tallgrass prairies.* New York: Oxford University Press.

Knapton, R. W. 1978. Behavioural ecology of the clay-colored sparrow (*Spizella pallida*). Ph.D. diss., University of Manitoba, Winnipeg, MB. See *Diss. Abstr. Int. B. Sci. Eng.* 39(5):2173 (1978).

———. 1979a. Breeding ecology of the clay-colored sparrow. *Living Bird* 17:137–58.

———. 1979b. Optimal size of territory in the clay-colored sparrow (*Spizella pallida*). *Can. J. Zool.* 57:1358–70.

———. 1980. Nestling foods and foraging patterns in the clay colored sparrow. *Wilson Bull.* 92:458–65.

———. 1987. Intraspecific avoidance and interspecific overlap of song series in the eastern meadowlark. *Auk* 104:775–79.

———. 1988. Nesting success is higher for polygynously mated females than for monogamously mated females in the eastern meadowlark. *Auk* 105:325–29.

———. 1994. Clay-colored sparrow (*Spizella pallida*). In *The Birds of North America*, ed. A. Poole and F. Gill, no. 120. Philadelphia: Birds of North America.

Knick, S. T., and J. T. Rotenberry. 1995. Landscape characteristics of fragmented shrub-steppe habitats and breeding passerine birds. *Conserv. Biol.* 9:1059–71. (Includes western meadowlark, horned lark, and Brewer's sparrow.)

Knight, D. 1994. *Mountains and plains: The ecology of Wyoming landscapes.* New Haven: Yale University Press. 336 pp.

Knopf, F. L. 1986. Changing landscapes and the cosmopolitanism of the eastern Colorado avifauna. *Wildl. Soc. Bull.* 14:132–42.

———. 1994. Avian assemblages on altered grasslands. *Stud. Avian Biol.* 15:247–57.

———. 1996a. Mountain plover (*Charadrius montanus*). In *The Birds of North America,* ed. A. Poole and F. Gill, no. 211. Philadelphia: Birds of North America.

———. 1996b. Prairie legacies—birds. In *Prairie conservation: Conserving North America's most endangered ecosystem,* ed. F. B. Samson and F. L. Knopf, 13–48. Covelo, CA: Island Press.

———. 1998. Foods of mountain plovers wintering in California. *Condor* 100:382–84.

Knopf, F. L., and J. R. Rupert. 1996. Reproduction and movements of mountain plovers breeding in Colorado. *Wilson Bull.* 108:28–35.

Knopf, F. L., and F. B. Samson, eds. 1997. *Ecology and conservation of Great Plains vertebrates.* New York: Springer. 320 pp.

Knopf, F. L., J. A. Sedgwick, and D. B. Inkley. 1990. Regional correspondence among subshrub bird habitats. *Condor* 92:45–53. (Discusses Brewer's sparrow and green-tailed towhee.)

Knue, J. 1997. Nebraskaland magazine wildlife viewing guide. *Nebraskaland Magazine* (special issue) 75(1):1–96.

Kopachena, J. G., and R. M. Evans. 1990. Flock recruitment in Franklin's gulls. *Colon. Waterbirds* 13:92–95.

Krause, H. 1968. *The McCown's longspur: A life history.* Manila, Philippines: MDB Publishing House.

Krueger, H. O. 1981. Breeding adaptations of the vesper sparrow (*Pooecetes gramineus*) in a fire-altered ecosystem. Master's thesis, Central Michigan University, Mt. Pleasant. 71 pp.

Küchler, A. W. 1966. *Potential natural vegetation of the coterminous United States.* Am. Geog. Soc. Spec. Publ. 36, New York.

Kurten, B., and D. C. Anderson. 1983. *Pleistocene mammals of North America.* New York: Columbia University Press.

Lanyon, W. E. 1956. Ecological aspects of the sympatric distribution of meadowlarks in the north-central states. *Ecol.* 37:98–108.

———. 1957. The comparative biology of the meadowlarks (*Sturnella*) in Wisconsin. Pub. no. 1. Cambridge, MA: Nuttall Ornithol. Club.

———. 1994. Western meadowlark (*Sturnella neglecta*). In *The Birds of North America,* ed. A. Poole and F. Gill, no. 104. Philadelphia: Birds of North America.

———. 1995. Eastern meadowlark (*Sturnella magna*). In *The Birds of North America,* ed. A. Poole and F. Gill, no. 160. Philadelphia: Birds of North America.

Lauber, R. 1991. Birds and the Conservation Reserve Program: A retrospective study. Master's thesis, University of Maine, Orono. 252 pp.

Laughlin, S. B., and D. P. Kibbe, eds. 1985. *The atlas of breeding birds of Vermont.* Hanover, VT: University Press of New England.

Least Heat-Moon, W. 1991. *PrairyErth.* Boston: Houghton Mifflin.

Lehman, R. N., L. B. Carpenter, K. Steenhof, and M. N. Kochert. 1998. Assessing relative abundance and reproductive success of shrubsteppe raptors. *J. Field Ornithol.* 69:244–56.

Leopold, A. 1949. *A Sand County almanac.* New York: Oxford University Press.

Leopold, E. B, and M. F. Denton. 1987. Comparative age of grassland and steppe east and west of the northern Rockies. *Annals Missouri Bot. Gard.* 74:841–67.

Lindmeier, J. P. 1960. Plover, rail and godwit nesting on a study area in Mahnomen County, Minnesota. *Flicker* 32:5–9.

Lingle, G. R. 1994. *Birding Crane River: Nebraska's Platte.* Grand Island, NE: Harrier Publishing.

Locke, B. A. 1992. Lek hypotheses and the location, dispersion and size of lesser prairie chicken leks. Ph.D. diss., New Mexico State University, Las Cruces. 69 pp. See *Diss. Abstr. Int. B. Sci. Eng.* 53:2647 (1992).

Lokemoen, J. T., and H. F. Duebbert. 1976. Ferruginous hawk nesting ecology and raptor populations in northern South Dakota. *Condor* 78: 464–70.

Long, C. A., C. F. Long, J. Knops, and D. H Matulionis. 1965. Reproduction in the dickcissel. *Wilson Bull.* 77:251–56.

Lorenzana, J. C., and S. G. Sealy. 1999. A meta-analysis of the impact of parasitism by the brown-headed cowbird on its hosts. *Studies in Avian Biol.* 18:241–53.

Lowther, P. E. 1977. Old cowbird breeding records from the Great Plains region. *Bird-Banding* 48:358–69.

———. 1979. Nest-selection by brown-headed cowbirds. *Wilson Bull.* 91:118–22.

———. 1993. Brown-headed cowbird (*Molothrus ater*). In *The Birds of North America,* ed. A. Poole and F. Gill, no. 47. Philadelphia: Birds of North America.

Lynch, W. 1984. *Married to the wind: A study of the prairie grasslands.* N. Vancouver, BC: Whitecap Books.

Macwhirter, R. B., and K. L. Bildstein. 1996. Northern harrier (*Circus cyaneus*). In *The Birds of North America,* ed. A. Poole and F. Gill, no. 210. Philadelphia: Birds of North America.

Madden, E. M. 1996. Passerine communities and bird-habitat relationships on prescribed-burned, mixed-grass prairies in North Dakota. Master's thesis, Montana State University, Bozeman.

Madson, J. 1993. *Tallgrass prairie.* Helena, MT: Falcon Press. 112 pp.

———. 1995. *Where the sky began: Land of the tallgrass prairie.* Ames: Iowa State University Press. 323 pp.

Maher, J. L. III. 1982. Nest site habitat and productivity of the prairie falcon (*Falco mexicanus*) in Harding County, South Dakota. Master's thesis, University of South Dakota, Vermillion. 68 pp.

Maher, W. J. 1979. Nestling diets of prairie passerine birds at Matador, Saskatchewan, Canada. *Ibis* 121:437–52.

Mahon, C. L. 1995. Habitat selection and detectability of Baird's sparrows in southwestern Alberta. Master's thesis, University of Alberta, Edmonton, AB.

Malin, J. C. 1969. *The grassland of North America: Prolegomena to its history, with addenda and postscript.* Gloucester, MA: Peter Smith.

Manning, R. 1998. *Grasslands: The biology, politics and promise of the American prairie.* New York: Penguin Books, USA.

Martin, S. G. 1967. Breeding biology of the bobolink. Master's thesis, University of Wisconsin-Madison.

———. 1971. Polygyny in the bobolink: Habitat quality and the adaptive complex. Ph.D. diss., Oregon State University, Corvallis.

Martin, S. G., and T. A. Gavin. 1995. Bobolink (*Dolichonyx oryzivorus*). In *The Birds of North America,* ed. A. Poole and F. Gill, no. 176. Philadelphia: Birds of North America.

Martin, S. G., and R. J. Robertson, 1992. Honest advertisement in flight displays of bobolinks (*Dolichonyx oryzivorus*). *Auk* 109:869–73.

Martin, T. E., and D. M. Finch, eds. 1995. *Ecology and management of Neotropical migratory birds: A synthesis and review of critical issues.* New York: Oxford University Press. 489 pp.

Marzluff, J. M., B. A. Kimsey, L. S. Schueck, M. E. McFadzen, M. S. Vekasy, and J. C. Bednarz. 1997. The influence of habitat, prey abundance, sex, and breeding success on the ranging behavior of prairie falcons *Condor* 99:567–84.

Matthiessen, P. 1973. *The wind birds.* New York: Viking Press. 159 pp.

Maurer, B. A., E. A. Webb, and R. K. Bauers. 1989. Nest-site characteristics and nestling development of Cassin's and Botteri's sparrows in southeastern Arizona. *Condor* 91:736–38.

McCaffery, B. J., T. A. Sordahl, and P. Zahler. 1994. Behavioral ecology of the mountain plover in northeastern Colorado. *Wader Study Group Bull.* 40:18–21.

McCallum, D. A., W. Graul, and D. R. Zaccagnini. 1977. The breeding status of the long-billed curlew in northeastern Colorado. *Auk* 94:599–601.

McClaren, M. P., and T. R. Van Devender, eds. 1995. *The desert grassland.* Tucson: University of Arizona Press. 346 pp.

McConnell, S. D., R. van den Driessche, T. D. Hooper, G. L. Roberts, and A. Roberts. 1993. First occurrence and breeding of Sprague's pipit, *Anthus spragueii,* for British Columbia. *Can. Field-Nat.* 107:222–23.

McGregor, R. L., and T. M. Barkley, eds. 1986. *Flora of the Great Plains.* Great Plains Flora Association. Lawrence: University Press of Kansas.

McNair, D. B. 1985. A comparison of oology and nest record data in evaluating the reproductive biology of lark sparrows, *Chondestes grammacus. Southwestern Nat.* 30:213–24.

McNicholl, M. K. 1988. Ecological and human influences on Canadian populations of grassland birds. In *Ecology and conservation of grassland birds,* ed. P. D. Goriup, 1–25. ICBP Tech. Publ. no. 7. Cambridge, UK.

Meanley, B. 1963. Nesting ecology and habits of the dickcissel on the Arkansas Grand Prairie. *Wilson Bull.* 75:280.

Means, B., and R. Means. 1992. *Audubon to Xantus.* London: Academic Press and Harcourt Brace.

Mengel, R. M. 1970. The North American central plains as an isolating agent in bird speciation. In *Pleistocene and recent environments of the Central Great Plains,* ed. W. Dort and J. K. Jones, 280–340. Lawrence: University Press of Kansas.

Messmer, T. A. 1990. Influence of grazing treatments on nongame birds and vegetation structure in south-central North Dakota. Ph.D. diss., North Dakota State University, Fargo. 164 pp. See *Diss. Abstr. Int. B. Sci. Eng.* 51(10):4670 (1991).

Mickey, F. W. 1945. Breeding habits of McCown's longspurs. *Auk* 60:181–209.

Mitchell, G. J., and P. W. Riegert. 1994. Sharp-tailed grouse *Tympanuchus phasianellus* and grasshoppers: Food is where you find it. *Can. Field-Nat.* 108:288–91.

Moriarty, L. J. 1965. A study of the breeding biology of the chestnut-collared longspur (*Calcarius ornatus*) in northeastern South Dakota. *S. Dakota Bird Notes* 17:76–79.

Morrison, M. L., L. S. Hall, S. K. Robinson, S. I. Rothstein, D. C. Hahn, and T. D. Rich, eds. 1999. Research and management of the brown-headed cowbird in western landscapes: Symposium proceedings. *Studies in Avian Biology* 18:1–312.

Moynihan, M. 1958. Notes on the behavior of some North American gulls. II. Non-aerial hostile behavior of adults. III. Pairing behavior. *Behaviour* 12:95–182; 13:112–30.

Munson, E. S. 1992. Influence of nest cover on habitat selection in clay-colored sparrows. *Wilson Bull.* 104:525–29.

Murphy, R. K. 1993. History, nesting biology, and predation ecology of raptors in the Missouri Coteau of northwestern South Dakota. Ph.D. diss., Montana State University, Bozeman. 212 pp. See *Diss. Abstr. Int. B. Sci. Eng.* 54(9):4464 (1994).

Murray, B. G. Jr. 1983. Notes on the breeding biology of Wilson's phalarope. *Wilson Bull.* 95:472–75.

Mutel, C. F. 1989. *Fragile giants: A natural history of the Loess Hills.* Iowa City: University of Iowa Press. 284 pp.

Nagel, H. G., ed. *The Loess Hills prairies of central Nebraska. (Platte Valley Review),* Kearney: University of Nebraska-Kearney.

The Nature Conservancy. 1974. *Nature Conservancy preserve directory.* Arlington, VA: TNC. For more recent summaries of TNC preserves, see their Great Plains website: <http://www.greatplains.org/resource/biodiver/biosig/map.htm>.

Nelson, P. W. 1985. *The terrestrial natural communities of Missouri.* Jefferson City: Missouri Dept. Nat. Res.

Newman, G. A. 1970. Cowbird parasitism and nesting success of lark sparrows in southern Oklahoma. *Wilson Bull.* 82:304–9.

Nicholson, C. P. 1997. *Atlas of the breeding birds of Tennessee.* Knoxville: University of Tennessee Press.

Nicholson, R. A., and G. K. Hulett. 1969. Remnant grassland vegetation in the Great Plains of North America. *J. Ecol.* 77:599–612. (Botanical analysis of central Great Plains communities.)

Nordin, K. E., B. McGillivray, and G. C. Biermann. 1988. Courtship feeding in Brewer's sparrows (*Spizella breweri*). *J. Field Ornithol.* 59:33–36.

Noss, R. F., E. T. Laroe III, and J. M. Scott. 1995. Endangered ecosystems of the United States: A preliminary assessment of loss and degradation. *Natl. Biol. Serv. Biol. Rep.* 28:1–58.

Nowicki, T. 1973. A behavioral study of the marbled godwit in North Dakota. Master's thesis, Central Michigan University, Mount Pleasant. 109 pp.

Ohio Dept. of Natural Resources. 1978. *Directory of state nature reserves.* Columbus: Ohio Dept. of Natural Resources.

Olendorff, R. R. 1972. The large birds of prey of the Pawnee National Grasslands: Nesting habits and productivity, 1969–1971. Int. Biol. Programme, Grassland Biome Tech. Rept. no. 151. Ft. Collins, CO. 59 pp.

———. 1993. Status, biology and management of ferruginous hawks: A review. *Spec. Rept. U.S. Bur. Land Manage.,* Raptor Res. and Tech. Asst. Cntr., Boise, ID.

Olson-Edge, S. L., and W. D. Edge. 1987. Density and distribution of the mountain plover on the Charles M. Russell National Wildlife Refuge. Prairie Nat. 19:233–38.

Omerik, J. M. 1987. Ecoregions of the coterminous United States. *Annals of the Assoc. of Amer. Geographers* 77:118–25.

Ortega, C. 1998. *Cowbirds and Other Brood Parasites.* Tucson: Arizona University Press.

Overmire, T. G. 1963. The effects of grazing upon habitat utilization of the dickcissel (*Spiza americana*) and Bell's vireo (*Vireo bellii*) in north central Oklahoma. Ph.D. diss., Oklahoma State University, Stillwater. 57 pp.

Owens, R. A., and M. T. Myers. 1973. Effects of agriculture upon populations of native passerine birds of an Alberta fescue grassland. *Can. J. Zool.* 51:697–713.

Palmer-Ball, B. Jr. 1996. *The Kentucky breeding bird atlas.* Lexington: University Press of Kentucky. 372 pp.

Pampush, G. J. 1980. Breeding chronology, habitat utilization and nest site selection of the long-billed curlew in north central Oregon. Master's thesis, Oregon State University, Corvallis. 49 pp.

Pampush, G. J., and R. G. Anthony. 1993. Nest success, habitat utilization, and nest site selection of long-billed curlews in the Columbia Basin, Oregon. *Condor* 95:957–67.

Parrish, T. L., S. H. Anderson, and W. F. Oelklaus. 1993. Mountain plover habitat selection in the Powder River Basin, Wyoming. *Prairie Nat.* 25:219–26.

Patterson, M. A., and L. B. Best. 1996. Bird abundance and nesting success in Iowa CRP fields: The importance of vegetation structure and composition. *Am. Midl. Nat.* 135:153–67. (Includes horned lark, dickcissel, and Savannah, grasshopper, and vesper sparrows.)

Peattie, D. C. 1938. *The prairie grove.* New York: Literary Guild of America.

Peck, G. K., and R. D. James. 1983 and 1987. *Breeding birds of Ontario: Nidology and distribution.* 2 vols. Toronto: Royal Ontario Mus.

Peritt, J. E., and L. B. Best. 1989. Effects of weather on the breeding ecology of vesper sparrows in Iowa crop fields. *Am. Midl. Nat.* 121:355–60.

Pernanen, S. K. 1994. Behavioral and ecological interactions of Brewer's (*Spizella breweri*) and clay-colored (*S. pallida*) sparrows. Master's thesis, University of Toronto, Toronto, ON.

Peterjohn, B., and J. R. Sauer. 1993. North American breeding bird survey annual summary. *Bird Populations* 1:52–67.

———. 1999. Population status of North American grassland birds from the North American breeding bird survey, 1966–1996. In *Ecology and Conservation of Grassland Birds of the Western Hemisphere,* ed. P. D. Vickery and J. R. Herkert, 27–44. Cooper Ornithological Society, Studies in Avian Biology no. 19. 299 pp.

Petersen, K. L. 1986. Avian ecological studies in a sagebrush community: Bird responses to fire and territory dynamics in a sparrow population. Ph.D. diss., Iowa State University, Ames. 100 pp. See *Diss. Abstr. Int. B. Sci. Eng.* 47(11):4399–4400 (1987). (Includes horned lark, Brewer's sparrow, and vesper sparrow.)

Petersen, K. L., and L. B. Best. 1985. Brewer's sparrow nest-site characteristics in a sagebrush community. *J. Field Ornithol.* 56:23–27.

———. 1986. Diets of nestling sage sparrows and Brewer's sparrows in an Idaho sagebrush community. *J. Field Ornithol.* 57:283–94.

Petersen, R. A. 1995. *The South Dakota breeding bird atlas.* S. Dak. Ornithologists' Union, Aberdeen.

Peterson, M. J., and N. J. Silvy. 1996. Reproductive stages limiting productivity of the endangered Attwater's prairie chicken. *Conserv. Biol.* 10:1264–76.

Pezzolesi, L. S. 1994. The western burrowing owl: Increasing prairie dog abundance, foraging theory, and nest site fidelity. Master's thesis, Texas Tech. University, Lubbock.

Picozzi, N. 1984. Breeding biology of polygynous hen harriers *Circus c. cyaneus* in Orkney. *Ornis Scand.* 15:1–10.

Pilz, W. R. 1983. Nesting ecology and diet of Swainson's hawk in the Chihuahuan Desert, south-central New Mexico. Master's thesis, New Mexico State University, Las Cruces. 30 pp.

Platt, S. W. 1981. Prairie falcon: Aspects of population dynamics, individual vocal identification, markings and sexual maturity. Ph.D. diss., Brigham Young University, Provo, UT. 91 pp. See *Diss. Abstr. Int. B. Sci. Eng.* 42(2):528 (1981).

Pleszcynska, W. K., and R. I. C. Hansell. 1980. Polygyny and decision theory: Testing of a model in lark buntings (*Calamospiza melanocorys*). *Am. Nat.* 116:821–30.

Plumbe, J. Jr. 1839 (reprinted 1925). Sketches of Iowa and Wisconsin. *Annals of Iowa* 14:483–531, 595–619.

Plumpton, D. L., and R. S. Lutz. 1994. Sexual size dimorphism, mate choice and productivity of burrowing owls. *Auk* 111:724–27.

Poole, A., and F. Gill, eds. 1990 et seq. *The Birds of North America.* Philadelphia: Birds of North America.

Porton, I. J. 1977. Some aspects of the breeding behavior of Swainson's hawks. Master's thesis, University of Arizona, Tucson. 127 pp.

Poston, B., D. M. Ealey, P. S. Taylor, and G. B. McKeating. 1990. *Priority migratory bird habitats of Canada's prairie provinces.* Edmonton, AB: Canadian Wildlife Service.

Potter, P. E. 1972. Territorial behavior of Savannah sparrows in southeastern Michigan. *Wilson Bull.* 84:48–59.

Powell, A. N., and C. L. Collier. 1998. Reproductive success of Belding's Savannah sparrows in a highly fragmented landscape. *Auk* 115:508–13.

Price, J. 1995. Potential impacts of global climate change on the summer distributions of some North American grassland birds. Ph.D. diss., Wayne State University, Detroit.

Price, J., S. Droege, and A. Price. 1995. *The summer atlas of North American birds.* London and New York: Academic Press. 364 pp.

Pylypec, B. 1991. Impacts of fires on bird populations in a fescue pasture. *Can. Field-Nat.* 105:346–49.

Pyne, S. 1982. *Fire in America: A cultural history of wildland and rural fire.* Princeton: Princeton University Press. 654 pp.

Quayle, W. A. 1905. *The prairie and the sea.* Cincinnati: Jennings and Graham.

Ramakka, J. M., and R. T. Woyewodzic. 1993. Nesting ecology of ferruginous hawk in northwestern New Mexico. *J. Raptor Res.* 27:97–101.

Redmond, R. L. 1984. The behavioral ecology of long-billed curlews (*Numenius americanus*) breeding in western Idaho. Ph.D. diss., University of Montana, Bozeman. 154 pp. See *Diss. Abstr. Int. B. Sci. Eng.* 45(3):796 (1984).

———. 1986. Egg size and laying dates of long-billed curlews *Numenius americanus:* Implications for female reproductive tactics. *Oikos* 46:330–38.

Redmond, R. L., and D. A. Jenni. 1986. Population ecology of the long-billed curlew (*Numenius americanus*) in western Idaho. *Auk* 103:755–67.

Reed, J. M. 1986. Vegetation structure and vesper sparrow territory location. *Wilson Bull.* 98:144–47.

Reichman, O. J. 1987. *Konza Prairie: A tallgrass natural history.* Lawrence: University Press of Kansas. 226 pp.

Reinking, D. L., D. A. Wiedenfeld, D. H. Wolfe, and R. W. Rohrbaugh. In press. Status, habitat selection, and nesting ecology of Henslow's sparrows in Oklahoma. *Wilson Bull.*

Renken, R. B., and J. J. Dinsmore. 1987. Nongame bird communities on managed grasslands in North Dakota. *Can. Field-Nat.* 101:551–57.

Renward, J. D. 1977. Effect of fire on lark sparrow nesting densities. *J. Range Manage.* 340:283–85.

Reynolds, T. D., and C. H. Trost. 1981. Grazing, crested wheatgrass and bird populations in southeastern Idaho. *Northwest Sci.* 55:225–34.

Rice, W. R. 1982. Acoustical location of prey by the marsh hawk: Adaptation to concealed prey. *Auk* 99:403–13.

Rich, R. 1980. Nest placement in sage thrasher, sage sparrow and Brewer's sparrow in southeastern Idaho. *Wilson Bull.* 92:362–68.

———. 1986. Habitat and nest-site selection by burrowing owls in the sagebrush steppe of Idaho. *J. Wildl. Management* 50: 548–55.

Rich, T. D. 1978. Cowbird parasitism of sage and Brewer's sparrows. *Condor* 80:348.

Rich, T. D., and S. I. Rothstein. 1985. Sage thrashers reject cowbird eggs. *Condor* 87:561–62.

Ricklefs, R. E. 1969. An analysis of nesting mortality in birds. *Smithson. Contrib. Zool.* 9:1–48.

Ridgway, R. 1901–1907. *The birds of North and Middle America: A descriptive catalogue.* Part I (1901), Part II (1902), Part III (1904), Part IV (1907). Washington, DC: U.S. Natl. Museum Bulletin (50).

Riley, T. Z., C. A. Davis, M. A. Candelaria, and H. R. Suminski. 1994. Lesser prairie-chicken movements and home ranges in New Mexico. *Prairie Nat.* 26:183–86.

Rising, J. D. 1996. *A guide to the identification and natural history of the sparrows of the United States and Canada.* San Diego, CA: Academic Press.

Risser, P. G., E. C. Birney, H. D. Bloeker, S. W. May, W. J. Parton, and J. A. Wiens. 1981. *The true prairie ecosystem.* US/IBP Synthesis ser. 16. Stroudsburg, PA: Hutchinson Ross Publishing Company. 557 pp.

Roberts, T. S. 1932. *The birds of Minnesota.* 2 vols. Minneapolis: University of Minnesota Press.

Robbins, C. S., ed. 1996. *Atlas of the breeding birds of Maryland and the District of Columbia.* Pittsburgh: University of Pittsburgh Press.

Robbins, C. S., B. Bruun, and H. S. Zim. 1983. *Birds of North America: A guide to field identification.* New York: Golden Press.

Robbins, C. S., D. Bystrak, and P. H. Geissler. 1986. *The breeding bird survey: Its first fifteen years, 1965–1979.* U.S. Fish and Wildlife Service, Resource Pub. 157, Washington, DC.

Robbins, M. B., 1998. The display behavior of male Sprague's pipits. *Wilson Bull.* 110:435.

———. 1999. Sprague's pipit (*Anthus spragueii*). In *The Birds of North America,* ed. A. Poole and F. Gill, no. 439. Philadelphia: Birds of North America.

Robbins, M. B., and D. A. Easterla. 1992. *Birds of Missouri, their distribution and abundance.* Columbia: University of Missouri Press.

Robins, J. D. 1971a. A study of Henslow's sparrow in Michigan. *Wilson Bull.* 83:39–48.

———. 1971b. Differential niche utilization in a grassland sparrow. *Ecol.* 52:1065–70. (Ecology of Henslow's sparrow.)

Rodenhouse, N. L., and L. B. Best. 1983. Breeding ecology of vesper sparrows in corn and soybean fields. *Amer. Midl. Nat.* 110:265–75.

Rodenhouse, N. L., L. B. Best, R. J. O'Conner, and E. K. Bollinger. 1993. Effects of temperate agriculture on Neotropical migrant landbirds. In *Status and management of Neotropical migratory birds,* ed. D. M. Finch and P. W. Stangel, 280–95. USDA Forest Service, Rocky Mtn. Forest and Range. Exp. Station, Gen. Tech. Rept. RM-229. Fort Collins, CO. 422 pp.

Rogers, E. I. 1998. Foraging patch selection by shrubsteppe sparrows. *Ecol.* 79:1160–73. (Includes Brewer's and sage sparrows.)

Rohrbaugh, R. W., D. L. Reinking, D. H. Wolfe, S. K. Sherrod, and M. A. Jenkins. 1999. Effects of prescribed burning and grazing on the nesting and reproductive success of three grassland passerine species in tallgrass prairie. In *Ecology and conservation of grassland birds of the Western Hemisphere,* ed. P. D. Vickery and J. R. Herkert, 165–70. Cooper Ornithological Society, Studies in Avian Biology no. 19. 299 pp.

Roosa, D. 1984. Iowa's prairie preserves. *Iowa Conservationist* 43(9):22–26.

Root, T. 1988. *Atlas of wintering North America birds: An analysis of Christmas bird count data.* Chicago: University of Chicago Press.

Rotenberry, J. T., and W. D. Klimstra. 1970. The nesting ecology and reproductive performance of the eastern meadowlark. *Wilson Bull.* 82:243–67.

Rotenberry, J. T., and J. A. Weins. 1989. Reproductive biology and shrubsteppe passerine birds: Geographical and temporal variation in clutch size, brood size and fledging success. *Condor* 91:1–14. (Includes Brewer's sparrow.)

———. 1998. Foraging patch selection by shrubsteppe sparrows. *Ecology* 79:1160–73. (Compares Brewer's and sage sparrows.)

Rotenberry, J. T., M. A. Patten, and K. L. Preston. 1999. Brewer's sparrow (*Spizella breweri*). In *The Birds of North America,* ed. A. Poole and F. Gill, no. 390. Philadelphia: Birds of North America.

Roth, S. D., and J. M. Marzluff. 1989. Nest placement and productivity of ferruginous hawks in western Kansas. *Trans. Kans. Acad. Sci.* 92:132–48.

Rothfels, M., and M. R. Lein. 1983. Territoriality in sympatric populations of red-tailed and Swainson's hawks. *Can. J. Zool.* 61:60–64.

Rothstein, S. I. 1976. Cowbird parasitism of the cedar waxwing and its evolutionary implications. *Auk* 93:498–509.

Rothwell, R. 1993. Antelope, sage grouse and Neotropical migrants. In *Status and management of Neotropical migratory birds,* ed. D. M. Finch and P. W. Stangel, 396–401. USDA Forest Service, Rocky Mtn. Forest and Range. Exp. Station, Gen. Tech. Rept. RM-229. Fort Collins, CO. 422 pp.

Rowher, S. A. 1972. Distribution of meadowlarks in the central and southern Great Plains and in the desert grasslands of eastern New Mexico and west Texas. *Trans. Kansas Acad. Sci.* 75:1–19.

Runde, D. E. 1987. Population dynamics, habitat use and movement patterns of the prairie falcon (*Falco mexicanus*). Ph.D. diss., University Wyoming, Laramie. 181 pp. See *Diss. Abstr. Int. B. Sci. Eng.* 48(6):1588 (1987).

Ryan, M. L., L. W. Burger Jr., and D. P. Jones. 1998. Breeding ecology of greater prairie-chickens (*Tympanuchus cupido*) in relation to prairie landscape configuration. *Am. Midl. Nat.* 140:111–21.

Ryan, M. R. 1982. Marbled godwit habitat selection in the northern plains. Ph.D. diss., Iowa State University, Ames. See *Diss. Abstr. Int. B. Sci. Eng.* 43(11):3426 (1983).

Ryan, M. R., R. B. Renken, and J. J. Dinsmore. 1984. Marbled godwit habitat selection in the northern prairie region. *J. Wildl. Mgmt.* 48:1206–18.

Ryder, R. A. 1980. Effects of grazing on bird habitats. In *Workshop proceedings: Management of western forests and grasslands for nongame birds,* ed. R. M. DeGraff and N. G. Tilghman, 51–56. USDA, Forest Service, General Tech. Report INT-86. Ogden, UT.

Salt, W. R. 1966. A nesting study of *Spizella pallida*. *Auk* 83:274–81.

Salt, W. R., and J. R. Salt. 1976. *The birds of Alberta*. Edmonton, AB: Hurtig Publishers.

Sample, D. W. 1989. Grassland birds in southern Wisconsin: Habitat preferences, population trends, and response to land-use changes. Master's thesis, University of Wisconsin, Madison. 588 pp. (See Sample and Mossman 1997.)

Sample, D. W., and M. J. Mossman. 1997. *Managing habitat for grassland birds: A guide for Wisconsin*. Madison: Wisconsin Dept. of Natural Resources. (Includes upland sandpiper, horned lark, western and eastern meadowlarks, bobolink, dickcissel, vesper sparrow, and grasshopper sparrow.)

Samson, F., and F. Knopf. 1994. Prairie conservation in North America. *BioScience* 44:418–21.

———, eds. 1996. *Prairie conservation: Conserving North America's most endangered ecosystem*. Covelo, CA: Island Press.

Sauer, J. R., J. E. Hines, G. Gough, I. Thomas, and B. G. Peterson. 1997. The North American breeding bird survey results and analysis. Version 96.4. Patuxent Wildlife Research Center, Laurel, MD. URL =http//www.mbr.nbs.gov/bbs/bbs.html.

Schartz, R. L., and J. L. Zimmerman. 1971. The time and energy budget of the male dickcissel (*Spiza americana*). *Condor* 73:65–76.

Schmutz, J. K. 1984. Ferruginous and Swainson's hawk abundance and distribution in relation to land use in southeastern Alberta. *J. Wildl. Manage.* 48: 1180–87.

Schmutz, J. K., G. Wood, and D. Wood. 1991. Spring and summer prey of burrowing owls in Alberta. *Blue Jay* 49:93–97.

Schmutz, J. K., S. Schmutz, and D. Boag. 1980. Coexistence of three species of hawks in the prairie-parkland ecotone. *Can J. Zool.* 58:1075–89. (Discusses red-tailed, ferruginous, and Swainson's hawks.)

Schnase, J. L. 1984. The breeding biology of Cassin's sparrow (*Aimophila cassinii*) in Tom Green County, Texas. Master's thesis, Angelo State University, San Angelo, TX. 108 pp.

Schroeder, M. A., and C. E. Braun. 1992. Seasonal movement and habitat use by greater prairie-chickens in northeastern Colorado. *Colorado Div. of Wildl. Special Report* no. 68:1–52 .

Schroeder, M. A., and L. A. Robb. 1993. Greater prairie-chicken (*Tympanuchus cupido*). In *The Birds of North America*, ed. A. Poole and F. Gill, no. 36. Philadelphia: Birds of North America.

Schroeder, M. A., and D. L. Sturgess. 1975. The effect on the Brewer's sparrow of spraying big sagebrush. *J. Range Manage.* 28:294–97.

Scott, G. J. 1995. *Canada's vegetation: A world perspective*. Montreal and Kingston: McGill-Queen's University Press.

Sealy, S. G. 1999. Cowbird parasitism on lark bunting: Frequency, acceptance and fledging. *J. Field Ornithol.* 70:182–86.

Sears, P. B. 1969. *Lands beyond the forest.* New York: Prentice-Hall. 206 pp.

Semenchuk, C. P., ed. 1992. *The atlas of breeding birds of Alberta.* Edmonton, AB: Fed. Alberta Nat.

Shackford, J. S. 1991. Breeding ecology of the mountain plover in Oklahoma. *Bull. Okla. Ornithol. Soc.* 24:9–13.

Shackford, J. S., D. M. Leslie Jr., and W. D. Warren. 1999. Range-wide use of cultivated fields by mountain plovers during the breeding season. *J. Field Ornithol.* 70:114–20.

Shane, T. G. 1974. The nest site selection behavior of the lark bunting, *Calamospiza melanocorys.* Master's thesis, Kansas State University, Manhattan.

———. 2000. Lark bunting (*Calamospiza melanocorys*). In *The Birds of North America,* ed. A. Poole and F. Gill, no. 543. Philadelphia: Birds of North America.

Shantz, H. L., and R. Zon. 1924. Natural vegetation. In *Atlas of American agriculture,* 1–28. Washington, DC: USDA.

Short, H. L. 1984. Habitat suitability index model: Brewer's sparrow. U.S. Fish Wildl. Serv. FWS/OBS–82/10.83. Fort Collins, CO. 16 pp.

Shimek, B. 1911. The prairies. *Iowa Univ. Bull., Lab. of Nat. Hist.* 6:169–240.

Simmons, R. E. 1983. Polygyny, ecology and mate choice in the northern harrier, *Circus cyaneus* (L.). Master's thesis, Acadia University, Wolfville, NS. 177 pp.

———. 1988. Honest advertising, sexual selection, courtship displays and body condition of polygynous northern harriers. *Auk* 105:303–7.

Sims, P. L. 1988. Grasslands. In *North American terrestrial vegetation,* ed. M. G. Barbour and W. D. Billings, 265–86. Cambridge: Cambridge University Press.

Sisson, L. 1976. The sharp-tailed grouse in Nebraska. Nebraska Game and Parks Comm., Lincoln. 16 pp.

Skinner, R. M. 1974. Grassland use patterns and prairie bird populations. Master's thesis, University of Missouri–Columbia.

———. 1975. Grassland use patterns and prairie bird populations. In *Prairie: A multiple view,* ed. M. K. Wali, 171–80. Grand Forks: University of North Dakota Press.

Skinner, R. M., T. S. Baskett, and M. D. Blendon. 1984. Bird habitat on Missouri prairies. Terrestrial series no. 14:1–37, Missouri Conserv. Dept., Jefferson City.

Skipper, C. S. 1998. Henslow's sparrows return to previous nest site in western Maryland. *No. Amer. Bird Bander* 23:36–41.

Smith, A. 1996. *Big bluestem: Journey into the tall grass.* Tulsa, OK: Council Oaks Press.

Smith, A. R. 1995. *Atlas of Saskatchewan birds.* Special Publ., no. 22. Regina, SK: Sask. Nat. Hist. Soc.

Smith, C. R. 1992. Henslow's sparrow, *Ammodramus henslowi.* In *Migratory nongame birds of management concern in the Northeast,* ed. K. J. Schneider and D. M. Pence, 315–30. U.S. Fish and Wildl. Serv., Newton Corner, MA. 400 pp.

Smith, J. N. M., T. L. Cook, S. I. Rothstein, S. K. Robinson, and S. G. Sealy, eds. 2000. *Ecology and management of cowbirds and their hosts.* Austin: University of Texas Press. 496 pp.

Smith, R. L. 1963. Some ecological notes on the grasshopper sparrow. *Wilson Bull.* 75:159–65.

Snow, C. 1974. Habitat management series for unique or endangered species. Report no. 13: Ferruginous hawk *Buteo regalis.* USDI, Bur. Land Manage. Tech. Note. T-N-255. 23 pp.

Sodhi, N. S. 1992. Comparison between urban and rural prairie Saskatchewan: Urbanization and short-term population trends. *Can. Field. Nat.* 106:210–15.

Sousa, P. J., and W. N. McDonal. 1983. Habitat suitability models: Baird's sparrow. USDI, FWS/OBS 82/10.44.

South Dakota Ornithologists' Union. 1991. *The Birds of South Dakota.* 2d ed. Aberdeen, SD: Northern State University Press. 410 pp.

Southern, W. E., and L. K. Southern. 1980. A summary of the incidence of cowbird parasitism in northern Michigan from 1911–1978. *Jack-Pine Warbler* 58:77–84.

Sparling, D. W. Jr. 1979. Reproductive isolating mechanisms and communication in greater prairie chickens (*Tympanuchus cupido*) and sharp-tailed grouse (*Tympanuchus phasianellus*). Ph.D. diss., University of North Dakota, Grand Forks. 255 pp. See *Diss. Abstr. Int. B. Sci. Eng.* 40:2963 (1980).

———. 1981. Communication in prairie grouse. II. Ethological isolating mechanisms. *Behav. Neural Biol.* 32:487–503.

Squires, J. R., S. H. Anderson, and R. Oakleaf. 1993. Home range size and habitat use of nesting prairie falcons near oil developments in northeastern Wyoming. *J. Field Ornithol.* 64:1–10.

Steenhof, K. 1998. Prairie falcon (*Falco mexicanus*). In *The Birds of North America,* ed. A. Poole and F. Gill, no. 346. Philadelphia: Birds of North America.

Steenhof, K., M. N. Kochert, L. B. Carpenter, and R. N. Lehman. 1999. Long-term prairie falcon population changes in relation to prey abundance, weather, land-use and habitat conditions. *Condor* 101:28–41.

Stegner, W. 1962. *Wolf Willow: A history, a story and a memory of the last plains frontier.* New York: Viking Press. Reprinted 1990, New York: Penguin Books USA.

Steigman, K. L. 1993. Nesting ecology of the dickcissel (*Spiza americana*) in a tallgrass prairie in north central Texas. Ph.D. diss., University of North Texas, Denton. 133 pp.

Stewart, R. E. 1975. *Breeding Birds of North Dakota.* Fargo, ND: Tri-college Center for Environmental Studies.

Stillwell, J. E., and N. J. Stillwell. 1955. Notes on songs of lark buntings. *Wilson Bull.* 67:138–39.

Stone, E., J. Smith, and P. Thornton. 1994. Seasonal variation and diet selection from pellet remains of short-eared owls (*Asio flammeus*) in Wyoming. *Great Basin Nat.* 54:191–92.

Strong, M. A. 1971. Avian productivity on the shortgrass prairie of north central Colorado. Master's thesis, Colorado State University, Fort Collins.

Sugden, J. W. 1933. The range restrictions of the long-billed curlew. *Condor* 35:3–9.

Sutter, G. C. 1996. Habitat selection and prairie drought in relation to grassland bird community structure and the nesting ecology of Sprague's pipit. Ph.D. diss., University of Regina, Regina SA.

———. 1997. Nest-site selection and nest-entrance orientation in Sprague's pipit. *Wilson Bull.* 109:462–69.

Sutter, G. C., and M. Brigham. 1998. Avifaunal and habitat changes resulting from conversion of native prairie to crested wheat grass: Patterns at songbird community and species levels. *Can. J. Zool.* 76:869–75.

Sutter, G. C., D. J. Sawatzky, D. M. Cooper, and R. M. Brigham. 1996. Renesting intervals in Sprague's pipit, *Anthus spragueii. Can. Field-Nat.* 110:694–97.

Sutter, G. C., T. Troupe, and M. Forbes. 1995. Abundance of Baird's sparrow, *Ammodramus bairdii*, in native prairie and introduced vegetation. *Ecoscience* 2:344–48.

Sutton, G. M. 1927. Flocking, mating, and nest-building habits of the prairie horned lark. *Wilson Bull.* 39:131–41.

Swanson, D. A. 1996. Nesting ecology and nesting habitat requirements of Ohio's grassland-nesting birds: A review. Ohio Fish and Wildlife Rep. 13, Ohio Div. of Wildlife, Dept. of Nat. Res., Columbus. 60 pp. (Includes upland sandpiper, bobolink, eastern and western meadowlarks, dickcissel, and Savannah, grasshopper, Henslow's, vesper, and lark sparrows.)

Svedarsky, W. D. 1979. Spring and summer ecology of greater prairie chickens in northwestern Minnesota. Ph.D. diss., University of North Dakota, Grand Forks. 183 pp. See *Diss. Abstr. Int. B. Sci. Eng.* 40:2923 (1980).

Svedarsky, W. D., T. J. Wolfe, and J. E. Toepfer. 1997. The greater prairie-chicken in Minnesota. *Minn. Wildl. Rep.* no. 11:1–19.

Taylor, S. V., and V. M. Ashe. 1976. The flight display and other behavior of male lark buntings (*Calamospiza melanochorys*). *Bull. Psychonomic Soc.* 7:527–29.

Temeles, E. 1989. Effect of prey consumption on foraging activity of northern harriers. *Auk* 106:353–57.

Terborgh, J. 1989. *Where have all the birds gone?* Princeton: Princeton University Press.

Terrill, L. M. 1961. Cowbird hosts in southern Quebec. *Can. Field-Nat.* 75:2–11.

Thompson, C. D., and S. H. Anderson. 1988. Foraging behavior and food habits of burrowing owls in Wyoming. *Prairie Nat.* 20:23–28.

Thompson, F. R. III, ed. 1995. *Management of midwestern landscapes for the conservation of Neotropical migratory birds.* USDI, North Central Forest Experiment Station Bulletin. Gen. Tech. Rep. NC-187, Detroit.

Thompson, F. R., S. J. Lewis, J. Green, and D. Ewert. 1993. Status of Neotropical migrant landbirds in the midwest: Identifying species of management concern. In *Status and management of Neotropical migratory birds,* ed. D. M. Finch and P. W. Stangel, 145–55. USDA Forest Service, Rocky Mtn. Forest and Range. Exp. Station, Gen. Tech. Rept. RM-229. Fort Collins, CO. 422 pp.

Thompson, L. S., and D. Sullivan. 1979. Breeding birds of prairie grassland and shrubland habitats in northeastern Montana—1978. *Am. Birds* 33:88–89.

Thompson, M. C., and C. Ely. 1989, 1992. *Birds in Kansas.* 2 vols. Lawrence: University Press of Kansas. 404 and 424 pp.

Thompson, T. 1994. *Birding in Ohio.* Indianapolis: Indiana University Press.

Thurow, T. L., and C. M. White. 1983. Nest site relationship between the ferruginous and Swainson's hawk. *J. Field Ornithol.* 54:401–6.

Thwaites, R. G. 1904–1905. *Original journals of Lewis and Clark.* 8 vols. New York: Dodd, Mead.

Trainor, J. M., and B. S. Peltz. 1996. Song repertoire of the bobolink: A reassessment. *Ethology* 102:50–62.

Trost, C. H. 1972. Adaptations of horned larks (*Eremophila alpestris*) to hot environments. *Auk* 89:506–27.

Tsuji, L., J. S. Daniel, R. Kozlovic, M. B. Sokolowski, and R. I. C. Hansell. 1994. Relationship of body size of male sharp-tailed grouse to location of individual territories on leks. *Wilson Bull.* 106:329–37.

U.S. Dept. of Agriculture. 1948. *Grass: The yearbook of agriculture.* Washington, DC: U.S. Gov. Printing Office.

U.S. Dept. of Interior, Geological Survey. 1970. *The national atlas of the United States of America.* Washington, DC: U.S. Gov. Printing Office.

Vander Haegen, W. M., and B. Walker. 1999. Parasitism by brown-headed cowbirds in the shrubsteppe of eastern Washington. *Studies in Avian Biol.* 18:34–40.

Vankat, J. L. 1979. *The natural vegetation of North America.* New York: John Wiley and Sons.

Vickery, P. D. 1996. Grasshopper sparrow (*Ammodramus savannarum*). In *The Birds of North America,* ed. A. Poole and F. Gill, no. 239. Philadelphia: Birds of North America.

Vickery, P. D., M. L. Hunter, and S. M. Scott. 1994. Effects of habitat area on the distribution of grassland birds in Maine. *Conserv. Biol.* 8:1087–97. (Includes upland sandpiper, bobolink, eastern meadowlark, and grasshopper, Savannah, and vesper sparrows.)

Vickery, P. D., and J. R. Herkert, eds. 1999. *Ecology and conservation of grassland birds of the Western Hemisphere.* Cooper Ornithological Society, Studies in Avian Biology no. 19. 299 pp.

Vorhies, M. 1990. Nebraska wildlife: Ten million years ago. *Nebraskaland* (June 1990):8–17.

Vorhies, M. and R. D. Worthington. 1979. Fossil grass anthoecia within Miocene rhinoceros skeletons: Diet in an extinct species. *Science* 206:331–33.

Walk, J. W., and R. E. Warner. 1999. Effects of habitat area on the occurrence of grassland birds in Illinois. *Am. Midl. Nat.* 141:339–44.

Walkinshaw, L. H. 1939. Notes on the nesting of the clay-colored sparrow. *Wilson Bull.* 51:17–21.

Watson, D. 1977. *The hen harrier.* Berkhamstead, UK: T. and A. D. Poyser.

Watts, B. D. 1996. Social strategy and cover in Savannah sparrows. *Auk* 113:960–63.

Weatherhead, P. J. 1989. Sex ratios, host-specific reproductive success, and impact of brown-headed cowbirds. *Auk* 106:358–66.

Weaver, J. E. 1954. *North American prairie.* Lincoln, NE: Johnson Publishing Company.

Weaver, J. E., and F. W. Albertson. 1956. *The grasslands of the Great Plains.* Lincoln, NE: Johnson Publishing Company.

Wells, J. V., and P. D. Vickery. 1994. Extended flight-songs of vesper sparrows. *Wilson Bull.* 106:696–702.

Wells, P. V. 1970. Postglacial vegetational history of the Great Plains. *Science* 167:1574–82.

Wendt, K. M. 1984. *A guide to Minnesota prairies.* St. Paul: Minn. Dept. Nat. Res.

West, N. E. 1988. Intermountain deserts, shrubsteppes, and woodlands. In *North American terrestrial vegetation,* ed. M. G. Barbour and W. D. Billings, 209–30. Cambridge: Cambridge University Press.

Wheelwright, N. T., and J. D. Rising. 1993. Savannah sparrow (*Passerculus sandwichensis*). In *The Birds of North America,* ed. A. Poole and F. Gill, no. 45. Philadelphia: Birds of North America.

White, R. P. 1983. Distribution and habitat preferences of the upland sandpiper (*Bartramia longicauda*) in Wisconsin. *Amer. Birds* 37:16–22.

Whitmore, R. C. 1979. Temporal variation in the selected habitats of a guild of grassland sparrows. *Wilson Bull.* 91:592–98. (Discusses Savannah, grasshopper, and vesper sparrows.)

———. 1981. Structural characteristics of grasshopper sparrow habitat. *J. Wildl. Manage.* 45:811–14.

Wiens, J. A. 1963. Aspects of cowbird parasitism in southern Oklahoma. *Wilson Bull.* 75:130–39.

———. 1973. Pattern and process in grassland bird communities. *Ecol. Monogr.* 43:237–70. (Includes data on fourteen spp. of grassland endemics.)

Wiens, J. A., and M. I. Dyer. 1975. Rangeland avifaunas: Their composition, energetics and role in the ecosystem. In Proceedings of the symposium on management of forest and range habitats for nongame birds, ed. D. R. Smith, 146–82. USDA, Forest Service, Washington, DC. (Includes data on twenty-one spp. of grassland endemics.)

———. 1977. Assessing the potential impact of granivorous birds in ecosystems. In *Granivorous birds in ecosystems,* ed. J. Pinowski and S. C. Kendeigh, 206–66. Cambridge: Cambridge University Press.

Wiens, J. A., D. L. Reinking, D. H. Wolfe, S. K. Sherrod, and M. A. Jenkins. In press. Nest site microhabitat of grasshopper sparrows (*Ammodramus savannarum*) in tallgrass prairie. *Wilson Bull.*

Wiens, J. A., and J. T. Rotenberry. 1979. Diet niche relationships among North American grassland and shrubsteppe birds. *Oecologia* 42:253–92. (Includes upland sandpiper, western meadowlark, horned lark, dickcissel, grasshopper sparrow, and chestnut-collared longspur.)

———. 1980. Patterns of morphology and ecology in grassland and shrubsteppe bird populations. *Ecol. Monogr.* 50:287–308.

Wiens, J. A., B. Van Horne, and J. T. Rotenberry. 1990. Comparison of the behavior of sage and Brewer's sparrows in shrubsteppe habitats. *Condor* 92:264–66.

Wiens, J. A., J. T. Rotenberry, and B. Van Horne. 1989. Territory size variations in shrubsteppe birds. *Auk* 102:500–505. (Includes Brewer's sparrow).

Wilcove, D. S. 1999. *The condor's shadow: The loss and recovery of wildlife in America.* New York: W. H. Freeman. 339 pp.

Williams, F. C., and A. L. LeSassier. 1968. Cassin's sparrow. In Life histories of North American cardinals, grosbeaks, buntings, towhees, finches, sparrows, and allies, ed. A. C. Bent, 981–90. Part 2. *U.S. Natl. Mus. Bull.* 237:1–1889, Washington, DC.

Wilson, J. K. 1976. Nesting success of the lark bunting near the periphery of its breeding range. *Kansas Ornithol. Soc. Bull.* 27:13–22.

Wilson, S. D., and J. W. Belcher. 1989. Plant and bird communities of native prairie and introduced Eurasian vegetation in Manitoba, Canada. *Conserv. Biol.* 3:39–44.

Winter, M. 1994. Habitat selection of Baird's sparrow in the northern mixed-grass prairie. Diplomarbeit, University Tübingen, Germany.

———. 1998. Effect of habitat fragmentation on grassland-nesting birds in southwestern Missouri. Ph.D. diss., University of Missouri, Columbia.

———. 1999a. Nesting biology of dickcissels and Henslow's sparrows in southwestern Missouri prairie fragments. *Wilson Bull.* 111:515–25.

———. 1999b. Relationship of fire history to territory size, breeding density, and habitat of Baird's sparrow in North Dakota. In *Ecology and Conservation of Grassland Birds of the Western Hemisphere,* ed. P. D. Vickery and J. R. Herkert, 171–77. Cooper Ornithological Society, Studies in Avian Biology no. 19. 299 pp.

Wisconsin Dept. of Natural Resources. 1977. Wisconsin scientific areas—preserving native diversity. *Wisc. Dept. Nat. Resources Tech. Bull.* 102, Madison.

With, K. A. 1994a. McCown's longspur (*Calcarius mccownii*). In *The Birds of North America*, ed. A. Poole and F. Gill, no. 96. Philadelphia: Birds of North America.

————. 1994b. The hazards of nesting near shrubs for a grassland bird, the McCown's longspur. *Condor* 95:1009–19.

Wittenberger, J. F. 1976. Habitat selection and the evolution of polygyny in bobolinks (*Dolichonyx orizivorus*). Ph.D. diss., University of California, Davis. See *Diss. Abstr. Int. B. Sci. Eng.* 37(6):2715 (1977).

Wolf, L. L. 1977. Species relationships in the genus *Aimophila*. *AOU Monogr.* 23:1–230.

Wolf, R. C. 1991. *Iowa's state parks: Also forests, recreation areas and preserves.* Ames: Iowa State University Press.

Wrege, P. H., and T. J. Cade. 1977. Courtship behavior of large falcons in captivity. *Report Res.* 11:1–27.

Wyckoff, A. M. 1986. A relict population of chestnut-collared longspurs in western Minnesota. *Loon* 58:3–11.

Wyoming Game and Fish Dept. 1997. *Atlas of birds, mammals, reptiles and amphibians in Wyoming.* Lander: Nongame Program, Wyoming Game and Fish Dept. 187 pp.

Zelenak, J. R., and J. J. Rotella. 1997. Nest success and productivity of ferruginous hawks in northern Montana. *Can. J. Zool.* 75:1035–41.

Zelenak, J. R., J. J. Rotella, and A. R. Harmata. 1997. Survival of fledgling ferruginous hawks in northern Montana. *Can. J. Zool.* 75:152–56.

Zimmerman, J. L. 1971. The territory and its density dependent effect in *Spiza americana*. *Auk* 88:591–612.

————. 1982. Nesting success of dickcissels (*Spiza americana*) in preferred and less preferred habitats. *Auk* 99: 292–98.

————. 1983. Cowbird parasitism of dickcissels in different habitats and at different nest densities. *Wilson Bull.* 95:7–22.

————. 1985. The birds of Konza Prairie Research Natural Area, Kansas. *Prairie Nat.* 17:185–92.

————. 1988. Breeding season habitat selection by the Henslow's sparrow (*Ammodramus henslowii*) in Kansas. *Wilson Bull.* 100:17–24.

————. 1993. *The birds of Konza: The avian ecology of the tallgrass prairie.* Lawrence: University Press of Kansas. 186 pp.

————. 1996. Avian community responses to fire, grazing, and drought in the tallgrass prairie. In *Ecology and conservation of Great Plains vertebrates,* ed. F. L. Knopf and F. B. Samson, 125:167–80. Ecological Studies. New York: Springer.

Zimmerman, J. L., and S. T. Patti. 1988. *A guide to bird-finding in Kansas and Western Missouri.* Lawrence: University Press of Kansas. 244 pp.

Species Index

Birds, mammals, and plants that are mentioned in the text and are identified to species (or in most cases to generic or larger groups of these taxa) are included in this index. Pages of individual life history accounts of grassland birds are shown in boldface; those of bird illustrations that are placed outside of their respective species accounts are indicated by italics. The appendices are not indexed.